D1598777

TALES OF OLD ODESSA

TALES OF Old Odessa

NORTHERN ILLINOIS UNIVERSITY PRESS / DEKALB

CRIME AND CIVILITY IN A CITY OF THIEVES

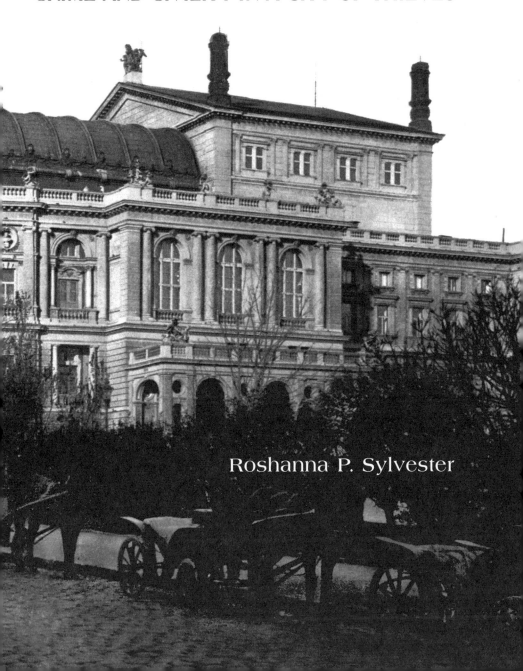

Roshanna P. Sylvester

© 2005 by Northern Illinois University Press

Published by the Northern Illinois University Press, DeKalb, Illinois   60115

Manufactured in the United States using acid-free paper

All Rights Reserved

Design by Julia Fauci

Library of Congress Cataloging-in-Publication Data

Sylvester, Roshanna P.

Tales of old Odessa : crime and civility in a city of thieves / Roshanna P. Sylvester.—
1st ed.

   p.   cm.

Includes bibliographical references and index.

ISBN-13: 978-0-87580-346-3 (clothbound : alk. paper)

ISBN-10: 0-87580-346-6 (clothbound : alk. paper)

1. Odessa (Ukraine)—Social conditions. 2. Jews—Ukraine—Odessa—History. I. Title.

HN530.9.O34S95 2005

306′.09477′2—dc22

2005007276

To Robin,

my joy and my passion,

my *muzh-geroi*

Contents

Acknowledgments

• This book has been a long time in coming, its appearance the direct re-sult of the advice, encouragement, and support of a wonderful set of col-leagues, mentors, friends, and family members. I initially discovered Odessa thanks to Paul Bushkovitch, who aside from a distinguished career as professor of Russian history at Yale also happens to be the grandson of one of the medical school pathologists who carved up my favorite pachy-derm. Once I came to know Odessa a bit better and started to try to make sense of its many tales, I benefitted enormously from the comments of Ka-terina Clark, Joan Neuberger, James von Geldern, and especially Louise McReynolds. Thanks are also due to John Bushnell, the late Reginald Zel-nik, the editors and anonymous reviewers of my articles and this book—especially Jane Hedges and Mary Lincoln—and those whose comments and questions at conferences and workshops helped me to think more deeply about my material. My biggest intellectual debt is to Mark D. Stein-berg, mentor and friend, who has done more than anyone else to shape my understanding of the complex dynamics of late imperial Russian soci-ety. As he may recall, this project is about the same age as "little" Sasha. I only hope that it has matured with the same grace and joie de vivre.

During its metamorphosis from dissertation to monograph, *Tales of Old Odessa* has moved back and forth with me across the country. Along the way, I have received aid and comfort, not to mention critical insights, from a wonderful group of colleagues and friends. At the top of the list are Tom Trice and Sally West, who have talked me down from the ledge on more than one occasion. In sunny SoCal, a tip of the hat to my over-worked, underpaid comrades in arms at Cal State Fullerton, especially Re-nae Bredin, Gayle Brunelle, and Terri Snyder. Here in Chicago, thanks go out to Rachel Bohlmann, Robert P. F. Buerglener, Paul Jaskot, Peter Zep-pieri, and my colleagues in the history department at DePaul. My writing-group pals, Anne Calcagno and Caroline Kraus, helped me find my voice. And as for Nina Barrett, who always encouraged me to just forget the analysis and tell the stories already, all I can say is, well, what can I say. I also have hearty thank yous for my comrade *odessitka* Patricia Herlihy and especially for Elena Shulman, a native daughter of "little Paris." I am grateful to both for their intellectual generosity and for sharing local contacts that proved to be invaluable at crucial moments. In Odessa, I owe a huge debt of gratitude to Olena Igina for her indefatigable energy and good cheer in the face of adversity. Lena, you saved the day. I also would like to thank Elena Karakina, Valeria Kukharenko, Aleksandr Kumbarg, Sergei Lushchik, Andrei Nevzorov, Valentin Volchek, and the staff of the State Archive of the Odessa Oblast. Thanks are also due to Anna Gerasimova and Aleksei Radov for research assistance in Moscow and to the intrepid detectives at the University of Illinois's Slavic Reference Service.

Financial support for this project was provided by grants from the American Council of Teachers of Russian, California State University at Fullerton, DePaul University, the Henry Hart Rice Foundation, University of Illinois's Center for Russian, East European, and Eurasian Studies, and Yale University. Some of the material included in chapters three, four, and five appeared elsewhere in earlier incarnations and is used with permission: "City of Thieves: Moldavanka, Criminality, and Respectability in Prerevolutionary Odessa," *Journal of Urban History* 27, no. 2 (January 2001): 131–57; "Cultural Transgressions, Bourgeois Fears: Violent Crime in Odessa's Central Entertainment District," *Jahrbücher für Geschichte Osteuropas* 44, H. 4 (1996): 503–22; and "Making an Appearance: Urban 'Types' and the Creation of Respectability in Odessa's Popular Press, 1912–1914," *Slavic Review* 59, no. 4 (Winter 2000): 802–24. Thanks to Sage Publications, Franz-Steiner Verlag, and the American Association for the Advancement of Slavic Studies for their permissions. Thanks also to Tom Willcockson for the creation of the maps. Unless otherwise noted, all translations are mine.

As is customary, I reserve the last word for my family. It makes me very sad that my father, Richard Sylvester, did not live to see this book in print. But in my mind's eye I can picture his smile had he done so. My mother, Irene Morgan, has been a constant source of inspiration and support since the day I was born or, more accurately, nine months before. My sister and brother, also known as Rebecca Kühn and David Sylvester, have kept the jokes coming, thick and fast. To Becca especially, all I can say is thank god long distance has gotten cheaper. I would also like to salute that large contingent of aunties and cousins out there in Packerland (wherever it may be). Thanks as well to Quentin, Ellen, and Victoria Burke, and to my father's widow, Eve Sylvester. At the end of the day and in the mornings too and sometimes in the middle of the night, there are Robin and Ian Burke, and Lily Sylvester, my own little family. If possible, I think they will be even happier than I am when I dot this one last *i*.

TALES OF OLD ODESSA

Introduction

The Modern Odessan

As the whole Qualification which intitles People to this *middling*
Rank is founded upon good Manners and Industry; the violation
of these Rules will serve, on the Contrary, for their Exclusion
from it; as for Instance, *Perfidiousness* and *Breach of Promise,* especially if *caused* by *Idleness* and *Treachery.*
—Catherine the Great[1]

• Vladimir Jabotinsky declared in his memoirs that Odessa before the
First World War was "one of those few cities which create their own type
of people." In the whole of the prewar empire there were only three such
cities, Jabotinsky continued: Moscow, St. Petersburg, and Odessa. But even
within this small universe Odessa was unique. If there was "a question
whether the Petersburger was really a native type or only a farrago of other
concepts: bureaucracy, capital, careerism," about the Odessan there was no
doubt. "In Odessa everybody was an Odessan." It was a type as clear "as if
hewn from marble." Other native Odessans concurred with this assessment. From early Soviet times down to the present day, the late-imperial
world of "old Odessa" has been enshrined in song and story, its memory
summoning up images of a freer, more irreverent world full of sunshine
and possibility.[2]

Given the special place Odessa continues to occupy in the public imagination, it is surprising that relatively few historians have examined the
complex interplay of cultures that gave rise to the Odessan type Jabotinsky
and others so vividly remembered.[3] Those who have studied the city suggest that Odessa's distinctive personality was the result of a combination
of factors: the city's strategic Black Sea location, its commercial raison
d'être and accompanying capitalist ethos, its relative newness and self-
conscious modernity, its vibrant mix of peoples, and its notorious criminal
underworld. While each element was vital in its own right the last one was
crucial, for if Odessa made its reputation as a Russian "El Dorado," it
achieved infamy as a city of thieves.

The Odessa of popular imagination produced the likes of Babel's Benya
[Benia] Krik, Il'f and Petrov's Ostap Bender, and the slew of underworld
types who frequent gangster songs. Representations such as these portrayed
Odessans as people with a strong distaste for authority and a penchant for

subversion; they liked to break the rules and enjoyed a caustic wit. While not disinclined to violence, they preferred stealth and cunning to cruder forms of persuasion. They also had a way with words, thwarting conventions of grammar and syntax to formulate a Yiddish/Russian argot described by one late-nineteenth-century observer as "not even a language, but a language salad."[4] And then there was the famed Odessa sense of humor, local "borscht belt" comics cracking mother-in-law jokes when not engaged in more pointed forms of satire.[5]

The tendency to mock the darker side of life underscores the mischievous playfulness that, with the criminal mystique, forms the bedrock of Odessan essentialism. Could the world so vividly described by Babel and the rest have ever really existed? What did it feel like to be in Odessa in the waning years of tsarist rule? How did Odessans understand the city and their place in it? What cultural influences flavored their sensibilities and led to differentiation and community within their metropolis? What did it mean for an Odessan to be modern?[6]

This book examines these questions through dissection of stories appearing in Odessa's mass-circulation Russian-language periodical press during the last years of tsarist rule.[7] Then as now, sensationalism sold papers. Colorful tales about crime and criminality often dominated local reporting, as newspapers covered everything from acid-throwing women to villainous "gentlemen-vampires" and even a rampaging elephant, whose "conviction" and eventual execution formed the basis of a civic epic. Such tales of everyday life, appearing as they did not only on the pages of popular periodicals but also in the annals of the city prefect, in police inspectors' reports, judicial records, memoir literature, and popular fiction, are windows into broader issues. They offer unique insights into relationships between self and society, anxieties provoked by modernity and urbanity, strategies for resistance and accommodation, and contestations for social dominance in a multicultural environment.[8]

Analysis of these sources suggests that, just as for Chicagoans of the Capone era, crime emerged for Odessans as a tangible aspect of identity, the reputations of city and residents alike closely tied to visions of regularized, businesslike criminality.[9] Some social critics of the day saw the brutality and vice of their metropolis as symptomatic of moral degeneracy and the decline of civilization. But it would be a mistake to dwell only on such dark interpretations. Press reports revealed not only Odessans' anxieties and fears but also their irreverence, sophistication, and ironic sense of humor. Some Odessans took great pride in the antics of successful criminals, especially those who perpetrated their "arts" with a wink and a smile. The celebration of criminal panache was part and parcel of crime reporting, the flamboyance of successful thieves and con artists providing Odessans with another form of middlebrow entertainment, the tales of derring-do lending excitement and a certain stature to their own workaday lives.[10]

Like their contemporaries in other cities, Odessans in late-imperial Russia grappled with the contradictions and anxieties that emerged with modernity even as they reveled in the possibilities and delights offered up by their metropolis. Clearly much of what they experienced was part of a larger dynamic. But the nuances of Odessa's particular geographic and demographic situation—the specific quality of its diversity—made its case singular, adding layers of complexity that contributed to Odessans' strong sense of place.[11]

To begin with, it should be remembered that Odessa sat quite literally on the edge of Russia, its back turned to St. Petersburg, its eyes on the sea. The implications of its geographical location cannot be understated. Odessa's population came not only from the Russian hinterland, most notably the Pale of Settlement, but also from other Black Sea societies and points further afield. As Odessa evolved, it became a conglomerate of minorities, the city's population split roughly into thirds: Russians, Jews, and everybody else. As a result, despite the fact that Odessa served as an incubator for both virulent Russian nationalism and Zionist activism, and that a series of violent pogroms marred the city's history, most Odessans took pride in their cosmopolitanism, asserting the primacy of local over national identity.

In the absence of a clear ethnic majority, social-class status emerged as the sine qua non of individual identity. Unsurprisingly to those familiar with western cities of the era, middle-class culture predominated in fin-de-siècle Odessa. But unlike in London, Paris, or New York, Odessa's middle-class sensibilities were infused not only with highly gendered, western bourgeois notions of propriety but with popularized moral ideals of the Russian intelligentsia. Further, in contrast to emerging middle-class societies in other Russian cities, Jews played a pivotal role in the creation of Odessa's dominant culture. Indeed, unlike in Berlin, Vienna, or Vilnius, let alone St. Petersburg, a secularized Jewish culture in a very real sense *became* the dominant culture. Moreover, this was not the exclusive culture of Odessa's rarefied Jewish haute bourgeoisie but of the much disparaged lower middle class, called in Russian the *meshchanstvo*.

This book explores the complexities of this hybrid form of middle-class identity, examining the dynamic cultural interrelationships that underlay the Odessan variety of modernity. It takes as a given that class identity is a cultural construct, that "middle-classness" emerged as a function of shared attitudes, practices, and experiences.[12] Thus, it strongly supports the view that Russia's middle class was not "missing," but instead was a vigorous force on the urban social scene, its influence discovered most readily through analysis of the products of mass culture.[13]

The Odessa Press

The world of "old" Odessa in all its richness and complexity comes alive in the pages of the popular press. Since Odessa was a publishing center, newspapers there were in no short supply. According to the 1914 city directory, there were more than sixty periodicals published regularly in

Odessa, written in a number of languages and catering to a wide variety of audiences.[14] The most widely read mainstream liberal papers were *Odesskie novosti* and *Odesskii listok,* both of which boasted annual sales of five to seven million. The most popular "boulevard" publication was *Odesskaia pochta,* described by a Soviet historian as "intended for the tastes and interests of the petty bourgeoisie and philistine masses;" it claimed *daily* sales of some 70,000.[15]

In addition to dailies, there were a number of serial publications printed in Odessa, magazines and journals of appeal to more specialized audiences. These included the local theater review journal *Odesskoe obozrenie teatrov,* the children's newspaper *Gudok,* the "first ever in Russia" weekly women's magazine *Zhenskaia gazeta,* and *Krokodil,* a weekly journal of humor and satire. A variety of local clubs and voluntary associations also published regular journals, including *Iuzhnyi avtomobilist,* the organ of the Odessa Automobile Society, and *Zaria aviatsii,* published by the local aviation club.

While I looked at the full range of available periodicals, my interest in mainstream experience drew me to rely most heavily on *Odesskii listok* and *Odesskaia pochta. Odesskii listok* was Odessa's oldest continuing periodical, founded in 1872. The editor-publisher S. M. Navrotskaia assumed control of the paper in 1911 upon the death of her husband, the previous editor-publisher, V. V. Navrotskii. Destined in 1917 to become the official organ of Odessa's Kadet party, the political bias of *Odesskii listok* tended toward moderate progressivism, evoking notions of enlightened Orthodox Christian ethics, prim respectability, and self-conscious modernity. As such, it was most likely to appeal to professionals, businessmen, and others on the middle to upper rungs of the white-collar ladder.

Odesskii listok consciously promoted a liberal social-reform agenda. It regularly (and critically) reported on the activities of the local government and endorsed progressive candidates in local and national duma elections. Beyond this, it boosted the activities of reform-minded voluntary associations (such as charities, mutual aid societies, workers' organizations, and educational clubs), reviewed a wide variety of entertainment and recreational events, covered international news (with special attention paid to Great Britain and France), kept tabs on the local business and financial scene, and was full of gossipy stories of appeal to "men of commerce." Further, the paper commonly ran family-oriented features (especially on Christian holidays, when such stories dominated) as well as feuilletons and other commentaries aimed at raising public consciousness about important issues of the day.

Unlike *Odesskii listok, Odesskaia pochta,* founded in 1908, was a paper clearly of the "boulevard" genre. Under the guiding hand of editor-publisher A. Finkel', a man with a reputation for activism in Odessa's Jewish community, *Odesskaia pochta* spoke to the concerns of the *meshchanstvo.* In terms of general style, choice of story line, and language of presentation, the paper was closer to the street than the more consciously high-brow *Odesskii listok.* Where *Odesskii listok* spoke with the voice of educated society, *Odesskaia pochta* catered to the tastes of Odessa's Jewish "everyman." This said, it is crucial to note that *Odesskaia pochta*, like *Odesskii listok*, conceived of itself consciously as a tool for liberal social change, as an organ of the new intelligentsia.

As was the case with most newspapers of the day, these two Odessa dailies dedicated significant attention to stories about crime, using them to articulate a cultural geography of the city as well as to sell papers. Reporters were highly attentive to the geographical component of crime, the location of a given incident a crucial data point to be plotted on the cultural map of the city. Likewise, the sociocultural identity of both villain and victim were key facts used by newspaper contributors to interpret a given crime. The unsurprising result was that, to varying degrees, both publications stigmatized lower-class neighborhoods and their residents, especially young men.[16]

While both *Odesskii listok* and *Odesskaia pochta* perpetuated to some extent negative stereotypes about crime, there were significant differences between the two in terms of tone and emphasis. Superficially, *Odesskii listok*'s principal crime column, "Diary of Local News" *(Dnevnik proisshestvii)*, was fairly evenhanded. It rarely included the kinds of lurid drawings or unabashedly sensationalistic headlines found in the boulevard press. *Odesskaia pochta* approached crime reporting somewhat differently. Finkel' and his reporters were well aware of the entertainment value of certain kinds of crime stories. They enhanced popular fascination with crime, describing violent incidents in vivid detail, putting words in the mouths of a story's principal actors, and playing up the most sensationalistic aspects of a given "drama." Even as it linked violence and spectacle, however, *Odesskaia pochta*, like *Odesskii listok*, used its crime reporting to pursue a pedagogical agenda rooted in liberal social ideology, deeply informed by the sensibilities of Odessa's unique hybrid form of "middle-classness."

A third publication highly revealing of the Odessan mentality, especially of secular Jewish attitudes toward modernity, was *Krokodil*, a short-lived but influential weekly humor magazine published from April 1911 through June 1912. The journal's two leading figures, credited as publishers from mid-1911 onwards, were Boris Denylovich Flit, a twenty-nine-year-old writer and son of a local pharmacist, and the artist Fedor Berngardovich Segal', whose father was the head of a local Jewish primary school. They were joined by a number of young men in their early twenties, most of them Jewish, many of them students at either the university (several studying law) or the art school. These included Ilia Il'f's older brother Aleksandr Ariol'dovich Fainsil'berg, whose drawings appeared under the pseudonym Sandro Fazini, the artist Boris Antonovskii, once described as the "Paganini of caricatures," and the writer-poet Emanuel Iakovlevich German who, under the name Emil Krotkii, went on to greater fame (as did several other of these early colleagues) as a contributor to the much more famous Soviet incarnation of *Krokodil*.[17]

Free of nostalgia, distinctly secular, and stridently irreverent, *Krokodil* offers a window into the minds of a young group of secular *intelligentnyi* moderns, focusing explicitly on what they thought funny, and worthy of ridicule, in their society. The journal's pages were filled with highly satirical stories, anecdotes, cartoons, and caricatures that offer rich commentaries on urban experience, from the personal to the political. Self-deprecating humor in the realm of Odessan Jewishness was a *Krokodil* staple, as were pillories against professional journalism, such as parodies of the meetings of the Literary-Artistic Society. Whether slyly critiquing courtship and marriage practices or ruminating about the fate of the Devil should he try to sit down for coffee at a swank café, *Krokodil's* spotlight shone mercilessly on the foibles and follies of the essential Odessan.

Contributors to Odessa's popular press were astute observers of the urban condition, offering daily critiques of the state of Odessan civilization. Anticipating Norbert Elias and Erving Goffman, savvy journalists understood modern identity in performative terms, emphasizing the intimate connection between improvements in manners and public behavior and the broader evolution of society.[18] But in their view, civilization was a function not only of "correctness." Instead, journalists synthesized western notions of propriety with the intelligentsia's disdain for the self-absorbed individualism and concomitant moral lassitude of the bourgeois order.[19]

While some writers were relentlessly earnest in their efforts to elevate the "spiritual" level of the public, others appeared to share their readers' penchant for the middlebrow. Since journalists' personal livelihoods depended on remaining popular with their audiences, newspaper contributors had much to gain by indulging public tastes. They regularly reported on the spectacles of urban life, covering in great detail the exploits of local celebrities in the worlds of entertainment, high finance, politics, or crime. The pedantic exhortations of serious-minded journalists were leavened by the writings of those journalists who used humor and arch wit to relate tales of Odessan life, not to scold readers for their lack of refinement but to join in the fun. Even as they fed the public's ravenous appetite for sensationalism, however, these lighter-minded journalists did not abandon the intelligentsia's "civilizing mission." On the contrary, journalists clearly savored their own *intelligentnyi* identities. They constantly appealed to the public to behave with more dignity, mocking their readers' (and perhaps their own) shameless interests, exhorting Odessans to think twice about the things they did and said as they moved about the city.

Manners, Morals, and Masquerade

At the heart of the complex calculus that underlay the performance of modern identity in Odessa were attitudes about manners, morals, and masquerade. Popular press writers understood that if one wanted to be deemed civilized, one must adhere to bourgeois conventions of dress, manners, and deportment. Keenly aware that in the modern city individual identities were inextricably bound up with the everyday rituals of public display and behavior, journalists emphasized that external "correctness" would be read by others as reflections of interior character. Indeed, journalists themselves engaged in this practice. Using newspapers as their rostrum, they set out for their readers a clear definition of what it meant to be proper, describing that which was dangerous, safe, normal, barbaric, insolent, cultured. They sorted out and named the faces in the crowd, describing a city inhabited by a range of social "types," each fitted neatly into a schema of respectability. Newspaper stories were laced with positive role models, mostly middle-class figures whose exemplary appearances mirrored pristine inner qualities. Likewise, papers were full of powerfully negative portrayals, primarily lower-class people whose unkempt appearances and uncouth manners proclaimed them to be uncivilized "savages," "barbarians," and "hooligans," products of the *narod,* the great unwashed Russian peasantry.[20] But journalists spotlighted, too, the more subtle flaws in taste and character that announced *meshchanskii* values: vulgar materialism and "spiritual" vacancy.

Even as journalists encouraged the notion that the visible self accurately reflected inner substance, they understood that visual criteria alone were insufficient indicators of moral reliability. In the vernacular of the press, the label that carried the most social weight was *intelligent* (or more commonly its adjectival form *(intelligentnyi* or *intelligentnaia),* which became journalistic shorthand for a civilized person. When used generically, the term implied a well-educated, well-spoken, properly mannered and respectably dressed middle-class person. *Intelligentnyi* in this sense was often a judgment of appearance, a journalist referring to an *"intelligentnyi*-looking" man or woman. Having said this, it is important to note that reporters would on occasion refer to an *intelligentnyi* worker or poor but *intelligentnaia* woman (usually a young woman or mother). When they did so, journalists employed the term as a judgment of character, clarifying and emphasizing that while the person being discussed might not look like an *intelligent,* he or she was in fact respectable (as opposed to all those *other* workers and lower-class people generally who were not *intelligentnye).*

As we will see throughout this book, journalists were fascinated by cases in which identities were in some way obscured. Popular press writers were by turns amused and horrified by insidious urban characters whose pristine appearances masked immorality. They celebrated the exploits of imposter ladies and gentlemen from Moldavanka who turned out to be ruling aristocrats in the netherworld of crime. But they utterly condemned "well-dressed men" and their ilk, dangerous sexual predators who lurked in the central city. Likewise, they were deeply troubled by the fact that *intelligentnye* people who did not look the part led lives of pain and suffering in the slums of urban decadence.

Journalists put a premium on authenticity, seeing duty to society and individual conscience as its chief guardians. Crime and masquerade undermined this notion, standing directly in the path of the successful accomplishment of the "civilizing mission." Crime by its very nature exposes the weaknesses of society, the desperation and social unrest that undermine faith in progress and defeat the idea that modernity necessarily leads to social harmony and economic plenty.[21] Even if they laughed at it on occasion, journalists for the most part read crime as a sign of disintegration, albeit in a positivistic way as a disease that could be cured, particularly through changes in the urban environment. And yet journalists were not blind to the notion that crime could also be read as rebellion, whether against state authority, the traditional structures of ethnic, class, and gender relations, or the increasingly exacting standards of social convention, all of which writers themselves saw as interfering to one degree or another with human progress.

Journalists routinely demonstrated that Odessans shared with other moderns the understanding that the city allowed for manipulation of identities. Indeed, in the Odessan case, this notion was positively vital, for the ability to become someone new was a key part of why people, especially Jews, had come to the city in the first place. But the possibility of reinvention, while exciting, aroused disquiet. The modern city was a world of disguises, the products of mass culture making it infinitely easier to assume an identity. Buy an outfit off the rack (stylish but affordable), brush up on etiquette to affect a proper demeanor, set the mood by going to a popular melodrama (perhaps a film by Evgenii Bauer or somebody French), and voilà, transformation was within reach. But did everyone really behave in this way? How was it possible to tell who was who?

In his evolving work on masquerade and modernity in fin-de-siècle St. Petersburg, Mark Steinberg notes that "masquerade reminds us of the inescapability of uncertainty, of the impossibility of full knowledge of the world, and hence of the impossibility of full control." He speaks of the mask as a device that "destabilizes certain knowledge of what is true and what is deception" while simultaneously revealing what Efrat Tseëlon called "the multiplicity of our identity." Thus, Steinberg concludes, silently invoking Ernest Goffman, masks enable "complex performances of cultural desire, play, and possibility, of alternative public selves."[22]

The idea of masquerade is a particularly fruitful one when considering how Odessans understood the possibilities and dangers of modern urban life.[23] I use the term in several ways to refer to the behavior of various groups that John Kasson has called "social counterfeits."[24] Most obviously, it applies to imposters such as con artists and expert thieves, usually from the lower classes, who perfected the art of "correctness" in order to move freely among and victimize the "better" circles of society. While journalists warned readers about the dangers of this sort of masquerade, they nonetheless reported such happenings with a fair amount of glee, underscoring the idea that people enjoyed watching others get away with deception of this sort (as long as they themselves were not the victims).

A second group of masqueraders that attracted the attention of the press were those I call "betrayers": people who thanks to their material success, educational level, degree of refinement, and "proper" upbringing were legitimately entitled to the identity they presented but who behaved in ways that were morally reprehensible. Journalists were much less inclined to laugh at betrayers, seeing not playfulness but malice in the acts of those who would exploit their superior social positions in order to win the trust of those destined to become their victims.

The third kind of masquerade refers to people who were trying to "pass" in a more subtle sense, not to commit crime but to raise or maintain their stature in society.[25] This kind of masking, more difficult to pin down, speaks to the psychological insecurities of social aspirants such as *meshchane* who, because of lack of wealth or refinement or perhaps a sense of "spiritual" inadequacy, did not feel legitimately entitled to the identity they were asserting. Such people were constantly worried about discovery, fearing that some slip in behavior would allow those whose respect and validation they most coveted to unmask them as frauds. Closely related were those individuals who had skeletons in their closets, people trying to hide secrets they feared could destroy their own and their family's reputations. Journalists revealed mixed feelings when it came to such cases, showing marked impatience with the meshchane's tentative grasp on respectability, a subject of much derision on the pages of the popular press. And yet they were not without sympathy for the plight of those who wanted to pull themselves up the social ladder. Indeed, it was precisely the people in this group who were the objects of *intelligentnye* journalists' "civilizing mission."

"Where is the Intelligentsia?" Journalists and the Odessa Literary-Artistic Society

Journalists' pretensions as well as their "civilizing" ambitions prompted some of the most prominent among them to found the Odessa Literary-Artistic Society, an association they hoped would serve as a vehicle for cultural enlightenment in the fin-de-siècle era.[26] The club's founders had two main goals. First, they sought to create a space where members of the intelligentsia could get together to exchange ideas. Second, they wanted to introduce "cultural life to those who by education and mode of life *(sklad zhizni)* have not had the possibility to taste the bittersweet fruits of knowledge."[27] The society's main activities, designed to be educational, intellectually stimulating, morally uplifting, and entertaining, included Thursday-evening lectures and literary discussions and Saturday-evening performances.[28]

As one observer commented, the group's high-minded goals were bound to garner the attention of "all *intelligentnaia* Odessa." By March 1912, however, two months after the club's foundation, the daily newspaper *Odesskii listok* reported with some chagrin that, contrary to expectations, "with the

exception of journalists and artists," members of educated society were failing to flock to the fledgling organization. Per the association's charter, full
membership in the Literary-Artistic Society was open only to writers, journalists, artists, and others with "definite literary, academic, or artistic qualifica-
tions."[29] Others interested in the goals of the club were invited to become
guest members, thus opening the door for "doctors, lawyers, engineers, architects, pedagogues, civil servants, and others." "But this is not happening,"
Odesskii listok's reporter complained. "The intelligentsia without distinction
of nationality have not moved into the ranks of guest members of the club
in a broad wave." This was a "strange paradox," the writer continued, a "phenomenon . . . even more strange since one so often hears complaints among
the Odessa intelligentsia that they are tired of the daily grind of business and
are starving for cultural displays, thirsting to devote themselves to the creation of something spiritually valuable."[30]

The people who *were* taking advantage of the opportunity to join in the
life of the Literary-Artistic Society were the "middle *meshchanstvo*," primarily Jewish men employed in semi-professional and lower white-collar positions. As the author of the *Odesskii listok* piece noted, it was the very presence of these "representatives of the lower spiritual categories" that kept
the more genteel element away from the club. Not only did the old intelligentsia wish to avoid standing in line to get into the "crowded and stuffy"
environs of the club, where they would be forced to "hob nob" with a
"crushing throng" of the "*meshchanstvo* public," they also spurned the
club because the level of discourse did not satisfy their "more refined
taste." The "middle *meshchanstvo*," meanwhile, were not only "satisfied"
with the "amateurish" essays presented by insufficiently authoritative
speakers but "even glad that everyone in the club could so easily understand them." The claim that club organizers catered to this less refined audience was underscored by the fact that one of the biggest and most popular events in the 1912 season was a decidedly middlebrow evening of
humor featuring famous Petersburg comedians.[31] By sponsoring such
events the Literary-Artistic Society did in fact broaden its appeal, the
columnist concluded, but it did so at the cost of alienating those members
of the old intelligentsia who "want more."[32]

If the Literary-Artistic Society was something of a disappointment as a
means to build community among established *intelligents,* journalists in
Odessa could take solace in the fact that at least some among the "middle
meshchanstvo" responded to the invitation to further their "spiritual development."[33] Those who crowded in as guest members wanted nothing more
than to "hob nob" with Russia's self-appointed elite, to be publicly acknowledged as themselves *intelligentnyi.* Journalistic usage of the terms *intelligentsia*
and *meshchanstvo* in discussions of the Literary-Artistic Society is highly suggestive not only of the animosity between people in the two categories but of
their fundamentally hierarchical alignment. Indeed, it is reminiscent of the
relationship between the categories of bourgeois and petty bourgeois in fin-

de-siècle France. Odessa journalists, confident in their self-appropriated role as the vanguard of the new intelligentsia, assumed the right to publicly initiate others into their ranks. Just as the Parisian bourgeois-aspirant waited for the day when he was called *monsieur,* so the *meshchanin* strove to be publicly acknowledged as an *intelligent.*[34]

Jews and the Odessan Path to Modernity

The astute reader would have noted several references to "nationality" in the journalistic discussion of the Literary-Artistic Society quoted above. For instance, at one point the columnist noted that "the intelligentsia without distinction of nationality have not moved into the ranks of guest members of the club in a broad wave." Thus he invoked the official Russian state category of "nationality" as a means to classify Jews. He did so, however, within a sociocultural rather than a political context, suggesting the elastic nature of the official designation in popular usage. Further, the quote acknowledges not only that Jews were an integral part of the intelligentsia but that they were as likely as their Russian counterparts to disdain the company of the "*meshchanstvo* public."

The question of how best to classify Jews is notoriously complex. Although at root a religious affiliation, Jewry in the modern period has been variously described in Russia and elsewhere as constituting a nationality, an ethnic group, and/or a race. The meanings of these highly fraught terms were (and continue to be) dependent on who deployed them and for what purposes. What is clear, as Benjamin Nathans points out, is that Jews in Russia's Pale of Settlement had a "distinctive way of life" that "together with the persistence of officially sanctioned legal discrimination, helped preserve Judaism not only as a religion but as a distinct social order." Nathans sums up the characteristics of that distinctive Jewish identity in terms of "languages (Yiddish or Hebrew), forms of dress, characteristic economic pursuits (commercial, financial, or artisanal, as opposed to agricultural), and a dense network of religious, educational, legal, and charitable institutions whose task it was to sustain tradition as well as to secure the basic needs of the poor."[35]

Odessa's Jewish community did not fit the standard model. Indeed, Jews came to Odessa precisely because they wanted to flee from the "distinctive way of life" that trapped them elsewhere in the Pale. Odessa functioned as what John Klier has called "a kind of anti-shtetl,"[36] a city made up of what Nathans has dubbed "new Jews": "modern, cosmopolitan, and strikingly successful in urban professions (such as law, banking, and journalism)."[37] Ilya Gerasimov also agrees that "Odessa Jews behaved and felt themselves to be different from Jews in other parts of Russia." Importantly in his view, Jewish criminality was a fundamental aspect of that distinctive identity, the Odessan Jewish practice of crime different from either the "typical immigrant" kind of gangsterism found in the United States or from more traditional forms of Jewish illegality in central Europe. Odessa Jews found "their own roads to modernity," Gerasimov concludes: They "participated en masse in various activities that crossed all traditional lines and boundaries— legal as well as ethnic—in their quest for adaptation to the challenges of the day, and for greater security and prosperity."[38]

Whether their pursuits were criminal or otherwise, newcomers to Odessa acculturated into an urban environment that was secular, modern, and, most importantly, largely of the Jews own making. True, Odessa Jews still had to deal with the discriminatory policies of the Russian state. Likewise, they had to fend off the periodic attacks of violent anti-Semites, including some in the ranks of local officialdom and the police. Despite these impediments, however, Odessa Jews were fully integrated into the life of the city—Jewish experience absolutely central to what it meant to be a modern Odessan.

Historians of modern Jewry have long been preoccupied with a paradigm that focuses on the process of Jews becoming someone else. In their view, the slow march to assimilation—a process Nathans describes as "culminating in the disappearance of a given group as a recognizably distinct element within a larger society"—begins with acculturation ("adaptation to the surrounding society that alters rather than erases the criteria of difference, especially in the realm of culture and identity") that allows for integration (social, institutional, geographic, economic) into a world that someone else has made.[39] Such a formulation does not allow for the notion that Jews themselves had the power to shape the society they came to occupy, that non-Jews in the city acculturated to *them*.[40] But this is exactly what happened in Odessa, the Odessan brand of modernity a function of a reciprocal relationship between the Russians and Jews who co-occupied the middle rungs of the urban social ladder.[41]

There has been much discussion of late in certain historical circles about "the port Jew" as a social type that played a central role as "a pacesetter in the saga of Jewish modernization."[42] David Sorkin and Lois Dubin originated the concept; Patricia Herlihy, John Klier, and Maria Vassilikou have offered preliminary thoughts on its applicability to Odessa.[43] David Cesarani sums up Sorkin's five-point model as follows: "Port Jews were associated with migration and commerce; they lived and operated in milieux that valued commerce; they eschewed the traditional autonomous Jewish community and enjoyed improved legal status which permitted voluntary affiliation to the Jewish collectivity; they were enthusiastic about Jewish education, or re-education, and engaged in vigorous intellectual debate among themselves and with Christians; they questioned Jewish religious tradition, having been estranged from it for so long, and displayed a form of ethnic Jewish identity."[44]

Despite the fact that Odessa Jews did not "enjoy improved legal status" after 1882, except with respect to other Russian Jews both in and outside of the Pale of Settlement, they seem to fit this model well. But I would push it a bit further. Their activities and reform efforts in the social, political, and cultural realms placed Odessa Jews firmly in the ranks of the city's liberal intelligentsia. Thus evidence is strong that the influence of Odessa's secular Jewish educated elite went well beyond the Jewish community itself. In the Odessan context, this made them pace-setters not only of Jewish but of Russian modernization, most notably in the sphere of everyday social relations, including interethnic ones.

However, there was a strong class component to all this. The Port Jew *intelligents* might set the pace, but they had to convince the rank-and-file *meshchanstvo,* not to mention the working class, to follow their lead. Odessa Jewry was not a monolith; intra-community tensions were frequently quite pronounced. But again, the issues dividing Odessa Jews were patently class-based. Jewish intellectuals might debate amongst themselves about various movements of the day—Zionism, Territorialism, Autonomism, socialism—but the average *meshchanin* on the street had more basic concerns: getting ahead and moving up. The question then becomes, was Odessa's Jewish *meshchanstvo* a modern element in its own right. My answer is an unqualified yes, the meshchanin and meshchanka more responsible than any others for giving texture to the Odessan form of modernity.

Crime and Civility in a City of Thieves

With all of this in mind, we may proceed with our tales of old Odessa. Chapter 1, "Dangertown," provides a brief narrative history of Odessa's development from its founding through the last years of tsarist rule. The second chapter sets out Odessa's cultural geography, concentrating especially on journalistic descriptions of the "Horrors of Life" in the lower-class Russian and Ukrainian neighborhoods on the city's periphery. In chapter 3, we enter into the heart of Odessa's "City of Thieves," investigating crime and criminality in the primarily Jewish world of Moldavanka. From there we move on to chapter 4 to discuss nefarious goings-on in Odessa's central city "Under the Cover of Night."

Chapter 5, "Making an Appearance," shifts the focus to crime in a metaphorical sense, looking at authenticity and masquerade among the middle class through examination of unseemly public behavior, urban spectacles, and "vulgar" entertainments. Chapter 6, "The Little Family," follows up with exposure of private sensibilities concerning love and marriage. Chapter 7, "Revenge of the Queen of Stylish Hairdos," returns to crime in a darker sense, looking especially at bloody domestic dramas involving the violent acts of the seemingly respectable. The star of "Iambo's Fate," the eighth chapter and finale, is neither man nor woman but beast, specifically an ill-fated elephant whose "crime" and eventual execution allowed for journalistic rumination on the fate of the modern Odessan.

16

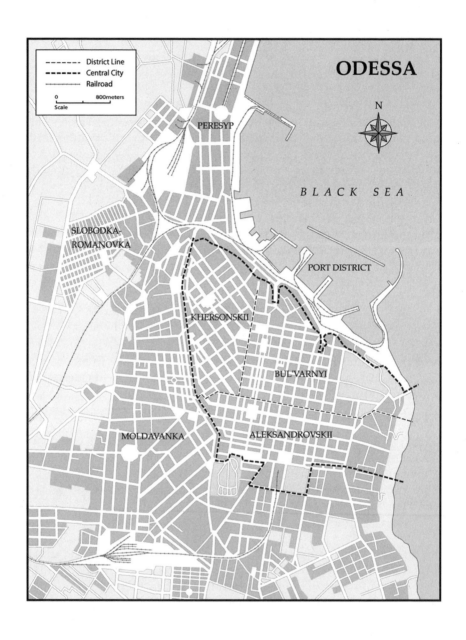

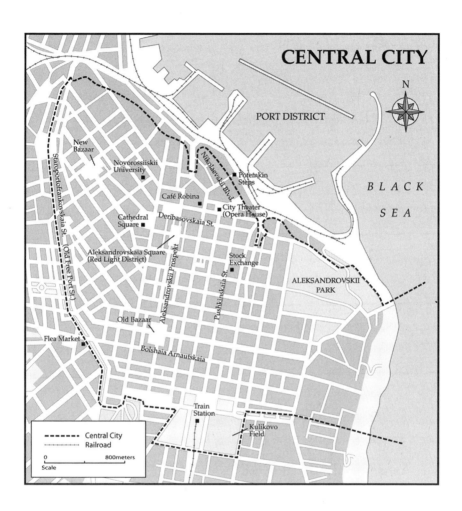

CENTRAL CITY

PORT DISTRICT

BLACK

SEA

New
Bazaar

Novorossiiskii
University

Staroportofrankovskaia St. (Old Free Port St.)

Potemkin
Steps

Nikolaevskii Blvd.

Café Robina

City Theater
(Opera House)

Cathedral
Square

Deribasovskaia St.

Aleksandrovskaia Square
(Red Light District)

Aleksandrovskii Prospekt

Pushkinskaia St.

Stock
Exchange

ALEKSANDROVSKII
PARK

Old Bazaar

Flea Market

Bolshaia Arnautskaia

Train
Station

Kulikovo
Field

Central City
Railroad

0   800meters
Scale

1 Dangertown

Odessa did not have any tradition, but it was therefore not afraid of new forms of living and activity. It developed in us more temperament and less passion, more cynicism, but less bitterness. Were I asked, I would not choose to be born in any other city.

—Vladimir Jabotinsky[1]

• In the closing decades of the tsarist period, St. Petersburg and Moscow, Russia's two great northern capitals, were in the throes of the industrial revolution, their populations and economies swelling at astronomical rates. Meanwhile in the provinces, sleepy agricultural towns were fast evolving into bustling urban centers with people, produce, and manufactured goods flowing freely on the rails laid at the behest of the determined Sergei Witte. In the south of the empire, on the coast of the Black Sea, sat a city unlike the others, the lively port of Odessa, Catherine the Great's commercial St. Petersburg, New Russia's window onto bountiful western markets. Founded in 1794 to exploit trade through the Black Sea, Odessa was one of the great cities in the empire long before the industrial boom of Russia's late nineteenth century. Already by the 1850s, the bustling southern seaport was the "Russian El Dorado," a glittering metropolis built on the profits of free trade, unbridled speculation, and entrepreneurial chutzpah.[2]

By the close of its first century, Odessa was imperial Russia's third-largest city (not counting Warsaw), a highly diverse locality populated by some half million Russians, Jews, Greeks, Turks, Ukrainians, Romanians, western Europeans, and many others. More than fifty languages were spoken on the streets of the city and dozens of religions practiced there.[3] The city on the Black Sea was the empire's "little Paris," distinctly un-Russian in manner and disposition, strikingly unlike other imperial cities.[4] Born of an empress who insisted that "she" be named in the feminine, Odessa was a volatile modern metropolis, a coquette in open flirtation with the West, sophisticated yet untamed, lively and exciting but dangerous.[5] Catherine's city had little in common with gray-bearded Moscow—an overgrown village struggling to break the bonds of peasant tradition—or with tense, conflicted St. Petersburg—a city caught in the throes of an identity crisis.[6] Odessa had different interests, different expectations, different aspirations.

"Piter" was cold, dark, and moody, caught up in the intricate quadrille of state power; Odessa was warm and bright, a dancer in the sultry tango of commerce, "a bourgeois, middle-class city *par excellence*."[7]

This chapter provides a brief overview of Odessa's historical development from its founding in the last years of Catherine's reign through the tumultuous first decades of the twentieth century. In part, this is a story of the allure of capitalism, cosmopolitanism, and the promise of modernity. But it also speaks to the paradoxes of those phenomena, Odessa emerging as a world rife with possibilities and dangers.

The Promise of "Little Paris"

From its inception, the port was Odessa's heart, and grain its lifeblood. During the city's first half century, virtually all of the empire's outgoing wheat and cereals trade was funneled through Odessa, the Black Sea port clearing more than 100 million silver rubles in goods annually. This made Odessa first in Russian exports, second only to St. Petersburg in terms of overall volume.[8] Lured by the siren song of quick profit, not to mention generous financial incentives put up by the state to encourage emigration to New Russia, people flocked to the frontier boomtown at a startling rate.[9] Some of the most prominent early arrivals were foreigners, who by 1819 comprised three-quarters of the population.[10] Among them was a group of men invited by Catherine and, later, her grandson Alexander I to design and build the new city; their contributions were crucial to Odessa's transformation from frontier outpost to capitalist mecca. These men included the Neopolitan solider of fortune Don Joseph de Ribas (born of Spanish and Irish parents), Franz de Voland, an engineer of Dutch origins, and two notable French nationals—the duc de Richelieu and Count Alexander F. Langeron, who served as city prefects.[11] Foreign merchants also arrived early. Italian emerged as the city's first lingua franca of commerce, and Greeks rapidly came to dominate the highly lucrative grain trade.[12]

While the foreign imprint ran deep, Odessa's meteoric growth was largely the result of migration from within Russia. As the nineteenth century progressed, Odessa became a favorite destination for Russian and Ukrainian peasants abandoning the countryside in hopes of forging better futures in the thriving metropolis. Unlike in European Russia's other metropolitan areas, however, ethnically Slavic groups did not predominate. Russians were the aristocrats of officialdom and landed leisure, and, with Ukrainians, filled the urban depths. But ranging across the broad middle spectrum of society was the vibrant community of Odessa Jews, who came by the tens of thousands from within the Pale of Settlement and Austrian Galicia, drawn to the city by opportunities and experiences unavailable in the shtetl.[13]

The presence in the city of so many different kinds of people heightened Odessa's reputation as a place that tolerated differences and nurtured innovation. Odessa was fresh and optimistic, providing a modern psychological and intellectual milieu rare in the empire. Known as "a haven for freethinkers," Odessa was a hospitable oasis, especially for Jews, less confining, less restrictive, less discriminatory than other more traditional Russian cities.[14] In the fin-de-siècle era, it was precisely these qualities that made Odessa a focal point for Jewish Enlightenment activities as well as a hub for the Zionist movement.[15] As Lucy Dawidowicz suggests, however, in the Jewish popular mind Odessa was rarely associated with high-minded pursuits. Instead, within Jewish folklore the word Odessa became "synonymous with disbelief, sinfulness, and frivolity."[16]

A large part of Odessa's appeal was that it afforded Jews (and others) the opportunity to define themselves in secular terms. They integrated fully into the fabric of Odessan society, participating vigorously in economic, cultural, and to the point that the law allowed, municipal affairs. Some Jews achieved stunning success in the worlds of commerce and industry, made names for themselves in the ranks of educated society, and otherwise dominated Odessa's bourgeoisie. By 1910, Jews controlled 50 percent of Odessa's wholesale trading houses, 61 percent of the handicraft shops, 64 percent of the industrial enterprises, 69 percent of the trade and commercial establishments, 70 percent of the banks, 83 percent of the membership in the first two merchant guilds, and 88 percent of the grain trade. Jews were also actively involved in the professions, comprising 70 percent of Odessa's physicians and 56 percent of its lawyers.[17] The success and high-profile presence of Jews further fueled the notion that in Odessa almost anything was possible.

The prosperity of Odessa's commercial and financial elite, Jewish or otherwise, led to a wave of building that laid into stone the city's bourgeois credentials. Bankers, businessmen, and entrepreneurs commissioned ostentatious trading houses, an expansive new stock exchange, and palatial private residences built in a variety of styles reflecting the latest in Continental tastes. Office buildings and banks, restaurants and shopping arcades, museums and libraries, cafés, cabarets, theaters, concert halls, and a glorious opera house (modeled on its architectural older sister in Vienna) all appeared in central Odessa in the mid- to late-nineteenth century. Add to these a growing list of churches, synagogues, and educational facilities—primary, secondary, commercial, and technical schools as well as the distinguished Novorossiiskii University—and one saw in place by 1900 all the essential trappings of western bourgeois civilization.[18] Further, although Odessa's international contingent declined steadily over time, it continued to impart to the city an aura of sophistication and ambiance, adding a special luster to the "pearl on the Black Sea." As one historian noted, "[t]he cultural influence of German, Italian, Greek, French, English, and Swiss residents and visitors permeated Odessa through the import of luxury items, the opening of restaurants and hotels that duplicated the atmosphere of the Continent, and even the hiring of French governesses by both Russian and West European residents in Odessa."[19]

Unfortunately for many, the charms of Odessa's central districts, home to the bulk of the city's aristocratic and middle-class elements, did not extend into lower-class neighborhoods. Odessans bedding down in the port district or living in the suburbs—Jews in Moldavanka, Russians and Ukrainians of peasant stock in the newer factory suburbs of Peresyp and Slobodka-Romanovka—enjoyed many fewer amenities than did their neighbors in the center. Residential housing in those areas was generally of poor quality, overcrowded, and unsanitary. Even well into the twentieth century, many Odessans continued to live without benefit of clean water, modern plumbing, and electricity, so neglected were they by local officials, who privileged the "haves" over the "have nots."[20] Despite disparity in living conditions, however, Odessa maintained its reputation as a place of possibility.

The Furies of 1905 and Tolmachev's "Reign of Terror"

But even in Odessa, opportunities were far from limitless, and diversity, if a hallmark, was not celebrated by all. Odessa in its first bloom had been "the darling of the tsars," the city benefitting tremendously from the largesse of imperial patrons.[21] But as the city approached its centenary, the winds of fortune began to shift. In the period of reaction following the assassination of Alexander II, increasingly security-conscious central administrators in St. Petersburg began to think that the things that made Odessa unique also made it dangerous. The city was too far from the center, too independent and self reliant, too full of Jews, students, and foreigners, too western in its ways, too prone to corruption, insubordination, and unrest. St. Petersburg expressed its displeasure by overlooking Odessa in favor of Kherson and Nikolaev when giving grants for the modernization of port facilities. Even more importantly, Odessa failed to become the southern terminus of a new railway freight line linking Russia's central agricultural region with the Black Sea. To make matters worse, poor harvests in the north, increasing competition from abroad, and nagging economic recession combined to threaten Odessa's preeminence.[22]

In the face of these troubles, city fathers and business leaders took aggressive action to diversify Odessa's economy and thus ensure its viability. In addition to securing foreign loans to modernize port facilities, they successfully developed midscale industry in the city, especially in the food-processing and metalworking sectors. Beyond this, they sought to entice more tourists to Odessa. Soon, a ring of modern health spas sprouted at the water's edge, offering all the latest scientific treatments. With them came luxury hotels, restaurants, and entertainment venues, and even a modern tram system to ferry vacationers as well as locals from the central city to suburban dachas and beach resorts.[23]

While such efforts helped stave off economic decline, they did not

alter the fact that St. Petersburg officials peered at Odessa through nar-
rowed eyes. Indeed, one of Odessa's own prefects described the city as
"the main hotbed of sedition in Russia," a position that found support in
the fact that, at different times in the nineteenth century, members of the
Greek, Bulgarian, and Polish national independence movements had all
used Odessa as a base of operations.[24] More to the point, homegrown
radicals—from Decembrists to Populists to Marxists—had found ready
support in the city. Odessan workers were among the first in the empire
to organize and strike. By 1900, their efforts were joined with those of
radical students and professors at Odessa's Novorossiiskii University.[25]
These developments proved to be but a warm-up for the events of 1905—
increasingly militant revolutionary strike actions, the June mutiny of the
Black Sea fleet's battleship *Potemkin* (later immortalized in Sergei Eisenstein's famous film), still more student demonstrations, and the coup de
grâce, a vicious pogrom in October—all of which showed indisputably
just how disorderly Odessa could be.[26]

It is important to note that for Odessa the pogroms of 1905 were not
without precedent. In its short history, Odessa had repeatedly been the
scene of ethnic strife, especially at moments when economic downturn
prompted fierce competition between rival groups. In the nineteenth century, clashes on the docks between Greeks and Jews had escalated on occasion into full-fledged pogroms. In the fin-de-siècle era, tensions between
Jewish laborers on the one hand and Russian and Ukrainian peasants on
the other resulted in moments of explosive unrest. But as 1905 made crystal clear, pogroms were not just a function of ethnicity. Much to the horror
of liberals and, for different reasons, conscious revolutionary workers who
sought to channel their fury productively into organized political activism,
the frenzied rage of pogromists—most of them unskilled day laborers
known as "black" *(chernyi)* workers—was expressive not only of anti-Jewish
hatred but of loathing for middle-class dominance in Odessa.[27]

The 1905 pogrom was the last of its kind in Odessa, seeming to quell
whatever popular appetite existed for violent anti-Semitism. But pogrom-
mongering and individual acts of harassment did not completely disappear in the reactionary years following 1905. Instead, anti-Semitism became de facto city policy, thanks to the arrival of General Ivan Tolmachev,
the new ultrareactionary prefect charged by St. Petersburg with the task of
reasserting order in the rebellious city. If Tolmachev had been a different
sort of man, his first priority might have been to attend to Odessa's flagging economy, which had suffered enormously in the turbulent early years
of the twentieth century.[28] He might also have taken steps to heal the rifts
that divided Odessan society. But instead of minimizing class and ethnic
tensions that continued to rise with unemployment, the new prefect's
policies only exacerbated them.

General Tolmachev was a tyrant by nature, seeing enemies everywhere,
blaming Jews especially for all the city's woes. Finding ready allies in the

local branch of the ultra right-wing Union of the Russian People (URP), otherwise known as the Black Hundreds, Tolmachev set out on a deliberate campaign of terror. He first decapitated the radical labor movement by jailing its leaders. Then he took aim at Odessa's newly assertive liberals, siccing his thugs on supporters of the Kadet party, especially its highly visible Jewish leadership. He bullied, threatened, and intimidated liberal voters, sponsored pro-monarchy demonstrations, encouraged pogrom-mongering, and blatantly interfered with the conduct of elections. In the words of no less a personage than Count Sergei Witte, "Tolmachev threw himself into the arms of the Black Hundred party, openly spitting on the law and introducing absolutely arbitrary rule."[29]

Despite their severity, it soon became apparent that Tolmachev's policies were by and large ineffective. Even at the height of the "reign of terror," St. Petersburg continued to receive disturbing reports about conditions in Odessa. In spite of massive arrests, a new wave of strikes broke out in 1910, signaling growing militancy among the working classes.[30] Meanwhile, the student movement also reasserted itself with renewed vigor, causing still another closure of the university. Further, reform-minded professors were pushing hard for autonomy, including the lifting of restrictive anti-Jewish admissions quotas.[31] Moreover, Odessa liberals managed to cling tenaciously to their seats in the national legislature.[32]

As if news of sedition and revolutionary activism was not enough, reports of pervasive crime kept Odessa in the official spotlight. Long before Isaak Babel wrote of Benya Krik, the prowess of Odessa's thieves was already the stuff of legend. From almost the moment of the city's foundation, dock workers were regularly implicated in smuggling rings and theft schemes. Contrabandists hid illegally imported luxury goods in the catacombs below old limestone quarries.[33] Some even ran guns and smuggled literature for revolutionaries, including the Bolsheviks.[34] Meanwhile, corrupt gangs of dockers pried brass fittings and portholes from the decks of visiting ships, their "work" unhampered by constables and customs officers routinely bribed to look the other way.[35]

As this suggests, Odessa's growing national reputation as a criminal capital was based not only on the activities of professional thieves, but of their supposed watchdogs. Indeed, members of the city's criminal investigations division seemed to do more aiding and abetting than detaining of criminals. Police agents were known to engage in strong-arm tactics, extorting money from people they threatened to arrest. One group of constables became a bona fide gang, pillaging their way through a string of southern towns before finally getting caught. Tellingly, such corrupt behavior proved to be inspirational. Certain entrepreneurial swindlers found profit masquerading as officers of the law in order to extort rubles from intimidated victims.[36]

Communiqués from Odessa describing powerful organized crime operations and rising corruption were cause for great concern among imperial administrators. Especially disturbing was the fact that Odessa had become a major exporter of crime. The registers of investigative police agents from St. Petersburg and Moscow to Warsaw, Kherson, and Nikolaev were heavy with the names of Odessa thieves, "kings" and "queens" of crime whose mug shots graced "rogues' gallery" albums circulated widely throughout the empire.[37] Likewise, the exploits of nefarious Odessans were documented in the national police gazette, which cited the city's primarily Jewish Moldavanka district as the wellspring of the criminal flood.[38] Though under pressure to close the criminal tap, local police in Odessa were hard-pressed to control or even keep tabs on all of the city's "shady characters," including many of their own. Finally in late 1911, faced with charges of official corruption and with incontrovertible evidence of the ineffectiveness of his tactics, the much-despised Tolmachev was forced to resign.

The New Year's Eve of Possibility

The general's fall from grace was the source of much rejoicing as Odessans celebrated the New Year on December 31, 1911. There were gala performances, charity balls, and private parties at virtually all the first-class clubs, theaters, and restaurants. Top bankers and entrepreneurs settled into the luxurious digs of the Londonskaia Hotel on Nikolaevskii Boulevard for an evening of high-stakes baccarat. Not far away, at the Petersburg Restaurant, a group of landowners, industrialists, and representatives of the judicial world raised their glasses in toast to a strong exchange rate. Members of the recently founded Literary-Artistic Society, including journalists, theatrical performers, and artists, turned the glittering new restaurant at the Paris Hotel into a New Year's Eve salon, singing festive songs and reciting poetry to musical accompaniment. A more family-oriented event took place at the Commercial School, where artisans and craftsmen gathered for a night of revelry. The Merchants' Club was the scene of another lively celebration, cut short in dramatic fashion by a blazing kitchen fire that sent panicky guests fleeing for the exits.[39]

If spirits were running high as the New Year dawned, so too were expectations, especially about the new prefect, I. V. Sosnovskii. While certainly no liberal, at least Sosnovskii appeared to have some respect for the law and was known in the city for his philanthropic activities.[40] Taking advantage of the New Year's holiday, Sosnovskii made two high-profile appearances well calculated to reassure a jittery public that a new era was at hand. The prefect began his evening at the Bolshaia Moskva Hotel, where he issued a stern reminder to upper-echelon police officials gathered for a banquet that members of the public who chose to voice legal opposition to official policy were free to do so without fear of heavy-handed repression. In these new, good times, the police would "serve the people, not the other way around," Sosnovskii declared. The prefect's next stop was the lavishly decorated main hall of the Odessa Stock Exchange where, with his wife on his arm, Sosnovskii presided over a gala charity masquerade. One of the reporters on the scene commented that those in attendance— luminaries from the worlds of city administration, the military, and "various layers of society"—outdid themselves in terms of the creativity of their costumes and the beauty of the ladies' toilettes. Unlike at most such events, the journalist quipped, "the masquerade intrigue" at Sosnovskii's party "was really quite witty."[41]

The witty new faces that civic officials donned for Sosnovskii in the waning hours of 1911 symbolized the beginning of a new era in Odessa, one in which the city's educated public might exercise greater influence. The moment was not lost on a reporter writing for *Odesskii listok,* who penned a New Year's Day article titled "Educated Society in Odessa." Because "Odessa is a port city with a mixed population and a mercantile spirit," the report began, educated society *(obshchestvennost')* never had much of an opportunity to develop the city as a cultural center.[42] Tolmachev and his followers *(Tolmachevshchini)* made the situation even worse by engaging in "mental terror," persecuting "anyone progressively minded" and paralyzing "every attempt at cultural work." As a result, Odessa was fast becoming a "cultural wasteland." Both the city government and the university had stopped working for the betterment of society, the reporter lamented. Further, Tolmachev's repressive policies meant that "no new social associations were founded, and the old ones dragged on a pitiful existence." Now that the yoke finally had been removed from the necks of educated Odessa, the reporter reassured his readers, things could begin to change for the better.[43]

A Change in the Weather

The elation that greeted Sosnovskii's arrival was not long for the world. All too soon it became apparent that, despite educated society's predictions to the contrary, Sosnovskii was yet another champion of chauvinistic Russian conservatism. Then the weather took a turn for the worse. January 1912 was one of the coldest on record, so frigid in fact that the harbor froze over, forcing activities in the port to come to a screeching halt.[44] The arrival of summer brought strong winds and torrential rainfall, a single storm in late May causing tens of thousands of rubles worth of damage to commercial establishments in the central city, where telephone and electric service was also cut off. Meanwhile, in the city's low-lying neighborhoods—Peresyp, Slobodka-Romanovka, and the port district—"water mixed with trash, stones and other debris swept down the hills in a torrent," knocking pedestrians and horses off their feet, whisking goods off piers, washing out bridges, downing telephone and electricity poles, flooding buildings, and turning streets and parks into rivers of mud.[45]

As if this was not bad enough, 1912 ushered in a series of economic crises brought on by escalating labor unrest, uncertain supplies of raw materials, and the increasingly unstable situation in the Balkans.[46] The repeated closing of the Black Sea straits added further to the city's misery, keeping thousands of dock workers unemployed even when the weather improved. Unsurprisingly, these unfortunate circumstances led to an upsurge in crime. According to Chief Inspector fon-Kliugel'gen, head of Odessa's investigative police force, forty to fifty thefts were committed daily in the city at this time, a fact he blamed on the "commercial crisis" and unemployment on the docks. While fon-Kliugel'gen claimed that these figures were "no worse than in Petersburg, Moscow, or Warsaw," Odessans remained unconvinced.[47]

Needless to say, the spirits of Odessa's commercial and industrial elite were dampened considerably by the bleak economic outlook. Their mood did not improve with the advent of a new round of political struggle that pitted conservatives, led by Sosnovskii, against a group of western-style progressives, including high-profile Jewish businessmen, professionals, and other members of Odessa's intelligentsia. The trouble started in October 1912 when popular progressive candidates unexpectedly suffered resounding defeats in elections to the Fourth Duma. To no one's surprise, reports immediately surfaced charging the notorious Union of the Russian People with seeking to use "all possible means of intimidation in order to secure the victory of their favorites in both curiae."[48]

Sosnovskii's "honeymoon period" was now definitely over. The prefect himself deepened tensions by naming URP members to serve as special commissioners investigating the alleged electoral irregularities (of which the URP were the main perpetrators). Needless to say, it was no surprise to anyone when Sosnovskii's commission, although it did adjust the vote count somewhat, failed to overturn election results.[49] But the war for local control was far from over. Less than a year later, in what newspapers described as a sweet victory for Odessa's "commercial interests," the progressive New Duma party *(novodumtsy)* won seventy-two of the ninety-two available positions in local city council elections. It was striking and more than a little suspicious, however, that all of the party's leaders and many of its most active members failed to win office.[50]

The political missiles flying between progressives and the far right were only part of the story during the stormy early years of Sosnovskii's tenure as prefect. Other fireworks erupted in 1912 when radical workers took to the streets to protest the tsarist government's unprovoked slaughter of miners at the distant Lena gold fields. Leading the charge were employees of the city's largest shipping firm, the Russian Society of Shipping and Trade (ROPiT), whose strikers demanded increased wages, an eight-hour day, compensation for work-related injuries, the right to elect their own leaders, and the assurance that they would be treated with respect and dignity by foremen and other management personnel. Other militant workers, including veterans of 1905, soon joined the fray, speared on by skilled metalworkers at the port district's Bellino-Fenderikh iron foundry and several large enterprises in Peresyp.[51]

By the summer of 1914, strikes and street demonstrations in the industrial suburbs and the port district were in full swing, providing Odessans with a highly charged variety of diversion and spectacle.[52] Peresyp workers in particular became the standard-bearers of radicalism, their neighborhood's main thoroughfare, Moskovskaia Street, becoming a stage for revolution on which workers spilling out of factories paraded, shouted antigovernment slogans, waved red flags, and sang the "Marseillaise."[53]

Conclusion

The period from 1912 through the first years of the Great War form the backdrop for the following tales of old Odessa. Within this incendiary climate, social critics, politicians, and pundits rose to the public rostrum to attempt to control the definition of morality, a construct that gained critical importance as fears of war and revolution provoked tensions and unrest that in turn gave rise to mounting anxieties about crime. The meaning of "civilization" was likewise in play as a jittery public confronted the panoply of paradoxes ushered in by modernity. As the next chapter demonstrates, local journalists were among the most vocal in their attempts to fix clear boundaries separating the civilized from the savage, their efforts exposing the dark side of life in the sunny seaside city of Odessa.

2 | Horrors of Life

You think that Odessa is one city? No, there are several Odessas.
It is something like a federation. The center is one Odessa. Mol-
davanka is another, Peresyp a third, and Slobodka a fourth
Odessa.

—Leonid Utesov[1]

• In the opening pages of his 1913 guide to Odessa, the travel writer Grigorii Moskvich advised his readers that, "Whether you arrive by sea or by
train, you immediately land in one of the central parts of the city." "For a
newcomer, especially a tourist," the writer adds later, "it is exactly this part
of the city that is most interesting, the most well equipped, the richest, the
most diverse, the most high spirited and lively." In Moskvich's opinion,
the best of the central neighborhoods was the Bul'varnyi district, Odessa's
most prestigious and exclusive quarter, an area populated primarily by upper-
and middle-class families headed by businessmen and professionals. Many
of Odessa's oldest noble families, meanwhile, lived in the stately Khersonskii district, known as the city's most *intelligentnyi* quarter, thanks to the
presence there of Novorossiiskii University and other educational and cultural institutions. The Aleksandrovskii district, noticeably less affluent but
still respectable, was the outside edge of the center, home to a large number of upwardly mobile, lower-middle-class *meshchanskie* families.[2]

In his descriptions of the central neighborhoods, Moskvich portrayed
Odessa as a model of civilization and modernity. He enthused about the
center's "streets, boulevards, gardens, parks, theaters, restaurants, and cafés
[that were] always full of people." Tree-lined promenades beckoned, shops
were bursting with luxury goods, entertainment options abounded, and
"music rings out everywhere until late into the evening." Visitors would
also be favorably impressed with the good arrangement and public amenities *(blagoustroistvo)* of the center, Moskvich continued. One would find
there "a fine water-supply, an exemplary sewer system, excellent roadways,
beautiful greenery," and clean, paved streets furnished with sidewalks for
the convenience of pedestrians. The beautiful multistory neoclassical
buildings of the center were equipped with electricity and, in many cases,
with telephone lines. Modern electric power illuminated the streetlights
and cinemas of the center's major avenues and drove an efficient tram

system—the *"electrichka"*—which by 1913 traversed the length and breadth of the central districts along thirty-two separate routes.[3]

Moskvich's guide was intended to provide visitors to Odessa with safe passage through a "lively" *(ozhivlennyi)* port of call. For this reason, the writer steered his readers away from the other Odessas, lower-class neighborhoods sporting few attractions and fewer amenities. Lying outside of the center but home to half the city's population, these neighborhoods included the factory suburbs on the "outskirts" *(okraina)*, populated largely by Russians and Ukrainians of peasant extraction. Moskvich judged the first of these, Peresyp, to be "the most vile part of the city," poorly equipped with services and utilities, a neighborhood without a hint of beauty. Meanwhile, the second factory district, Slobodka-Romanovka, was in the writer's view exceedingly provincial, "not even Odessa anymore." Moving on to the port district, Moskvich acknowledged that it was "the nerve center of Odessa, its pulse, the source of its well-being and the axis around which all of its life revolves." And yet his guidebook urged visitors to leave the port behind as soon as possible, partaking of it only as scenery from the vantage point of fashionable Nikolaevskii Boulevard. As for Moldavanka, Odessa's most infamous quarter, Moskvich was mute on the subject of organized crime or even Jews, instead dismissing the neighborhood out of hand as offering "little of interest" for tourists.[4]

Like Moskvich in his travelogue, Odessa's journalists promoted the view that everything worthwhile in the city could be found in the center. Indeed, they extended this judgment one step further, consistently conflating the physical appearance of neighborhoods with the moral characteristics and respectability of their inhabitants, propounding a cultural geography of the city with "good" people in the center and "bad" ones on the periphery. By strongly linking respectability and morality with class, ethnicity, and neighborhood, journalists drew cultural boundaries that mirrored physical geographical separations literally dividing the city. The central districts sat atop a high plateau, several hundred feet above the tiny port territory and the factory suburbs of the outskirts. The port, meanwhile, was visible but physically cut off from the center, connected to the city above only by a series of steeply descending alleyways *(spuski)* and a monumental stone staircase, made infamous in Sergei Eisenstein's 1925 film, "Battleship Potemkin." Likewise, physical barriers separated the center from Peresyp and Slobodka-Romanovka, the former abutting the port but otherwise geographically isolated, lying below and to the north of central Odessa, the latter at the foot of a wide ravine that cut it off from the rest of the city.

In the pages of the popular press, the steep descent from Odessa's center to the port district and the outskirts was a metaphor representing declining socioeconomic and moral status. The divisions on the plateau itself were more subtle but still visible to the geographic eye. The civilized center reached southward, spreading out to Pirgovskaia Street, beyond which lay open steppe and, along the shore, a string of dacha communities—Arkadia and the three Fontans (Malyi, Srednyi, and Bolshoi)—with their beaches, resorts, entertainments, and health spas. Beyond the city limits, these small seaside villages were nonetheless outposts of the center to which they were connected by Frantsuzskii Boulevard and a tiny suburban train line installed to convey summer residents, tourists, and weekend revelers from the city to the shore. To the west, meanwhile, the center ended abruptly at Old Free Port Street *(Staroportofrankovskaia ulitsa)*, the city's original boundary, beyond which lay Moldavanka.

This chapter begins to explore Odessa's cultural geography by considering descriptions of life on the periphery, in the port district and the factory suburbs of Peresyp and Slobodka-Romanovka. Journalists writing about the outskirts and the inhabitants thereof focused especially on the "horrors of life" in those neighborhoods, employing tropes of darkness, filth, disease, and barbarity to underscore the moral inferiority of those residing on the urban periphery. When they invoked such images, redolent of high colonialism, journalists married traditional stereotypes of the backwardness of the peasant *narod* with bourgeois fears of the allegedly innate immorality of the lower classes. Even as they reinforced a moral hierarchy that favored the "civilized" center over the "savage" periphery, however, some journalists appealed for compassion, suggesting that "wild beasts" could be tamed if exposed to civilizing forces. Thus, journalists assumed roles as modern civic activists—à la Jacob Riis in New York, George Sims in London, and others—displaying marked sensitivity to the notion that squalid living conditions had a deleterious impact on physical as well as spiritual well-being. Beyond this, their explorations of Odessa's periphery made the outskirts "legible" and "knowable" to readers, suggesting that these neighborhoods could and should be ordered and integrated into the modern metropole. Acknowledgment that the urban environment itself was at least partially responsible for the "horrors of life" on the outskirts and that the savage lands on the city's periphery were, in fact, governable, led crusading journalists to call on local officials and readers alike to take corrective action. Despite this progressive, well-intentioned agenda, however, journalistic dispatches from the port and the outskirts may well have served not to alleviate but to heighten the fears of respectable readers, especially about that idea of "the street" as an active agent of contagion and corruption.[5]

The Port District

The year 1912 was a busy one for the Odessa port. Despite cold weather and record-breaking rainfall, more than eight hundred steamers docked in the harbor, carrying with them over 400,000 passengers and close to 30 percent of the year's 1.62 million tons of freight, the rest of which arrived on barges that plied Black Sea coastal waters. Of the steamers that arrived, slightly less than half were Russian and about a quarter British. Others sailed under the flags of Austria, Germany, Greece, Holland, France, Italy, Bulgaria, Rumania, and the Ottoman Empire. Regular passenger service was available daily from Odessa to the Crimea and the Caucasus, once weekly to Constantinople, and several times a month to more distant ports like Genoa, Marseilles, and London. Freight traffic, meanwhile, continued year-round at Odessa, only rarely curtailed by severe weather.[6]

For those arriving by sea, the first glimpse of the city was of the Great Stairway, designed by the Italian architect Boffo and completed in 1842, a monumental structure that immediately invited ascent from the port to the city center. Indeed, few lingered in the port unless they had business there or had come as so many did in hopes of finding work on the docks. But even a passing glance established the fact that Odessa's port territory was alive with activity. Although the district was relatively small, containing only three miles of coastline, every inch of it was developed. Thanks to the extensive installation of electric lighting, the port's shipyards, dry docks, engine shops, and machine-works could operate twenty-four hours a day. The transporting of grain and other freight also proceeded around the clock. Cereals were delivered directly to the district by elevated rail lines that ran the entire length of the port. Once it arrived, the grain was cleaned, weighed, and dried in huge elevators, then reloaded into railcars and ferried out to the major piers, where longshoremen used conveyers to load it onto waiting freighters at the rate of eighteen tons an hour. While moving grain was a highly mechanized operation, other goods had to be loaded and unloaded by hand. Thus, a common sight in the port was one of stevedores and carters hauling crates and barrels to and fro on the docks.[7]

Although the port was the source of the lion's share of Odessa's wealth, its environs did not constitute much of a neighborhood. The district had one main avenue, Primorskaia Street, that ran the length of the territory from Customs Square in the southeast to the border of Peresyp in the northwest. A hash of small streets and alleys crisscrossed Primorskaia, providing sites for the district's few lodging, eating, and retail establishments, the neighborhood's only church, and its scant handful of elementary and trade schools. Official statistics show that less than 1 percent of Odessa's permanent residents actually lived in the district. Of those, the great majority were unmarried Russian men of lower-class origins, most of whom had been born outside the city.[8] While many in the port came to Odessa from Russia's central regions, a small but highly visible minority hailed from the Caucasus, Moldavia, Greece, and the Ottoman Empire.[9] Unsurprisingly, there were quite a few more people living in the port territory than the statistics implied. Indeed, one contemporary report indicated that almost 95 percent of those actually residing in the district had no official address.[10] In general, anyone who could afford to do so moved away from the port as soon as possible, especially those with families, who did their best to rent cheap rooms or "corners" in other parts of the city, Russians and Ukrainians in Peresyp, Jews in Moldavanka.[11] Those without sufficient means, however, had little choice but to remain on the waterfront.

As a group, inhabitants of the port district were severely disadvantaged. While some men were lucky enough to secure regular positions in workers' cooperatives *(artels)*, most stayed in the ranks of unskilled day laborers, known as "black workers" *(chernorabochii)*. By one estimate, on any given day in the port as many as seven thousand men were available for temporary work. Of these, as many as half were destined to remain jobless, even when trading activity was at its peak. When times were bad, unemployment was massive. In the early spring of 1912, for example, when the pace normally should have picked up, more than five thousand workers idled on the docks.[12] At moments such as these, even veteran stevedores like the "banabaks" (primarily Georgians and Tatars) were forced to accept lower-than-normal wages in order to keep working.[13] For day workers, large-scale unemployment meant the rekindling of ethnic rivalries and fears of possible violence, especially between Jewish and non-Jewish laborers who were ever wary in each others' presence.[14]

Even when work was readily available on the docks, residents of the port did not have easy lives. Because their incomes were so tenuous, most could not secure regular dwelling space, which in any case was scarce in the district. "Home" thus became a squalid bunk in an overcrowded flophouse or room above a tavern, rented by the night, sometimes at inflated prices. The unemployed, meanwhile, bedded down dockside or simply slept on the streets. For food and drink, port dwellers turned to the cheap cafeterias, tea houses, and food stalls that dotted the district's streets. But, once again, many preferred to eat in taverns, which were pivotal institutions in dock workers' lives. In a neighborhood with no theaters, cinemas, or clubs and only one reading room, taverns were centers of sociability, places where dockers came to unwind after long hours of hard physical labor. Beyond this, taverns served a crucial function as impromptu employment offices, where *artel* bosses and labor contractors came every morning to recruit that day's complement of temporary workers. Moreover, tavern keepers frequently provided workers with an exploitative kind of welfare, happily extending credit on the promise of future employment.[15]

The central irony of life for port workers was that, while their labor was indispensable to the city's prosperity, they were at the bottom of the heap in terms of social status and reputation. Further, although surrounded by potent symbols of modernity and progress—electric lights, mechanized transport equipment, and the like—technology that was part of their daily experience, they themselves became icons of backwardness and innate savagery, thanks in part to pervasive stereotypes in newspapers and elsewhere. Journalists describing life in the port did not place dockers within the environs of the modern workplace. Instead, these writers focused on conditions in functionally domestic spaces, district flophouses, and taverns. Their stories underscored the point that people in the port were as dangerous and disorderly as their surroundings.[16]

Stories about life in flophouses appeared regularly in the Odessa press. Journalistic "explorers" routinely portrayed dockers as uncultured and "dark," dirty and diseased, so barbaric that they would literally kill each other for a kopeck, or for the sheer joy of it. One reporter described a scene in which some four thousand workers—men and women alike—paid four to five kopecks a night to "crowd together like sardines" in large, cold, drafty rooms, where skirmishes broke out regularly between patrons vying for dirty cushions, moth-eaten blankets, or space to lie down on the cold concrete floor.[17] Another story described a round of inspections carried out by the city prefect Sosnovskii, who with his team of doctors, police, and civil officials, visited eight port-district flophouses in March 1912. The resulting report confirmed that "disorderly conditions" prevailed in the flophouses, the majority of which were found to be unsanitary and overcrowded.[18] Still another press dispatch told readers about the outbreak of infectious disease in a flophouse, further underscoring the dangers one might encounter if one came into direct contact with residents of the port.[19]

Other dispatches from the district further emphasized the base immorality of neighborhood inhabitants. Journalists regularly told of large-scale police raids in which dozens if not hundreds of "shady characters" were arrested for a variety of offenses ranging from living in the city without permission or under false credentials to theft, clandestine prostitution, or desertion from the army.[20] Other reports described official efforts to limit vodka consumption in the district by capping distribution. Even with such measures, sales of *merzavchiki* (one-hundred-gram bottles of vodka) at the district's seven state liquor stores topped four thousand daily.[21] Despite severe restrictions on hours of sale, one writer asserted, demand for vodka was so great in the port that it remained readily available at any hour of the day or night.[22]

Although the overwhelming majority of newspaper stories depicted port district residents in a negative light, the *Odesskii listok* contributor Boris Isaev made it his project to rehabilitate port workers in the eyes of the public. In the tradition of contemporary western liberal reform journalism, Isaev's tours of taverns and flophouses were intended to raise public consciousness. Like other observers covering the district, Isaev vividly illustrated for his readers the "horrors" of life in the port. He did so, however, not to vilify "barbarians" *(dikari)* but to humanize the individuals he portrayed as victims of those horrors and, equally importantly, demand that local government and civic society do something to improve conditions.[23]

Regardless of Isaev's intentions, the series of feuilletons penned by the columnist in 1912 contains some of the most damning images of port district "otherness" to be found in the pages of the popular press. Darkness, dirt, and disease were dominant motifs in his writings, applied in equal measure to both the people and the domestic spaces of the port. Isaev's columns portray the neighborhood's flophouses, taverns, and eateries as "dark, smelly, and sepulchral," more like "stables" and "coal warehouses" than sites fit for human occupation. In summer, these places were hot and humid, in winter cold and damp. The furnishings within the establishments were likewise "unbelievably filthy," while the food was "strange" and "unfresh." The air itself was befouled, Isaev continued. It was "poisonous" and "asphyxiating," so filled with "thick, acrid smoke" and the "terrible smells" of rotting food, trash, and unwashed human bodies that it "chokes the throat" and makes it "difficult to breathe." Even the bright southern sun could not penetrate the "frightful," "repulsive" blackness of port district interiors, the columnist concluded.

The people who moved in these spaces were likewise described by Isaev as dangerous and disorderly. In terms of appearance, they were "unpleasant looking" and "ragged," their bodies bearing the marks of unhealthy, physically abusive lifestyles. They were "emaciated," "sick" men with "watery red eyes," faces "distorted by disease," and "sunken chests" wracked by "terrible assaults of coughing." Their "black eyes" and "broken noses" spoke of bar fights and flophouse skirmishes while their incoherent speech and staggering gaits were testaments to long hours of hard drinking. There were "bodies everywhere" in port district establishments, the writer explained, the "dirty," "half naked," "falling down" bodies of men, the shameless, "barely covered," "public" bodies of women. Taverns and flophouses were filled with both, said Isaev, men "ready to work all day just for a little vodka," women and girls ("of the type it is not pleasant to talk about") ready to sell themselves to those with whom they drank, smoked, and swore.

Isaev portrayed the port as a place apart, an "otherworldly" locale where people were "cramped shadows" and "ghosts" who "lived their whole lives" in the neighborhood and had "never been to the city." The columnist's depiction of the district's sole reading room evokes metaphorically the oppositional relationship between those "above" in the city and those "below" in the port. Simultaneously, however, Isaev promotes the elevation of his subjects, invoking "light" as a trope to demonstrate the value not only of his subjects' attempts at self-improvement but of his own reformist project and the larger civic responsibilities of modern citizens. "There is a big, light, and clean room, very comfortable and full of people," the columnist begins. "On the walls are several portraits in old frames . . . and geographic maps," he continued. "Everything is quiet" in the room, wrote Isaev, with only the tinkling of tea glasses and the sound of the door breaking the peaceful silence. Within this pure space—so unlike all others he sketched in the port—could be found "tired and hungry" but "serious" workers, tattered and unkempt, who examined the maps or sat on benches "turning with dirty fingers" the clean pages of newspapers and books. The reading room was a sanctuary, one of the few places a port worker might "forget about his suffering and the unhappiness of the workday and let his mind take him somewhere far away." It was there, Isaev told his readers, that these humble people read and discussed the news of the world or struggled to understand Kant, Tolstoy, and the works of other great philosophers. It was there, too, he said, that workers composed their letters and petitions, some even turning their hands to poetry.[24]

Isaev wanted his readers to see another side of port workers. While not denying that they were often drunk, dirty, and sometimes wild in their actions, the columnist tried to explain the underlying reasons for these behaviors. Port workers drank to escape from their deeply troubled lives, Isaev asserted. The camaraderie of drinking and tavern life was one of the few amusements available to them, especially because they felt themselves unwelcome in the city above, and few of them ever ventured beyond the immediate environs of the port district.[25]

Odesskii listok further developed this theme by printing letters to the editor ostensibly from port workers, including one Tikhon Degterev, who regularly responded to Isaev's columns. Isaev was telling "the honest truth" when he described the "nightmarish" life of a port worker, filled as it was with "heavy drunkenness, dirt, and hunger," said Degterev. But not all of those who lived and worked in the district were hopeless drunks, he asserted. "Many, very many" of those forced to live on the streets "are not drunk but hungry, old, and sick."* Those who did drink were lured into dissipation by tavern keepers, Degterev claimed. "The tavern is the main evil and source of unhappiness for port workers. If they didn't have this 'monster' around their necks, they could save some money against future unemployment and their wages wouldn't fall into the greedy hands of immoral people." Tavern keepers in the port were "robbers" who stole from sleepy, drunk workers. They were the worst "exploiters" on the docks, villains who "squeezed" port workers for all that they had. "A port worker could respect himself if he didn't have drunkenness in his life," Degterev went on. But "nobody pays any attention to the protests of sober workers" who want the taverns shut down, he continued. Taverns were always there, inviting workers to drink away their troubles and their paychecks.[26]

By running stories and letters like those described above, *Odesskii listok* attempted to integrate port workers into the civilized city by making their lives and environs legible to the respectable public. Thus the paper called on readers to understand that the souls of those laboring on the docks were as heavy as the loads they hauled. Modern citizens in the world above the port should not turn a blind eye to the plight of these hard-working but spiritually deprived people, who too often found comfort and consolation in bottles and brothels. They were but victims of a corrupt, immoral system that forced them to frequent taverns in order to find and keep work, and of disreputable tavern keepers, who provided false friendship and easy credit to those seeking shelter and solace in an unfriendly world.

But simply recognizing the humanity of port workers was not enough. *Odesskii listok*'s columns suggested that action had to be taken to improve conditions in the port. First, they compelled city officials to do more to support workers, especially in times of high unemployment. Second, shipping companies and other port district employers had also to provide protections for workers, including insurance that would compensate them in the event of work-related injuries. Further, they should revamp hiring practices so that taverns were not the central site in the lives of morally vulnerable port workers. Finally, both public and private charities had to do more to help port residents improve themselves. They should provide clean, comfortable, healthy spaces, such as reading rooms and daytime shelters, where people might spend their idle hours. Moreover, they should supply more and better-maintained housing options, especially shelters equipped with bathing facilities. While such establishments should be available at a low cost, they should nonetheless provide high-quality services to those most in need.[27]

City prefect Sosnovskii offered a different set of solutions to problems in the port. After his tour of neighborhood flophouses, for instance, Sosnovskii declared that the establishments should be required to employ more cleaning personnel and that patrons there should be turned out during the day so that sanitary workers could thoroughly clean and disinfect the premises.[28] This action, meant to curtail the spread of infectious diseases, seemed designed more to protect residents in the city above rather than those in the port. Indeed, Sosnovskii's order actually served to worsen the lot of neighborhood dwellers whose options for daytime shelter were now even more severely limited. There were only a few day shelters in the district that together might accommodate perhaps 350 of the thousands of workers who stood idle on any given day. Since conditions in these establishments were as bad or worse than in their nighttime equivalents, many dockers simply wandered toward taverns, where they might spend an hour or two over food and drink ordered on credit before going back out on the street.[29] According to *Odesskii listok*, Sosnovskii's new directives were ill-conceived and counterproductive. "It used to be that drunk port workers could spend their days sleeping in flophouses. Now they will be mucking around on the streets in the dirt," the paper declared. "This will affect their health," especially given the poor weather and the fact that a typhus epidemic was in full swing.[30]

The lack of civic support for port district residents became glaringly apparent at times of crisis, as in 1912, when a variety of stormy conditions combined to create massive unemployment in the port.[31] The city duma did nothing substantive to alleviate the situation; instead duma members spent their time debating plans for improving mechanized facilities and constructing a new grain pier in the port.[32] As the crisis deepened and work became more and more scarce, even tavern keepers, who could usually be counted on to provide dockers with a kind of exploitative welfare, decided to cut off customers who were unable to repay their debts.[33] Dockers who were members of *artels* fared somewhat better than day workers since their organizations were able to distribute small grants to members. Others benefitted from "advances" given out to regular employees by several shipping firms.[34] Still others received free meals thanks to relief efforts mounted by the port district church and other private charity organizations.[35]

Regardless of such emergency measures, however, a great number of unemployed dockers spent much of 1912 in a state of near starvation. As one sympathetic columnist noted, the number of unemployed in the port was growing daily. Masses of "workers who have not eaten for several days" roam without purpose through the port, telling anyone who will listen that "hunger is conquering us," the journalist reported.[36] According to Chief Inspector I. V. fon-Kluigel'gen, head of Odessa's investigative police squad, things had come to such a pass that more and more idle dockers were resorting to theft, stealing old jackets and boots simply for survival. "Some try to get arrested just so they'll get food and a place to sleep," the chief inspector commented.[37]

The association of port district residents with crime was certainly not new in 1912. As mentioned above, popular press crime columns were full of stories about petty thefts and muggings in the neighborhood's flophouses and taverns as well as on the street. Beyond this, dockers had been implicated in smuggling rings and organized theft operations almost from the city's inception. British Consul General Charles Stuart Smith complained in one dispatch of "constant and uncontrolled thieving and robbery" in the port of Odessa, a view seconded in a series of complaints filed by masters of British merchant vessels. The master of the *Shandon* reported that "it takes the officers and several of the crew all their time to keep the deck clear of thieves and loafers" when his vessel docked in Odessa, adding that "in all my experience . . . I have never seen such a state of things in my life." The master of the *Gorsemore* concurred, declaring that he was "absolutely convinced that the police officers are working in collusion with these expert thieves," a charge that local officials for obvious reasons vehemently denied.[38]

The persistence of negative representations of port district inhabitants worked against the reformist agendas of crusading journalists like Isaev, who in the name of progress and modern civic duty, sought to change popular perceptions of the neighborhood. Perhaps more damaging still were vivid memories from October 1905 of violent mobs ascending from the port to rob, beat, and murder hundreds of Odessa Jews in the bloodiest pogrom ever recorded in the city's history. Such recollections were surely too fresh for at least some in the center, especially Jews, to be able to entertain the suggestion (even if it be metaphorical) that port district residents should be encouraged to rise. Indeed, as will be seen in chapter 4, evidence provided in press accounts of hooliganism and other kinds of rowdiness in the central city—especially in Bul'varnyi's central entertainment quarter—suggests that many among the respectable still feared the "invasions" of those from the port. Such fears were fueled further by rising labor unrest demonstrated in a series of increasingly militant strike actions led by stormy dock workers. Rather than tearing down borders, then, residents of the "civilized" center seemed eager to build higher defenses to better protect themselves against "barbarian" incursions. As it was with the port, so it was, too, with the outskirts, another environment rich in the "horrors of life."

The "Outskirts"—Peresyp and Slobodka-Romanovka

From the perspective of central city residents, the neighborhoods on Odessa's outskirts were worlds unto themselves. Originally incorporated into the city limits in the mid-nineteenth century, their populations swelled with industrial development. By the 1910s, the two communities were "quintessential Russian factory districts" housing the largest industrial manufacturing facilities in Odessa as well as sizable populations of Russian and Ukrainian peasant migrants.[39] Anecdotal evidence suggests that in Peresyp, the Ukrainian peasant presence was particularly strong while Russians predominated in Slobodka-Romanovka. For instance, the popular entertainer Leonid Utesov recalled that while Slobodka was full of "Ivanovs, Petrovs, and Antonovs," in Peresyp one was likely to run into "Ivanenkos, Petrenkos, and Antonenkos."[40]

Although the two communities on the outskirts shared many common characteristics, their physical layouts were noticeably different. Peresyp occupied a narrow corridor of coastal land adjacent to the port territory, only about five or six feet above sea level. Although it had frontage along the water, the neighborhood could not boast of a single park or beach. Instead, the district was almost entirely given over to industry, its skyline dominated by seemingly endless rows of smoke stacks. The Petroleum Harbor commanded Peresyp's waterfront, a massive set of structures originally constructed in the 1890s but undergoing significant retrofit in 1913. Along the shoreline itself were dozens of reservoirs and storage tanks for oil, kerosene, and other petroleum products, as well as a number of warehouses. Further north, the municipal stockyards, slaughterhouse, and various animal-product processing plants also had frontage on the water, which they polluted with impunity.

Running parallel to the waterfront was Moskovskaia Street, Peresyp's central thoroughfare, which traversed the entire length of the district. In its first leg—from its origin near the port territory to Kruglaia Square—Moskovskaia was primarily residential, crowded with one-story tract housing for workers. From that point north, however, the avenue was taken up completely by large factories, warehouses, and other industrial works, particularly food-processing, metal- and machine-making establishments. Further to the north, Moskovskaia widened into Market Square, site of Odessa's "lively" annual mid-September fair, one of the few events that attracted other Odessans into the neighborhood.[41] The square was itself surrounded by still more manufacturing plants, the stockyards, and slaughterhouse. Beyond Moskovskaia, the rest of Peresyp's territory was likewise

occupied by industrial establishments and their accompanying infrastructure. The neighborhood's factories produced everything from leather, can-
dles, and buttons to wine and industrial paints. Food warehouses, railroad
loading facilities, steam mills, and an electric power plant for the tram system were other features of Peresyp's landscape.

Peresyp provided few diversions to brighten up the bleak surroundings.
There were small shops and stands, a handful of restaurants, tearooms and
cafeterias, four taverns selling strong drink, and two cinemas in the district. Most of these establishments were located in the Moskovskaia Street
residential quarter or on other streets at the southern end of the district.
Another cluster of stores, and food and drink stalls, was located at the opposite end of the neighborhood on Market Square. There were also several
churches in the neighborhood, about a dozen elementary and trade
schools, and a free lending library.[42]

Slobodka-Romanovka was laid out quite differently from long, narrow
Peresyp. Founded as a housing development for low-income factory workers, the neighborhood was a tightly packed grid of narrow, unpaved lanes,
all of them lined with poorly constructed one- and two-story residential
buildings. Slobodka's huge industrial establishments, meanwhile, were
arranged in a semicircle that, in essence, cut the neighborhood off from
the rest of the city. Like Peresyp, Slobodka offered its residents all too few
diversions. Even the neighborhood's "best" avenue—Gorodskaia Street—
boasted only a few small shops, a couple of cinemas, a few taverns, and a
restaurant. But there was a people's auditorium in the neighborhood,
which featured free courses, lectures, concerts, theatrical performances,
and other cultural events.[43]

The face of Slobodka changed significantly in the immediate prewar
years, thanks to the construction on the neighborhood's western edge of
the huge New City Hospital complex. The addition of the modern hospital, its adjacent psychiatric unit, and a number of smaller medical clinics
as well as the city's central bakery and laundry facilities infused the
neighborhood with much-needed vitality. By 1912, the city government
was the district's largest employer, and Slobodka-Romanovka was known
as Odessa's "municipal village."[44] At that time, a deputation of Slobodka-
Romanovka property owners petitioned the city prefect to make their
community an independent police district, thus signaling to local authorities that their neighborhood had come of age and that it was high time
they received a fair share of the municipal pie.[45]

The geographical isolation of Peresyp and Slobodka heightened the impression that the neighborhoods were, in Moskvich's words, "not even
Odessa anymore," a notion furthered too by the fact that residents of the
outskirts had little opportunity for contact with people from other parts of
the city. As one historian noted, Peresyp residents "lived in a relatively in-
sular and self-contained community that was administratively and economically connected to the city at large but for the most part did not

share in its social, cultural, and political life."[46] Yet evidence suggests that this isolation was to a significant degree forced on the people on the outskirts, rather than being chosen by them. Neither Peresyp nor Slobodka was well served by public transportation systems that might have linked them with the rest of the city. As one column noted, trams in the central city came every five or six minutes, while in the outskirts, people had to wait a half hour or more.[47] With factory jobs and cheap housing located on the periphery and no reliable way to commute from center to outskirts, lower-class Odessans had little choice but to live in close proximity to their workplaces. Much as in the industrial sections of Moscow and St. Petersburg, then, residents who lived near each other in Peresyp and Slobodka—often on the same street or even in the same building—were also likely to work together in the same large industrial factories. The outskirts thus became "the locus of the lives of the vast majority of Odessa [industrial] workers."[48]

The fact that neighborhoods on the outskirts were systematically neglected and grossly underserved by Odessa's municipal government did little to breach the divide that separated center and periphery. As noted above, the lot of residents in Peresyp and Slobodka-Romanovka was eased somewhat through the work of private philanthropic and charitable associations that operated low-cost cafeterias, night shelters, an orphanage, and other such establishments.[49] Unfortunately, such small-scale efforts, however laudable, had only a marginal impact. The problems faced by residents of Peresyp and Slobodka-Romanovka were serious, even life-threatening. Yet, when those problems were duly documented and officially verified, the neighborhood dwellers' petitions fell on deaf ears.

The housing problem was a case in point. As Odessa expanded in the late nineteenth century, civic authorities were little able to cope with the phenomenal pace of growth. Faced with mounting municipal budget deficits, local officials showed a marked reluctance to devote scarce resources to new housing and the extension of public services and utilities to these fast-growing communities. Some of the larger industrial concerns stepped in to underwrite the construction of cheap tract housing. While such living space was affordable, it was far from comfortable. Most of the apartments were overcrowded, of inferior quality, and lacked the basic amenities common to virtually all central city residences: running water, electricity, gas, and good ventilation.[50]

In January 1912, an *Odesskii listok* column reported that city duma member M. Duditskii conducted a tour of a "typical" one-room Slobodka apartment. After his inspection, Duditskii declared that he was "horrified" that people, especially small children, were living in such cramped quarters, with earthen floors, mold-covered walls, small windows, stifling air, and no conveniences to speak of. "This is living death," Duditskii was quoted as saying. "It is impossible for a man unaccustomed to such conditions to stay in such a room more than three to five minutes." The construction of new low-income housing in the area was "absolutely essential," the duma member concluded.

While such remarks indicated sincerity, there is no indication that the city, private philanthropists, or local charities took sufficient action to improve the quality or quantity of housing available in Slobodka-Romanovka.[51] A group of private developers discussed their intentions to build low-income housing in both Slobodka and Peresyp.[52] They planned to do so, however, only after completing large new housing blocks for lower-middle-class residents in the central city. Thus, the lack of decent cheap housing remained a significant problem on the outskirts, one that local authorities did virtually nothing to ameliorate.[53]

Peresyp and Slobodka-Romanovka were at the bottom of the city's priority list in terms of the allocation of municipal funds, with each receiving significantly less support than any of the central districts or even Moldavanka. "In this neglect of the less privileged districts," comments one historian, Odessa's local government "betrayed its bourgeois bias. The standard Soviet charge that in the late Imperial city a sharp division existed between the well-built, modern center of the city and the poorer suburbs is amply borne out by the example of Odessa."[54]

The most egregious example of official neglect toward the outskirts involved the implementation in the late nineteenth century of Odessa's new municipal sewage system. The new system relied on gravity feed to pipe wastewater down from the central city to Peresyp. Once there, the waste water was directed through a series of open conduits to a "sewage farm" *(pole oreshenii)* at the edge of the district, where it was composted for use in agriculture. Gravity feed was impossible in low-lying Peresyp, however. Because of this, even though the district hosted the sewage treatment grounds, it could not itself benefit from the improved system. Ironically, then, by the turn of the century the vast majority of buildings in the central city were equipped with fresh running water and indoor plumbing, leading to precipitous declines in mortality rates for residents of those neighborhoods. Meanwhile in Slobodka-Romanovka (where only a few houses were hooked up to the new system) and especially in Peresyp, death rates were startlingly high, especially among infants.[55]

The lack of a modern sewer system was not the only public health problem facing residents of the outskirts. Soot from iron foundries and metalworking plants blackened the air. Factories funneled toxic waste into Black Sea waters. Vermin feasted on animal carcasses left to rot in the open in fields near the stockyards. Industrial accidents claimed the lives and limbs of countless workers. To make matters worse, because of the lack of plumbing, bathing facilities in the district were rare. The problem was particularly bad during the summer months when hot weather drove neighborhood dwellers to bathe in industrial drainage ditches or in the fouled shallows along the waterfront. This combination of factors meant that neighborhoods on the outskirts suffered more than any others in the city from epidemics of infectious diseases, like cholera and typhus.[56]

Although the deck was stacked against them, residents of the outskirts were not without their champions. For instance, when the city council failed to deliver on promises made before the 1912 elections to schedule much-needed street improvements in Slobodka-Romanovka, an enraged deputation of neighborhood residents went to the duma to confront officials: "Before the elections you are meek! You promise everything. Then after the elections you snub us."[57] In another example, physicians associated with the Peresyp Sanitary Inspectorate lobbied aggressively for the allocation of funds for a pump sewage system to service the district. Their efforts, too, were largely unsuccessful. Even though during the same period the city funded extensive street paving and paid for the installation of electric streetlights in the central neighborhoods, no money could be found in the municipal coffers to support the Peresyp project. Finally, in 1913, plans were drawn up for the much-needed sanitary improvements. Unfortunately, the outbreak of World War I interfered with city plans to follow through on the promised additions.[58]

The *Odesskaia pochta* columnist "Faust" (a pseudonym of the prolific writer Iakov Osipovich Sirkis) returned often to the topic of deplorable living conditions on the outskirts, never failing to put the blame squarely on the shoulders of city government. For instance, in a July 1914 column titled "By Boat around Slobodka," the columnist berated the duma for its decision "to supply the central parts of the city with magnificent roadways" while at the same time people in the outskirts were "sinking in the mud."[59] The feuilletonist raised the issue again a year later when he described the plight of residents of Mineavskaia Street in Slobodka who had to trudge daily through large quantities of horse manure. While they stoically endured these deplorable conditions in winter, with the spring thaw their street became a sea of filth. Invoking the image of Slobodka children playing in the unsanitary ooze, Faust again called on city leaders to do something about the problem "for the health of the city."[60]

The voice of "Faust" was a striking example of a popular press columnist who spoke out in favor of the humanity of lower-class Odessans. While many stories represented communities on the outskirts as squalid, polluted, disease-ridden environments unfit for human occupation, they did so in order to emphasize the "barbaric" nature of life in those neighborhoods. Indeed, some journalists went so far as to assert that the outskirts were not, in fact, populated by human inhabitants but by "wild beasts," creatures of instinct not reason, uncontrolled and uncontrollable.

Such images were particularly prevalent in crime reporting. Notices of street violence in Peresyp and Slobodka-Romanovka turned up regularly in terse accounts, with the two neighborhoods' main arteries—Moskovskaia and Gorodskaia—frequently identified as sites for muggings and street fights.[61] Such stories, which were treated by journalists as highly routine, often featured lower-class men who beat, knifed, or shot each other for reasons that to most middle-class readers would have seemed petty or trivial.[62] For example, a notice concerning an incident in a Moskovskaia Street flophouse described a man stabbing another in the chest over an unpaid debt of two kopecks.[63] Other items offered no explanation at all for brutality, suggesting to readers that violence in the outskirts was a normal part of everyday life. In one such report, a pedestrian was attacked for no apparent reason by a man wielding an ax near the stockyards on Moskovskaia Street.[64]

As with crime reporting in other lower-class districts, in order for a story about Peresyp or Slobodka to rate detailed exposition in the press it had to have some unique twist or had to highlight the exceptional dangers of life on the outskirts. For instance, when a young worker was killed by muggers on Naberezhnaia Street in Peresyp, the story seemed noteworthy not because of the murder itself but because a specially trained police dog named Spitz was employed to sniff out clues in the case.[65] Likewise, a story about a Peresyp street fight was notable not because one of the combatants was stabbed in the chest but because angry witnesses took justice into their own hands, surrounding and beating the knife-wielding man. Only with difficulty were police able to extract the villain from the hands of the crowd, *Odesskii listok* reported, leaving readers with the distinct impression that Peresyp residents as a group were excessively violent.[66] This impression was further heightened by the story of an investigative police agent who, while eating dinner at a Market Square restaurant, overheard a couple at the next table talking: "But do you remember how we cut up the corpse," the woman inquired. Her companion responded, "Shut up or there'll be trouble." The couple was later arrested for a previously unsolved 1908 murder.[67] Yet another story that supported the image of the implicit dangers of the Peresyp streets described a shoot-out between police and burglars that broke the peace of the dawn one morning on Market Square.[68]

The idea of "the street" itself as a dangerous player in the life of the city was a recurring motif in popular press reporting. The notion comes through clearly in an *Odesskaia pochta* story concerning a "bloody drama" in Slobodka-Romanovka, which centers on domestic troubles in the lower-class Stefanovskii family. The villains in the drama are several. First, there is Nikolai Stefanovskii, a loud, boorish, "despotic" man with a violent temper who terrorized his wife and children, then "threw them away" in order to set up housekeeping with "some woman." The second villain is the family's oldest son, seventeen-year-old Vsevolod, described as a young man "with a quarrelsome, tempestuous, vindictive character of the 'Slobodka hooligan' type" who "inherited" his father's "devilish soul" and "peculiarities of character," stepping in after Nikolai's desertion to "literally terrorize" his mother and siblings. The third villain is Slobodka's "street," a place filled with "rowdies and cutthroats" *(buiani i golovorezi)*, an "environment" that exercised a "corrupting influence" on Vsevolod, heightening the "hooligan inclinations" that had been apparent to all "almost from the cradle."[69]

If there are several villains in the drama, there is only one "hero": the younger Stefanovskii son, fifteen-year-old Valentin, who in the course of defending his mother beat his older brother to death with a hammer. Unlike the "tyrannical" Vsevolod, Valentin was reportedly "a gentle, compassionate youth" who could not stand the beatings and "tortures" inflicted by his brother. Neither could he tolerate the way Vsevolod "humiliated and insulted his mother." Given the set of circumstances, Valentin's actions were perfectly understandable, at least to the *Odesskaia pochta* reporter who covered the story. Rather than acting with malicious intent, Valentin had "unintentionally stained his hands with his brother's blood," the columnist concluded. The jury apparently agreed, acquitting Valentin Stefanovskii of his brother's murder.

To a certain extent, everyone involved in the "bloody drama" in Slobodka was represented as a victim. A cruel, unloving husband had abandoned Feoktista Stefanovskaia, depriving her of male protection and rendering her unable to meet the enormously difficult challenge of raising her sons in a violent, inhospitable environment. Symbolizing the essential powerlessness of the "good" lower-class woman, Feoktitsa could do little to protect herself or her children from the "horrors of life." The brutal Vsevolod, too, was something of a victim, a casualty not only of his father's dark peasant nature but of the destructive influence of Slobodka's mean streets.

The figure of Vsevolod Stefanovskii metaphorically symbolized what in the eyes of respectable society were the twin evils of life on the outskirts: the inborn barbarity of lower-class men and the corrupting influence of the environment that perpetuated it. Even Valentin himself, the hero of the story, was not an unambiguously positive figure. On the one hand, he was his mother's champion, doing what he had to do to protect her from harm. On the other hand, though, he signified the lengths to which one might have to resort in order to purge society of the various threats Vsevolod embodied. Valentin was above all a tragic figure, a desperate hero who was only able to save his mother by tapping into his own hitherto unexposed violent tendencies. Thus he too became a victim of the street.

A 1914 *Odesskaia pochta* column called "Horrors of Life" is a particularly vivid example of the tendency of the popular press to emphasize stories from the outskirts that highlighted violence and immorality. The story opens with the bucolic image of two teenage "country girls" going out for a walk in a field "near the Brodskii factory" in Peresyp. It was there that they met "a company of seventeen men who started making lewd suggestions to them." When the girls tried to run away, "the gang caught up with them and dragged them to the nearest ravine." "What took place there was horrible, wild, and inhuman," wrote the reporter. "The men absolutely brutalized them. One held the girls by the legs, a second by the arms, a third covered their mouths, and so continuously for four hours all seventeen took turns raping the unfortunate girls."

Only when the victims started to lose consciousness did the attack finally come to an end, the writer continued.[70]

A close look at the story suggests that it fulfilled several purposes. First, it provided shocking details of a sexual crime so heinous that it was bound to both fascinate and horrify respectable society.[71] Second, while not saying expressly that the rapists were factory workers, the author nonetheless established a link between class, neighborhood, and violence, weaving together in the article's lead paragraph references to Peresyp, the Brodskii factory, and the actions of "barbaric," "wild," "inhuman" men. The representation of the residents of Peresyp and Slobodka-Romanovka as more violent than the respectable people in the central city reflects a view whose currency was growing in prerevolutionary Russia, namely that crime and immorality were closely connected with industrial workers.[72] While not strictly synonymous, the words "worker" and "criminal" were nonetheless frequently put together in press reports of violent incidents. Coverage of the upsurge of labor unrest and consequent arrests of striking workers in Slobodka-Romanovka and Peresyp for "disorderly activities," not to mention the association of these neighborhoods with the violence of 1905–1907, served to further underscore this connection, drawing a straight line between workers' alleged criminality and their penchant for revolution.[73]

Beyond this, there is a strong implication in the report from Peresyp that lower-class men enjoyed the camaraderie of gang-raping women as much as they might like sharing the same bottle of vodka. The article offered more damning evidence that lower-class men were sexually uncontrollable, that they were in fact dangerous "wild animals," whose depraved sense of masculinity depended on violent public displays of physical strength and sexual prowess. This attitude comes through not only in stories about rape but also in reports of men fighting, even killing each other, over women (many of whom were themselves portrayed as "fallen").[74] Such a construction of lower-class masculinity was further reinforced in press accounts of the behavior of men at home—where they violently "disciplined" or sexually abused wives, lovers, or children—and at leisure, when they engaged in drinking contests and impromptu or staged fist fights.[75]

Another *Odesskaia pochta* story from 1914 that also carried the title "Horrors of Life" emphasized not only the sexual barbarity of men on the outskirts but also the special depravity of women there. The heroine in this tale was a fourteen-year-old girl who worked as a domestic servant in the home of a Peresyp couple. Not only did the master of the house repeatedly rape his servant, but the mistress, who was pregnant, reportedly "tortured her, beat her, and pulled her hair." The report went on to say that "the cruel treatment of the unfortunate victim at the hands of these monsters attracted the attention of soft-hearted neighbors who brought the beaten and tormented girl to the Society for the Defense of Women," where she found shelter. "The case was turned over to the procurer of the circuit court for prosecution," the story concluded.[76]

This report is notable in several respects. First, like other accounts of disorder and violence in domestic life, the story accentuated the moral irregularity of residents of the outskirts. But the behavior especially of the wife, herself a mother-to-be, increased the story's shock value, furthering the notion that such barbarity would be inculcated in a new generation. As will be discussed at length below, such a representation stood in stark contrast to a vision of "true" womanhood that saw mothers particularly as civilizing forces. The story also is revealing in that it hints at a phenomena that *intelligentnye* journalists sometimes succored, namely that even on the outskirts one might encounter good people such as the "soft-hearted neighbors" who delivered the young victim from her tormentors. The fact that the ultimate heroes in the case were not the neighbors themselves but the middle-class ladies of the Society for the Defense of Women emphasized that it was up to respectable Odessans who had the means as well as the will to save civilization.

Conclusion

Newspaper representations of life in the port and on the outskirts painted a grim portrait of lower-class existence in neighborhoods dominated by Russian and Ukrainian workers. Indeed, darkness as a trope, in both its literal and metaphorical senses, permeated most dispatches about the urban depths. But some *intelligentnye* journalists also invoked "light" as a cleansing force controlled by civilized society. Columnists such as *Odesskii listok*'s Boris Isaev and *Odesskaia pochta*'s "Faust" articulated the woes of the underprivileged and demanded social justice. These reporters and others delivered moral challenges that had political as well as social connotations, clearly expressing liberal reformist sentiments and calling for concrete action. Yet their voices, like those of their subjects, seemed to carry little weight. However sympathetic municipal authorities might have been to the plight of the deprived, they were unwilling to provide the material resources necessary for meaningful improvement in the conditions of life in the port and on the outskirts. Writers condemned government incompetence as vigorously as they applauded representatives of civil society who made efforts to provide for the material and "spiritual" needs of lower-class Odessans. And yet they were far from convinced that the respectable middle-class public was in fact doing its part.

Dispatches from the port and outskirts exposed deep political rifts between conservatives and liberals. But they also revealed considerable ambivalence about the root cause of lower-class immorality and hence its cure. Steadfast reformers like Isaev and "Faust" condemned the degraded physical environment of modern urban life, laying blame at the feet of conservative politicians, exploitative tavern keepers, unenlightened bourgeois employers, and the like. Yet even seasoned "civilizers" could not completely divorce themselves from the cliched notion that the lower class itself was at least partially responsible for its own plight and thus should be held accountable. While perhaps shying away from the belief that people born into society's depths were inherently evil, they nonetheless perpetuated fears of "the street" as an immoral force capable of massive corruption. The overwhelming strength of negative stereotypes of lower-class men as violent hooligans and thugs was not easily mitigated by stories about the occasional hero who might emerge ethically undamaged from the morass of immorality.

A subtle but important distinction that deserves a moment's scrutiny concerns hints of ethnic differentiation that surfaced especially in reports about port life filed by *Odesskii listok* and *Odesskaia pochta*. As discussed at length above, Boris Isaev expended considerable amounts of ink as he attempted to redeem port workers in the minds of *Odesskii listok* readers. *Odesskaia pochta*, meanwhile, which targeted a Jewish audience, never engaged in such a project. While not openly nursing a grudge against Russian and Ukrainian port workers for their participation in the 1905 pogrom, *Odesskaia pochta* reporters certainly did not go out of their way to dispel fears about the violent tendencies of non-Jewish dockers. The fact that "Faust" and other contributors to *Odesskaia pochta* did occasionally stand up for residents of Peresyp and Slobodka-Romanovka suggests that reporters did not always indiscriminately lump together all lower-class "types." Indeed, as the next chapter demonstrates, the characteristics ascribed to Russian and Ukrainian workers were of a distinctly different flavor from those attributed to Jewish Moldavankans.

3 City of Thieves

> "Monsieur Eichbaum," he had written, "have the goodness to deposit, tomorrow morning, in the entrance to No. 17 Sofievskaya Street, the sum of twenty thousand roubles. If you fail to comply with this request, something unheard of will happen to you, and you will be the talk of Odessa. Yours respectfully, Benya the King."
>
> —Isaak Babel[1]

• I. P. fon-Kliugel'gen, head of the local investigative police squad, declared in 1912 that more than thirty thousand "suspicious characters" lurked in Odessa. While "shady types" could be found "in every quarter of the city," the chief inspector continued, they lived "primarily in Moldavanka," where on some blocks "every single resident is a criminal."[2] Moldavanka—if even a tiny fraction of the stories were true it was unsavory terrain, a quarter filled with dark alleys, filthy streets, crumbling buildings, and violence. In the fictional world of Isaak Babel, it was the realm of Benya Krik, the brutal but charismatic gangster "king."[3] In the "real" world of newspapers, it was home to thieving "aristocrats," "gentlemen" burglars, and entrepreneurial kingpins purported to be heads of criminal dynasties.

This chapter examines journalistic depictions of Moldavanka, exposing several interrelated narrative threads that run through press accounts of life in Odessa's most notorious district. Much as they did in dispatches from the port and the outskirts, reporters "ventured" into Moldavanka in order to explore and thus map the neighborhood's public and domestic spaces. Some described Moldavanka unambiguously as an arena of menace, employing familiar tropes of darkness, disease, and squalor to stigmatize the neighborhood and its inhabitants. As in discussions of the outskirts and the port, such portrayals emphasized disorderly familial relationships and parental neglect of children, decrying the role of "the street" as an immoral force initiating each new generation into the world of brutality and vice.

But another set of newspaper accounts represented Moldavanka as a "distinct and peculiar little world," inextricably tied to Jewish experience. These articles did not focus on the brutal if banal crimes of everyday lower-class life. Instead, journalists were intrigued by the professional, businesslike criminality they associated with Jewish gangsterism. Their stories portrayed Moldavanka as a kind of "looking-glass world" in which the values, attitudes, and identities of respectable middle-class society were systematically subverted, where success in crime rather than in legitimate business led to high status and social prestige. The motifs of masquerade and authenticity are especially vivid in such portrayals. But the masks donned by successful criminals were not always black. Indeed, some journalists celebrated the achievements of Odessa's nefarious elite, thereby elevating the currency of the criminal world's best and brightest. Writers portrayed criminals as experts in their fields, people engaged in unlawful professions not because they were inherently immoral, but because they shared the same aspirations and beliefs as their neighbors in the central city. Indeed, these were criminal "gentlemen" who wanted nothing more than material security and social recognition; they valued hard work and education and understood the value of individual achievement. Likewise, men involved in the business of crime were represented as sharing some of the same fears as their legitimate counterparts, especially the fear of professional failure, which in their case might involve more than a metaphorical death. Although certainly not advocating crime as a career path, writers nonetheless offered subtle recognition that unlawful avocations had a certain appeal and provided possibilities for upward mobility and social advancement that might not otherwise be available, especially to lower-class Jews.

A handful of columnists writing in the popular Jewish daily *Odesskaia pochta* were particularly active in their efforts to demystify Moldavanka's criminal world, and the neighborhood more generally, envisioning it as a place not so very different from the middle-class center. The overarching message of their stories was unity. To begin with, they called upon Jewish readers to set aside class prejudices in order to embrace a shared ethnic identity that had little to do with religious practice. Beyond this, though, they appealed to readers, regardless of ethnicity, to see Moldavanka in human terms. These journalists stressed that some Moldavankans were helpless victims subject to the assaults not only of brutal criminals, from whom they could not escape, but also of modern urban life. Their only crime was being poor, their material need trapping them in an environment where they and their children were prevented from getting a fair chance to build decent lives. Like residents of the central city, respectable Moldavankans wanted nothing more than to live and raise children in a safe, healthy, comfortable neighborhood, free from the ravages of crime, pestilence, and urban decay. But instead of receiving aid and comfort, they were exploited by landlords and employers, neglected by public officials, and largely ignored by educated society. Thus journalists compelled their readers not only to "know" their honest, hard-working, but less fortunate neighbors, but also to help them. By failing to act, journalists suggested, privileged Odessans were themselves implicated in perpetuating criminality, immorality, and savagery in Odessa's "little city."

"A Distinct and Peculiar Little World"

In Odessa's early days, Moldavanka was the frontier, a largely undeveloped area save for a military barracks, a couple of limestone quarries, and a few country homes built by wealthy Odessans. By the 1850s, however, Moldavanka's complexion changed markedly. New manufacturing operations established themselves in the area, pulling in with them a flood of recent migrants, especially Jews. Soon, Moldavanka was legally drawn inside the city limits and rich Odessans abandoned the area, ensconcing themselves instead in new, even more ostentatious dachas along the shore.[4] By century's end, Moldavanka was a thriving manufacturing district, Odessa's "little city." While it was ringed by large warehouses, flour mills, and granaries, chemical plants, iron foundries, and metal-processing factories, breweries, wineries, and distilleries, much of the production in Moldavanka itself was pre-industrial in character. It was a neighborhood of artisan workshops and garment sweatshops, a "quintessential Jewish quarter," filled with shoemakers, tailors, milliners, jewelers, watchmakers, metal smiths, carters, porters, shop assistants, small traders, and more.[5]

Unlike the port district and factory suburbs on the outskirts, there was no physical barrier separating Moldavanka from Odessa's urban center. But the wide arcing boulevard of Old Free Port Street nonetheless demarcated a border, as the well-planned, grid-patterned streets of the center gave way there to more erratic spaces. Few avenues beginning in the center provided direct connections to Moldavanka. Of those few that did, none carried the same street name when emerging on the other side of the boulevard. This small but telling detail of Odessa's physical layout served to emphasize that things were *different* once one crossed the line, that the unpredictability of street patterns presaged the moral irregularity of residents. As noted by the travel writer Grigorii Moskvich, Old Free Port was one of Odessa's most important avenues, having until the mid-nineteenth century marked the edge of the city limits. In 1912, Old Free Port was the site of "a mass of charities and other civic establishments that follow each other endlessly around it." If one were to walk the avenue's length, one would pass the Sretenskii Philanthropic Society (that included a cafeteria serving low-cost meals to the poor), the city almshouse, the foundling home, the Massovskii night shelter, more than a dozen schools, the civic auditorium, a children's clinic and other such establishments. Some contemporary observers referred to this string of institutions as the civic "jewels" in "the beauty's necklace" (the "beauty" being the center). Others, however, might have seen these "jewels" as defense fortifications buffering the center of civilization against the wilds of the frontier.[6]

Moskvich suggested that the initial transition from the central city to Moldavanka was quite subtle. Indeed, he told readers that those parts of the neighborhood nearest to Old Free Port Street differed little from the streets of the center. As one progressed, however, one entered the environs of the "less wealthy part of the population." One might "occasionally find attractive three- and four-story buildings" there, complete with all the modern amenities, said the writer. For the most part, however, Molda-vankans made do with fewer of the "comforts of life."[7] Shopkeepers in kiosks and tiny windowless storefronts proffered groceries, dairy goods, to-bacco, and liquor. Entertainment options were limited, with only a smat-tering of theaters and cinemas, a public auditorium, and a couple of read-ing rooms. Moldavanka did have a fair number of cafeterias, buffets, and restaurants (none of which rated mention in Moskvich's guide), and more than a few taverns, beer halls, wine cellars, and brothels, which by all indi-cations did a thriving business.[8]

Popular press journalists were more explicit than Moskvich in their de-pictions of conditions in Moldavanka, portraying its streets and buildings as inhospitable and inherently dangerous. Several reporters noted that roads in the neighborhood were a morass of mud, poorly paved and with few sidewalks for pedestrians.[9] As the *Odesskaia pochta* columnist "Faust" said, "The devil himself would break a leg" on the streets of Moldavanka, so full were they with "piles of stones, pits, and pot holes."[10] Buildings, meanwhile, were described as dilapidated, poorly constructed one- and two-story slums, packed to bursting with cramped, overcrowded apart-ments so neglected by landlords that residents justly feared the dire effects of crumbling walls, collapsing floors and ceilings, poor ventilation, and faulty stoves and chimneys.[11]

The association of physical squalor with moral degeneracy was a com-mon theme in popular press reports of Moldavanka, on view especially in dispatches from the flea market located on Prokhorovskaia Square. Just barely on the Moldavankan side of the Old Free Port Street divide, the flea market was a potent symbol of the neighborhood's many and various evils. The *Odesskii listok* columnist Boris Isaev branded the flea market a "distinct and strange little world," a dirty, densely crowded bazaar where petty traders sold used clothing, furniture, household items, and other "junk" to a primarily lower-class clientele of "factory hands and workers."[12]

Isaev's characterizations of the flea market's physical environs and its denizens articulated what to him were appallingly dangerous conditions. Upon entrance to the marketplace, the visitor was immediately over-whelmed and disoriented by the noise and bustling pace, Isaev warned his readers. Like in a beehive, "everything is in motion," with "ragged" and "very dirty" "junk dealers, cake sellers, and boys" swarming around every new entrant. The vendors, too, were aggressive and fast-talking, their words shooting out "like bullets from a gun." Moreover, they were "greedy, rude" and unethical, complained the columnist, not businessmen as much as thieves, who fenced stolen goods or repainted "trash" and sold it as new. "I don't know why, but a majority of customers think that they can buy something good for cheap at the flea market," wrote Isaev. "Actually it isn't true. We won't even talk about the quality of the products, which is certainly awful," he continued. "And instead of being cheap they are even more expensive than things that are brand new." Flea market traders were no better than "parasites," Isaev concluded, their goods themselves infested with "microbes."

Similar to his dispatches from the port district (discussed in chapter 2), Isaev portrayed the flea market as a highly masculinized world dominated by the naked aggression and virulent power of lower-class men. But unlike his columns about port life, Isaev's studies of the flea market offered no hint of redemption for the "shady characters" who "swarmed" around and "infected" Prokhorovskaia Square. Rather than championing their plight, Isaev further condemned them, warning readers away from the many and various dangers of the "distinct and strange little world." The key difference here is ethnicity. Although the writer did not consciously mark the flea market as a predominantly Jewish space, one can nonetheless discern anti-Semitic undertones in Isaev's stories. The association of Moldavankan men with unethical commercial practices, not to mention out-and-out criminality, clearly perpetuated negative stereotypes about Jewish men of business. Moreover, Isaev's columns directly implicated Jewish men in the spread of dirt and disease, their bodies as well as their goods represented as sources of contamination. Stories by others about the flea market further reinforced such images. One article described the visit of city sanitary inspectors to the bazaar's *"obzhorka"* (literally, "little gourmand"), a row of refreshment stalls: "The floor had not been washed in months, the walls and ceiling were filthy, the dishes were disgusting, and the serving people had dirty hands."[13] Similar reports were posted regarding the market's row of barbershops, where instruments were never disinfected.[14] Still other stories told of visitors who fell prey to petty thieves, pickpockets, thugs, and rapists, all of whom were portrayed as regularly "prowling" through the crowds in Prokhorovskaia Square.[15]

Importantly, representations such as these invested lower-class Jewish men with considerable power. Yet from the perspective of decidedly anxious "civilized" observers, the masculinity of these men, if robust, was a function of innate immorality. While most flea market denizens were portrayed in this light, Isaev introduced another type that symbolized a different kind of menace. Among the "parasites" and thieves on Prokhorovskaia Square, Isaev warned his readers, were men who had once been "talented and even gifted." "But gradually they sank, gradually they became 'former people' [*'byvshie liudi'*]." There was a "hungry army" of such men hanging around the market trying to get odd jobs as porters, offering to transport customers' purchases to homes or businesses, the columnist wrote. "Among [them] it is possible to meet former artists, former students, engineers, mechanics, and others." In the end, Isaev concluded, "all roads are closed to such people. . . . They wander together through the market from early in the morning until late at night, emaciated, ragged, and hungry. . . . And if they make a little money, they joyfully drink it up before they sleep, praising God for their luck and hoping for more the next day."[16]

Few images spoke as powerfully to the fears of the respectable man than those that turned on the possibility of economic failure. For the middle-class gentleman, the loss of earning potency meant public shame and humiliation. More than this, it denoted emasculation and thus doom for his conception of self, his fall sure to devastate not only himself but his dependents. Isaev's emphasis on the special misery of the "former people," moving ghostlike through the filth and treachery of Prokhorovskaia Square, added poignancy to a scene that already spelled dread on many levels to respectable Odessans. And yet these fears did not translate into compassion, either for "fallen" men of the middle class or those from the social depths, who might be attempting to pull themselves up. Neither Isaev nor any of his colleagues took it upon themselves to acknowledge the existence, let alone champion the plight, of petty traders who might have been trying to earn an honest living at the flea market. On the contrary, negative imagery in the press worked against the interests of small-scale traders attempting to compel local officials to improve conditions on Prokhorovskaia. For instance, city prefect Sosnovskii responded coolly to suggestions that he allow several hours of Sunday trading to accommodate the schedules of working-class customers. Instead of taking measures to expand trading, local officials sought instead to close down the flea market or at the very least move it to a location further from the center.[17]

Although the question came up repeatedly, city authorities never took any definitive action to close, relocate, or clean up the flea market. It seems likely, however, that the duma's indecisiveness was due less to successful lobbying on the part of flea market traders than to more pressing government concerns, especially the outbreak of the First World War. Interestingly, despite the reformist sympathies of some journalists and civic leaders, no one in a position of influence seemed to believe that improving physical and business conditions on Prokhorovskaia Square might promote the moral betterment of flea market denizens. On the contrary, the prevailing view, as expressed by officials as well as journalists, was that any space devoted to petty trade carried out primarily by lower-class Jewish Moldavankans would necessarily remain tainted. Indeed, there is no evidence to suggest that Sosnovskii, duma members, or any other local officials thought of the flea market as anything but a blight, an image more than confirmed in the pages of the popular press.

"In the Criminal World"

Reports from the flea market offered vivid testimony to the assumption that the physical appearance of a neighborhood bespoke the moral values of its inhabitants. The attitudes of local police officers toward Moldavankans were certainly colored by such beliefs. These attitudes, inflamed by long years of official anti-Semitism, meant that when police were looking for a criminal, from the petty thief to the organized racketeer, they turned their eyes first to Moldavanka.[18] Chief Inspector fon-Kliugel'gen once again underscored the point: When Moldavankans come home at night, they "do not have to trouble the *dvornik* [concierge] to get him to open the gate," he declared. "Since everyone has got their own set of lock-picks, they can get in on their own."[19]

Given such beliefs, it is unsurprising that, as an *Odesskii listok* correspondent pointed out, Moldavankans had to accept "extra curtailment of freedom" compared to residents of other Odessa neighborhoods, especially in the form of increased police surveillance. The intrusion of police authority into the daily lives of Moldavankans occurred at several levels. *Dvorniki* were on duty in almost every apartment building in Moldavanka, charged with responsibility for keeping tabs on building residents. Because of their quasi-official status, these men could and did wield a good deal of power over their charges, especially in Moldavanka, where much more than in the center, their chief function was to act as police informers. "As everyone knows, fear of *dvorniki* is one of the many fears with which Odessa residents have to cope," *Odesskii listok* reported. But "Moldavankans are especially afflicted." If a central city resident does not want to deal with providing explanations to the "Cerberus" at the door, he must be in by eleven in the evening, the story continues. A Moldavanka resident, on the other hand, had to "hurry to hearth and home at ten."[20]

Any indignities Moldavankans suffered at the hands of tyrannical *dvorniki* paled in comparison to those inflicted by raiding policemen, who were frequently ordered into the neighborhood to conduct apartment-by-apartment searches.[21] During these forays, police arrested anyone who looked "suspicious," could not produce a valid passport, did not have the legal right to live in Odessa, or was found to be in possession of stolen goods or burglary tools. Large-scale raids also occurred in the central city, especially in the summer when the investigative police were under pressure to keep Odessa clean and safe for tourists. The crucial difference was that, when police staged raids in the central districts, they targeted brothels, flophouses, third-class hotels, boarding houses, taverns, bars, and wine cellars.[22] In Moldavanka, however, police burst into private homes, rounding up anyone they considered to be a "shady character."

An *Odesskii listok* report from October 1912 offers a vivid description of one large-scale raid on three huge residential buildings, during the course of which police took into custody nearly five hundred people charged with a variety of offenses. *Odesskii listok's* coverage of the event took readers inside the private world of Moldavanka, employing the familiar technique of representing the appearance of a place as synonymous with the moral traits of its inhabitants. All the apartments "look like dog kennels," the reporter observed, with "large families huddled together in the filth." Residents had few household furnishings, the report continued. Instead, people slept on the floor side-by-side surrounded by dirt and piles of trash.

The air itself was putrid, the writer proclaimed. It was in such insalubrious dwellings that "so many thieves of various specializations were arrested," the story concluded.[23]

Reports such as these connected Moldavankans with the disorderly world of lower-class domesticity. And yet dispatches suggested that, when it came to Moldavanka, all was not clear to the naked eye. Journalists represented Moldavankans as stealthy and cunning masters of subversion, professional masqueraders who moved with ease between the realm of the respectable and the covert criminal underworld, unhampered by conscience and disdainful of sincerity. Just as unscrupulous traders brushed on fresh paint to disguise inferior goods at the flea market, so too did Moldavankan thieves use tools of deception to mask their true selves.

Newspaper accounts described Odessa's most successful thieves as those who skillfully exploited middle-class conventions of fashion, manners, and speech in order to move freely in spaces where a person clearly marked as lower class would be considered suspicious.[24] Master pickpockets known as *maravikhery*[25] dressed up as gentlemen in order to "work" in the center's fashionable theaters and restaurants, at the lectures and meetings of educated society, in banks and post offices, at the stock exchange, on the streets, and in fancy shops and hotels. Their compatriots were the *subbotniki* (Saturday men) and *voskreseniki* (Sunday men), thieves who circulated through weekend crowds on Deribasovskaia Street and Nikolaevskii Boulevard. Another disguised thief was the *chistil'shchik* (cleaner), who in his role as an amiable gentleman would clean off the back of a victim's coat while lifting his wallet.[26] Then, too, there were *kliukvenniki*, sinners masquerading among the pious in order to pickpocket in churches.[27] Businesses, too, were frequently victimized by thieves, including some who relied on masquerade. A "lady" shopper might turn out to be a *shopenfellersha*, a female shoplifter who specialized in stealing luxury goods from fancy stores in the center.[28] Shopkeepers were also on guard against *kukol'niki* (puppeteers), "gentlemen" who passed counterfeit money.[29]

Another set of thieves who worked in disguise infiltrated private homes. *Skokari* specialized in stealing from apartments, usually by gaining entrance under false pretenses. A number of female thieves took jobs as domestic servants in order to perpetrate inside jobs. These were the *golubiatniki* (pigeon-hawks), who stole from the master's attic, and *prachki* (laundresses), maids who wound wet linens around their bodies under their dresses. Some thieves, the so-called *domushniki*, moved into better apartment buildings specifically to steal from neighbors. Still others got into houses by presenting themselves as poor, distraught individuals in need of a cup of tea or a bit of bread. While burglars in general did not work in disguise, they were nonetheless known to rely on tactics of stealth and cunning. *Tsiperi* (zippers), for instance, climbed into houses or apartments through open windows, usually at dawn, in order to "work" while the household slept. (This variety of thief was also known as an *utrennik* or *fortochnik.*) Then, too, there were thieves who relied on strength and speed. *Shniferi,* for example, broke down doors to get into apartments; purse snatchers, who were called *bugaishchiki* or *basamanshchiki,* simply grabbed the goods and ran.

The wide variety of specializations available to the aspiring criminal mirrored the possibilities offered by expanded professionalization in the modern business economy. As in the legitimate world, specialists in crime were far from equal in terms of social status, with criminal aristocrats at the top overseeing workaday types below. But social mobility was definitely possible, both up and down through the criminal ranks, success being a function not only of skill but of hard work and opportunity. As will be discussed below, journalists frequently portrayed criminals as industrious. But at the same time, they tended to blur the lines between work and play, representing successful thieves as celebrity entertainers. Notorious "kings" and "queens" of theft came to Odessa "on tour" to "perform" for an appreciative audience.[30] Cast in a variety of roles, they were applauded as acclaimed actors on the criminal stage. Master thieves "worked gracefully, with deftness and dexterity," one reporter enthused; they were "artistes" and "ballet dancers" who "cleansed the pockets of the careless almost without risk."[31] One particularly theatrical thief literally transformed himself into a female cabaret singer, whose true identity was not uncovered until, at the insistence of a police supervisor, "she removed her headdress and became . . . a young fellow."[32]

Odessans understood that the criminal world was a liminal one, a fluid space where identities were mutable, where the meanings of class, gender, and ethnically charged symbols could not be pinned down. The element of masquerade was completely crucial to a professional thief's success, elevation to the ranks of aristocracy being dependent not only on sleight-of-hand ability or the mastery of other criminal arts, but on skill as a performer. Take, for example, the "queen of thieves" Ol'ga D'iachanko, one of Odessa's most successful professional female criminals, who assumed a variety of identities in order to exercise her craft. On one occasion, she appeared as a pregnant bourgeois wife who gained entrance to the home of a midwife by asking for the address of a famous obstetrician. On another occasion, she disguised herself as a chic lady in need of a new apartment. On still other occasions, she played the role of that indispensable middle-class accessory, the trustworthy lady's maid.[33]

Popular press reports about criminal aristocrats often represented such "heroes" as celebrities living lives of luxury. A 1912 story that clearly revealed this tendency told of the pomp and circumstance surrounding the arrival in Odessa of Faivel' Rubin, "the internationally notorious king of pickpockets." According to the account, the crème de la crème of the criminal world assembled at the main railroad station to meet the elegantly dressed young man as he emerged from his first-class compartment. The drama of the moment was further heightened when police lying in ambush scuttled the regal proceedings.[34]

Regardless of its outcome, the article about Faivel' Rubin fueled the illusion that successful thieves lived lives of glamour. Another tale that explicitly reinforced that image concerned the appearance in Odessa of a mysterious couple, the handsome and extremely well-dressed Apollon Dubin and his stunningly beautiful wife. The pair took up residence at the opulent Londonskaia Hotel, soon becoming the darlings of high society. According to the article, the charming couple supped at the best cafés and restaurants, attended all the hit shows, and were invited to the most fashionable salons and balls. But even though Dubin and his wife were obviously wealthy, the report continued, no one seemed to know much about them. Chief Inspector fon-Kliugel'gen thought the couple's unexplained appearance in Odessa was suspicious, the article maintained. His unexpected visit to their hotel room revealed that Dubin was in possession of a large cache of diamonds and other precious gems. When fon-Kliugel'gen asked for an explanation, Dubin freely admitted that he was an international jewel thief, wanted in France, Germany, and America, among other places. The chief inspector immediately took the man into custody, but was later forced to release him when it turned out that there were in fact no outstanding warrants for his arrest in Russia. The story ended with the glamorous thief's declaration that, having traveled the world over, he had never found a city he loved more than Odessa. It was because of that love that he decided to relocate with his wife and settle down there to "live as an honest man," vowing never to commit a crime in Odessa.[35]

"Mr. Thief"

More than any other Odessa popular press contributor, *Odesskaia pochta*'s main feuilletonist Faust displayed a fascination with life in the criminal world. But where other journalists played on images of aristocracy (with all the ease and luxury that word implied), Faust's criminals were hard-working, middle-class professionals, personified in the character of "Mr. Thief," a type who displayed the material, and to some extent moral, affect of his legitimate counterpart. Mr. Thief was a savvy entrepreneur who worked hard to perfect his skills and firmly establish his business. Once these goals were accomplished, Mr. Thief himself no longer needed to perpetrate crimes, said Faust. Instead, he became a criminal manager, "skillfully lead[ing] the work of his assistants," choosing promising protégés whose careers he nurtured. In his personal life, too, Mr. Thief lived a solidly middle-class life. He "rents a nice apartment," he and his wife "dress decently in up-to-date styles, and his children go to school."[36]

Just as Faust differentiated the industrious middle-class thief from the leisured criminal aristocrat, so, too, did he distinguish Mr. Thief from the "good-for-nothing" *(propashchikh)* sort who wandered "from flophouse to flophouse." Faust described Moldavanka's middle-class thieves as having infinitely more finesse, talent, and skill than the thuggish amateurs who plied their trades in the port and on the outskirts. Moldavankan thieves were chameleons of inconstant appearance, who metamorphosed seamlessly from worker to "gentleman" to thief. These "lovers of other people's property" were cunning, secretive, and insidious, working meticulously in the criminal profession, while at the same time holding legitimate jobs as tailors, shoemakers, bakers, and the like. Crime in Moldavanka was sophisticated and institutionalized, Faust asserted. Theft was a family business to be passed from father to son. There were even whole schools of the thieving arts run by skilled practitioners such as the notorious "Morozhenshchik" (the ice cream vendor), who taught his nephews as well as other "children of the street" how to steal "at first a handkerchief from a pocket, then a wallet, then how to break into an apartment through a window."[37]

While not disputing the notion that crime and Moldavanka were intertwined concepts, Faust worked to reinterpret popular understanding of both ideas. Unlike many of his colleagues, Faust's project was not to romanticize crime, to serve it up as entertainment, or to use it as a means of demarcating borders, be they spatial or cultural. Instead, the writer seemed intent on debunking rather than reinforcing stereotypical images, on blurring rather than clarifying boundaries. Faust used his columns to educate his readers, emphasizing particularly that criminal occupations were neither consistently profitable nor necessarily glamorous. He described theft precisely as a profession, one that required education, skill (both technical and managerial), hard work, and perseverance. Imbedded in Faust's columns is a vision of thieves who, like professionals in the legitimate world, saw their occupations as a means to attain not only material security but high social status. While the writer did not condone crime as a means to upward mobility, his columns nonetheless suggest that practitioners of theft shared many of the same aspirations and fears as their respectable middle-class victims.

Such views come through clearly in Faust's 1912 multipart series, "In the Criminal World," one installment of which recounted the criminal career of a celebrated Moldavankan thief, the notorious R. Freidenberg, whose exploits had been well chronicled in the popular press. In recognition of his celebrity status, journalists bestowed upon Freidenberg a variety of honorifics including "the king of thieves," "the papa of Odessa thieves," and "the professor." Those who followed Freidenberg's exploits knew him to be an inveterate recidivist. In fact, Freidenberg's name had turned up in *Odesskaia pochta*'s crime column barely a week before the appearance of Faust's feuilleton, when the famous thief was arrested for pickpocketing on Kulikovo Field during the hundredth-anniversary celebration of Russia's victory over Napoleon at the Battle of Borodino.[38] Readers knew, too, that Freidenberg was purportedly the head of a Jewish criminal dynasty. Journalists portrayed him as an accomplished master who ran a school of the thieving arts and groomed his children for criminal careers. Proof to the point was supplied by the thief's son, Iser, who was first arrested at age twelve and, by his mid-twenties, had already spent ten years behind bars.[39]

Faust's column was devoted to a letter ostensibly sent to the journalist by this very same son, who wanted to clear up some misconceptions about his infamous father. To begin, the younger Freidenberg took issue with the idea that his sire lived like a king. The Freidenberg family home was more like a pigeon coop than a mansion, the thief's son declared. "We pay eight rubles a month for our apartment, and the only furnishings we have in the place are a table, two chairs, a bed, and a trunk. Such is the life of the king! We are cold by night, hungry by day. But for that we delight in our 'kingly' rewards!" True, there had been better days when "my father had it all," Iser confided. In his heyday, the elder Freidenberg provided his family with a big apartment, "rich furnishings, luxurious carpets." But all that ended one cold winter night eighteen years before, when "a thick layer of snow covered our Moldavanka" Iser recalled. "A theft occurred somewhere that night," Freidenberg continued. "The head of the investigative police and his agents were searching everywhere for the stolen goods." Meanwhile, all was gay in the Freidenberg flat as the family sat down to tea accompanied by four young thieves who "simply by chance" happened to be visiting. Just then, the police burst in. "They searched everything but found nothing," Iser remembered. Then "they had a little chat with my father and our guests and dragged them all away." "Of course he was freed the next day," Iser remarked, "but by then they were reporting in the newspapers that my father was a 'professor' who operated a school for thieves in his home. Since then this name has made the rounds in Odessa and stuck," the younger Freidenberg declared. Regardless of what the public thought, Iser continued, the title was unwarranted. At this point in his life, the elder Freidenberg was but a poor, sick old man leading a "meager existence . . . just trying to make ends meet." The nickname tormented the "professor," his concerned son testified. "Enough! Let's leave my unhappy father in peace."[40]

Even if Iser Freidenberg's aim was to downplay his father's culpability in the face of a recent arrest, the son's telling of his father's tale remains a fascinating demystification of one of Odessa's most legendary thieves and a hearty rejection of the romanticism and hype surrounding criminal Moldavanka. By using the letter as the basis for his column, Faust challenged his readers to look past stereotyped images of criminal Moldavanka. The criminal's perspective was not often reported in the pages of the press. Under Faust's pen, the Freidenberg story became the drama of a middle-class father struggling to take care of his wife and family, a drama to which respectable readers could surely relate. By taking aim at black-and-white images of the criminal world, Faust exposed the ironic fact that professional thieves and their middle-class victims shared similar aspirations. The notion of criminality as individual enterprise in which daring and ingenuity might lead one from poverty to prosperity seems to have been a Moldavankan equivalent of the "American dream." This suggests that, for young Moldavankans, professional criminality assumed some of the same characteristics as any other contemporary middle-class career path.

As Boris Briker shows, this idea finds further expression both in the fictional writings of Isaak Babel and in 1917 *Odesskie novosti* newspaper reports of criminal raids. "A typical raid in Odessa would begin with a letter of extortion received by the owner of a business," Briker explains. "In this letter the extortionist would demand that the owner amass a prescribed sum of money and deliver it to a designated place. Such letters invariably contained some of the same clichés found in business letters." While Briker concludes that "because of the intent of these letters, the correspondence ultimately produces a pure parody of business correspondence," the evidence offered by Faust's column suggests that some criminals might, indeed, have seen themselves as serious professional businessmen. Briker's discussion of the fictional Benya Krik's insistence on propriety, both in his personal appearance and conduct, in the conduct of his subordinates, and in the conduct of the raid itself, lends additional (if anecdotal) support to the notion that the criminal code of behavior mirrored (albeit in a distorted way) its respectable counterpart.[41]

Like so much else from Faust's pen, the story of the rise and fall of "Professor" Freidenberg was not so much a morality tale as a rumination on the life of the modern Odessan, in this case the Jewish man. Freidenberg was a tragic figure not because he engaged in a life of crime. Rather, Freidenberg was compelling because, despite the fact that he was skilled, industrious, and sacrificed much for the benefit of his dependents, he ultimately failed in his efforts to provide for and protect his family. At his height, the thief achieved the goals to which so many aspired. He was materially well off, his talents were publicly recognized, he was famous. And yet in the end he fell, losing everything he had worked so hard to achieve. Given that the thief's success was gained through illegitimate means, some would undoubtedly consider Freidenberg's demise as inevitable and just. But to Faust, Freidenberg's story emphasized the multifaceted pressures men had to endure in their quest to fulfill their duties, and the consequences for themselves and others if, in the end, they came up short.

Thief as Victim: The Tale of the *Skokar*

Faust continued to explore these issues in the next installment of his series when he interviewed another representative of the criminal world. "Here he sits before me in the editorial office, pale, worn out, and pitiful," the column begins. "He is a young man but already an old Odessa thief." "I have committed a great many crimes," the unnamed thief confessed. "But I have nothing to show for it but the hair on my head!" "It's my father's fault," the thief contended. "He didn't take care of me. He left me at the mercy of God." As a consequence, the young man came to know criminal Odessa "like the palm of my hand." "I know the life of the thief," the man continued. "And I will tell you frankly, there is no such thing as a happy professional thief!"[42]

When asked about his particular specialization, the thief explained that he was a *skokar,* a master in the art of stealing from apartments. In order to exercise his craft, he and a female accomplice scanned classified ads to locate the addresses of flats for rent in central city neighborhoods. Then, in the guise of a respectable couple, the pair would appear at a building, obtain the key, search for valuables, pocket any they discovered, and disappear. The whole operation took less than fifteen minutes. If the landlord or landlady came into the apartment while they were working, the two of them would simply jump out the window and make a run for it.

Needless to say, such a specialty was not risk free. After one particularly close call, the thief vowed to go straight. "I was robbing an apartment on Uspenskaia Street [in the center] when the lady of the house came back from the bazaar and caught me red-handed. I rushed at her, threw her to the floor, and bolted out to the street with pursuers hot on my tail." After this narrow escape, the young man was determined never to do anything so dangerous again. But building a legitimate life proved to be difficult. "How can we live honest lives when we are labeled 'thief' and all doors are closed to us," he inquired. With a wife and children at home "demanding bread," there was nothing to be done but to "go out and steal." "Once I truly loved the thieving profession," the *skokar* confessed. But after a time it became a disease for which there was no cure.

With this column, Faust introduced the notion that there were at least some in Moldavanka who would rather not live in the criminal world, that in fact there were those who tried to "go straight." But the story also emphasized the difficulty, if not impossibility, of such a radical transformation. The unnamed thief was prompted to reassess his definition of self at the very moment—after his narrow escape—when his chosen career had almost failed him, yet the pressure to keep bread on the table drove him to return to the same profession. A self-described slave to his line of work, his story surely had resonance in the legitimate middle-class world, where one's occupation formed such a vital component of one's identity. Further, the column underscored the point that, because occupations leading to middle-class status were for the most part beyond the reach of those in the lower class (especially to those marked as thieves), a career in crime was perhaps the *only* way one might acquire the material wealth necessary to live a comfortable life.

The tale of the *skokar* is primarily one of victimization. The first villain in the picture was the thief's father, a "typical" lower-class man who ignored his son's upbringing and abandoned him to the street. The second villain, then, was the street itself, which funneled the boy quickly into the criminal world. The final villain, though, was not the force of the street but the fortress of respectability, which would not admit a known thief to its midst, would not help "cure" him of his "disease." Thus, Faust implicated his civilized audience in the propagation and maintenance of criminality, calling into question middle-class assertions of moral superiority.

"Their Motherland Is the Street"

Ambiguous identity and moral ambivalence frequently fell by the wayside in press reports about violent crime in lower-class neighborhoods. As noted in dispatches from the port and outskirts as well as Moldavanka, a main culprit in such cases was not an individual but "the street," a complex symbol meaning modern urban life, the larger cultural milieu of neighborhood and city. "The street" in Moldavanka was a theater of corruption and vice, an image conveyed through a barrage of documentary accounts of muggings, assaults, knife fights, and murders.[43] As with coverage of violent incidents in other lower-class neighborhoods, reporters treated violence in Moldavanka as commonplace, even banal, rarely voicing outrage or indignation, instead simply writing up terse accounts included in daily crime columns with little if any commentary. Indeed, only stories that underscored the "special depravity" of Moldavanka and emphasized its otherness found detailed expression in the papers. For example, one report featured a pair of "workers" who doused a cat with kerosene and burned it alive.[44] Other stories told of Moldavankans who drank to excess and were sexually dangerous. Cases of gang rape and domestic abuse were seemingly endemic, with children as well as women portrayed as the victims.[45]

An incident that raised the ire of one popular press writer involved the murder of Moisei Blembe, who while driving his cart down a Moldavanka street, noticed a would-be thief attempting to pick a worker's pocket. When he called out a warning, the villain rushed up to Blembe's cart and stabbed him to death.[46] The *Odesskaia kopeika* correspondent covering the case was highly impassioned in his response to the crime. "Odessa's gentlemen thieves are becoming perfectly insolent, particularly here in our Moldavanka, where there is nowhere to hide from them," the column began. Blembe's assassination was "the ignoble act of a wild beast disguised as a human being. But he doesn't even deserve to be called a 'wild beast,' for wild animals are much more humane than he is." "How can one not be disturbed" by such crimes, the reporter queried. How long would Odessa allow "the wild bacchanalia" of the "apaches" to continue?[47] This column is notable not just because it invokes vivid images of Moldavankan savagery but because it highlights the fate of good people who attempted to stand up to the brutal power of the street.

Journalists suggested that children growing up in such an uncivilized environment had little choice but to adapt to the evils of their world. Writers told of disputes between teenagers that ended in stabbing,[48] of boys aged ten and younger raping girls as young as three.[49] "A two-year-old boy was made drunk and died," Faust reported one day in *Odesskaia pochta*. "True, this was done by his own little sister, who is also a baby. But whose example are they following? That of their parents and those around them." Such "unenlightened" behavior, like the displays of "wild drunkenness" so common in Moldavanka, was "corrupting" and "pernicious," the columnist declared. "Adults, dark people, you are your children's executioners!"[50]

Faust was deeply concerned with the fate of Moldavanka's children. Yet his columns set forth conflicting explanations for the cause of their corruption. Sometimes he painted lower-class parents as inherently evil. But more frequently he blamed the larger urban environment—the street—as an agent of contamination, a hungry demon that preyed on the pure innocent souls of the young. Such a view comes through clearly in one of Faust's columns, when he compares the children of Moldavanka to a "huge collection of sparrows hundreds strong that fly from place to place in summer." Walk down any Moldavanka street and you will see them, "dirty, ragged, and barefooted, but so carefree and joyful!" But soon the street would become "the major attraction of their lives," exposing them too early to all life's secrets. "The curses of passersby, the fights, violence, and debauchery, all this leaves an early imprint on the impressionable souls of children." In the end, the writer lamented, these "children of the street" would be corrupted "to the core."[51]

The victim motif was often on view in journalistic portrayals of street children. A frequent scenario described the exploitation of innocent youngsters by immoral adults, as on the occasion when a group of eight- and nine-year-olds at the behest of their "guardians" performed various acrobatic feats on a street-corner carpet. The children's faces were "like stone," the reporter noted. "They never smile or laugh." Instead, they went about their grim business, doing gymnastics and begging money from spectators in the crowd.[52]

If such reports were disturbing to respectable readers, they were not nearly as unnerving as stories depicting lower-class girls forced into prostitution.[53] It has "become the most commonplace occurrence for mothers to drive their daughters onto the street" in order to sell them as prostitutes, asserted the author of a column in *Odesskaia pochta*. Older sisters were also guilty of the crime. Then, once in the hands of exploitative madams or pimps, the little girls were dressed up in school uniforms with books in their hands, the report maintained. One twelve-year-old girl, hospitalized with a severe case of venereal disease, confided to her doctor that she contracted the disease from a "visitor" who had paid her fifteen rubles because she looked like his daughter.[54]

Regardless of the particular evil that forced children onto the streets and thus into a world dominated by the depraved, writers asserted that once there children quickly adapted, learning to emulate adult behaviors. Once again the voice of Faust spoke out on the issue. Little Moldavanka girls of four or five years of age were already "humming little songs" about getting married, Faust said. But their dreams would not come true. Once on the street, girls would start frequenting taverns and wine cellars, where "one can hear rakish songs, wine flows, laughter rings out, and sometimes a knife gleams." Girls would "morally perish" in this "intoxicating atmosphere," falling under the tutelage of experienced prostitutes and thieves, "the kind of women who found refuge, support, and attention in such places." Then the girls themselves would begin their careers, joining the ranks of those women, "the majority of whom are Moldavankan," who are "given a bad name by passersby," Faust concluded.[55]

Although probably unintentional, Faust's statements served to perpetuate stereotypes of Jewish involvement in prostitution, thus labeling Jewish women especially as wanton and immoral.[56] While many reports about Moldavanka children stressed their victimization at the hands of adults, both women and men, others portrayed children themselves, especially girls, as conveyers of corruption. One such report told of young girls lured into prostitution by their own "fallen" friends, who proudly "flaunted" the material rewards of their sordid trade.[57] The figure of the deviant child thus was transformed from victim to villain. A number of journalists described the street as a place without parents, an environment in which children could create a powerful counterculture marked by juvenile crime and defiant amorality.[58] Indeed, the image of children dominating the street was one frequently invoked on the pages of the popular press. "There are children at every crossroads" in Moldavanka, declared *Odesskaia pochta*'s "Satana," "children whose unwashed faces are marked with blemishes and disease," children playing heatedly on the pavement as cigarettes hang from their teeth.[59] *Odesskii listok*, too, portrayed lower-class children as running rampant on the street:

> One can meet them everywhere, on the street counting kopecks, lying curled up near gates and porches at night, in taverns stealthily approaching leftover food and drinking vodka like adults. . . . Whose are they? You will not get an answer to this question. They were born on the streets of the big city. Here they were born, here they grow up. . . . Their motherland is the street.[60]

Far from being docile innocent figures, children of the street were powerful creatures who defied all authority. In one of his "In the Criminal World" columns, Faust spoke of a father who petitioned the court to "save" him from his thirteen-year-old daughter, described as an uncontrollable thief: "I'm worn out with her," the father reportedly cried. "As much as I admonish her, nothing seems to help. She is being led down the path by her street friends from Moldavanka."[61] In another column, penned three years later, Faust described parents who pleaded with a justice of the peace to send their son, a recidivist thief, to a reformatory: "'We're sick of dealing with him. He doesn't care what happens to him. We've already worn ourselves out. . . . He's stealing again. . . . We will not take him home!' And a special constable is invited to take the boy away under arrest to be sent for correction."[62]

The street became a symbol of juvenile delinquency run wild, a place where children could not be restrained by outside authority but instead controlled each other. It was a training ground where veteran children initiated new recruits into their ranks, preparing them for a variety of sordid careers. To make matters worse, such children knew no borders, moving freely throughout the city, often as a crowd. An investigative police agent interviewed by Faust told of an encounter with a twelve-year-old boy who was begging in the central city: "His father testified in court that the boy runs away everyday and hangs out with a gang of youths on the street. Then, together or in small groups, they go to the center of the city to beg for alms." "How can I keep an eye on him," complained the father, "when he just takes off. I've beaten him for the last time. But how can one not beat such a convict!"[63]

Moldavanka was famous for its aggressive corps of juvenile beggars, who "run around . . . impudently soliciting alms from passersby [and] then use the money they collect to play 'orlianka' (pitch-and-toss) right next to the constable's post."[64] But begging was but one of the "professions" open to children. Those with the skills turned to more lucrative trades, especially theft. The popular press regularly reported incidents in which children of the street were caught "working" in cinemas, churches, markets, restaurants, taverns, and wine cellars, strongly suggesting that both boys and girls used petty theft, particularly pickpocketing and shoplifting, as the point of entry into the criminal world.[65] Girls in particular were accused of "systematically stealing from passengers on the tram system." On one occasion, reported in Odesskaia pochta, police arrested a group of eight girls who had formed themselves into a "bouquet of the criminal world." All of those apprehended had "rich histories" and were "old friends of the investigative police," the report declared. Among their party were girls whose aliases included "Man'ka the Devil," "Nastia the Lump," "Pashka the Black," "Man'ka the Cossack," and the "Snub-Nosed Pole."[66]

"From the introduction in Odessa of the electrichka [electric tram], the number of young female thieves specializing in 'working' the streetcars has greatly increased," asserted the investigative police agent interviewed by Faust. "They are all juveniles and there are as many as fifteen hundred of them. It is a horrible figure!" Even though "they look so small, thin, and naive," the agent warned, these girls were actually accomplished thieves, "darting in and out everywhere and setting an example for other children of the street, who idolize them." One such child thief was Sashka Vorob'eva, also known as "the golden hand," a "wunderkind" whose work often landed her in the chambers of the justice of the peace. During one of her visits, the longtime and highly respected judge S. I. Snamenskii asked Vorob'eva how many crimes she had committed. Without hesitation, the young thief proudly reported: "Your honor, you may congratulate me on my jubilee! I've committed exactly one hundred thefts."[67]

The testimony supplied in the popular press by journalists, parents, investigative police agents, and youngsters themselves strongly suggests that children on the street created substitute families, finding in each other the comfort and companionship that may for the most part have been absent at home. Bribery, prostitution, and certainly theft became means not only to survive but to earn the respect of one's peers. For Vorob'eva, convictions were a source of pride, not shame, a measure of her self-worth rather than her deviance. She reveled in her fame, her identity secured by the knowledge that she was the idol of younger thieves on the street who were just cutting their teeth in the criminal world.

While Moldavanka was most frequently cited as the ancestral homeland of street children, sometimes the young villains hailed from other parts of the city. An *Odesskii listok* reporter described an interview with a young boy on the street:

> "Where do you live?" "There" (vaguely gesturing toward the port). "What does your mother do?" "She's a beggar." "And your father?" "He's there" (vaguely gesturing toward the port). "Is he a worker?" "No . . ." "A sailor?" "I don't know . . ." "And you yourself. What do you do?" "I ask for bread . . . Give some, baron."[68]

The boy would surely become a thief, a drunk, or a pimp, the journalist prophesied. "Is it true that there is no one in all the city who is interested in the fate of these street children?"[69]

Stories about "children of the street" highlight the tension between the two most common explanations provided in the popular press for criminality in the city. The first hinged on the by now familiar assumption that members of the urban lower classes were morally unredeemable. This view comes through most clearly in stories that highlight adult behavior described as "savage" and "depraved" as well as in reports about amoral children who willfully defied authority. The second explanation rested on the assumption that children *became* evil, that they were in fact products of their environment.[70] To Faust, citing poverty as a key source of parental neglect in Moldavanka, the main enemy was material need. There were in society's depths, fathers and mothers who tried desperately to be good role models for their children, the writer maintained. But because of their never-ending struggle to put food on the table, their offspring themselves were left to the devices of the street. "How can parents 'supervise' their children, when they are occupied from morning till night trying to earn enough for a crust of bread? . . . The children grow up without supervision from the start, begging for handouts, and then move on to theft under the instruction of experienced 'teachers' of the art of stealing, like the notorious Freidenberg."[71] "There is nothing the parents of these children suffering on the streets of Moldavanka can do," the columnist noted. "They are consumed by need, by the struggle to eke out a pitiful living." "Who will supervise the children of these unlucky individuals?" queried Faust. "Who will raise them? The street is raising them!"[72]

(above) The City Theater, modeled on the opera house in Vienna.

(left) Children playing in the city garden, with a university building in view, early twentieth century.

Flower sellers on Deribasovskaia
Street, early twentieth century.

(left) The Grand Stairway ("Potemkin Stairs"), linking the port district to Nikolaevskii Boulevard and central Odessa.

(below) A view of the city from the vicinity of Aleksandrovskii Park, early twentieth century. The port district is center right, the City Theater in the upper left.

Cafe Fankoni, a favorite of Odessa's financial elite, early twentieth century.

(left) A view of the port district, early twentieth century.

(below) Corner of Preobrazhen-skaia and Elisavetinskaia streets in central Odessa, near the university, early twentieth century.

Rishelevskaia Street, looking
toward the City Theater, early
twentieth century.

A tram station at the corner of Tiraspolskaia and Nezhinskaia streets in the central
city, early twentieth century.

Cathedral Square, a favorite with local hooligans.

Central Odessa, early twentieth century.

"Moldavanka—Her Enemies and Friends"

Faust and others repeatedly lectured public officials as well as their readers about the need for social reform as a civilizing tool. Such journalists challenged their audience to put aside assorted ethnic- and class-based prejudices to see in Moldavanka a community of respectable people crying out to be saved. Beyond this, the writers demanded action. They wanted the individuals and institutions responsible for poor conditions in Moldavanka to be held to account, be they government officials, landlords, businessmen, or others who had the means to be civilized.

This was certainly the point the feuilletonist "Satana" was trying to make in his four-part *Odesskaia pochta* series, "Moldavanka: Her Enemies and Friends." Satana opened with an image that was more than familiar: "There is in Odessa a completely separate, peculiar world with its own distinct interests, its own sufferings and joys, habits and opinions, prospects and hopes. . . . This little world is Moldavanka . . . a city within a city." He wanted to get better acquainted with the "out-of-the-way, supernumerary, poor little city," Satana asserted; he wanted to leave behind the "'streets of luxury, fashion, and gentlemen'" of his own central city neighborhood and instead "stand face to face . . . with streets of sorrow, suffering, disease, destitution, and vice."[73]

Satana came to his project with the perspective of many contemporary middle-class, would-be social reformers, protecting his readers by maintaining a discreet distance between the center and Moldavanka.[74] The reporter went "slumming," describing Moldavanka as foreign territory, a place to be explored by the intrepid urban traveler. The neighborhood was wretched, the columnist noted, filled with "small one-story buildings, gray with chipping plaster." Those who dwelled inside those "Lilliputian houses" were equally forlorn: one could discern through the misted-over window glass "the sick faces of wrinkled old women or the beautiful ones of girls with dirty calico dresses and tangled, uncombed hair," wrote Satana with a sigh. True, there were some larger houses in the neighborhood, but "do not think that rich people live in them." Instead, the residents there were "poor but decent people who maintain decorum." They try to drape their homes in the trappings of "aristocratism" while all the time supporting themselves by giving cheap lessons, having dinner at home, and renting out corners to lodgers, Satana declared. For most people, though, life in Moldavanka meant sharing overcrowded apartments where "semi-white bread and a bowl of borscht" were luxuries.

Faust, too, told his readers of the deprivations and despair endured by the residents of Moldavanka, describing the neighborhood as an "ant hill of endless poverty and work" where the struggle for survival began at sunrise:

> Teenagers hurry to the factories and seamstresses to the city, where by the sweat of their brows, they will work to exhaustion. A midwife with her case

hurries to a pitiful hovel in order to present Moldavanka with a new sufferer. . . .
A funeral hearse emerges from a gray house, heading to the cemetery. It car-
ries the body of a youth, dead from consumption. His mother hopelessly
pounds her withering hands against the coffin.

Those most affected by this oppressive atmosphere were Moldavankan
children, almost all of whom would someday say that it was their lot in
life to have a sad childhood, the reporter observed.[75]

The Moldavankans evoked by Faust and Satana were the deserving
poor, innocent victims of their squalid environment, people who needed
to be "saved." As Satana pointed out, there were in fact "angels of mercy"
who operated establishments like the children's refuge in Moldavanka,
where boys and girls could find shelter, "breakfast, dinner, tea, and spiritual sustenance."[76] Such efforts, while helpful, were alone not enough. Individuals of sufficient means were morally obliged to support the work of
organized charities and social reformers, Satana declared. But, he emphasized, they were failing to do so. "If you think that [charitable organiza-
tions] are supported by rich Jews, you will be cruelly mistaken," the
columnist pointed out. Moldavankans themselves donated the funds necessary to operate charitable facilities, while *intelligentnye* workers volun-
teered to staff them. Most people in the center did not even know that the
charities existed, Satana asserted. But it was high time that situation
changed.[77] "Do not forget that at the same time that you are living a rich,
comfortable, cultured life in a big fashionable city, there are next door to
you, in Moldavanka, those who are dirty, poor, and hungry," Satana lectured his readers.[78]

Odesskaia pochta reporters often found it necessary to scold middle-class
Odessans for their poor treatment and neglect of Moldavanka. The behavior of Moldavanka landlords (many of whom lived in the center) was especially subject to journalistic scrutiny. Property owners' neglect forced
dozens of families to huddle together in "impossibly filthy, dilapidated"
apartment buildings, where people lived lives of "endless torment, eternal
hunger, and poverty from which there was no escape."[79] One story told of
a cruel landlord—the lawyer Kerner—who had no pity for a poor tailor
and his family, who suffered great losses when the roof of their apartment
collapsed. Even though the landlord himself had once lived "in the terrible claws of poverty," the reporter noted, he nonetheless "felt no responsibility for the destruction of [the family's] belongings, and did not feel it
necessary to give them another apartment."[80]

The author of another story demanded that readers start paying attention to conditions in Moldavanka. The specific objects of castigation in the
story were owners of Moldavanka buildings who allowed their properties
to deteriorate to the point that they were like the "lairs of wild animals."
The "anti-sanitary condition" of the buildings led to the outbreak of "all
sorts of epidemics and contagious diseases," the journalist's reprimand

continued. In fact the houses themselves were "a continuous threat to all the population of Odessa."[81] One landlord refused to set foot in his own Moldavanka building for fear that he might contract consumption.[82] Other landlords were portrayed as calculating and greedy. Some even hired "managers" to extort rent from poor tenants by threats, court actions, confiscation of household goods, and eviction. "Such 'managers' carry out their roles remarkably well," the author of the story noted. "The residents are not allowed a half-kopeck in arrears."[83]

Reports such as these upended the standard connection between the external appearance of neighborhood and the inner qualities of inhabitants. To Faust, Satana, and others, the squalor of Moldavanka masked the goodness of respectable Moldavankans. Going one step further, the columnists reproached middle-class property owners for creating the environment that prevented the deserving poor from living productive, healthy lives. The far-reaching ramifications of their greed and inhumanity showed that these men were not only uncivicminded and irresponsible, they were immoral. Their neglect of Moldavanka was so extreme that they were in fact *creating* "wild animals." Landlords such as these were true menaces to society, their actions undermining civilization and thus endangering all of respectable Odessa.

Landlords were not the only ones to blame for dangerous conditions in Moldavanka. A pair of stories in Faust's "Days of Our Lives" columns included medical professionals, too, in the list of Moldavanka's enemies. In the first story, Faust complained that Robinson Crusoe on his desert island would have an easier time getting a doctor than a poor Moldavankan in need of emergency medical treatment.[84] The second story, written more than two years later, showed that the problem had yet to be solved. "I do not advise residents of Moldavanka to get sick," Faust began, "not old people or women or children. It is bad to get sick in Moldavanka. It is especially bad to suddenly fall ill at night when one cannot find a physician" and every doctor's apartment becomes "an impregnable fortress." "Many doctors 'start out' their careers in Moldavanka, where it is easy for a physician to become 'popular,'" the columnist noted. "But with the coming of 'popularity' the doctor becomes less responsive and less sensitive to the suffering of those around him. I do not know whether this occurs because a doctor's nerves are dulled by an abundance of human suffering. Would that it were never so. Would that a doctor would not for one second forget his duty."[85]

Journalistic attacks such as these brought the problems of Moldavanka squarely into the middle-class center. Other *Odesskaia pochta* columnists, led again by Faust, implicated industrialists and city officials as well as landlords and professionals. A June 1912 article focused on the complaints of a group of Moldavanka residents who asked Faust to call attention to the fact that poisonous emissions from a chemical-products factory were "causing suffering and illness among all the residents," including children.

The "sufferers are asking me to help them save their lives and the lives of their families by bringing this situation to the attention of those 'who are required to be in charge of this,'" Faust continued. The concerned citizens themselves had already confronted the owner of the factory, a certain Vainshtok. The entrepreneur responded to their pleas by offering a paltry five rubles per family, Faust noted, a sum the afflicted rightly refused.[86] Faust was incensed about the entire affair. Why was such a "dangerous factory [allowed] to exist in a densely populated neighborhood?" Faust demanded to know. "Where are the sanitary inspectors? Where are the other people responsible for the factory's existence?" "If the Vainshtok factory really is infecting the air and causing illnesses," Faust concluded "it must be closed down immediately. The life and health of poor toilers is worth more than the pocket interests of business owners!"

Journalistic indictments of city officials for complicity in the suffering of respectable Moldavankans were not rare in the popular press. Complaints about official indifference toward the trials and tribulations of Moldavankans ranged from stories about poor or non-existent public services in the neighborhood to laments about the repeated failure of city government to do something about the "dens of debauchery" that peppered the quarter. A good example of the latter was a letter from a Moldavanka resident complaining about the prostitutes who "circulated" near a seedy local flophouse. These women were drunk, exposed their breasts, and used crude language, the Moldavankan asserted. "Honest working people live in the area," the writer contended. "Upright, respectable women live near there, too; they have to face this scene when they come home after a hard working day." Regardless of the fact that such complaints made in the center on the same grounds drew immediate attention, public officials did nothing to resolve the situation in Moldavanka.[87]

It is doubtful that Moldavankans had much faith in the capacity of either city government or social reformers to improve their material conditions let alone deliver them from evil. Petitions from irate business and home owners regarding everything from the poor quality of housing and public services in their community to the disruptive, corrupting influence of excessively "lively" brothels and bars were politely accepted and roundly ignored by the city prefect. Even the frequent protestations mounted by fiery members of Moldavanka's duma delegation failed to make a difference.[88]

Rather than relying on others, enterprising Moldavankans tried to protect themselves by founding a variety of mutual-aid organizations, consumer cooperatives, and voluntary associations.[89] The tradition of self-help in Moldavanka was advanced in part as a result of the highly destructive pogroms unleashed on the neighborhood in October 1905. In the aftermath of that violence, Moldavankan property owners, small businessmen, and employers joined forces to create a self-defense brigade and hire private guards to patrol the streets with police constables and night watch-

CITY OF THIEVES | 79

men.[90] By the 1910s, however, such measures appeared necessary not so much to protect Moldavankans against the possibility of marauding pogromists but to keep themselves safe from the dangers of "the street."

Conclusion

The majority of writers in the popular press perpetuated the notion that Moldavanka was a "distinct and peculiar little world," where the "normal" and "proper" relations of society were turned upside down. Thieves and con artists were neighborhood monarchs, who lived like kings in comfort and luxury. Children, meanwhile, were masters of the street, aggressive and powerful in their assertion of values that ran counter to those of mainstream society. Journalists who authored such images based their interpretations of Moldavankan criminality on well-established notions of Odessa's cultural geography and class-based moral hierarchy. Thus they emphasized the special depravity of a neighborhood in which parents schooled their children in "the thieving arts" and abandoned them to "the street" for an education in immorality. But, as this chapter has shown, Moldavanka had some friends in the press, columnists who tried to dethrone the criminal aristocracy, to humanize the neighborhood, to minimize differences and build cultural ties. But even the most zealous crusaders seemed to find it difficult to free themselves completely from entrenched conceptions about the "little city." The pertinent questions are, first, why was it necessary to identify criminal tendencies so strongly with the residents of Moldavanka and, second, who benefitted from this distortion.

One can postulate that the equation of Jewish, lower-class Moldavanka with criminality was sustainable and potentially satisfying to several constituencies. First, and most obviously, anti-Semitic Russians and Ukrainians, including right-wing chauvinists in local government whose identities rested on notions of their own national cultural superiority, would have little trouble blaming Jews for all of Odessa's ills, including crime. Second, local authorities especially the police, hoping to contain fears of rising crime, at times relied on very public displays of power exercised in the name of social order. By taking aim at Moldavanka, local officials might minimize the risk that their heavy-handed actions would alienate the politically advantaged or anyone else who might publicly question their arbitrary and repressive use of power. Third, Odessa's criminal "aristocracy" might have benefitted by using popular images of Moldavankan criminality to secure for itself a realm in which it, not respectable society, made the rules. Even the lowliest petty thief could feel that there was a place for him in such a neighborhood. If he was skilled and smart, he might even work his way up through the ranks until he, too, was crowned "king of thieves," becoming a power to be reckoned with in Moldavanka's criminal underworld and constructing for himself a powerful modern identity.[91] Likewise,

Odessa Jews in general, especially men, may have gained stature from images that portrayed their brethren as commanding and passionate, authoritative and successful.[92] This was precisely the point Isaak Babel brought home, when in his story "How It Was Done in Odessa," he advised *intelligentnyi* readers to be more like Benya Krik:

> [F]orget for a while that you have spectacles on your nose and autumn in your heart. Cease playing the rowdy at your desk and stammering while others are about. Imagine for a moment that you play the rowdy in public places and stammer on paper. You are a tiger, you are a lion, you are a cat. You can spend the night with a Russian woman, and satisfy her.[93]

In the eyes of journalists and readers ensconced in the central city, Moldavanka and its streets powerfully symbolized urban adventure, masculine possibility, and the allure of danger. For some, the district was too close for comfort, not below and away like the outskirts and the port, but a near neighbor in a variety of senses. Its inhabitants, too, could not be kept at a distance. They came on the street in their subtle masks of deception, moving with stealth and cunning into the world of the respectable, "the street" enabling their circulation into the very heart of Odessa. The exploits of skilled thieves—be they larger-than-life "kings," diligent professionals, or vicious desperados—could be titillating and romantic, amusing and highly entertaining. Such portrayals frequently emphasized the robust masculinity of Jewish men living in the criminal world. But they also served to underscore men's vulnerabilities, stressing that professional failure could and did lead to devastation, not only for themselves but for wives and children. Such contradictions permeated newspaper accounts of Odessa's "little city," revealing not only ambivalence about modern urban society but growing anxiety about the malleability of identity in the modern city, themes explored further in tales of crime in central Odessa.

4 Under the Cover of Night

In the Centre lived "the rich," those special beings who traveled first class, who could go to the theatre every day, who for some strange reason had their dinner at seven o'clock in the evening, who kept a *chef* instead of a cook and a *bonne* instead of a nursemaid, and often even "kept their own horses," something indeed beyond human imagination.

—**Valentin Kataev**[1]

• Deribasovskaia Street was Odessa's Nevskii Prospect, the "nerve center" of the city. A high-end retail hub, the street was a magnet for lady shoppers and gentlemen of business, mirroring the self-images of its most conspicuous patrons. "When bathed in the hot light of the southern sun," one journalist intoned, Deribasovskaia was "ostentatious . . . peaceful, well-fed, and satisfied," the place where "all of aristocratic Odessa . . . roll[ed] by in their carriages and automobiles." Like the city itself, this high-profile promenade was often personified in female form. By day "she" was "clean, beautiful," "splendid and luxurious." In the evening hours, she was "still more charming," when, "illuminated by the burning lights of the cinema," the center's most "fashionable public" crowded the pavement, "joyful and carefree" with their "brand new attire, grandiose smiles, idle conversation, and carefree laughter." It was then that she was at her best, with "flaneuring people" "promenading back and forth" to see, be seen, and "gain an 'appetite' for a full dinner." But "as soon as the stars start burning in the sky," Deribasovskaia's "physiognomy sharply changes," an anxious commentator warned. By ten o'clock in the evening, as the fashionable crowd went to their suppers, Deribasovskaia became "an untidy woman wearing a chic dress with a dirty hem," with "not a single honest woman remaining on the street." Instead, "creeping out from dark alleys like ghosts, like mice from their holes," appeared prostitutes and their "knights." So it was that Odessa's finest shopping avenue was transformed into a "slave market," a "non-stop market in women's bodies," where proprietor "tomcats" sought out "brutal, lustful baboons" with a taste for "living goods."[2]

Deribasovskaia's two faces were deliberately set in dramatic opposition—day versus night, light versus darkness, respectability versus immorality, civilized promenade versus savage jungle. But the situation was more complicated, some journalists warned, for even in broad daylight, Deribasovskaia was not completely in the hands of the respectable. "Whispering, secretive 'gentlemen'" loitered on the street, seeking out "old men and corruptible youth" to whom they quietly sold "pornographic artwork" and pamphlets of "piquant literature"—"Night of the Newlyweds," "Alone with Venus," and "Oy, Mama, I Have Fallen!"[3] On the street, too, were ladies "dressed in the best taste and elegance," who were not ladies at all but sophisticated courtesans,[4] women like those John Kasson described as "involved in a masquerade of class as well as virtue," "seducing gullible men, corrupting family life, and tainting virtuous women."[5]

Popular press writers returned again and again to the image of Deribasovskaia, "the street" in its central city guise as a powerful symbol of modernity, a metaphorical formulation juxtaposing the pleasures and the dangers of contemporary urban life. It was no accident, then, that the street was a woman, described by turns as virtuous and fallen. Newspaper columns suggest that for the middle-class men who called the central districts home, "she" was the site of both desire and fear, a space where secret passions might be unleashed with unpredictable results. These men wanted to be seduced by "her," taking advantage of the sexual license that urban anonymity allowed, and yet they sought to sanitize "her," purifying the street for virtuous wives and children.

Journalists intertwined reality and image to shape a complex portrait of central Odessa, one highly expressive of conflicting attitudes about the possibilities and anxieties of modern metropolitan life. Like their counterparts in the West, press correspondents in Odessa imagined their city as divided into distinct cultural geographical spaces, into "zones of light and dark, with certain areas off-limits to the respectable."[6] As seen in chapter 2, journalists considered the port and outskirts to be dangerous places, their representations of those neighborhoods clearly linking unrespectable, immoral, and certainly criminal behavior with the urban lower classes. But as known from chapter 3, such clear boundaries were difficult to maintain when it came to Moldavanka's sophisticated brand of criminality. This chapter continues to explore the fin-de-siècle city as a place where "the difference between the middle and the margin of the social order became blurred."[7]

Dispatches about street life in Odessa's central entertainment district— Deribasovskaia and its environs—were full of troubling images, representations of the city as contested social and cultural terrain, journalistic portraits suggesting that people, "formerly confined to the edges of society, had more and more usurped the centre of things and seemed to be making the city over in their image."[8] But stories from the central entertainment district and elsewhere in the center also indicated rising apprehension about middle-class "betrayers," gentlemen (and a few ladies) who either could not or did not choose to control the beast within. A significant number of sources portrayed the middle-class man as his own worst nightmare. To a surprising extent, the term "hooligan" was applied not only to "invaders" of lower-class birth but also to middle-class students, the privileged sons of the bourgeoisie, whose disreputable, sometimes violent, assaults drove fears of societal degeneration. Another ominous type was the "well-dressed man," his dishonorable deeds (notably sexual violence) belying his impeccable appearance. A character of indeterminate origins, the villain presented himself as the epitome of correctness. The fact that it was impossible to know (unless he was caught) whether the "well-dressed man" was a cunning impostor or a gentleman gone wrong made stories of his already unsettling activities even more disturbing to the public.

A smaller but important set of stories likewise shed doubt on the social origins of prostitutes, some of whom reporters claimed were daughters of the middle class. Prevailing stereotypes denied respectable ladies any claim to libidinal interests, instead casting lower-class women exclusively into the role of erotic temptress. Yet the press took pains to report the "discovery" of ladies amongst the ranks of the "fallen," journalists using such stories to warn readers yet again about the dangers of the modern city. These revelations, too, were cautionary tales rooted in the anxious knowledge that little could be judged by the naked eye, even in Odessa's best neighborhoods.

In the Heart of the City

By all accounts, the Bul'varnyi district, with its distinctly European ambience, was Odessa's premiere address, a place of special beauty, home to the very best that the city had to offer. Its beautiful tree-lined streets were straight and wide, graced with elegant multistory stone buildings of neoclassical design. Landscaped parks and squares, secluded courtyards and gardens, and majestic monuments and fountains added to the neighborhood's overall appeal. Thanks to the potent combination of old nobility and new money, Bul'varnyi was rich in the institutions of bourgeois culture and respectability. It was the seat of the financial district, including most of the city's large brokerage firms, trading houses, and banks. Many of Odessa's largest and wealthiest churches and synagogues were also located there, as were the headquarters of major charities and philanthropic organizations. Further, Bul'varnyi was the center of high culture in the city, the location of several important museums, a symphony orchestra, and the famed Odessa opera house, "the finest example in Russia of European baroque theater design of the 19th century." Middlebrow entertainments were also well represented in the district: the best restaurants and cafés, popular *estrada* theaters, and a growing number of cinemas, especially along Deribasovskaia. Shoppers with money to spare frequented the district's high-end department stores and luxury shops.[9]

Other popular Bul'varnyi attractions were its promenades, parks, and gardens. Overlooking the port at the top of the Grand Stairway was Nikolaevskii Boulevard, its magisterial architecture, stunning sea views, tree-lined pedestrian lanes and pleasure grounds making it a favorite with the public. On the boulevard, too, was the posh Londonskaia Hotel, where luxury suites could be had for the staggering rate of twenty rubles a night, and an elegant alfresco café, weather permitting, provided free orchestra concerts for the enjoyment of patrons and passersby alike.[10] Aleksandrovskii Park's sixty-five acres of greenery were another Bul'varnyi favorite, anchoring the district on its eastern edge. An additional popular spot was the central city garden, fronting on Deribasovskaia and Preobrazhenskaia streets, which offered benches for tired shoppers, pavilions selling ice cream and other dairy treats, and a fountain and play area for children.[11]

As the city garden reached Preobrazhenskaia Street, Bul'varnyi eased into the Khersonskii district, the evenly spaced, grid-patterned streets shifting forty-five degrees. Above all else, Khersonskii was Odessa's center of learning. The main buildings of Novorossiiskii University were located on Peter the Great Street; the main branch of the public library was several blocks to the north. In addition, the neighborhood was home to primary and secondary schools of all types, from kindergartens and grammar schools to specialized artistic, commercial, and trade schools. In the northern corner of the district, at the intersection of Ol'gievskaia and Khersonskaia streets, was an area known as the "medical village," site of the main building of the university medical school, the anatomical institute, a number of faculty clinics, and some private medical offices. Also nearby was the Old City Hospital, the local bacteriology station, the offices of the Society of Odessa Physicians, and the headquarters of the city ambulance service. Like Bul'varnyi, Khersonskii's physical appearance reflected the combined influences of both noble and bourgeois patrons, especially in the university quarter and the blocks closest to the sea. Khersonskaia Street, one of Odessa's prettiest avenues, was lined with block after block of gracious three- and four-story buildings, many of which housed educational institutions. The seaward end of Torgovaia Street, meanwhile, showcased some of the most luxurious mansions in the city, most of them complete with beautiful gardens and brilliant views.

The most conspicuous residents of Odessa's best neighborhoods were the nouveau riche. As a group, the ladies and gentlemen promenading in Bul'varnyi were affluent, attractive, and had a penchant for things modern. Odessa's "in crowd" enjoyed the highest standard of living in the city and had the most political, economic, and cultural clout. The men exercised their right to vote and hold public office; they sat on the boards of prominent banks, educational institutions, and philanthropic societies; they smoked imported cigars, wore well-tailored suits, and filled the rosters of gentlemen's and sporting clubs. The ladies, meanwhile, adorned in the latest French fashions and perfumes, were also involved in civic activities, organizing and working for charities, attending educational lectures, and patronizing artistic associations. In their leisure hours, they shopped, had tea had in the women's sections of better cafés, visited friends, and received guests. The living spaces of Odessa's elite were expansive, expensive, and well equipped. They had electric lights, indoor plumbing, and telephones. Their household furnishings included pianos and gramophones, original artwork and Louis XV furniture, gilded mirrors and crystal chandeliers, potted plants and silver samovars. Many of them also had dachas along the eastern shore, to which they motored on weekends in their state-of-the-art autos.[12]

While affluent residents tended to attract the urban eye, even Bul'- varnyi and Khersonskii were not the exclusive domain of the privileged. Indeed, the districts were places of significant social, religious, and ethnic diversity. In general Khersonskii was more heavily Russian than Bul'varnyi and had more residents of noble birth. This was counterbalanced, however, by the presence in Khersonskii of a diverse student body, including representatives of many social, ethnic, and religious groups.[13] Students in the district tended to live modestly. They rented rooms or "corners" in the homes of Khersonskii professionals or in tenement-style boarding houses near campus; they ate at subsidized student cafeterias or low-cost cafés on Peter the Great Street. A number of students were frankly impoverished, supplementing their stipends by doing odd jobs or giving lessons.[14] Others living less than luxurious lives in the center were domestic servants: maids, cooks, governesses, laundresses, chauffeurs, and *dvorniki,* who often lived in the same buildings as the families they served. Mid-level managers and trading-house employees maintained modest residences with central city addresses. Sales and office clerks lived more modestly still, renting small corners in basements and garrets.

Abutting Bul'varnyi and Khersonskii to the south was Aleksandrovskii, the least well-to-do of Odessa's three central districts. Some parts of the neighborhood were similar to residential sections of Bul'varnyi, with tree-lined streets of beautiful, well-maintained buildings. Overall, however, Aleksandrovskii was more densely populated, more Jewish, and decidedly more *meshchanskii* in character than the other central city neighborhoods. In most of the district, large apartment houses lay in close proximity to workshops, while small retail stores crowded in with tiny manufacturing operations. Aleksandrovskii was home to clerks, teachers, lesser civil servants, and others who labored in semi-professional, low-white-collar positions. Many in Aleksandrovskii were small-scale artisans and traders, people who lived where they worked—above, behind, or below their shops.[15]

According to Grigorii Moskvich, of all the central neighborhoods, Aleksandrovskii had the least to recommend it, its busy streets so filled with "crowds of Jews" that there was "for tourists, little of interest." Indeed, most of Moskvich's coverage of Aleksandrovskii involved how to get out of it quickly, particularly by means of the electric tram system, several lines of which converged near the main passenger-train station at the south end of the district.[16] Moskvich pointedly did not direct tourists to Aleksandrovskii's main hub of activity: the thriving commercial corridor that ran along Aleksandrovskaia Street from the Privoz market to Old Bazaar.

According to the newspapers, the two large outdoor markets were dense mazes of booths and kiosks dealing primarily in foodstuffs, household products, and seasonal specialty items. Likewise, Aleksandrovskaia Street itself was portrayed as teeming with activity. Small shops lined both of its sides while out front masses of street vendors hawked their wares directly from crates and wheelbarrows set out on the pavement. At particularly busy times of the year, especially around spring and year-end holidays, reporters described the entire corridor as "practically impassable."[17]

In the pages of the press, Aleksandrovskii and its lower-middle-class residents were seen as literally and figuratively but one step removed from Moldavanka. This perception came through vividly in newspaper stories and police records describing unsavory activities in Old Bazaar, a dangerous, crime-ridden quarter, packed with cheap boarding houses and hotels, third-rate bars and buffets, and not a few brothels.[18] Pickpocketing and petty thefts were regular occurrences in the area.[19] Sometimes police were called in to deal with more serious kinds of crime: muggings, armed assaults, drunken brawls, and street fights.[20] One *Odesskii listok* reporter warned that Bazarnaia Street in particular had become especially dangerous. Several blocks of the street were "lined with the kind of entertainment establishments that are unmentionable in respectable society," the author explained. "Highly dubious characters pour out of these places at night and harass passersby unrelentingly," he continued. "Stay away from this street!"[21]

Journalistic descriptions of criminal activity and immoral behavior in Aleksandrovskii set that district's problems firmly within the context of respectable society's growing concerns about increasing danger throughout central Odessa. Having said this, however, it should be noted that journalists covering such incidents in Aleksandrovskii were not so quick to claim that "outsiders" were responsible for trouble in the district. Instead, readers were often left to wonder whether the culprits there were "invaders" or district residents themselves. The overall tone, then, was quite different from dispatches emanating from Bul'varnyi's central entertainment district.

The Tavern Evil

For much of Odessa's history, Bul'varnyi's central entertainment district had been shared urban territory, sporting a diverse assortment of establishments catering to a wide variety of tastes. The Gambrinus on Deribasovskaia was famous to sailors from the Black Sea to the ports of New York, Sydney, and Ceylon.[22] University students frequented the Bavariia, which many called their "mortuary," thanks to the quality of hangover one experienced after an evening's revelry there. Merchants and entrepreneurs preferred the comforts of the Café Fankoni, which after 1910 also had a separate women's salon.[23] Well-to-do couples enjoyed the ambiance of the area's fine restaurants and theaters, often bringing their children to the fashionable Café Robina on Ekaterininskaia for dessert.[24] Theatrical and music hall personalities were also neighborhood habitués, lending an aura of celebrity to the nightlife scene. Meanwhile, other central entertainment district establishments, particularly lower-rated taverns *(traktiry)*, catered to a less glamorous (but no less theatrical) crowd—lower-class "rabble" and "women of easy virtue"—actors in violent "dramas" that often found narration in newspaper crime columns.

Even though people of various walks of life had been a part of the central entertainment district's nightlife scene since the city's inception, by 1912 popular press journalists were stressing the dangers rather than the pleasures of the area. It was precisely the presence of people who did not "belong" in the district that most troubled writers, who complained in their columns that Deribasovskaia and its environs were fraught with peril and uncertainty for the respectable, especially after dark. Reporters vividly described the threatening mix of unsavory types to be found in the area, portraying the place as a region where cultural boundaries were repeatedly transgressed. Cunning thieves, shoplifters, and con artists assumed guises of "correctness" to infiltrate the world of the respectable, while stealing valuables as well as pride from neighborhood residents and businesses. Master pickpockets dressed as gentlemen "worked" the lobbies of fashionable theaters, the central post office, and stock exchange. Other "imposters" included courtesans playing the part of "ladies." Popular press contributors also told of other individuals who did not bother with disguises: "invaders" from lower-class neighborhoods, thugs, hooligans, and floozies, who terrorized the respectable with their "indecent," "immoral," "insolent," and violent behaviors.

According to popular press contributors, lower-class men came to the center from the outskirts or the docks in search of entertainment in one of Bul'varnyi's less-than-prestigious taverns, where they displayed an assortment of behaviors considered highly typical of their ilk. They drank to excess, acted tough, cursed, consorted with prostitutes, insulted each other, and picked fights, some of which escalated into full-scale battles. Newspapers chronicled their disorderly behavior relentlessly if routinely in small-print dispatches lining the daily crime columns. Bar fights were the most typical kind of incident reported, with women, money, wounded pride, or bravado the most commonly ascribed reasons for such disputes. While the items themselves included few details beyond the location of the incident and the names of key participants, together they reinforced the unflattering portrait of lower-class men as dangerous barbarians capable of murdering one another over some petty disagreement or alleged insult.[25]

Thanks to the disreputable behavior of such clientele, certain central entertainment district taverns developed particularly bad reputations. The Parizh, for instance, became known as the kind of place where a customer might steal the owner's coat and hat in the middle of January, where a person might be accosted and robbed by a gang of ruffians. One might also run into a colorful character like "Tishka Krasnoglaz" ("Tishka Redeye"), whose nom de guerre made its way into the press after he stabbed a man with whom he had been trading insults over the billiard table.[26] Such incidents were also common at the nearby Iubilei, where on at least one occasion, a fight between two groups of drunken men escalated into a full-scale riot.[27] Taverns also attracted dangerous lower-class women, who threatened civilized society with their "unwomanly behaviors."

The dangers posed to society by the lower-class female tavern habitué were the subject of a June 1914 *Odesskaia pochta* column: "A woman, as the pearl of the universe, as the emblem of beauty and elegance, must always remain a woman," the report began. "No matter what level of the social ladder on which she stands, no matter how intellectually developed she may be, her purpose on earth (apart from her purely physiological functions) is to serve as a counterbalance to the rougher half of the human race—man—to soften the coarse, sharp tone of his way of life, speech, and manner." It was a woman's job to "vanquish" a man, to "convert him from his (by nature) rough and egotistical self into a knight." Her "weapon" of conquest was "femininity, that attractive, inviting, and captivating charm of her soul, that unyielding and, by definition, all-conquering strength that the Delilahs have used to subjugate the Samsons of all times and epochs." Without femininity, a woman "loses all her charm," the author declared. "Without this strength, her influence on men quickly evaporates."[28]

The notion of gender difference embedded in this passage is firmly rooted in the idea that men and women were destined "by nature" to play different roles in society, that a woman's natural morality empowered her to tame the savage beast that was man.[29] The biblical reference especially serves to underscore the author's belief in the fundamental, eternal power of womanhood, the columnist emphasizing the positive influence women supposedly exerted over men and, by extension, over society in general. Tellingly, as the column unfolded, the writer revealed that his central concern was not the feminine woman but the "unwomanly" one, setting up a familiar dichotomy between the virtuous and the fallen, a representation fraught with patriarchal values and Victorian sensibilities. "Women who play cards, smoke, and drink are no longer women," the columnist wrote. "These are the inalienable rights of men. The vulgar habitué woman who smokes and drinks with bravado is unpleasantly startling," he went on, concluding that, "if a drunken man makes an unpleasant impression, then a drunken woman inspires loathing. She loses all her charm and femininity. For when drunk she is more cynical and vile than a man."

Odesskaia pochta's coverage of a "drama" set at the seedy Iubilei, written up in an article titled "Under the Cover of Night," provides a particularly vivid depiction of the various evils associated by journalists with lower-class types and the social world they populated. The "central figure in the drama" was one of the "Iubilei's permanent habitués," a woman identified only as "the queen of love" *(koroleva liubvi)*. On the night in question, the "queen" was sitting as usual at the center of a group of men, one of whom was her frequent companion, a jealous, bad-tempered sort inclined to pick fights with potential rivals. Heedless of the presence of her possessive beau, the devilish "queen" began to flirt blatantly with a sailor, Grigorii Mamaev. Thus incited, it was not long before the two men rose to battle. The reporter left the reader with the spectacle of a murderous street fight set in the heart of Bul'varnyi. The two men faced off, each supported by his loyal retinue. Vodka bottles smashed, knives were drawn, and the blood started flowing. In the end, the sailor Mamaev died on the street as he struggled to drag himself back down to the port.[30]

"Under the Cover of Night" was the stuff of high drama, narrated by journalists who clearly played up the story's most sensationalistic aspects. Mamaev's murder was spectacular, the actors' performances over the top. The evil antics of the principal players and their out-of-control passions—for strong drink, sex, and violence—were sure to fascinate readers whose own reputations demanded moderation. But if such dark tales were entertaining for some, to the columnist Faust they were abominations, acts of barbarity committed by lower-class invaders whose presence in the city was anything but laughable. In a column titled "The Tavern Evil," Faust declared that central entertainment district establishments like the Parizh and the Iubilei were "breeding grounds for violence." They were the scenes of "horrible spectacle" (uzhasnoe zrelishche), places where "bottles and plates flew through the air and the smell of vodka mixed with blood." It was bad enough that savage battles took place inside tavern walls, Faust continued. Worse still, "to the horror and disgust of peaceful passersby," bar fights often spilled out onto the streets, where "screams and wild outbursts exert[ed] a corrupting influence on residents."[31]

Faust's heated commentary clearly goes beyond the facts of Mamaev's murder to discuss the larger dangers posed to respectable citizens by the presence of lower-class tavern-goers in the city center. Interestingly, Faust did not argue against the existence of taverns themselves. As far as he was concerned, no one could complain about the "peaceful businessmen" (kommersanty) who gathered for meetings in the "noble" (dvorianskiia) sections of taverns. Indeed, the columnist suggested, men should have fun in a controlled sort of way, should be able to come together in a place where men could be men. It was "in the terrible and disgustingly filthy 'common rooms' (obshchie zaly) with their specific brand of rabble (spetsificheskim sbrodom) that all sorts of scandals and bloody skirmishes take place, up to and including murder," Faust concluded.

Faust's logic at this point took a revealing turn. The real villain was the tavern keeper "who, in the interest of profit, permits ["rabble"] to turn a peaceful inn into a center (ochag) for every kind of outrage," the columnist declared. In Faust's view, the businessmen were negligent, uncivic-minded, even immoral. Not only were they shirking their personal responsibility to uphold high moral and ethical standards, they were failing in their duty to promote the general welfare of society. Just as a good middle-class father was expected to control his children absolutely and discipline them firmly (without mistreating them), so a respectable innkeeper was to keep a sharp eye on his clients and make sure that they were staying out of trouble. In not calling for a prohibition on the sale of alcohol or for the closing of troublesome taverns, Faust revealed a sympathy for tavern life not shared by other observers or, indeed, by local officials. In Faust's opinion, such radical steps were unnecessary if patrons within taverns exercised the self-control one expected of the respectable man and if innkeepers exercised vigilance at their entrance doors.

Faust clearly had little faith in the efforts of local authorities to deal with "the tavern evil." With unabashed derision, the writer told readers that in the aftermath of the Mamaev incident, city government was once again "busying itself" with the "eternal question" of how to curtail street disturbances in the center. But no new solutions were forthcoming from a city council that could only put forward its perennial proposal to force low-rated taverns to relocate to the outskirts. Would such a policy really solve the problem? No, Faust concluded emphatically, "[i]t would be even worse. If such scandals take place in the center of the city, what would happen on the outskirts? Any tavern there will turn into a den *(vertep)* for all sorts of shady characters *(temnye lichnosti)* and crimes."

Both Faust and city authorities wanted lower-class "invaders" to be kept out of the central entertainment district. The city's plan called for increased insertion of state authority into the worlds of business and entertainment. Faust's proposal proceeded from the bourgeois belief that individual citizens should be responsible for their own behavior and for the enforcement of respectability within the premises they controlled. This important difference aside, however, both plans rested on similar assumptions: first, that members of the lower class were the source of trouble in the central neighborhoods; and second, that because of this, the problem would be solved if invaders could be excluded from respectable neighborhoods. But try as they might to uphold this tidy conceptualization of how to sanitize the central city, local officials and social reformers, including *intelligentnyi* journalists, could not overcome the fact of middle-class involvement in unsavory activities.

"Women of Easy Virtue"

As might be expected in a "lively" port town, prostitution was big business in Odessa. According to one account, there were some fifteen thousand registered prostitutes in the city, with another twenty thousand or so working clandestinely.[32] Odessa sported around forty licensed brothels, ten of which were "first-class" and the others "less luxurious." City officials were well aware that the central entertainment district was a mecca for prostitution, and they took repeated action to try to "clean it up." Police raided the area with great regularity, especially during the summer months, when tourists flooded the fashionable Bul'varnyi district.[33] Beyond this, special night watchmen were posted in an effort to limit the activity of illegal streetwalkers.[34] Occasionally, too, even more forceful measures were taken. In June 1914, for example, police chief Baron S. V. fon-der-Khoven ordered his forces to engage in a full-scale "struggle against prostitutes, pimps, and nighttime debauchery" in the center. Prostitutes in the central entertainment district displayed wanton behavior "right under the eyes of family women and youngsters," fon-der-Khoven complained. They move "unceremoniously . . . leaning up against passing men . . . their insolence even allowing them to grab hold of the men's clothing."[35]

Fon-der-Khoven's comments underscored the view repeated in the popular press that the presence of prostitution in central Odessa was corrupting. The lower-class woman was particularly marked as the carrier of danger. A prominent stereotype saw her as an evil temptress, a pathological, disorderly creature wanton in her carnal proclivities and malicious in her desire to "ruin" respectable men and thus despoil respectable women.[36] As one observer put it, "when flaneuring on Deribasovskaia . . . you collide at every step with the Frinas and Lauras of whom three are sick, two are *khipesnitsy* [con artists], and one is a thief."[37]

The sickness was of course venereal disease, especially syphilis, a malady generally reported to afflict 95 percent of all prostitutes.[38] A police doctor corroborated this testimony, concluding after one raid in Bul'varnyi, which netted more than two hundred prostitutes, that "almost all" of the women exhibited symptoms, their bodies marked with "repulsive sores."[39] "In no other city, not even in Paris, is prostitution so monstrously notable," an *Odesskaia pochta* columnist lamented. "In no other place are newspaper galley proofs of first and fourth pages so abundant in [advertisements for] physicians of venereal diseases." Another columnist warned his audience that, "every second or third seeker of extramarital delight— are you listening, reader?—runs the risk of catching a terrible disease."[40]

Not all urban observers were so preachy in their discussions of prostitution in the central city. The satirical journal *Krokodil* frequently poked fun at those engaged in illicit relationships, as in a cartoon depicting a well-dressed man in a bedroom with a prostitute: "What are you thinking about, dear?" she asks. "About how quickly time flies, little dove," he replies. "Not long ago there was '606' and now already there is '914'," the numbers referring to drugs widely used to treat syphilis.[41] This playful but sharp little dart was clearly aimed at exposing men of the privileged classes whose immoderate cravings drove the trade in sex. A 1912 *Odesskaia pochta* report underscored the point, describing a fancy aristocratic "salon" that catered exclusively to the young bourgeois crowd. The French madam of this "chic, first-class brothel" passed out engraved visiting cards to clients and set up reservations over the telephone, said the reporter.[42]

Even if some commentators could see the humorous side of gentlemen's entanglements, most stories concerning the involvement of privileged men in the world of prostitution stressed the dark side of things. While one might laugh at an ostensibly respectable husband who ended up with syphilis, few thought it funny when wives ended up suffering as a result. As Laura Engelstein notes, educated men "bore full moral responsibility for their sexual acts."[43] But their culpability went beyond the dangers their actions posed to those at home. Playing strongly on traditional notions of women's vulnerability and moral corruptibility that denied female agency even in the realm of her own body, some writers portrayed prostitutes, too, as victims of their gentlemen callers.

Popular press columns were full of stories that spoke of prostitutes as "victims of social temperament" *(obshchestvennago temperamenta)* or, more simply, "victims of the street."[44] Representations such as these set out three categories of "villains" described as responsible for a prostitute's "fall." The first group was comprised of immoral lower-class parents who "drive their daughters onto the street" or "sell" them to pimps or brothel keepers. A second set of villains were lower-class men, who mistreat and then desert women, leaving them to fend for themselves on the "cold, indifferent street." Finally there were women who turn to prostitution after being "ruined" by "scoundrel-baboons," immoral men of the privileged classes who took advantage of and then discarded them. A large contingent of prostitutes in this third category were described as former domestic servants who fell victim to their masters' advances. As one woman testified, she "slaved" for the mistress in the kitchen all day, then at night for the "baron [who] would not give me peace." "So many [prostitutes] give this explanation that it is clearly not groundless!" *Odesskaia pochta* declared.[45] The opinion was further upheld by the assistant lawyer Mr. Gol'dbaum who said in a lecture titled "Prostitution and the Social Struggle against It" that nearly half of all prostitutes had been or were domestic servants who fell in this way.[46]

If lower-class women were represented as the most likely victims of modern urban life (their fall seeming to be inevitable), it was fear of the moral fall of middle-class women (and the greater societal implications of that fall) that evoked the most passionate journalistic commentary. As one columnist explained, "often, very often" the "ladies" entertaining "gentlemen" clients in "aristocratic" brothels were none other than "the wives of *chinovniks* [bureaucrats] or men of the *intelligentsia* professions." The "sad list" of "fallen" middle-class women included, too, "the wife of a local lawyer with a baby daughter (!), a physician's assistant, a *kursistka,* and . . . and . . . and . . . ."[47] Another reporter depicted a "salon" in which "hundreds of women from society bury their honor and sell their caresses for silk, velvet, and perfume."[48] Yet another commentator, describing the scene at the Bul'varnyi police station after a large-scale raid, told readers that among the mass of prostitutes brought in "are those from the middle and even upper circles of society." "Here are two sisters, both former *gim-nazistki*, and now habitués of night taverns," he went on. "They are fallen and ragged, with bruises on their tired, tormented, emaciated faces," the marks on their body betraying their current social as well as moral status.[49]

The notion that middle-class women would voluntarily renounce respectability in order to become prostitutes was rarely entertained by popular press reporters. Instead, like their lower-class counterparts, middle-class women were represented as having "fallen" because they had been victimized. For instance, a highly sympathetic report appeared in *Odesskii listok* about a "young woman from an *intelligentnyi* family," who wound up in a brothel after being brutalized and abandoned by a cruel husband. The penultimate moment of the story came when the offending husband by chance visited the "salon," only to "come face to face with his wife." The climax itself occurred when the brutal husband, suddenly struck by the gravity of his "crime," attempted to kill himself. Shortly thereafter, the fallen woman, too, tried (unsuccessfully) to take her own life.[50]

Performance was once again center stage in this melodrama of urban life. The scene might easily have been drawn from a popular novel or film, such as Alexander Kuprin's *The Pit* or Semion Iushkevich's *The Street*, both of which prominently featured Odessa brothels. Stories involving "white slavery" were likewise spectacular parables of city life focusing on the fate of women who fell for the wrong man.[51] Odessa's position on the Black Sea made it a hub of international commercial sex operations since the late-nineteenth century. Stories surfaced regularly about unscrupulous men and women, many of them Jewish, who procured "fresh goods" in Odessa for bordellos in Constantinople or as far afield as Calcutta and Buenos Aires.[52] While it remains unclear how many of the women who set off for foreign shores went willingly into prostitution, sensationalized newspaper accounts screamed about "good" girls who were tricked or abducted outright. One such report told of the fifteen-year-old daughter of a Kiev merchant who was rescued in Odessa from a band of "white slavers."[53] Another story described the agony suffered by a Jewish father in Odessa, who discovered that his daughter had been lured away by an "elegantly dressed young man," also Jewish, who was later discovered to be a "seller of living goods."[54]

There is a strange silence in the press on a crucial point that one might expect to be aired, namely the matter of Jewish involvement in the world of prostitution. Authorities at both the local and higher administrative levels perpetuated the view that Jewish women predominated in the ranks of brothel keepers and prostitutes.[55] Jewish men and women were also widely implicated internationally in commercial sex operations during the fin-de-siècle era.[56] Although Jewish names regularly appeared in stories about prostitution and "white slavery," the almost complete absence of open discussion about such linkages in the mainstream press is worthy of note. Part of the explanation might be that the mere mention of a Jewish name was enough to confirm already existing negative associations. Another factor may have been the reluctance on the part of liberal *intelligentnyi* journalists to enter, even indirectly, into anti-Semitic discourse that at this point was confined mainly to the political right. Still another factor may have been that the most frequent "victims" of Jewish procurers in the commercial sex trade were not gentiles but other Jews.[57] It would be understandable if a consciously Jewish newspaper such as *Odesskaia pochta* took pains to avoid identifying either "white slavery" or prostitution as particularly Jewish practices. But there was enough concrete evidence of Jewish participation in both that the paper could not openly deny Jewish involvement.

In any event, it was issues of social class rather than considerations of ethnicity that seemed uppermost in the minds of journalists as they interpreted for their readers stories about prostitution and other kinds of sexual danger. And while writers expressed high concern for female victimization, they nonetheless continued to emphasize that women, especially lower-class ones, posed a threat to respectable society. Such fears found articulation especially in tales that involved prostitutes who disguised themselves as ladies.

"My Husband's Back"

The crime known as *khipesnichestvo* was a con game that targeted respectable middle-aged "family men." According to *Odesskaia pochta,* the scheme unfolded as follows: an attractive young prostitute, the "criminal cat" *(blatnaia koshka),* assumed the role of a bored housewife and set out to "catch a fish." Dressed for the part, she "prowled" the streets of certain likely districts in the central city (especially in the vicinity of New Bazaar) until she "accidently" made the acquaintance of a friendly "friar." Beginning to flirt, the woman explained to her new friend that her husband, a "lesser *chinovnik*" or "head clerk," was so overworked that she hardly ever saw him. Wouldn't the gentleman come for a visit just to "keep her company?" If the mark (duped man) took the bait, the couple retired to a nearby apartment, her "den" *(khovir)* or "little lair" *(gnezdyshko),* where the seduction began in earnest. Then, while the *khipesnitsa* "worked over" her gentleman friend, a carefully concealed accomplice "cat" stealthily cleaned out the victim's pockets, quietly left the apartment, then knocked excitedly on the door exclaiming, "Your husband's home!" With this announcement, the distraught victim quickly retrieved his clothes and beat a hasty retreat. Only when the gentleman realized that he had been robbed did the real nature of this encounter occur to him.[58] There were other variations on the *khipesnichestvo* theme. In one case, "elegant young men worked with the 'criminal cat' to bring in clients: 'I'd like to introduce you to a charming blonde' whose husband works from nine to nine. 'The poor thing is bored.'" In another version of the con, a male "operative" *(deiatel')* actually appeared on the scene as the wronged "husband," adding injury to insult by punching the victim for fooling around with his "wife."

Khipesnichestvo was a crime of humiliation as well as of property. The key to the con was the thieves' assumption that the victim's concern for reputation and respectability would overrule his outrage and thus keep him from reporting the matter to the police. If the victim went to the authorities, it would mean public disclosure of his indiscretions. Such a course of action would undermine the gentleman's own respectability as well as that of his family. It was the fear of loss of reputation, of not being able to continue to associate with his friends or to move unencumbered by shame through his usual cultural milieu, that would prevent the "friar" from taking action. Journalistic coverage of these crimes was once again steeped in the language of performance, with all of the principal actors playing their roles on the stage of the city.

If the prostitute/*khipesnitsa* was the masked villain in the story, she was also the one empowered to unmask her victim. The fact that the con was repeatedly staged shows that criminals themselves recognized, and hence were able to take advantage of, middle-class obsessions with the appearance of respectability. The disguise of the thieves was a means to uncover the forbidden desires that middle-class respectability hoped to deny. But a strange thing happened on the rare occasions when such affairs did become public. Rather than condemning the middle-class mark for his moral indiscretion, journalists scrupulously protected his identity and hence his respectability, representing him as a hapless dupe who was "lured" into a trap or simply "fell into the affair by chance." He was "captivated" by the seductive powers of the *khipesnitsa* (who was, after all, disguised as a middle-class woman), then naively "swallowed the bait." Aside from the sarcastic comment made by one columnist that the "middle-aged gentlemen" approached by the con artists were "completely unsusceptible to this kind of thing," the victim's sexual agency was by and large denied. Any lapse of moral judgment he might have exhibited in his dalliance (which had, after all, rendered him vulnerable) was at least to some extent negated by the gross immorality of the *khipesnitsa*. Thus once again one sees the figure of the lower-class woman cast as a malevolent force. Some urban men reading about these cases might have become a bit more wary about the possibility of chance encounters. But others seeking the thrill of an anonymous tryst might still have been willing to take a chance that the bored wife of a chinovnik might turn out to be a "criminal cat."

The "Well-Dressed Man"

The wily *khipesnitsa* focused societal attention on criminals who worked in disguise. A far more dangerous kind of counterfeit that appeared regularly in the crime column was the "elegantly" or "well-dressed man," a decidedly ominous figure who embodied anxieties about ambiguous identity. On a superficial level, he looked the part of the respectable gentlemen. His behavior, however, was anything but gentlemanly and his "true" identity open to speculation. Was he a lower-class "imposter" or a middle-class "betrayer"? Even if the answer to this query could not be ascertained, what was overwhelmingly clear was that his very existence sullied the reputations of authentic gentlemen. Thus middle-class men themselves became objects of suspicion, especially to lower-class women who were the most frequent victims of the "well-dressed man."

Journalists were disparate in their treatments of "dramas" involving the "well-dressed man." Frequently the key consideration coloring their interpretations was not the identity of the "hero," however, but the social status and moral character of his female victim. If the woman who was ill-treated by the "well-dressed man" was judged to be respectable, she was portrayed sympathetically in the popular press. But if journalists saw her as a "fallen" woman, her suffering was in some measure turned against her so that she herself was revealed as deserving of her fate.

An example of the second tendency can be found in an *Odesskii listok* story billed as "An Everyday Drama" that told of Aleksandra Bukhtoiarova, a nineteen-year-old Bul'varnyi chambermaid, who one evening after work went to the Gambrinus on Deribasovskaia for a few drinks with her father and sister. After an hour or so, the "visibly intoxicated" young woman left the bar alone, intending to go to a girlfriend's house to spend the night. En route, a "well-dressed man" approached her to ask if he could "assist" her. She accepted his offer and got into his carriage. The stranger then abducted Bukhtoiarova, took her to a port district boarding house, then stripped, robbed, beat, and possibly raped her.[59]

The most notable feature of the *Odesskii listok* story is its *lack* of indignation. Given the representation of the young woman's moral character, however, this is not surprising. To begin with, Bukhtoiarova was identified as a domestic servant, and thus was automatically assumed to be sexually disorderly. Her subsequent actions confirmed her to be both "unwomanly" and "indecent." First, she went to a notorious tavern and, once there, became visibly intoxicated. Then, even though it was nighttime, she went out alone onto Deribasovskaia (!) where, rather than proceeding directly to her destination, she stopped to speak with the stranger and voluntarily got into his carriage. The fact that her father escorted her to the Gambrinus, was a party to her inebriation, and then failed to ensure her safe passage home served to underscore the "inadequacies" of Bukhtoiarova's moral upbringing. The incident was an "everyday drama" because Bukhtoiarova was represented as a "fallen" woman.

At the "Grand-Otel"

As noted in the opening, a particular concern of the journalists was the "occupation" of Deribasovskaia Street by prostitutes, pimps, and other unsavory types. But Deribasovskaia, at least, had a sunny side, one marked by

light, fashion, and ostentatious displays of wealth. Just blocks from Deribasovskaia, around Aleksandrovskaia Square, lay an area journalists and
other observers portrayed as impenetrably dark: a notorious red-light district including the old Greek bazaar and two of Odessa's oldest streets,
Krasnyi and Kolodeznyi lanes. The travel writer Grigorii Moskvich warned
his readers to steer clear of the sector, noting that "despite their closeness
to the best of the city center," he could not recommend the second-rate
hotels and Greek coffeehouses that lined Krasnyi Lane. As for Kolodeznyi,
Moskvich declared, "This lane is one of the least attractive corners of
Odessa. . . . All sorts of dubious characters huddle together there in unpre-
sentable old buildings that house third-rate hotels, boarding houses, cafeterias, and little shops." In fact, the writer concluded, the whole of the
area was "in essence a cesspool."[60] An *Odesskaia pochta* columnist concurred, reporting that in "the dark, suspicious bars and taverns of Krasnyi
and Kolodeznyi Lanes, Grecheskaia Square, and other adjacent central
streets . . . house after house is a clandestine brothel." In this corner of the
Bul'varnyi district, where the buildings themselves were corrupt, "block after block is a prostitute."[61]

An *Odesskii listok* column concerning the rape of seventeen-year-old
Dariia Vasilenko highlights fears about the area while at the same time ex-
ploring again the problematic figure of the well-dressed man and moral as-
sessments of his victim. According to the initial report of the rape, the facts
of the case were these. In order to keep up with household expenses and
save for the future, Vasilenko and her husband decided that she should get
a job. To that end, the young wife put a "work wanted" ad in the newspaper. Shortly thereafter, a "well-dressed man" appeared at the Vasilenkos'
petty bourgeois Aleksandrovskii district apartment, saying that he had a
friend who needed a nanny for her son. The stranger said he would be glad
to provide the necessary introductions if Dariia was interested. Vasilenko
readily agreed. The unknown man escorted the young wife to the notorious
"Grand-Otel" on Kolodeznyi Lane, took her to an empty room, and "entertained" her with refreshments to pass the time while they waited for the arrival of the friend. Then the unidentified man spilled onto Vasilenko's dress
some "strong-smelling liquid" that rendered her insensible, and he raped
her. When Vasilenko recovered, the man was gone.[62]

Although, as shown above, the press treated the assault of the servant
Bukhtoiarova as an "everyday drama," the rape of the young *meshchane*
housewife Vasilenko engendered an impassioned response. *Odessii listok's*
regular feuilletonist "N. Moskvich" was particularly outraged by the case,
using his "Modest Speech" column to spell out for his readers the various
dangers the incident represented. His first warning was addressed to
"pretty, innocent, young married ladies," whom he implored to be wary of
male strangers, even those who appeared to be "wholly proper-looking, *intelligentnyi* young men." "But the real danger," wrote the columnist,
"greater still than the 'well-dressed young men'" were the "'Grand-Otels'

and 'Otel de-Europes' lodged in various Krasnyi and Kolodeznyi Lanes along which, day or night, it is terrifying to walk."[63]

Moskvich described Bul'varnyi's notorious red-light district as the perfect stage for the "well-dressed man," mirroring the dark interiors of his corrupt soul. The buildings themselves with their "rooms for non-residents" were "dangerously arranged," the columnist stressed. They were "dens" [vertepy] with multiple entrances and exits as well as "secret passages," all of which were "absolutely unlit," so that "[n]o amount of police vigilance" could prevent "a whole string of 'violent rapes' from happening there."

Moskvich's column fell short of openly condemning city officials for allowing such a salacious space to exist in the heart of central Odessa. Nonetheless, the implication was clear: it would be impossible to keep "vultures" from "preying" on the innocent if the red-light district was not closed down or at least cleaned up. As noted above, city authorities were well aware that the hive of brothels and bordellos nestled together in the narrow alleys surrounding Aleksandrovskaia Square was a dangerous place, especially for women.[64] Local residents had in fact been complaining about the area for some time.[65] Yet, no matter how much pressure was brought to bear on local officials by citizens or journalists, the authorities could never quite manage to clean up Bul'varnyi's red-light district. Despite repeated threats from the city prefect to shut them down, places like the "Grand-Otel" continued to operate.[66]

Part of the explanation for official inaction might be connected to the fact that respectable women were not often the victims of violence in Aleksandovskaia Square's red-light district. Bearing in mind that, as Moskvich asserted, "naive, gullible, innocent women and girls" were no doubt reluctant "to make public the 'unhappy occurrences' that go on in those dens," the fact remains that, on the record, prostitutes were the ones who suffered most from brutalization by the men (well-dressed or otherwise) who frequented the area.[67] Not surprisingly, newspaper coverage of such incidents tended to be perfunctory. In 1915, however, the murder of a twenty-one-year-old prostitute in the Grand-Otel drew a storm of press attention not because yet another "woman of easy virtue" came to a bad end on the street but because her assailant was eighteen-year-old Maior Stroker, the son of a respectable, well-to-do central city businessman.

The first reports of the "bloody nightmare" at the Grand-Otel portrayed Maior Stroker as a rebellious bourgeois youth who, much to his parents' horror, began to drink heavily, patronize bordellos in the red-light district, and consort openly with prostitutes. When the wayward son announced that he had "fallen in love" with one of the "fallen" women, a certain Vasil'eva, his parents threatened to disown him. Upon hearing of the parents' demand, Vasil'eva pleaded with Stroker not to leave her, claiming that she could not live without him. Stroker responded by stabbing his lover thirty-two times with a dagger.[68]

In the opinion of one reporter, Stroker's trial had everything an audi-

UNDER THE COVER OF NIGHT | 99

ence might want from a crime story, "love, blood, and filth."[69] The public obviously agreed, for on the day that the accused took the stand, the courtroom was packed, admission by ticket only. "Do you plead guilty to the murder of Vasil'eva?," the prosecutor asked. "No, I do not know myself how it all happened. I do not even know if I am to blame," Stroker responded. When asked about his relationship with Vasil'eva, Stroker explained that he had befriended the woman because she was "sick of life in the brothel" and wanted him to "save her." When asked if he loved the prostitute, Stroker said that she was a "nice girl and I was a spoiled boy."

The Stroker case was the most highly publicized crime story of the year in Odessa, with any bit of gossip relating to it finding its way into the papers. When the trial finally opened, the sensationalism had reached fever pitch. One of the first witnesses to take the stand for the prosecution was Professor Kosorotov, an expert in psychology who had testified in the Beilis trial.[70] Was Stroker in his right mind when he committed the horrifying murder? Yes, said the professor, Stroker was an arrogant, self-absorbed, hot-tempered young man who killed Vasil'eva in a fit of pique.[71] Odesskaia pochta's reporter immediately picked up on the question of Stroker's sanity: "A purulent boil is being lanced in the courtroom today and the court of public conscience awaits the verdict: Did Stroker intentionally take from Vasil'eva nature's most precious gift—life—or is he a madman . . . who belongs in a lunatic asylum?"[72] The next day's headline read simply, "Madman or criminal?"[73]

In the end, the insanity defense mounted by Stroker's attorney proved to be more compelling to the jury than the testimony of the string of experts put forward by the prosecution to prove the young man's criminality. Stroker was remanded to the custody of the city psychiatric hospital for observation. If the doctors determined that he was indeed of sound mind, the case would again be heard by the circuit court.[74] Tellingly, the two defense witnesses identified by the Odesskaia pochta reporter as the most important were not professional physicians or psychologists but rather the arresting officer and the mother of the accused, both figures with differing claims to authority, who offered "medical" explanations about Stroker's behavior. The arresting officer concluded succinctly that Stroker was "not a normal man." The defendant's mother confirmed that view, tearfully explaining that "[m]y son is not normal. They gave me chloroform while I was delivering him. I was so sick then. . . . And he caught that illness."

By turning the matter over to physicians, the jury deferred the final verdict of what was to blame for Stroker's murderous behavior and thus Vasil'eva's bloody demise. The reluctance to condemn Stroker outright—to see him as a "madman" rather than a criminal—speaks to the strength of cultural assumptions separating criminality from the middle class. Stroker was not a "child of the street," a party from his earliest days to violence, depravity, and vice. Instead, he was the product of a privileged bourgeois family complete with an attentive mother who attempted to raise him well. According to the grieving mother, responsibility for Stroker's behavior fell not at her own doorstep nor that of her society but was the result of modern medical science, specifically as practiced by the doctor who, she asserted, poisoned her baby during delivery. By combining the mother's testimony with her son's version of events, Stroker's actions could be read as a perverted version of the standard narrative in which a well-meaning, middle-class hero attempts to "save" a fallen prostitute. But because of his medically induced abnormality, Stroker saw the prostitute's "salvation" as death.

Stroker's psychiatric confinement made the case easier for the middle-class public (including journalists) to explain and accept. The portrayal of Stroker as an aberration was in some ways reassuring, ruling out the possibility that his deranged behavior was symptomatic of a larger social evil: the moral decline of privileged youth. It is highly doubtful, however, that had Stroker been a Moldavankan or hailed from the outskirts or port, a jury would have interpreted his actions as anything less than criminal. Likewise, the crime would have been interpreted quite differently if Vasil'eva, his victim, had been of higher social status. The death of yet another "woman of easy virtue" was hardly to be mourned. Journalists did not try to redeem her, seeing in the murder her inevitable fate. Such reassurances aside, the Stroker case reaffirmed the troubling fact that seemingly respectable men could fall prey to their own savage desires.

No Woman Is Safe

Press reports from the central districts about crimes involving the victimization of women crystalized fears about the dangers of life in the modern city. These fears were especially apparent in stories that pitted one of civilized society's most visible enemies—the hooligan—against the person who more than any other symbolized middle-class morality—the respectable woman. According to Joan Neuberger, the prototypical hooligan was a young, lower-class "tough" who "threatened, harassed, and assaulted respectable pedestrians on the streets" by doing everything from "whistling and shouting or careening about in a drunken stupor, to more aggressive acts such as bumping into passersby or yelling obscenities in ladies' ears, to genuinely dangerous, even life-threatening crimes such as the back-alley stabbings and muggings that seemed to demonstrate contempt for human life." While such "rowdy, exuberant, crude behavior" was "shocking and offensive" to the respectable, standing "in sharp contrast to bourgeois public propriety," the harassment of women was especially threatening to the security of middle-class sensibilities. "Hooliganism was first and foremost a struggle over power: the power to define street behavior and to assert control over the streets," says Neuberger. "Not only was pestering women a relatively effortless display of hooligan power, it had the added benefit of threatening the ability of respectable men to protect their womenfolk from the dangers and vices of the street."[75]

Neuberger's assessment of the deleterious consequences of hooliganism for the bodies of middle-class women and the masculinity of middle-class men finds ample support in Odessa's popular press. "Hooliganism in Odessa goes on every day around the clock," announced an *Odesskaia pochta* report in September 1913. "And in the majority of cases, the victims are women with no one around to defend them." "There was a time when women were only subject to insult and assault late at night and only in dark alleys or when they found themselves by some unforeseen circumstance alone on the streets," the story continued. "Now women aren't safe anywhere at anytime. Not during the day, not at night. Not in the outskirts nor even in the very center of the city, at the very edge of Deribasovskaia." "Nothing can stop the hooligans once they've set their caps on a particular victim, even if she's walking on the arm of her husband."[76]

A reporter describing another hooligan incident expressed frustration and a profound sense of powerlessness when faced with such a recalcitrant and pervasive enemy: "Isn't it true that we can't walk along the street at night without subjecting ourselves to the risk of, if not a shove, then the rude and often cynical mockery of the street's 'golden youth'? Isn't it true that we're afraid to let go of our wives, daughters, and sisters for one moment, even on crowded streets?" Odessans understood and could deal with the activities of beggars, petty thieves, cheats, and thugs on the street, the reporter continued. But "impertinent, reckless hooliganism" was a phenomenon that "we still haven't managed to, don't know how to, understand."[77]

Even if hooligans' motives were deemed enigmatic, *Odesskaia pochta* reported that at least the attackers' appearance betrayed physical marks to alert the respectable to the possibility of impending danger: "The street hooligan—insolent, cynical, and malicious—roams our streets, hat cocked at a jaunty angle, hands thrust in his pockets, proud of his free and easy ways." Thus the hooligan became another portrait in the gallery of "types." Being able to see hooligans was not the problem. (They did, after all, go out of their way to be seen). What journalists and other middle-class observers wanted was for city authorities to do something to protect the respectable public from the violent, socially dangerous, culturally transgressive behavior exhibited by hooligans. Such calls became even more impassioned with the apparent increase in hooligan "intrusions" into formerly safe middle-class territory—Aleksandrovskii Park, the central city garden, Cathedral Square.[78] Public officials, meanwhile, appeared impotent, a fact that did not escape the *Odesskaia pochta* columnist who complained that, after a "rumble" in the city garden sent fearful residents running for their lives, officials responded by vowing to install extra street lights. "At least now the hooligans will be able to see what they are doing," the writer quipped.[79]

Perhaps the most telling incident highlighting the inability of the authorities to protect Odessa's most respectable residents, especially women, appeared in a September 1913 issue of *Odesskaia pochta*:

Night before last around 2:00 a.m. a group of drunken students walked through Cathedral Square talking loudly, laughing and shouting at passersby. Even the prostitutes moved away from them as quickly as possible. A minute later a taxi came into the square with a couple in the back. By the glow of the street lamp the company could tell that the woman looked young and interesting. That was enough for them to storm the taxi and throw the driver to his knees.[80]

The couple in the cab turned out to be the chief of Odessa's investigative police force I. V. fon-Kliugel'gen and his wife. Because the chief inspector was carrying a gun, he was able to protect his wife from further "indignities" at the hands of the hooligans. Still, the damage was done. What was the world coming to if even the wife of a powerful police official was subject to random assault on Cathedral Square?

Stories about hooliganism in the local press heightened public perceptions that, even in the very heart of central Odessa, streets were increasingly becoming unsafe for respectable citizens. The fears engendered by such alarmist reporting were deepened and complicated by revelations of student involvement in hooligan activities. The presence of Novorossiiskii University in the Khersonskii district meant that students were not "invaders" into respectable space. Instead, they were for the most part sons of the middle class, young men entitled by their social origins as well as their student status to residency in the center. Thus their blatant transgressions of the lines of respectability were in various senses more unsettling than those of their lower-class counterparts.

Like the residents of any city housing a major university, Odessans in the central neighborhoods had come to expect a certain level of student rowdiness. A "typical" incident took place one evening at the Neapol restaurant on Spiridonovskaia Street near the university, where a debate over a legal question escalated into a full-fledged fight. The commotion began with the combatants pounding their fists on the table, progressed to the hurling of plates and assorted pieces of tableware, and ended when one high-flung siphon bottle brought the restaurant's enormous chandelier crashing to the floor.[81] Another example highlights a different kind of disorderliness associated with students. According to an official report, the Lanzheron beach, situated on the shore below Aleksandrovskii Park, was on more than one occasion the scene of "orgies" wherein groups of several dozen students were observed "drinking wine, swinging each other around, throwing empty bottles into the air, and singing various songs."[82] Still other reports told of student hooliganism at the high-profile Café Robina.[83]

The larger cultural implications of the student disturbances surfaced in an *Odesskaia pochta* column called, "About the Scandal at the Robina." Since "Odessa only has three cafés where families can spend time together," the reporter declared, customers there had every right to be outraged by the offensive behavior of "insolent" students. In order to guard against future attacks, all possible measures should be taken to ensure the safety of regular café patrons. Alcohol was the root of the problem, the reporter suggested. Respectable people could only be protected if "half drunk subjects" were kept out of first-rate cafés. Café owners in Odessa did take measures to increase security by hiring doormen, the columnist explained, but, given "these radical times," sterner measures were required.[84] As this report suggests, the activities of the rowdy students could not be divorced from the nationwide escalation of revolutionary activity in the period from 1912 to 1917 or from the memory of student involvement in the 1905 revolution. Indeed, there is strong evidence to conclude that local authorities in Odessa (as elsewhere) viewed student behavior not simply as aimless rowdiness but as conscious radicalism.[85]

Revelations of student involvement in hooligan activities introduced an element of ambiguity into press analysis of violent incidents in central city neighborhoods. In general, journalists placed a high value on education, praising the efforts of parents often portrayed as making great sacrifices to ensure that their children could attend and succeed at school. Columnists were also generally sympathetic toward students themselves, representing them as good, respectable, liberal citizens in the making, hard working, thrifty, and wholly dedicated to the improvement of self and society. Student-hooligans, however, did not fit this mold. Rather than future pillars of civilization, newspapers portrayed them as morally bankrupt. They drank to excess, were sexually promiscuous, "flirted" with death, had a "passion" for suicide, and might even engage in revolutionary activism as well as violent hooliganism. Given that most students were from privileged backgrounds, their "insolence" could not be simply explained away by reference to the bourgeois belief that such blatant immorality was clearly associated with the lower class.[86] Instead, middle-class Odessans had to confront the unsettling possibility that some of their own sons could and in fact sometimes did pose a dangerous threat to respectable society, that in fact their children might have already morally "fallen."[87] More than this, middle-class parents, especially mothers, would be forced to admit that they themselves must be held to account for failing to provide their offspring with a "good upbringing."[88]

This was precisely the point alluded to in a column titled "Bitter Truth" in which *Odesskaia pochta*'s regular contributor Faust printed a tirade against "modern women" drawn from a letter he received from one of his readers. "Everybody knows that all sorts of crimes are preceded by poor upbringing," the letter begins. "And just look at the kind of upbringing '*intelligentnye* mamas' give to contemporary youth!" A young man "goes out onto Deribasovskaia and what does he see?" the writer asks. Women promenading on the street "practically in bathing suits." "Why do they permit women" to appear so immodestly, he demanded to know. Why are women "trying to augment certain parts of their torsos? Is this for the moral education of youth?"[89] While the misogynistic tone of the letter's author is difficult to miss, the incensed writer nonetheless identified yet another "they" whom he thought were to blame: the men who controlled Odessa's government and, in his view, who should control women.

The presence of vice, not to mention violence, in the heart of an otherwise beautiful and well-heeled neighborhood was the cause of genuine fear for many central city residents, who likewise called on local authorities to do something about cleaning up Deribasovskaia and its environs. While some urban "explorers" might have enjoyed moving in this hazardous space, others surely steered clear of the central entertainment district, hoping to avoid its multifarious evils.[90] Respectable Odessans wanted action. Prominent individuals wrote letters to the editors of important newspapers and petitions to the city prefect, which were hand-delivered by well-respected and influential representatives in the name of the "public." Meanwhile, others in educated society who hailed from the center delivered speeches and lectures on decaying morality or inadequate civic protection. Unlike the pleas of less-privileged Odessans, the demands of central city residents did not fall on deaf ears. On the contrary, the central neighborhoods as a whole enjoyed the unrivaled favoritism of city officials, partly because of the ability of savvy residents to articulate their concerns and apply pressure to "work" the system. Complaints about muggings and purse snatchings in the center resulted in the installation of electric streetlights and the establishment of new police posts. When too many prostitutes congregated in the red-light district, police raids swept the area clean. Hooligans and perverts were arrested, vagrants and street urchins were sent packing.

Conclusion

Popular press journalists narrated the skirmishes that broke out in the central entertainment district, articulating as they did so conflicting views of city, self, and society. Writers represented the area as the most highly contested terrain in Odessa, both geographically, by citing the incursions of lower-class invaders, and morally, by suggesting the breakdown of established (if stereotypical) class and gender linkages to respectability. Even though newspaper contributors continued when possible to rely on familiar references in order to explain trouble in the center, the interpretive authority of such explanations became less and less effective as the social roots of danger became more and more ambiguous.

The pages of the popular press reflected clearly the frustration of respectable middle-class men with their inability to influence, let alone control, the turf they had claimed for themselves in the central city. Regardless of their economic power and political clout, they still had not been able to realize their reformist agenda. Although middle-class calls for official action were heard at city hall, government officials consistently failed to deliver on their promises to "clean up" the central districts—a fact that could be attributed variously to ineptitude, corruption, lack of resources, or, perhaps, will. In any event, middle-class opinion alone was not enough to dissuade lower-class citizens from moving freely though the city, especially to their favored "haunts." Indeed, some openly mocked those who saw them as invaders. Student "hooligans" likewise appeared little inclined to bow to the dictates of polite society, using the street as a site to aggressively assert their contempt for the social milieu of their birth, deliberately defying the sensibilities of the respectable.

The fight for control of central Odessa was very much about the intersection on the street of commerce, entertainment, violence, power, and women's bodies. So, too, was it about the performance of identity; the incidents considered most troubling by journalists (and, by extension, their audience) involved the blurring or distortion of the lines separating the civilized from the savage. It was precisely when a person appeared to act "against type" that his or her underlying motivations (and inner character) came under the closest scrutiny. The resulting dissonance is highly revealing of the range of fears plaguing Odessans, setting into stark relief the unsettled nature of identity in the modern city. The *Odesskaia pochta* columnist Satana captured this sentiment: "Odessa is beautiful, magnificent, well-proportioned, and graceful," the columnist wrote. But "do not trust this beauty. She is utterly infected with syphilis."[91]

There is little doubt that newspaper stories about street life in the center heightened fears among the respectable. But there was another side to all this. Masquerade could be dangerous but it could also be fun. The dramas of the metropolis were the stuff of spectacle, full of titillation, enhancing the city's appeal as a world of intrigue and adventure. Journalists spoke of central Odessa especially as a venue for performance, a stage filled with masked players who may or may not be what they seemed. As will be seen in the next chapter, in their roles as urban spectators, popular press writers encouraged readers to enjoy the show, but from a safe distance. For if the city could conceal, it could also expose, a lesson some learned the hard way under the cover of night.[92]

5 Making an Appearance

Every season arrives with new fashions and colors of ladies' clothing. Two years ago it was considered almost indecent not to dress in lilac. This winter green was the reigning color. Now the spring season has arrived from abroad—it's white.

—*Odesskii listok*[1]

• In his 1913 guide to the city, Grigorii Moskvich wrote that the dream of the "essential Odessan" was to strike it rich and immediately acquire a house, a carriage, and everything else he needed in order to "transform himself (by appearance, of course) into an impeccable British gentleman or blue-blooded Viennese aristocrat." Then, "[i]mmaculately dressed, with an expensive cigar in his teeth," the remade Odessan was ready to meet his public. Whether "getting into a carriage or sitting down in one of the better cafés, on the boulevard or in the park," the Odessan was "out to impress by his appearance, aware of his own worth, looking down on everyone and everything below." "Odessans are proud of themselves (not without foundation), flaunting their ability to dress as well as any purebred Parisian or Viennese." Women, too, were always well turned out, "no husband carrying the expenses of his wife's toilette as uncomplainingly as the Odessan." "This passion for fashion, the desire to impress by external appearances, penetrates all of Odessa society, from the counts to the cooks," the writer declared. "The petty bank clerk, cashier, or salesclerk at the haberdashery, the barber, and lackey, everyone in Odessa is superlatively dressed and mingles in the variegated street crowd, full of the consciousness that on the street, in the restaurants, on the promenades, everyone is equal." In Odessa, "appearances get a lot of attention," Moskvich concluded.[2]

In the writer's estimation, the "essential Odessan" was a quintessential arriviste, caring only for money and the social status it imparted in bourgeois society. Even more than the residents of fabled Nizhnii Novgorod, the Odessan was defined by "the passion for quick enrichment, the spirit of enterprise and a rare resourcefulness and shrewdness in business," Moskvich declared. Indeed, "the cult of profit penetrates to the innermost recesses of [the Odessan's] heart," his soul given into the hands of the "pagan idol" Mercury, Roman god of commerce and thievery. The Odessan was obsessed with image while giving little regard to "spiritual development" or "the inner content of public life," the writer complained. Even "in questions of serious books, journals, the theater, and art," the Odessan was "fashion obsessed," "fickle," and "capricious." As a result, despite the fact that Odessa was "the intellectual center of New Russia, the Crimea, and the Caucasus," the city was culturally inferior to St. Petersburg, Moscow, Kiev, Warsaw, or even Kharkov. The Odessa "public" *(publika)* concerned itself only with that which was "in keeping with the spirit and mood of the moment," concluded the author.[3]

Moskvich's judgments about the questionable refinement of the Odessa public were confirmed by the city's popular press journalists. Speaking to their readers from the perspective of *intelligentnyi* gentlemen, contributors to mass circulation dailies supported the view that "spiritual development" lagged quite considerably behind the cultivation of image among the city's would-be bourgeoisie. To Moskvich, the explanation lay in the fact that Odessa's *intelligentsia* was "comparatively small," its civilizing efforts "lost among the huge half-million population of traders."[4] An *Odesskii listok* columnist concurred, complaining that Odessan society was dominated by the "middle *meshchanstvo*," people with material means and a degree of refinement but who lacked the qualities of mind and morals that characterized the truly civilized.[5]

As this chapter shows, journalists used stories about individual and group behavior in public to articulate a calculus of respectability that juxtaposed the virtues of idealized *intelligentnyi* types with the flawed behavior and indecent appetites of their moral inferiors. Stories such as these take the reader into the realm of "crimes" of taste and refinement, some involving misdemeanors and others full-blown felonies. These are tales of spectacle and spectatorship that do not involve blood, narratives of a lighter genre than those dealing with the violent theater of the streets. But performance in both its literal and metaphorical senses is still very much in evidence here. The dramatis personae include bourgeois "ladies in white," icons of purity and light who take control of the street for a charity fundraising campaign, and dandified "Robinists," gentlemen of the café, pristine in appearance but rogues within. This chapter will also consider the appearances of celebrities and entertainers, including a fabulously corpulent wrestler and an exotic troupe of Africans who came to Odessa on tour.

Notions of masquerade and authenticity remain a crucial part of the story as journalists invoke highly nuanced criteria to separate "real" ladies and gentlemen from pretenders and philistines. But once again it becomes apparent that identity performance in the modern city resisted clear-cut classification, with journalists themselves caught in the paradox of appearances. Writers were quick to mock the Odessan's penchant for vulgarity even as they themselves fueled popular fascination with middle-brow entertainments that were a far cry from *intelligentnyi*. Paradoxically then, stories about public behavior and popular tastes simultaneously critiqued and perpetuated the *meshchanskii* values so closely tied by Moskvich and others to the tainted character of the "essential Odessan."

Ladies in White

Odessa's middle-class women, like their counterparts in the West, were a growing public presence on the streets of the city. They routinely appeared to shop or run errands, go for walks, visit the library, or take tea in the "ladies' sections" of the better cafés. Women traveled through the city, the elite in carriages or automobiles, the thrifty on foot or by streetcar, bound for the venues of polite society. They attended committee meetings and public lectures. They made charity calls or did volunteer work. Some also appeared in professional roles, as teachers, nurses, clerks, and the like. In the evenings, too, the ladies of Odessa were a familiar sight on the streets, on the arms of male escorts who accompanied them to sites of respectable sociability: restaurants and theaters, balls and concert halls, art exhibitions and readings, the circus, the skating rink, the cinema, the park, the boulevard.[6]

Although as a group the ladies of the middle class were becoming more visible, individually they took pains to remain inconspicuous. Social conventions of the day, as articulated in etiquette books, stressed that cleanliness, simplicity, and modesty were "the most important of charms," emblems of decency revealing a woman's strong character. Only the vulgar drew attention to themselves with rich materials, bright colors and excessive displays of jewelry, or by wearing clothes that were "prettier than necessary" or "too fashionable," etiquette writers opined. A proper lady sought to avoid the public gaze and thus elevate her own beauty. She dressed carefully and conservatively, usually appearing on the street in subdued colors and always with a hat and gloves. In the warm summer months, too, the respectable woman preserved her modesty, wearing lighter colors, particularly white, but with a parasol in addition to the mandatory hat and gloves. Under no circumstances did she appear in public with heavily rouged cheeks or smelling obviously of strong perfume.[7]

Once on the street, a lady knew that not only her clothing but her manner of walking would indicate to others her degree of refinement and hence respectability. A lady took light, measured steps, moving "neither too quickly nor too slowly." She held her torso erect and her head high "without affectedness or arrogance," making sure that her arms moved in an easy, relaxed, and natural manner. Touching others on the street, even by accident, was very bad form, and it was considered sheer madness when walking to speak loudly, gesture wildly, or sing. A lady especially avoided meeting the eyes of passersby or speaking so that she might be overheard. Indeed, she scrupulously avoided contact of any kind with strangers. Under no circumstances did she stop to speak or flirt with a man on the street. Instead, she proceeded ahead purposefully but modestly with eyes forward and downcast.

Contemporary notions of proper behavior for women in public are demonstrated by the writer Valentin Kataev, who in his memoirs of growing up in a middle-class Odessa family, recalled vividly his mother's transformation when she went out on the street:

> At home, she was soft, pliable, warm, and usually without a corset—just an ordinary, cozy mamma. But in the street she was a severe, even slightly disagreeable lady, with a black-spotted veil over her face, and a dress with a train, which she held up to one side with her hand, on which hung a little moiré bag, embroidered with spangles. . . . [This woman was] not my mamma at all but "madam," as she was addressed in shops or by someone inadvertently brushing against her on a narrow pavement: "I beg your pardon, madam."[8]

Popular press reports suggest that dressing and behaving conservatively in public were for a woman more than simply matters of good form. Journalists warned ladies that appearing on the street was a dangerous proposition, that a woman's personal security was on the line every time she ventured out, especially unescorted. For even if a lady took special pains to present a properly modest public face, she might nonetheless subject herself to the unwelcome, potentially dangerous attentions of men. *Odesskaia pochta's* columnist Satana emphasized precisely this point in his cautionary tale of one lady's adventures in the wilds of the city. The heroine's trauma began when she went out alone in the evening in search of the apartment of a certain seamstress. Entering the courtyard of a large building in a remote corner of the lower-middle-class Aleksandrovskii district, the lady was accosted by a famously gruff *dvornik*. The veritable Cerberus[9] "growled" at the woman in an "insulting" tone, addressing her in the familiar *"ty"* form of address rather than the formal *"vy"* (which would have been more appropriate for a lady of her station). "[T]rembling with fear and indignation," the lady "reproached him for his rudeness and moved on." "Stop or I'll kill you," the "fearsome dvornik" snarled after her. "You can imagine for yourself the situation of the poor lady," wrote Satana. "There she is in a huge, unpopulated courtyard at eight o'clock in the evening with not a soul in sight except for a huge ferocious man with bloodshot eyes." At that point, "close to fainting" and "pale as death," the lady fled the scene, rushing out to the street where she was ministered to by kindly passersby.[10]

Satana's column pivots on the stark opposition of the vulnerable middle-class lady and the threatening lower-class "Cerberus." Dvorniki are not known for "delicacy and knightly subtlety," Satana declared. But rudeness of this particular character—harassing and even threatening a respectable middle-class woman—was so extreme that Satana labeled the dvornik a "hooligan." By thus invoking the specter of one of respectable society's most visible enemies, the columnist simultaneously deepened his vilification of lower-class men generally while castigating middle-class ones for their seeming inability to protect innocent ladies. But Satana did not stop there; he impugned respectable men still further. Not satisfied with laying blame for the incident solely on the impudent dvornik, (whose behavior while inexcusable was predictable), Satana found fault, too, with the "gentleman" landlord, who failed in his civic duty by hiring such a "monster." Going beyond this, the columnist implicitly admonished all middle- and upper-class men who took on employees, reinforcing the message that they themselves were ultimately responsible for the conduct of those they retained. Satana reserved his strongest counsel for middle-class women, his words a study in warning and reprimand. "If you value your personal safety, avoid [this building] at gunshot range," declaimed the columnist, underscoring not only the particular dangers of a specific address but the wider even more perilous ones that might await a lady who ranged too widely into the urban jungle. Like other men of his day, Satana was far from comfortable with the notion that respectable women should have free rein in the city.

Ambivalence about respectable women's growing public role is evidenced, too, in a series of stories about White Flower Day, a city-wide charity extravaganza held one day each spring to raise money for the Odessa Anti-Tuberculosis Society. If social convention demanded that decent women go out of their way to be inconspicuous on the street, the occasion of White Flower Day offered ladies a rare opportunity to upend this dictum. On the "holiday" in April 1912, for example, dozens of middle-class women took to the streets festooning themselves in white paper flowers that they "sold" throughout the city. Their efforts were met with stunning success. When the proceeds were tallied, organizers proudly announced that some 46,000 rubles had been collected in a single day.[11]

Odesskii listok covered White Flower Day as a major news happening, including splashy from-the-street accounts emphasizing the warm response people throughout the city showered on charity workers. In these reports, women volunteers were given the lion's share of the credit for the event's success. In their roles as philanthropy's saleswomen, they were portrayed as bright, charming, lively, compassionate, and indefatigable, bringing out the best in everyone they met. Indeed, in all of its coverage, the paper related only one minor incident that besmirched White Flower Day: One of the lady volunteers working on Nikolaevskii Boulevard, her hands overstuffed with coins, let slip a gold piece which fell to the ground. The coin was immediately swept up by a man who disappeared into the crowd.[12]

In their reporting of White Flower Day, popular press journalists offered uneasy acknowledgment that respectable women were entitled to a discreet but important place in the public world. Masters of the street, if only for a day, the ladies of the middle-class had license on White Flower Day to break the rules of polite society. While journalists did not represent charity workers as tempestuous, uncontrollable, "new women" whose activities fundamentally threatened traditional male authority, some writers were clearly uncomfortable with the notion that proper ladies would under any circumstances approach men on the street for money. Indeed, as the following report suggests, it seemed to some observers that it was the attentions of the ladies themselves that were up for sale:

> A well-groomed gentleman smiled good-naturedly at a young saleswoman adorned in white flowers. Not averse to paying a little attention to her, the man said, "Pin the flower on me yourself and it will mean gold in the collection box." The saleswoman answered smartly, "I'm really too busy but for gold, I agree."[13]

The insinuation of impropriety imbedded in the narrative hints at deeper anxieties about women's public roles. Journalists wanted to ensure that respectable women in public would never be confused with "public" women. This was especially important given that in Odessa, as in any port city, the culture of prostitution was particularly vibrant, seemingly immune to attempts at "eradication." Journalists strongly suggested that middle-class women should take great pains to present themselves unambiguously, prescribing visual criteria especially as a means to draw clear distinctions between "good" women and "bad."

Another of Satana's columns provides a classic example of oppositional characterizations aligning markers of appearance with qualities of character. "Go out onto Preobrazhenskaia Street near 'Passazh' at eleven in the morning, at two in the afternoon, at six in the evening," the columnist begins, summoning up the image of one of central Odessa's busiest intersections. There, with the "intoxicating sounds of a waltz" floating on the air, you will see sitting on the verandah of the fashionable Kvisisana restaurant "the flower and cream of society," "charming ladies" brilliantly turned out in the tastefully elegant white dresses of summer, the very "emblem of purity and innocence." Meanwhile, "on the pavement, close to the verandah, other women dart back and forth," Satana continued, "damned" women with "crudely painted faces" and "tastelessly loud florid attire." These were the "Frinas and Lauras of one-ruble love," Satana went on, lower-class women whose bodies were marked "with the seals of a shameful profession."[14]

Satana's use of symbolism is strong, if obvious: white versus florid, purity versus crudeness, elegance versus tastelessness, the innocent versus the damned, the respectable middle-class lady versus the immoral lower-class whore. Not only do his comments harken back to etiquette manuals with their dictates against bright colors, makeup, and improper carriage, they also suggest the extent to which journalists fitted all women into two categories—the virtuous and the fallen. Since such an opposition was only sustainable if there were clear visual signs separating the two, there was no room in this system for gradation or ambiguity. Journalists told women that the more they adhered in public to the "laws of good form" the less likely they were to be mistaken for "public" women.[15]

Journalists represented the middle-class "lady in white" as a model of impeccable virtue just as her lower-class counterpart was a portrait in vice. In both cases qualities of appearance and morality were studies in harmony. Dissonance arose when respectable women gave in to shortcomings in behavior to which they were deemed particularly "susceptible." Etiquette writers warned that vanity, pride, and curiosity were three vices against which women had constantly to fight. "Passions" for gold, idleness, apparel, jewelry, coquetry and the "immoderate craving for praise" were other defects that might stain a woman's character. Women as a group were also susceptible to gossip, cattiness, superstition, flattery, and, especially, talkativeness.[16] It is exactly these "vices," closely linked to the *meshchanstvo,* that were satirized in an *Odesskii listok* piece called "Ladies' Chatter," which began with the following exchange between two friends meeting on the street:

—"Akh, my dear, this is terrible! . . . It's . . ."
—"Don't tell me, cheri! . . . I've been sniffing my smelling salts all day already . . . C'est incroyable!"
—"It's terrible! . . . It's awful! . . . Today I should have bought myself a new spring hat but Bazel said: 'There will be no hat for you now, my dear! . . .' 'Mais pourquoi donc?' I asked . . . And he said: 'They say the Dardanelles are closed . . .' I laughed: 'But Vlasopulo [a boutique] is open!' . . . And then, my dear, he looked at me fiercely and said something that I simply can't repeat . . . and wouldn't give me any money!"[17]

The sprinklings of French dotting the ladies' speech were pure affectation. So, too, was the mention of smelling salts, with its intimation that the speaker was such a delicate flower that she could not possibly suffer another piece of news that might offend her gentility. The first speaker's lust for a hat and her shock at being denied the funds to acquire one revealed other vices: vanity, a passion for apparel, and lack of thrift. These faults in her character were highlighted still further when the speaker continued her tale of woe:

—"But that is nothing . . . Yesterday evening we intended to go to the [Café] Robina . . . We got in the carriage and arrived—where do you think—at Ditman's! . . . Imaginez vous! . . . I, of course, was astounded . . . But Bazel said: 'If the blockade of the Dardanelles lasts another few days, then there will not even be dinner at Ditman's' . . . How do you like that?"

The "conversation" becomes truly absurd when the two ladies begin to talk politics, blaming the Italians for the closing of the straits and, thus, for their own inability to buy new spring hats and eat dinner at the "right" cafés. "It is our duty to organize an 'anti-Italian' patriotic league," one of them suggests, calling for a boycott of Italian opera singers. "Banish pasta from the dinner menu!" she exclaims with enthusiasm. Still later, the ladies speak of Count Witte: "Is it true that he is in fashion again?" one asks. "Yes, yes. I have already seen an umbrella model called 'the Witte.' It is the height of fashion."

Although the "conversation" is clearly satirical, it serves to highlight the crucial importance of external signs (most of western provenance) in the assertion of respectable identity. Fashionable clothing, a carriage, shopping at an expensive boutique, and dinner out at a chic café were part and parcel of the bourgeois lifestyle. It is important to note that these markers of appearance in and of themselves were not skewered in the tale. Instead, the *intelligentnyi* author critiques the "ladies' chatter," ridiculing their failed attempts to appear cultured, well informed, and patriotic. Still, the author of the "conversation" treated his subjects gently. There is no doubt that the women represented in the piece were respectable, but they were also *meshchanstvo*, characterized by superficiality, excessive materialism, and a paucity of "spiritual development" but at least striving in the direction of goodness. In the hierarchy of crimes of taste, chattering ladies were misdemeanor offenders. Robinisti, on the other hand, were out-and-out felons.

Robinisti

The Café Robina was Odessa's most fashionable haunt, a main hub of middle-class sociability. Among its denizens were some of the city's most high-profile personalities: politicians, financiers, high-ranking officers, distinguished professionals, and "stars" from the world of entertainment. The presence of such luminaries did much to heighten the prestige of Odessa's premiere café. So, too, did the fact that journalists themselves liked to frequent the Robina, meaning that the presence of those luminaries did not go unreported. Part of the reason for the Café Robina's popularity with middle-class patrons was that it served so many purposes. Businessmen and politicians came there to work, negotiating deals or conducting meetings over coffee and sweets. Others came in search of work, hoping to strike up profitable acquaintanceships with successful entrepreneurs, exporters, merchants, or brokers. Many others, including women, came simply to relax, enjoy the company of friends, and catch up on the news of the day: When would the Dardanelles reopen? How high would wheat prices go? What was the latest exchange rate? Did you know that Libman is selling his house? Did you read the latest about Spitz the police dog? Have you heard? The tenor Ansel'ma's voice is gone![18]

For people who aspired to upward mobility, being a part of the café world meant being on the inside. "When Odessa infants start to talk, the first word they pronounce is "Robina!" wrote Faust, one of *Odesskaia pochta*'s regular columnists. "Especially clever ones utter the phrase, 'Robina and Fankoni!'" he proclaimed (referring to the other café favored by Odessa's financial elite). "The father rejoices," Faust continued. "'As I live and breathe, the baby will be a big merchant!'" The columnist Satana expressed similar feelings about the importance of the city's two most prominent cafés: "Every Odessan, regardless of social position, considers it necessary to go to the Robina or Fankoni at least once in their lives," Satana declared, "but especially to the Robina." "To live in Odessa and not go to the Robina is like being in Rome and not going to see the Pope," he concluded.

While every Odessan might have dreamed of going to the Robina, the astronomical prices charged there ensured that the café would remain the exclusive domain of the privileged. In return for their rubles, the Robina's patrons enjoyed luxurious surroundings and immaculate service. The verandah especially was a sight to behold, with neat "rows of snow white tables" set amongst "winding ivy, wild grapes, and tubs of exotic plants." Through the greenery moved exquisitely dressed waiters in black frock coats and white gloves, flawlessly serving the chocolate and cakes so "importantly" ordered by the "mesdames" and "monsieurs." Young people especially were drawn to the Robina's "fairy tale" atmosphere. As Faust declared, when "a bashful youth" wanted to "fix a meeting with a girl . . . he says shortly, 'To Robina!' . . . When a 'proper' lady wants to talk with a 'proper' gentleman, she whispers to him, batting her eyes, 'To Robina!'"

Among the "monsieurs" who frequented the café were the so-called Robinisti, a disparate assemblage said by journalists to include "artists without engagements," "unemployed salesmen," and "men waiting for the opening of the Dardanelles." The group's most conspicuous members—the most "typical" Robinisti—were profligate sons of the middle class, well-bred, well-educated young men of good families who should have been the pride of polite society but instead were its nemesis. According to journalists, who sardonically dubbed them "the golden youth," Robinisti were always immaculately dressed, giving every appearance of gentility. Instead of being true gentlemen, however, Robinisti were devious satyrs devoting themselves exclusively to the pursuit of pleasure. They did not work, as every middle-class person was duty-bound to do. Instead, they were idlers, gossiping aimlessly over coffee on the verandah by day and vodka in the billiard room by night. As if these sins were not enough, Robinisti also indulged in foolery, deception, and scandal. They gambled (and cheated) at billiards, insinuated themselves into the company of the rich to get free meals, and invited young women to join them at table only later to present them with the bill. If all else failed, Robinisti were known to order expensive meals and then walk out without paying.

Popular press contributors pitched a relentless attack against the Robinist, suggesting that this type of outwardly respectable man—a dandy who engaged in "a deliberate program of self-fashioning, designed to create the image of a man with taste and well-honed masculine manners"—posed more than a benign threat to polite society.[19] In a scathing column addressing the matter, Satana pointedly unmasked the young men as social frauds: "Look at them. They have chic visiting cards, collars brilliant and elegant, ties that are something delicious. All signs stamp them as higher gentlemen. But if you probe one, you will find a rogue *(zhulik)*, a thorough rogue."[20]

To those of bourgeois sensibilities, personal industriousness was a hallmark virtue of respectability. "A person is born to work; this is a law of nature," etiquette writers opined. "Only he who loves work is content, happy, and at peace." Idleness, on the other hand, was both an unnatural and an immoral condition, one fraught with negative consequences for self, family, and society. The rich man of leisure was an object of scorn, a morally bankrupt figure who did nothing to improve either himself or society. "One look is enough to see that boredom eats up the idle man . . . that riches and even entertainment cannot fill up the emptiness of the soul or excite its activity." Such a man was destined to destroy himself and ruin his reputation, succumbing in his boredom to all manner of corruption. Such a man had only himself to blame for his reduced circumstances. He was "guilty before God whose will it is that a man be obliged to toil."[21]

In journalistic writings, the Robinist was portrayed as a betrayer of his class, a man who blatantly mocked all of the values held dear by the sincerely respectable. The Robinist "lived with the wind," never lifting a finger to support his own penchant for luxury. Instead, he shamelessly exploited the generosity of others, especially young women, whom he charmed, then unceasingly manipulated. An *Odesskaia kopeika* contributor calling himself "An Enthusiast" characterized the type mercilessly in a poem called "A Robinist's Monologue," which read in part:

Thank the lord, I am twenty years old
and to strict laws I am true.
I am always well-fed, well-shod, well-dressed.
I am well-known to all, the entrance to high society
open to me as to few others.

How do I live? You know quite well.
A carefree bird is living?!
Aren't there billiards? Aren't there "belles femmes"?
I borrow and do not repay.
That is my skill and my habit.[22]

Yet another story starring a Robinist (found appropriately enough in the pages of a theater review) represents the "hero" as exactly the kind of man with whom etiquette writers warned readers not to associate. He was a lazy, selfish, immoral cad, the very antithesis of the respectable, hard-working, middle-class family man. The "drama" took place during the period of malaise that settled in after lunch, when the Robinisti were running out of ways to entertain themselves: "All the anecdotes had been told ten times. All the local gossip had been discussed. 'If only there was a little scandal,' someone sighed." Then, suddenly out of nowhere, a young woman "barged in," running straight up to an "artistic looking young man" (an unemployed actor) who was "sitting at one of the tables drinking coffee and eating sweets." "You worthless scoundrel," the woman cried. "How can you leave me alone at home to starve with a baby while you hang around in taverns and restaurants?"

> All the "Robinisti" were on their feet. The post-lunch laziness disappeared like smoke. From one of the tables someone said enthusiastically: "Look at him, he wanted a scandal. It's great!" The artistic-looking young man finally tore himself from the grip of the young woman and ran through the restaurant, with the woman in hot pursuit. They circled several times through the ladies' section, then flew into the street where the woman overtook her cowardly friend and got him into a carriage. The public watched until the pair disappeared from view. "They've gone," they said sadly, and went back to their coffee.[23]

The story is an indictment not only of the individual (unnamed) "scoundrel," whose indecent character was publicly exposed by his female "friend" (explicitly not his wife), but of all Robinisti, who as a group were shown to be morally bankrupt young men who thrived on scandal and enjoyed the misery of others. In this scene, there were no boundaries between actors and audience. The Robinisti played parts within parts and were their own best "public."

The dangers posed to the respectable by dissipated Robinisti were addressed explicitly in an *Odesskaia pochta* column titled "The Suffering of an Odessa Mother."[24] This morality tale, penned by Faust, featured a letter from an "intelligentnaia laborer" who feared that her beautiful eighteen-year-old daughter was, in the columnist's words, "perishing in the gilded patina of Odessa debauchery." According to the worried mother, the trouble started when her daughter asked permission to use a complimentary ticket to the skating rink. "Why not?" the mother thought. "Let the girl have a break from her daily work. After all, nice people go there." The daughter began going to the rink regularly, soon striking up acquaintanceships with a number of "young dandies who were vying to pay court to her." It was not long before a certain Kolia, one of the young courtiers, began escorting the daughter to the women's section of the Café Robina. "These 'women's sections' in cafés!" the mother moaned. "Why do they exist? To turn the heads of inexperienced young girls. . . . There, there is expensive finery, gay, carefree people, servants, lackeys, and the compliments of splendid cavaliers. And at home . . . at home there is everlasting toil and a meager dinner."

As the tale developed, the daughter moved further and further into the glittering circle of the young "intelligentnyi profligates." "After she became acquainted with the charms of the city," the young woman "started coming home at one, two, or even three in the morning." Worse still, the girl showed stunning disrespect for her mother, even calling her an "old witch" *(ved'ma)* and telling her to "shut up," all the while claiming that she was her own master. Finally one night, the mother went to the Café Robina in search of her daughter. When she described the girl to one of the young men there, he replied: "Don't worry. Your daughter is still honest." This comment outraged the mother still further: "You understand how impudent those words were, *still honest.*" Now the daughter did not come home at all, the mother told Faust. "They tore my daughter away from her mother's heart," the suffering woman cried. "I have lost her forever!"

Faust's column is revealing on a number of levels, not least for its dual usage of the term *intelligentnyi.* Faust inflected the usual meaning, using it in a positive sense to sanctify the lower-class mother, then employed it ironically to describe the "profligate" Robinisti. In doing so, the author emphasized the extent to which the Robinisti undercut the integrity of middle-class identity. In this representation, the halo of respectability rose over the lower-class woman whose sincere desire to protect her daughter's virtue won Faust's approval. The Robinisti, on the other hand, were marked as social counterfeits, betrayers who subverted the signs so heavily relied on by others of their own social class to create a collective self-identity. Journalistic representations of idle Robinisti lounging in their luxurious café "haunt" waiting to ruin those they should save summoned up images of decadence derided and scorned by the respectable. In the middle-class ethos, the well-bred, well-educated son was expected to be hard working and productive, honest and thrifty. The sons of the old upper class were the ones most closely associated with profligacy and dissipation, not the sons of good, upstanding, modern, moral, liberal citizens.

By breaking down the connection between appearance and inner quality, Faust, Satana, and other popular press contributors advised readers to distrust the very markers of propriety they themselves helped invest with significance. Tellingly, a damaging report from the city sanitary inspector's office gave reporters an opportunity to expose the café itself as a consummate Robinist. Although the Robina presented its public with a stainless facade, a tour of the kitchen revealed less-than-pristine conditions. The Fankoni, too, was found to be lacking. Publication of these revelations provided *Odesskii listok*'s columnist "Leri" with an opportunity to condemn the entire milieu of café life, which he characterized as patently indecent, the domain of *meshchanskie* values. The Robina charged "barbarian prices" for "tasteless luxuries" served in surroundings permeated by the "aroma of vulgarity," wrote the columnist. Nonetheless, it was "the shelter of 'all Odessa,' the marker of Odessa 'chic,' the last cry of Odessa 'comme il faut.'" But then, Leri wrote almost gleefully, "it suddenly turns out that there is no 'comme il faut' at all, no 'chic.'" Thanks to the sanitary inspectors, the Robina was revealed to be no better than a cheap lower-class eating house, the worst sort of *obzhorka*. But the protocols would change nothing, sighed the exasperated columnist. The owner would pay the "trifling fine," allow the unsanitary conditions to continue, and "laugh at the public."[25]

Thus both the Robina and its most notorious denizens were exposed and vilified. Yet, as Leri predicted, nothing changed. The inspectors wrote up protocols against Odessa's "best" cafés but dared not close them down. If the "aroma of vulgarity" was in the air, the "public" did not smell it. Instead, they continued to gather on the verandah and in the billiard room, the expectation of scandal elevating the excitement of the venue, perhaps even making it more popular than before. "Without the Robina and Fankoni all Odessa would commit suicide," Faust noted dryly. "Odessa would rather sacrifice the monuments to the duc [de Richelieu] and Pushkin or the Public Library . . . than throw down from their pedestals the favorites of modern Odessa."[26]

The Calculus of Respectability

Thus we return again to Moskvich's conclusion that Odessa was a city where image was preeminent in the assertion of social identity, where bourgeois appearance carried more currency than *intelligentnyi* moral virtue. However evolved they considered themselves, popular press journalists were unable or unwilling to divorce themselves completely from reliance on appearances as a valid measure of social worth. They defined respectability as a dependent variable determined by a complex equation involving values of appearance, taste, manners, deportment, lifestyle, material wealth, and finally moral fidelity. While a certain level of income was critical in the equation, morality rather than money was the most crucial component. The problem was that one's level of "spiritual development" was not immediately obvious to the eye. Thus it was on the strength of the visible self—generally assumed to be a good indicator of moral achievement—that initial judgments about respectability were based.

Journalists plotted "types" on the plane of respectability, the axes of which measured both one's visible "correctness" in the western bourgeois sense and one's level of *intelligentnyi* spiritual development. Authentic types, those whose external appearances accurately reflected inner character, could be found along one diagonal, the polar extremes occupied by the unmistakably unrespectable "fearsome dvornik" and the authentically cultivated "lady in white." Along the other diagonal were those whose external appearances often masked spiritual substance, the pole positions occupied by the Robinist and the *intelligentnaia* mama. In the middle of the plane stood the amorphous *meshchanin,* portrayed as one whose blind devotion to the material left him spiritually stunted but whose relentless desire to appear correct in dress and manners rendered him detectable only to the practiced eye.

Journalists loathed the denizens of the *meshchanskii* middle for their naive understanding of the respectability equation, fearing that to the *meshchanin's* literal eye, the Robinist was a figure to be admired, the *intelligentnaia* mother one to be scorned. *Intelligentnye* reporters struggled against this one-dimensional view, reminding their readers constantly of the hazards inherent in such a simple equation. Yet the conflicted writers themselves could not deny the power of appearances, cognizant as they were that the modern commercial city was a world in which visible things rather than inner qualities imparted identity and hence social status.

Even as they were aware of the power of correctness, popular press writers were likewise cognizant of, even trapped by, the paradox of appearances. Journalists constantly examined their subjects' dress, manners, and deportment, investing those signs with cultural meaning used to mark inner quality and moral worth. At the same time, however, they undercut the stability of that meaning, laying bare a vast array of ways in which external signs could be manipulated and subverted. Moreover, even as they called for authenticity of identity—publicly exposing those whose external appearances did not accurately reflect inner character— journalists nonetheless constantly (if inadvertently) reinforced the notion that individuals wanting to move up in the world had to learn to *assume* an identity, conceal their emotions, deny their desires, and otherwise mask their inner selves behind guises of "correctness." Correct appearance was therefore simultaneously a crucial course of study for the aspirant, a mask for the unscrupulous, an intricate code to be read by the urban spectator, and somehow still an honest reflection of a person's true character.

It was the divination of "true" character as much as the opportunity to shape it that fueled the journalistic project. Popular press writers, as the vanguard of the new *intelligentsia,* conceived of themselves as setting the benchmark for morality, stubbornly and relentlessly striving to create a perfect society. In working toward this goal, journalists assumed for themselves the right to publicly initiate others into the ranks of the respectable or, conversely, to ostracize those who failed to live up to moral expectations. The problem was that journalists and their medium functioned not just as chroniclers and shapers of modern urban culture but also as cultural products. Stories from the world of popular entertainment clearly exposed the paradoxical role journalists played as arbiters of civilization, highlighting ambivalent attitudes about the essential nature of the Odessan public.

The Indecent Appetites of the Respectable Public

According to etiquette advisors, attendance at operas, symphony concerts, and dramatic plays was the right kind of activity for those wanting to publicly display their good taste and refinement. The theater, the writers claimed, was "a school of morality," great performances having the power to improve a person's overall disposition, "soften coarse manners, annihilate prejudice, mock falsity, and inspire loathing of vices." An evening at the theater was thus elevated above the simple desire for entertainment to a higher moral plane. When one entered a theater or concert hall, one joined other like-minded individuals to become "that great organism that in society is known as the public *(publika)*." In order for everyone to get the most out of the experience, then, each member of the public needed to be respectful and disciplined in his or her spectatorship.[27]

To this end, individuals venturing out to the theater were expected again to exercise great control over both their bodies and their emotions. Restraint was the main course to be followed by spectators. One was to carefully avoid knocking into or rubbing against others in crowded lobbies or in adjoining seats and should take great pains not to crush a lady's dress. If one carried opera glasses or binoculars to a performance, one should keep them trained on the stage, certainly never using them to scan the audience or stare at ladies in the crowd. During the performance itself, one should be quiet and attentive. "Only common people and those of limited intellect" whistle, cheer, stomp their feet, or applaud out of turn. Applause was only appropriate at designated times. Even then, "ladies need only applaud lightly for appearances."[28]

An *Odesskaia pochta* piece titled "Sad Incident" showed the extent to which the Odessa public was failing to live up to the dictates of polite behavior, even in Odessa's most prestigious venue, the metropolitan opera house.[29] The Odessa City Theater was a magnificent auditorium presenting highbrow fare at high-end prices. For those in the middle and upper classes, an evening there meant public recognition of high social status and personal refinement. Ladies and gentlemen appeared at the theater in full evening dress. Whether seated in orchestra seats or the loge, in the ultra-prestigious dress circle or the less patrician balcony or gallery, everyone in attendance became part and parcel of the rich elegance of the venue. How could one not feel a heightened sense of refinement and self-worth when sitting in a red velvet seat surrounded by walls ostentatiously decorated with gilded stucco and ceilings graced by frescoed scenes from Shakespeare? Yet, as *Odesskaia pochta* reported, it was within this same hallowed hall that in February 1914 the "sad incident" took place.

At the beginning of the second act of a gala end-of-season benefit, the director appeared on the City Theater stage to announce that a famous diva scheduled to appear that night had been forced by illness to cancel. The crowd "took the news badly," said *Odesskaia pochta,* assaulting the diva's understudy with a storm of "whistles and catcalls." Several minutes later, the besieged artiste broke down in tears and ran from the stage. Hoping to calm the tempest, the director called an intermission, assuring the disgruntled audience that the star would in fact perform. After the break, the diva appeared on the boards, but only to chastise the audience for its poor behavior: "You seriously insulted my comrade on the stage. . . . It is too much for me to bear. Can't you see that I am ill?" Then she, too, burst into tears, leaving the stage with the words, "You should be ashamed of yourselves."

Odesskaia pochta's story was in essence a rebuke aimed at all respectable members of the theater-going public. The high refinement of the venue itself called on patrons to enjoy themselves with dignified restraint. When an individual failed to conduct himself accordingly, it was scandalous. When an entire audience behaved poorly, it threatened the reputations of all the respectable. Such indecent disturbances were expected from lower-class audiences at places like Moldavanka's Bolgarova Theater, where on one occasion police had to be called in to quell a riot that ensued because the famously volatile crowd failed to appreciate the humor of the celebrated satirist Vladimir Khenkin.[30] But audiences at the city's most refined venue should certainly have known better.

The sad incident at the City Theater suggests that not all members of Odessa's middle-class audience had been completely won over to the strictures of disciplined spectatorship required by good form within the venues of high culture. Moreover, while it cannot be denied that "being seen" at the City Theater had definite social benefits, in terms of overall popularity that venue was far surpassed by the haunts of *estrada*.[31] The public especially liked the theater Iumor, the Miniatiur, and the Malyi Theater, all of which featured light opera, song and dance, comedy, and specialty acts.[32] Despite his poor reception in Moldavanka, the humorist Vladimir Khenkin was an Odessa favorite for his satirical character anecdotes drawn from Jewish life, which dealt with "infidelity, high fashion, and in-laws."[33] Another popular estrada star was the female impersonator Nikolai Panin, whose fabulous portrayal in gypsy costume of the famous romance singer Anastasiia Vial'tseva propelled him from the slums of Slobodka-Romanovka into the central city's light theater spotlight.[34]

Middlebrow venues and the performers they showcased were appealing to the public precisely because they afforded middle-class audiences the collective opportunity to let down their guard, to bend if not break the laws of good form. A night at the theater, then, rather than being yet another exercise in restraint, became an opportunity to indulge in sensual pleasures (at least vicariously and always in moderation), and consume (if only with their eyes and to a limited extent) the forbidden fruits of bodily and emotional excess. The Odessa public's infatuation with "gypsies" (a passion they shared with estrada audiences throughout Russia) is a case in point. "The Gypsy was an emblem of freedom and looseness in Russia," says Richard Stites. The "gypsy idiom" appealed to audiences because it "contained violent and rhythmically exotic flourishes of uncontrolled passion—intimations of sex, hysteria, flights of fancy, and floods of champagne," all of which middle-class ladies and gentlemen were supposed to deny themselves in everyday life.[35]

Some patrons, especially those drawn to spicier estrada haunts, did more than flirt with such dangers; they openly courted them. For example, a popular destination for the late-night set was the Severnaia restaurant, which featured a lively *café-chantant* presenting variety shows of up to fifty acts.[36] But it was not only to watch famous dancers do the tango or to hear a "virtuoso" performance on bamboo rods that patrons came to the Severnaia. It was one of Odessa's most exciting nightspots, sexually charged,[37] a place where no evening was complete without a "scandal."[38] On one summer evening in 1912, for instance, a "strongly intoxicated" young man identified as "N. P.," the "famous heir of a large concern," presented Miss Kitty Florence, one of the Severnaia's popular cabaret dancers, with a "rude proposition." When the artiste rebuffed his advances, N. P. attacked her with his cane. Despite the efforts of "the son of a local merchant" to defend the besieged dancer, N. P. did not "calm down" until the police were called in to deal with him.[39] The Severnaia was not the only *café-chantant* in which such "scandals" occurred. Another *Odesskii listok* report described an incident at the Alkazar in which a "gentleman" approached the house chanteuse after one of her performances and "gave her an 'unambiguous proposition.'" Underscoring the view that female performers were sexually promiscuous, the reporter went on to say, that "[d]espite the fact that the affair took place in the 'Alkazar,' [the singer] 'turned away indignantly.'" The man then "grabbed her by the hair and forcibly pulled her to him."[40]

While nightclubs and cabarets offered sophisticated adults-only fare, other estrada stages appealed to a broader, more family oriented crowd. The circus in particular was an entertainment venue visited by "all Odessa."[41] As Valentin Kataev recalled:

> [The front rows] presented an elegant spectacle of the town's beauties, wearing large hats trimmed with ostrich feathers and boas round their necks, and men in bowler hats, silk top-hats, or officers' caps with coloured bands, stiffly upright in the Prussian manner. Among them, too, were fur coats, gaiters, narrow, sharp-toed patent-leather shoes, students' narrow trousers strapped to their soles, gold-tipped canes, and opera-glasses reflecting in their projecting lenses a miniature picture of the circus arena.[42]

Even if its audience was more diverse, however, the circus, too, unabashedly emphasized everything that was off-limits in the repertoire of middle-class behavior. Acrobats, trapeze artists, and tightrope walkers strutted and preened, inviting the audience to exalt in well-developed bodies shimmering gloriously under hot spotlights. Animal trainers and riders tantalized and unnerved spectators, using controlled danger masterfully to deliciously heighten emotional tension. Clowns then shattered that tension with slapstick humor, pointed jokes, and satire, allowing the audience to join them in ridiculing "a wide range of behavior by exaggeration and deflation."[43] Through it all, the orchestra played, arc lights hissed, and the sonorous voice of the announcer rose to the rafters.

As if the sensual explosion of traditional acts was not enough, Odessa circus audiences also thrilled to the performances of "infamous" wrestlers, with tournaments staged between champions like the aviator Zaikin, the famous "dragoon" Bogatyrev, and others.[44] Although more entertainment event than sport, these bouts nonetheless showcased the muscle-bound male body in action. In fact, it spotlighted two such bodies, totally and intimately involved with each other in intense physical activity. This combination of eroticism and physicality was too much for some *intelligentnyi* Odessans, who considered wrestling to be debasing and vulgar.[45] Regardless of this, more than a few middle-class patrons developed a passion for the sport.[46]

Kataev remembered that some of the most devoted wrestling fans were ladies who "made a habit of attending wrestling bouts." According to his testimony, the ladies were drawn to the events not so much by the competition as by the excitement aroused within them by the sight of the competitors' bodies. The wrestlers had "bulging Hercules-like biceps," "Grecian" profiles, "classical" statures, and "expanded" muscular chests, said Kataev. When they appeared from behind the curtain, the ladies "completely lost their heads . . . and unashamedly acclaimed them loud enough for the whole circus to hear." But the ladies went even further, "throwing at [the wrestlers'] feet lace handkerchiefs scented with l'Orian de Coty, gloves, and even handbags, from which small mirrors and powder-boxes scattered about the arena." As an impressionable boy, Kataev recalled that he, too, was completely overcome by the sight of a wrestler's body: "I could almost swoon as I gazed at the broad shoulders of the Estonian demigod under the arc lights, at his narrow hips and lumpy muscles protruding from the arms clenched behind his back, his whole body dusted with powder that gave his skin the tint of Carrara marble."[47]

There is much evidence to suggest that, rather than scolding readers for their prurient entertainment cravings, journalists shared and even encouraged public enchantment with the body. A sensational example marrying sensual fascination with vicarious craving for excess starred Foss the Wrestler, a gargantuan figure who in June 1914 quite literally gobbled up the attention of the Odessa public. Far from being notable for a well-sculpted physique, however, Foss was famous for his tremendous girth and enormous appetite.

The Incredible Fatness of Foss

Foss was fat, there was no denying it. He was so fat, in fact, that he could not "even sit in the barber's chair." To the appetite-suppressing middle class, the endless flesh was shocking but fascinating, almost pornographic. People wanted to see the corpulent wrestler, wanted to revel in his excess. Unfortunately for the hungry fans, as soon as Foss arrived in the city, he went into seclusion at the less-than-prestigious hotel Maibakh, in the Aleksandrovskii district's Old Bazaar quarter, the heartland of the Odessa *meshchanstvo*. Foss's reluctance to meet his audience served to swell public interest in the celebrity, which was fueled further by *Odesskaia pochta*'s periodic intelligence reports: "He is still eating huge amounts." He ate "seven portions of veal and a big loaf of bread, drank two barrels of water, then went to sleep." Later he drank a whole samovar of tea "at one sitting." Within days of the wrestler's arrival, the paper reported that the public was "thirsty for a look at the great one," that hotel staff were having a hard time controlling the growing crowd of curious fans besieging the Maibakh. Meanwhile, the owner of Odessa's Malevich circus, not blind to the potential profit involved in presenting the reclusive "athlete," sent his manager into the fray to negotiate with the star.[48]

It was at this juncture that an ironic fact surfaced in *Odesskaia pochta*: Foss was reluctant to leave his room because he was embarrassed by his "beggarly clothing." The star simply would not appear in public until he had a decent outfit. What the man really needed was a good pair of trousers. The matter of the pants turned out to be a difficult one to solve. The manager of the circus himself scoured central city stores in vain trying to locate a suitable garment. A couple of enterprising second-hand dealers did the same at the flea market, finally succeeding in finding a pair of Foss-sized trousers that they brought in triumph to the Maibakh. But an "insulted" Foss refused the offering, citing the garment's inferior quality and excessively high price tag. Meanwhile, the rumor spread among the public that Foss was finally going to leave the hotel. By evening, the street outside the Maibakh was filled with "a crowd of thousands." Police and mounted guards were called out to try to maintain order. The crowd waited for hours but still Foss did not appear. Finally, the principals cut a deal: Foss agreed to perform at the circus; the manager of the Malevich agreed to pick up the tab for the wrestler's provisions plus have a new suit tailored for the portly star.

Foss proved to be his own best promoter. Knowing that the public was more than eager to feast their eyes upon him, the king of corpulence decided to exploit his popularity by charging admission to his room. Anyone interested in watching him eat was welcome to attend, providing the person could pay the price. Knowing how to maximize profits, he set his rates at twenty-five kopecks for women, twenty for men, and ten for children, more evidence that "ladies" were especially enthralled by such entertainments. Almost a hundred spectators visited the wrestler on the first day of his hotel room "performance," netting Foss nearly fifteen rubles. During the program, the grandiose star gobbled up eight portions of borscht, ten portions of lamb, and five loaves of bread, all of which he consumed "in a couple of minutes washed down with three big samovars of tea."

A week after Foss's arrival, *Odesskaia pochta* reported that "Count de-Foss is obviously God himself judging from the growth of his celebrity in Odessa." When the day of Foss's debut at the circus finally arrived, the "cavalier" still remained in his room "fattening up" for the occasion. The bill for that day's provisions alone amounted to a whopping forty rubles, "this at a discount and without breakfast!" Meanwhile, a "sea of people" crowded into the circus, with several thousand others gathered on the street outside the Maibakh waiting to cheer their oversize hero. A detail of armed guards and policemen was dispatched to the scene to help maintain order. Then, at long last, Foss made his appearance. The crowd erupted in cheers as "the cavalier elegantly took his bows." They "swallowed up the sight of the legendary giant" with his "imperious gestures" and "colossally sized stomach." His circus performance, too, was a sight to behold. "In the final battle, it took only a few minutes to lay out his opponent, the wrestler Zharinkov. Then Foss set off for supper declaring, 'I have an appetite!'"

Foss was a living caricature, larger than life in every respect, the very embodiment of masculine excess. Unlike his contemporaries in the world of wrestling—Sandow the Magnificent, the "Jewish Samson" Siegmund Breitbart, Russia's "champion of the world" Ivan Poddubnyi—Foss's claim to fame was not athleticism.[49] His was not a disciplined physique. Indeed, nary a ripple of muscle could be detected beneath the mountainous layers of flesh. To those of cultivated sensibilities, Foss embodied vulgarity, serving as a foil for their own *intelligentnyi* values. Mavens of correctness would have seen the wrestler's girth as indecency incarnate, would have thought the wrestler's alleged "shame" over his "beggarly clothing" to be a mocking insult to those truly concerned with presenting themselves properly. Despite his masculine prowess and "elegant" airs, the wrestler was no gentleman. In fact, he was barely civilized.

To the columnist Faust, Foss's promiscuous appetite represented more than a threat to decency. In the following "conversation" the writer claimed he overheard near the circus, Foss was portrayed as a ravenous cannibal whose immoderate cravings were socially destructive:

> "Good gracious!" exclaimed an old woman. "When will they take Foss away from Odessa? Life has disappeared . . ." "And what is it to you, dear?" someone asked. "What has he done to you?" "Why, he has gobbled up everything, an exceedingly large amount. That is why everything is so expensive in Odessa, why it is so hard to get eggs, meat, beans, and potatoes in the bazaar. It is all because of Foss, they say. Let's just hope he doesn't gobble us up, too."[50]

Clearly, Foss as metaphor can be read a variety of ways, many of which are suggestive of the various excesses of consumer capitalism. He was the corrupt speculator so often portrayed in the press as the source of shortages and high prices. So too was he the satirical incarnation of a rich merchant, whose mounds of flesh were invoked in editorial cartoons (usually set opposite the emaciated figure of a poor worker) to symbolize selfishness, greed, and lack of humanitarianism. Foss consumed, but he was also an object of consumption. Like porn stars today, his exaggerated dimensions, his insatiable appetite, his immoderate cravings for flesh (the animals he ate, the men he wrestled), were shocking yet titillating. Like all other fads, the Foss phenomenon was destined to fade. Once it had finished gorging itself on the Foss spectacle, the Odessa public cleansed him from its palate, waiting expectantly for journalistic chefs to serve up the next sensational course.

The Civilized and the Savage—"Bare, Black & Wild"

The Foss story reveals the paradoxical role journalists played, when with one breath, they chastised Odessans for their vulgar tastes and unrestrained behavior, and with the next spurred on the public to greater heights of sensationalism. Another episode from the arena of popular entertainment is likewise expressive of tensions between journalists' efforts to civilize the public and their tendency to perpetuate the culture of the *meshchanstvo*. The stars of this story appeared at the beginning of the theatrical season in the fall of 1912, when Odessans were treated to an unusual entertainment event involving fifty-five "Somalians" who arrived in town for a month-long engagement at the club Oginski. Even though Odessans were used to a great deal of diversity in their cosmopolitan city, the presence of the Somalians added to the mix an element of racial difference to which they were less accustomed. The city, like the empire at large, had few connections with Africa, the aspirations of Russian imperialists falling a bit short when it came to the "dark continent." Interestingly, however, Odessa had been the staging ground for a famous misadventure in the late 1880s involving the botched efforts of a hundred and fifty Don Cossacks to claim Ethiopia for tsar and country.[51] While this episode may not have been in the front of the minds of Odessans over twenty years after the fact, the exoticism (and eroticism) of the Somalian act made the troupe a huge hit.

Similar to the kind of cultural exhibit presented on the Midway at the Chicago World's Fair in 1893, the show consisted of "black-skinned savages" who demonstrated for the public "how they live in their natural environment." The setting for the show was a recreated Somalian "village" in which the "natives"—men, women, and children, clad only in loincloths—displayed the "ceremonies . . . dances, military exercises . . . and fighting styles of the wild tribes" of Africa as well as skills such as sewing, boot making, and the fashioning of weapons. But it was not to see edifying displays of the "native arts" that crowds of Odessans flocked to the Oginski; it was to see flesh—"bare, black, and wild."[52] By far the most exciting part of the repertoire was the presence of Somalian women, some of whom were "unashamedly breast-feeding their babies right under the eyes of the public." Still more enticing was the fact that, for an additional charge of fifteen kopecks (on top of the thirty-kopeck ticket for general admission), curious Odessans could enter the "harem." A reviewer for one of the local theater journals described the erotically charged scene:

> We went in and were greeted by several Somalian "beauties." Really, they were very well built. Their shoulders and breasts were exposed and glistening with sweat. The Negro beauties were quite talkative. Near one tall, shapely Somalian, a large circle of men had formed. They talked to her all at once in ten different languages. In the crowd, too, we noticed Monsieur Khenkin, who was chatting with one of the Negro women.

The contrast between the "savage" Somalian "beauties" and Odessa's civilized "ladies in white" could not have been more stark. As noted above, the press portrayed women of refinement as cultivated, virtuous, modest, vulnerable, controlled, and controllable. The Somalian women, by contrast, were "bare, black, and wild"—primitive, unrestrained, spontaneous, openly sexual, disorderly, and highly seductive.

While the act had obvious appeal for men, reporters exclaimed that "all Odessa" was turning out for the show: "women, children, old people." Dispatches appeared in the theater reviews several times a week for the length of the run. Many of the items kept the public abreast of which local celebrities, like Khenkin, were stopping in to see the show. Others alerted the public to one-time-only events like, for instance, the marriage of two "natives," which took place as part of a special performance. The ceremony was "very much like a Jewish wedding," one reviewer observed.

The presence of the Somalians provided journalists with an opportunity to critique the degree of civilization (or lack thereof) that had been attained by the natives of their own city. By linking the rituals of Somalian "savages" with Jewish cultural practice, the reporter quoted above implied that both peoples were something less than civilized, essentially "blackening" Odessan Jews. *Odesskaia pochta*'s Faust, meanwhile, drew on concepts of class and ethnic difference, not to malign Jews but to vilify lower-class dock workers, who as a group were famous in Jewish circles for anti-Semitic brutality. Faust pointed out that the "savages from deepest Africa" had nothing on two "savages" in the port district, recently reported to have soaked a cat in kerosene and burned it alive. "What splendid amusement. . . . Very refined. Very cultured," the columnist spat. "I'm afraid the savage Africans will run away from Odessa in fear." Meanwhile, *Odesskii listok*'s regular feuilletonist Leri critiqued the values of the typical Odessan through a tongue-in-cheek piece that depended for humor on the lack of fluency of the Somalian guests. In Leri's imaginary tale, a long-suffering guide took the African men on a tour of the city, at every stop of which the visitors got into trouble. They were swindled by Robinisti, were threatened by the Black Hundreds, and created a scandal at the opera house. At the end of the day, they returned to the "welcoming hearth" of the Ognisko, told their wives about their day, and tried to hide the enormous bill they had rung up at a fashionable restaurant.

Portrayals of the Somalians as victims of Odessan savagery and, more generally, of modern urban life anticipated events in the real world. Shortly before the show was due to close, the troupe's impresario ran off with the proceeds. Panic stricken and penniless, the Somalians ran en masse to the police station, then on to the British consulate, where they threw themselves on the mercy of the consul general. In the end, "after a whole row of adventures," the British agreed to underwrite the cost of transporting the stranded Africans to Aden. On the day of their departure, the newspapers noted, over a thousand "curious onlookers" escorted the woeful "savages" down to the docks.

Conclusion

In the pages of the popular press, the Odessa public emerged as decidedly *meshchanskii* in terms of its tastes. Tellingly, journalists scolded the public for its lack of restraint as an audience, bemoaning "uncultured" behavior in the venues of high art. Simultaneously, however, writers encouraged prurient interest in the likes of Foss the wrestler or celebrated exotic/erotic "savagery" of the Somalian troupe. Headlines screaming "bare, black, and wild" were promises, not condemnations, sustenance for the indecent appetites of the *meshchanskii* public.

Journalists reporting on the spectacles of urban life revealed a mischievous playfulness, encouraging Odessans to venture into the city for fun and adventure. But they also warned readers to remain ever vigilant when it came to trusting strangers on the street, once again reinforcing the message that appearances deceived. Further, their stories underscored the point that, while a person aspiring to upward mobility might learn fairly easily how to present an acceptable appearance, character building was a significantly more challenging endeavor. They provided instructions on how to assume the public face of respectability even as they criticized the moral vacancy of a cultural system built on the edifice of proper appearances. The next chapter continues to explore this paradox within the context of domestic life.

6 The Little Family

"Well, so how is Iasha doing?"

"Ekh, it grieves me to talk about him, my friend."

"What's going on? Is he involved in politics?"

"No, even worse. He's going to marry for love."

—Text of a cartoon titled "Suicide," *Krokodil*

Daughter—a perishable good.

—*Odesskii listok*[21]

• Meet the Perel'muters, the fictional Jewish *meshchanskii* family whose domestic travails were the focus of a short comic play called "The Little Family, or Lady and Gentleman Odessans" penned by "the Stranger" ("Neznakomets") and published in serialized form in April 1912 in the Odessa weekly humor magazine *Krokodil*.[3] The family patriarch was Jacob, a not wildly successful "forty-something" commercial agent. His forty-year-old wife Rachel was the mistress of the family's "typical" *meshchanskii* home, supervising a household staff of one, the "good-for-nothing" maid Dunia. The four remaining members of the household were the couple's demanding children: Elijah, Gene, Mathilda, and Esther. At Jacob's insistence, both of his sons were on the road to careers in business. Elijah, the eldest, was a reluctant "man of commerce," while the younger son Gene, described as a "dandy," was still a student at Faig's Commercial School. Both of the Perel'muter daughters were recipients of a respectable upbringing. Mathilda, the eldest, had been trained to be a marriageable "lady" *(baryshnia)* and had mastered the feminine arts: she spoke French, "play[ed] a little," embroidered, and was "a marvelous housekeeper." Her sister Esther, on the other hand, was a modern *kursistka* (a female student enrolled in a higher-education course for women), who always seemed to have a book in her hand and "only talks about lofty matters."[4]

As these brief introductions show, "the Stranger"—a pseudonym for Boris Denylovich Flit, the driving force behind *Krokodil*—painted the personal characteristics of the Perel'muters in broadly exaggerated strokes, with each of the dramatis personae representing a distinctly modern type. Central to the action are attitudes about love and marriage, the main plot line involving the procurement of the right kind of husband for the capricious Mathilda, the spoiled older daughter whose shelf life as a potential bride was about to expire. Although a matchmaker was involved in the proceedings, the Perel'muters' main concerns in the marriage game were social status and money, bourgeois dreaming obliterating traditional Jewish ideals. Religious identity as a whole was nearly absent in "The Little Family," Flit portraying Jewishness as a distinctly secular endeavor, a modern identity rooted in Odessa in early adoption of enlightened *haskalah* reforms. Tellingly, the writer did not oppose his characters' crass materialism against older models of religious piety that in Odessa were beyond passé. Instead, his comedy explored contrasts between conventional bourgeois moderns and more evolved social types: the eldest son Elijah, who strove to transcend his *meshchanskii* roots to become *intelligentnyi,* and the younger daughter Esther, a radical "new woman" romantically attracted to a "sexual mystic," à la Oscar Wilde.

Billed as "a caricature in one act," "The Little Family" is first and foremost a comedy of manners, Flit employing exaggeration and irony to expose and skewer the values of the *meshchanin* and *meshchanka* at home. The author's sophisticated gaze pierced the manners and affectations of the milieu he explored, as he pilloried the exacting but morally trivial standards of bourgeois correctness and reveled in the crimes of taste and decorum so frequently linked in Odessa to middle-class Jewish life. As a critique of cultural mores, the play positively drips in *intelligentnyi* disdain for *meshchanskii* pretension and hypocrisy, serving to verify (and damn) the high degree to which western-style notions of propriety in appearance and style of life had permeated Odessan culture. Beyond this, Flit poked fun at the idealized world of home and the "cult of domesticity," desacralizing rather than sanctifying the family as "the institution most central to the cultural life and value systems of the bourgeoisie."[5] Further, the author interrogated the alleged divide between public and private identities, questioning the sureties offered up by mavens of bourgeois propriety, who glibly decreed that fathers were homebuilders and mothers homemakers, and that children happily assumed the roles prescribed to them by their sex.[6]

Before proceeding further, one might ask how much weight a historian should place on a short work of fiction published in a magazine that only existed for a couple of years and had a circulation of no more than six thousand copies, many fewer than a well-established newspaper such as *Odesskaia pocta,* which claimed to reach ten times that many readers on any given day. One reason to judge *Krokodil* highly as a historical source is because it attracted readers and contributors in at least a dozen other Russian cities, including the northern capitals. Moreover, many of the writers and artists who worked for *Krokodil* contributed regularly to major newspapers and specialty journals in Odessa and beyond. For instance, Flit penned feuilletons for *Odesskie novosti* as well as columns for the local theater review *Odesskoe obozrenie teatrov.* Plus, he wrote short plays and comic sketches that appeared on the boards of Odessa estrada theaters (perhaps including "The Little Family"). Moreover, the quality of satire found in *Krokodil* was sufficiently high that other publications felt compelled to steal from it; on more than one occasion, Flit and his publishing partners had to file plagiarism complaints against the popular St. Petersburg and Moscow satirical journals *Satirikon* and *Budil'nik*. Finally, with respect to the particular content of "The Little Family," the fact that nearly all of *Krokodil*'s contributors were well-educated young Jewish men who grew up in Odessa lends authority to Flit's humorous exposé of life in the fictional Perel'muter home.[7]

Man and Wife

The curtain rose on "The Little Family" to reveal Rachel Perel'muter vigorously dusting her "*meshchanskii*-type living room" where all was "symmetry . . . everything precisely placed *(vse akkuratnen'ko)*." With her first words, the reader discovers that Rachel was not at all satisfied with the arrangement and operation of her household. She complained about the incompetence of her "little idiot" of a maid and the laziness of her "mean" *(parshivyi)* daughters, neither of whom in her view did their fair share of the work. She was also unhappy with the furniture in her "salon," which was only "average." In Rachel's studied opinion, the room would have benefitted immensely from the presence of a few more opulent pieces, preferably "in the style of Louis Quinze" (using the French number but then mistranslating it into Russian as "the Seventeenth"), a desire deemed by her husband to be a "decadent joke." Rachel's mood did not improve when Jacob entered the living room after a long day at work. Far from offering comfort and support to her loving mate, the not so adoring wife dryly inquired whether Jacob had finally gotten the commercial order he had been after (and that she had been counting on to finance the purchase of a Louis "the Seventeenth"). After a long pause, the browbeaten husband made it clear that he had not.

The first exchange between man and wife made it abundantly clear that the Perel'muters' relations were far from tranquil. A chief source of disharmony was Rachel's dissatisfaction with the size of Jacob's income, a criticism sure to rankle since it impugned her husband's manhood. "The Stranger" thus lost no time in exposing Rachel's imperfections as a household manager, wife, and mother, casting into doubt her credentials as a "true woman." As for the *meshchanka*'s personal character, Rachel's lust for a "Louis Quinze—the Seventeenth" revealed a lack of good breeding and a crass desire to have for the sake of having. Flit thus cast aspersions at the bourgeois cult of domesticity, using Rachel's concern with the quality of the family furnishings to mock the pervasive belief, introduced with commercial capitalism, that possessions had the power to impart as well as convey identity.

While Flit aimed his first salvo at Rachel, the writer made sure that Mr. Perel'muter's inadequacies as breadwinner and father were also a main theme in "The Little Family." Indeed, throughout the play, the writer never resisted an opportunity to reveal the flaws in character that made Jacob a less then perfect role model. Jacob was neither the all-powerful Russian autocrat nor the firm but kindhearted bourgeois paterfamilias. And he certainly was no Torah scholar. Not measuring up to anyone's ideal, Jacob was simply a *meshchanin,* no more and no less. Likewise, Flit made Rachel into a textbook *meshchanka,* a woman who thought of her children much as she did her possessions: as a means to enable her own social rise. This patently *meshchanskii* ethic lay at the heart of the play's comic action, especially in the plot line concerning the marriage prospects of Mathilda.

The Matter of the Dowry

In her opening speech, Rachel informed the audience that, having already invested a substantial sum in Mathilda's education and refinement, the time had come for the Perel'muters to make the final payment and reap the social rewards that accompanied a profitable husband. The matchmaker had been called and negotiations were under way. But there was a problem. The would-be bride was "demanding a doctor." In order for her parents to procure one, however, they would need to come up with a dowry of twenty thousand rubles, twice the sum that Jacob was in a position to provide.[8] "The Little Family" quickly established itself as a farcical rendition of the dowry chase, with the Perel'muters aligned against an absurd set of adversaries: the prospective fiancé Dr. Berman (a "handsome" "Jewish careerist"), Berman's domineering mother (an "old-fashioned" woman of the "harridan" type), and Mr. Kogan, a "smooth-talking" matchmaker. Not surprisingly, Mathilda herself played only a peripheral role in the proceedings. Indeed, her big scene came not in service of her future marriage but against it, giving Flit an opportunity to brand Mathilda as "capricious":

> Mathilda: Papa, you know what I want to ask you?
> Perel'muter: Let's assume I don't know, but probably it has something to do with money.
> Mathilda: Papa, I want to go to theater school.
> Father: Have you lost your mind?
> Mother: This is some kind of a joke. Thank God there have never been any artists in the family. There were two converts, but so far we haven't had to live through any other disgrace.
> Perel'muter: Give me quiet . . . (then to the wife) This is your doing. This is how you brought her up.
> Wife (shouting): Why are you being so sharp! And you didn't spoil her? What do you mean to theater school? It's a dirty trick! This is all nonsense.

Perel'muter: I don't understand, Mathilda. Why do you suddenly have this urge?
Mathilda: I want to be an artiste! There are so many theater schools in the city now. And they are so cheap. I have talent. Remember when I was in that show at Fontan? There was an artiste there from the City Theater. He courted me all evening. Why should Dora German get to go to theater school? Why should Mania Bliuvshtein? And Manichka Lur'e? She already graduated and gets eighteen rubles a month in Akkerman . . . I am so bored, I want . . .
Wife: And what kind of match can you get! Boys without careers, without anything.
Mathilda: Mama, I don't want a match! I am artistic. I want to act.
Perel'muter: You know, when a daughter talks about wanting to be an artiste at age 17, she is indulged. But not at 22. And you, praise God, are 23. What, do you think fiancés will come to you on their own? A young lady is not like wine. The older she is, the worse!
Mathilda (crying): I want to be an artiste. I'm bored *(mne skuchno)* . . .
Perel'muter: If you want to find yourself a fiancé, it would be better to audit classes at the university . . .
Wife: Or at dentistry school . . .
Mathilda (capriciously): I don't want anyone. I want to be an artiste. I have talent. It's only 150 rubles for a whole year. (crying)

This scene confirmed that the Perel'muters' home life was anything but a study in bliss, especially for Jacob. Far from being able to put aside his cares and be completely free from domestic troubles at the end of a trying day, he was instead embroiled by family difficulties and harangued by wife and daughter. The family squabble managed to skewer in one turn the characters of all involved. Jacob lambasted his wife for her failures as a mother, therein dodging his own responsibility. Rachel returned the favor by criticizing her husband as a father, thus demonstrating her lack of submissiveness. The insufferable Mathilda, meanwhile, was portrayed as self-absorbed, manipulative, and whiny, not the qualities one would hope to find in a well-brought-up young lady.

The implicit ridicule in the scene went well beyond the Perel'muters' fictional living room. It derided bourgeois fears about the limited marketability of marriageable daughters, Flit joining other Odessan journalists who saw in the notion that girls were "perishable goods" still more damning evidence of the "typical" Odessan's innate *meshchanskii* character.[9] In a similar vein, the scene impaled the "capricious" natures and questionable refinement (not to mention the vacuous minds and limited spiritual capacities) of spoiled young women like Mathilda and her friends, who entertained the vulgar notion that theater school was an appropriate activity for cultured ladies.[10] But Flit also satirized bourgeois parents who strategically placed daughters in venues of higher education, not so that young women could improve their minds and morals, and thus become better mothers, but so that they could meet the "right" kind of husband.[11]

The notion that potential fiancés could be stacked up in a status hierarchy based on their professions was explicitly lampooned in scene 6, when the matchmaker Mr. Kogan arrived at the Perel'muter home to open negotiations:

Matchmaker: I have a doctor! But he doesn't want to listen for less than fifteen thousand.

Perel'muter: So, he'd be pained to take ten?

Matchmaker: Ten? For ten he could have taken some beauty long ago.

Wife: And my daughter isn't beautiful? The girl graduated from the gymnasium, she can do needlework, keep house, play the piano, speak a little French. She's a marvelous housekeeper. And the dowry!

Perel'muter (angrily): If there's not enough profit in it for you, you can go to the devil. Are there so few doctors now? They are like dogs, all you have to do is give a call and one will come running.

Matchmaker: Let's suppose that you can't find a doctor for ten thousand. How about a dentist? I have a marvelous one!

Wife: What do we need with a dentist? With our kind of money we should be able to get a doctor.

Matchmaker: Madame, the dentist would be much better than the doctor. His brother is a lawyer and his sister is married to a pharmacist in Poltava.

Wife: A pharmacist! I'm so honored.

Perel'muter: We order a doctor but he specializes in dentists and we don't want one.

Matchmaker: If you would like, I've got another doctor in Elisavetgrad. But his brother is a Christian.

Wife (sharply): That won't do.

Matchmaker: There is also a Christian among your people.

Wife: Where did you get that idea? That's a lie. It's a fabrication. How could I live with that.

Matchmaker: Madame Perel'muter, you can't deceive Kogan. Kogan knows everything. But this is not important. So, what is your final price?

Perel'muter: Ten thousand. I don't have more.

Wife: And we will sew her a trousseau.

Matchmaker: Good. I will pass it along. But I don't think that his mother will agree. She will hardly agree to fifteen thousand.

Perel'mutter: Ten thousand isn't enough for the sniveller, eh?

Matchmaker: In my opinion, personality is primary and the money is secondary. And maybe love is important to you? Love is possible.

Perel'muter: If there is love, I won't give money. (laughing)

Matchmaker: No, the money will be in advance. All of it. So, I will pass along the offer. Goodbye, madame.

Wife (seeing him out): I say! Please, husband . . .

Perel'muter: Not a kopeck more than ten. And he picks up the tab for the wedding.

This scene emphasizes two closely related and definitive aspects of *meshchanskii* mentality set into especially sharp relief by the matrimonial arrangement process: obsession with status and, once again, the quest for upward mobility. Strikingly, what mattered most to the parents (especially Rachel) was the occupation and thus class status of their prospective son-in-law. While Mathilda's husband most definitely had to be a Jewish doctor, there was no discussion here, or anywhere else in "The Little Family," about how Jewish he needed to be in terms of religious learning or practice. At first glance, it might appear that the secularized Perel'muters cared little about the qualities traditionally associated with the ideal Jewish husband and had instead fully embraced bourgeois ideals. But such a conclusion misses the mark. As ChaeRan Freeze points out, "if Torah study had once served as a means of upward social mobility, a university degree . . . now played a similar role among some strata of Jewish society. Little wonder that, by the early twentieth century, Jewish men began to advertise their diplomas in medicine and law to attract wealthy partners."[12]

Instead of reading the Perel'muters obsession with social status strictly as a function of their *embourgeoisement,* one can see it as a modernized version of the traditional Jewish emphasis on family wealth as a key criterion in spousal selection. In other ways, too, the Perel'muters did not turn away so completely from traditional Jewish marriage strategies. They had after all engaged Mr. Kogan, even though they obviously distrusted him, probably for good reason. Kogan's protestations that "love is possible" revealed at best a disingenuous character. The Perel'muters also put a premium on the pure family lineage of the prospective spouse. On this point, however, what stood out was Rachel's hypocrisy. Flit represented the mother as appalled in the extreme by the very idea that Mathilda might marry into a family that included a convert to Christianity. And yet in an earlier scene Rachel had disclosed privately that her own family line included Christians, a fact she vehemently denied to the matchmaker.[13]

Such considerations aside, when it came to evaluating a potential bride's worth, bourgeois values clearly prevailed in "The Little Family." Unlike the ideal woman of Jewish tradition, whose appeal as a potential life partner sprung from her ability to support her husband and family as the primary breadwinner, Mathilda cultivated few skills beyond the "feminine talents" required of the "true woman." Rachel's spirited defense of her daughter's worth during negotiations with the matchmaker showed that the mother was enlightened in the Jewish secular sense, believing that she had done her part to cement Mathilda's credentials as a good bourgeois wife. But Flit pointedly unmasked the daughter's ladylike pretensions. Mathilda's vacuous behavior and caprices betrayed her ill-breeding, the young woman's superficiality announcing to the world that she, like her mother, was nothing but a *meshchanka.*

It was precisely the marriage of enlightened Judaism and bourgeois culture that made the secularized Jew modern. But it was the Odessan *meshchanskii* versions of the modern Jewish man and woman—people who only imperfectly understood both what it meant to be bourgeois and what it meant to be Jews—that Flit roasted without pity on the spit of "The Little Family." A word should be said, too, about Jacob's comment that "doctors are like dogs." Jacob clearly held in contempt the supercilious attitudes of *intelligentnye* professionals toward the world of commerce. Unlike Rachel, who was clearly a social climber, Jacob seemed content with his lot in life and certainly was not ashamed that he was a gentleman of business. Through exchanges between the father and his eldest son Elijah, Flit gave Jacob a chance to lambaste *intelligentnyi* pretension, usually while attempting to set Elijah straight about the practical rewards of a career in commerce. In scene 3, "the Stranger" allowed both father and son to make their cases, and even let Mathilda get in a kopeck or two:

> Elijah (entering with a briefcase in hand; he imagines himself to be a lawyer): Oh, already fighting. Not a moment's peace.
> Mathilda: Be quiet, lawyer.
> Perel'muter: Quiet, children. You look like humans but you squabble like dogs.
> Elijah: Papa, it looks like they are going to let me take the law exam.
> Mathilda: Without a certificate from the gymnasium (secondary school)? Never. Ha, ha, ha.
> Elijah: I have influence *(protektsiia)*.
> Perel'muter: I don't understand why you want to be a lawyer so badly. Lawyers now go without trousers. Better to be a good businessman.
> Elijah: Don't say that, papa! A lawyer is this (waving his briefcase). Why did you send me to the commerce school anyway? Did I ask you to? I so want to be a lawyer. I already have the briefcase.
> Mathilda: You don't set your sights on trifles, do you. First a certificate from the gymnasium then a university diploma!
> Perel'muter: Children stop it.
> Elijah: Artiste!
> Mathilda: Lawyer!
> Elijah: Artistes are all drunks and charlatans.
> Mathilda: Papa, tell him to be quiet.
> Perel'muter (hammering on the table): Chil-dren! (pause)
> Elijah: Papa, Rozenberg only wants a ruble and twenty kopecks. Well???
> Perel'muter: Well, what. Let him wait.

The exchange between father and son turned on the relative merits of business versus the professions. Jacob valued material rewards (trousers) above all else. But Elijah craved recognition of his *intelligentnyi* status (the briefcase) and wanted to rise above the dirty world of commerce. As Mathilda correctly pointed out, there were formidable obstacles standing between a son of the Jewish *meshchanstvo* and a degree in law. Chief among them was a quota system (the notorious *numerus clausus*) that severely limited Jewish admissions to the university. Since Elijah, at his father's insistence, had gone to a commercial high school, he did not possess the requisite secondary degree required to apply for university admission. Instead, he was staking his hopes on being able to successfully bribe an official into letting him sit for the state law exam as an extern (a student who through independent study had gained an equivalency degree). In Elijah's mind, the payoff of a career in law was well worth the hassle. Not only would he gain considerable social capital and the right to relocate outside the Pale of Settlement, he would also instantly become *intelligentnyi*, a man with a right to carry a briefcase.[14]

But Flit would soon lacerate Elijah's pretensions too, exposing the son's *meshchanskii* character at a crucial moment in the dowry negotiations, which made up the whole of the play's final scene. The action commenced with the arrival of Dr. Berman (the prospective fiancé) and his mother. As soon as the maid announced the visitors, Rachel quickly decided that their first impression should be of the beautiful Mathilda at the piano. The daughter dutifully took her place behind the instrument, while the rest of the family beat a hasty retreat. Berman and his mother then entered the "salon." "Allow me to introduce myself. I am Dr. Berman. I have a clinic on Bolshaia Arnautskaia.[15] Allow me to present my mother! . . . Would you be kind enough to play?" Mathilda willingly complied. Berman's mother then held up a piece of needlework, asking the next vital question: "Did you embroider this yourself?" "Yes, myself!" Mathilda replied, proud of her command of the feminine arts and her ability to pass this impromptu exam. Berman nodded his approval, stating that, "In my opinion, the most important thing is that a wife be a housekeeper and know how to use a needle. I am not a supporter of all sorts of emancipations, you know." Once the "goods" had been displayed and the interest (and personal philosophy) of the "buyer" evinced, Mathilda's parents and eldest brother entered the room and she herself was dismissed. Jacob asked if the visitors had had a chance to get acquainted with his daughter. "Yes, we are all acquainted," replied Berman's mother. "Now let's get down to money."

> Mother: Kogan said that you will give twelve thousand.
> Perel'muter: Ten thousand, no more.
> Mother: Petia, we are going! (jumping up)
> Mrs. Perel'muter: Why are you hurrying? My daughter is a wonderful homemaker.
> Berman: But I need fifteen thousand. I won't take a penny for myself. I have a business. If you like I will put it in the bank under her name.
> Perel'muter: But you haven't even talked with the bride. Maybe you won't like her.
> Berman: Yes, I like her, but is the money reliable?
> Perel'muter: As in the State Bank.

Berman: Ten thousand is so little.

Perel'muter: That is a matter I can do nothing about . . .

Mother: Petia, we are going!

Mrs. Perel'muter: Why are you hurrying?

Mother: Maybe my son isn't worth it?

Mrs. Perel'muter: (starting to fight) What a big head. Doctors are like dogs. As if the family name "Berman" is such a great honor

Mother: The whole city knows that your father set two [arson] fires.

Mrs. Perel'muter: Well, at least my mother wasn't a market-woman in the bazaar . . .

Mother: You yourself are a market-woman! You are negotiating like a market-woman.

The satire in this fictional dialogue underscored the marriage game as a high stakes battle involving not just the qualities of the daughter, but the honor of the family. Likewise, it was not just the social rise of the bride but the advancement of her close relations that was the goal of a "good" marriage. As Marion Kaplan points out, "[a]ll participants understood that a family staked its prestige during dowry negotiations. For a bourgeois family, the dowry was a measure of its reputation. For the petty bourgeoisie, in particular, the dowry was a source of parental pride."[16] While all parties understood that more than money was on the table, the negotiating styles of the principal players as portrayed by Flit reveal gender differences. As the meeting commenced, both Jacob and Dr. Berman conducted themselves in a businesslike manner. Jacob was self-composed and efficient, if a bit curt. Berman was likewise controlled, albeit a bit churlish, as when he inquired if Jacob's money was "reliable." But Berman took pains to reassure Jacob that he would not squander the dowry, asserting that he needed it to further his professional practice. For a bourgeois man, this was a perfectly reasonable goal. Indeed, a gentleman had a duty to improve his business and to maintain sufficient savings to safeguard his respectability and position in society.[17]

If to this point in the proceedings Jacob and the doctor had been able to maintain at least the facade of gentlemanly decorum, Berman's mother and Rachel could not approach the negotiations with anything remotely resembling dispassion, let alone "feminine" delicacy. Their rapid descent into the realm of personal insult and slander revealed them as gross offenders of the rules of good form, stripping away any pretense that either of them were "ladies." Flit clearly exaggerated the women's flaws in order to make fun of their essential *meshchanskii* nature. Since the humor in the scene derived not only from the female characters' histrionics but from the quality of their taunts, the vitriolic barbs themselves deserve a bit of inspection. Most obviously, the women's insults took aim at family honor, but they also cast aspersions on individual moral fortitude. In the course of one short speech, Rachel called Berman's mother arrogant, pilloried the doctor's professional identity, and derided the Berman family name. Her adversary shot back with a well-aimed missile against Rachel's father, to which Rachel responded with an accusation against Dr. Berman's maternal grandmother, who she said was a "market-woman." "You yourself are a market-woman!" Berman's mother flung back. Indeed, at this point "The Little Family's" author casts both women as proverbial fishwives, embodying every negative stereotype society associated with sharp-tongued Jewish harpies manning stalls at the bazaar.[18]

As the negotiations continued, the pungent odor of vulgarity that permeated the interactions between the female characters spread to the male ones, including Elijah, who stepped into the fray to defend his family's honor by insulting Dr. Berman's manhood:

> Berman: Mama, stop it. Look, these are simple people *(prostye liudi)*!
> Elijah: We are simple. And you are so educated that you don't even have a pair of trousers.
> Berman: Let's get out of here, mama! I don't like the girl and they are trying to rob us.
> Elijah: Most of all a young man has to have trousers!
> Perel'muter (to Berman): Take the ten thousand and kiss your fiancée.
> Mother: Petia, I tell you we're going. This is a den of thieves.
> Mrs. Perel'muter: Go, go, and I will tell the whole town what kind of fiancé you are. Everyone will know . . .
> Mother: What? I will tell them how your whole family is starving. Then we will see . . .
> Perel'muter: Sh! Don't argue. Well, you want twelve thousand?
> Elijah: What do you mean twelve thousand? Papa, is it true that you only have one daughter? You are robbing us!
> Perel'muter: Be quiet. It's not your affair . . .

In the list of dramatis personae at the beginning of "The Little Family," Flit had identified Berman as a "Jewish careerist," making it clear to readers from the start that the doctor would willingly sacrifice ethics for the sake of social advancement. When Berman insulted the Perel'muters by calling them "simple people," he was implying that he and his mother were a cut above their *meshchanskii* adversaries. But Elijah would have none of it, blasting Berman's *intelligentnyi* pretensions and the doctor's lack of "trousers." Apparently having come around to his father's view that higher education alone did not make the man, Elijah attempted to take Berman down a peg by calling into question the doctor's masculinity. Berman's strong reaction showed that the physician obviously took the point.

Elijah's outbursts certainly did not help his father restore order to the proceedings. Jacob's vague attempts to rein in his wife and son were in any case futile. The "business" at hand soon degenerated into a no-holds-barred duel with all of the parties drawing on full arsenals of indignation and insult, each side threatening public exposure of the other family's crimes:

> Perel'muter: Will you take twelve thousand? . . .
> Berman's Mother: Well, now you're talking about a different matter! Twelve thousand. This is of course not much. Don't forget, he's a doctor.
> Perel'muter: Aye, aye, aye. A doctor! For a ruble I can have a doctor. And for three rubles a whole consul! An important thing, a doctor!
> Mother: Give us fifteen thousand and God will be with you.
> Elijah: This woman is disgraceful. Hold me down so that I don't strike her with all my might. I will throw the piano at her head.

Love or Money?

With the threat of a flying piano hanging in the air, Flit took a moment for a brief reflection on the subject of love. "You see, if I was marrying for love, it would be another matter," Dr. Berman commented to Jacob. But since he was not, the question of "the figure" remained the most important issue. This declaration led Jacob to interject a little anecdote: "You know, I once asked a man how he got married. He answered that he considered the figure and fell in love." "You mean, then he fell in love?" Berman inquired. "No," Jacob replied. "They wouldn't give him any money. Then he fell in love."

Flit had touched on the love/money equation a bit earlier in the play, just before the arrival of Dr. Berman and his mother, when Elijah himself received a letter from a matchmaker:

> Mr. Perel'muter. You don't know me but I am a matchmaker specializing in skeptics. If you agree that money is secondary and humanity primary, then at this happy moment I have the honor of suggesting to you a first-class party, the daughter of an exporter, a sweet beauty, light-brown hair, age twenty, plays the piano, speaks French, her brother is a doctor, and ten thousand. She is a marvelous housekeeper. She is favorably disposed toward you, but I must let you know in advance that you should not tarry because someone else might snatch her up.

"Well, how do you like that, papa," Elijah inquired. "Does it mean a wedding of love?" Jacob questioned in return. Needless to say, the matter of love was overshadowed tremendously in "The Little Family" by the matter of the dowry. Yet the modern notion of marrying for love had nonetheless made its appearance. Those of bourgeois sensibilities celebrated romantic love as the hallmark of a good marriage, as long as it came backed by the guarantee (or at least strong promise) of material security.[19] As Flit pointed out, matchmakers likewise gave lip service to the ideal of companionate marriage, even as they itemized the most saleable qualities of the clients they represented.

For those who sought to avoid the services of a middleman or who hoped to limit parental involvement in the spousal selection process, the modern world provided other options. In Odessa, as elsewhere, one available avenue to those seeking mates was the "marriage gazette." The mere existence of these weekly broadsheet publications, wholly devoted to what today are known as personal ads, confirmed that at least some Odessans attempted to circumvent traditional practices and parental authority in order to find spouses on their own.[20] Marriage gazette entries included self-representations that provide insight into what at least some men and women considered to be their own appealing qualities as well as those attributes deemed essential in an ideal mate. In describing themselves and possible life partners, ad writers commonly mentioned level of education, occupation, appearance, character, talents or interests, age, and religion. But just because some people preferred to select spouses on their own did not mean that material considerations no longer mattered to the aspiring bride or groom. Indeed, while most of the lines of copy in any given ad appeared in standard font size, important monetary sums were set out boldly in large type: the size of the dowry accompanying a prospective bride or the yearly income of a potential husband.[21] An *Odesskii listok* columnist could not let such crass commercialism pass without comment:

> Among the promenaders on Deribasovskaia scurry children of eight or ten who, in their thin voices, cry out, "Who wants a wife? Who wants a husband? The *Marriage Gazette* just came out!" A gentleman *(gospodin)* approached a little boy, asking jokingly, "Let us suppose that I want to get married. What should I do?" "Ah, here it is. Buy the *Marriage Gazette*. It will tell you everything." "And have you read it yourself?" "No, I can't read." Here is a rare occasion when one can say with pleasure, "it is good that this eight-year-old boy still cannot read."[22]

Tellingly, even if journalists branded the marriage gazette as an organ of *meshchanskii* materialism, would-be grooms who placed ads frequently labeled themselves *intelligentnyi*, using the term to signify that they were men of good character seeking like-minded women of similar circumstances.[23] As the following example demonstrates, however, some men still felt compelled to boost their appeal by referencing their material prospects, lending support to the notion that the economic potency of a potential match was still a crucial factor in this new version of the marriage game:[24]

> *Intelligentnyi* gentleman *(gospodin)*, 30 years old (Jewish), earning 100 rubles a month through *intelligentnyi* work, would like to make the acquaintance of, with intention to marry, an *intelligentnaia* young woman, not older than 27. Prefer a blond of respectable family *(solidnykh rodnykh)*. Dowry of 2,000 rubles (not mandatory).[25]

ChaeRan Freeze points out that while some Jewish men took out personal ads that "stressed more traditional qualities, such as an Orthodox background, strict observance, respectable lineage, and even rabbinical ordination,"[26] other would-be grooms articulated pointedly modern opinions about the qualities of an ideal spouse. This finding is borne out in an ad placed by an Odessan who was "seriously and openly seeking a wife-friend" who was a dentist and thus could work with him in his practice and "could understand me."[27] Another writer used his ad to emphasize his open-mindedness, thus accentuating the high level of his spiritual development (not to mention his romantic proclivities): "Lonely *intelligentnyi* young man thirsty for love seeks the acquaintance of an *intelligentnaia* individual. Age, social position, material circumstances, past life *(proshloe)* and religious persuasion *(veroispovedanie)* do not matter *(bezrazlichnyi)*."[28]

Ads such as these suggest that at least some Odessans were willing to entertain the idea of marrying "down" rather than up, privileging *intelligentnyi* ideals of moral virtue over philistine considerations of money.[29] It is tempting to read such emphasis, in concert with the downplaying of class and ethnicity (expressed as a function of religion or nationality), as a possible sea change in attitudes about qualities of difference in Odessa. As Ilya Gerasimov argues with respect to religious identity, however, even if some of those placing ads in the marriage gazette claimed that ethnicity did not matter, few were actually bold enough to marry across ethno-confessional boundaries.[30] Likewise, while some might claim that money was secondary, newspaper evidence strongly suggests that upward mobility via marriage remained the strategy of choice for men and women across the modern urban social spectrum.

Fiancées and Fiancés

As has become abundantly clear, the Perel'muters were not so evolved that they were willing to put material concerns on the back burner. Jacob had done his part, allocating a significant chunk of cash for his daughters' dowries. Like their middle-class contemporaries (fictional or otherwise), lower-class Jewish families saw marriage as a means to achieve upward mobility. In their eyes, too, the dowry took on tremendous importance. Even the poorest parents did what they could to put something aside for a daughter's future, knowing that her success could mean the rise of the entire family. In Odessa's Jewish community, there was even a special charity created to ensure that no respectable young Jewish woman would became "a girl without a dowry" *(bespridannitsa)*.[31] When no other means were available, however, respectable single women of the lower class fended for themselves, securing wage labor in factories, workshops, or sweatshops. The hopes and dreams of such women (as well as their pragmatic cynicism) were captured in an April 1914 *Odesskaia pochta* column called "Fiancées and Fiancés," based on a visit the columnist "Zhak" made to a millinery workshop somewhere "on the outskirts."[32]

According to Zhak, every young single woman who "crouched over sewing or tied together bouquets of bright flowers . . . for the hats of [Moldavanka] dandies" had the same dream: to marry a "good man" who would save them from the "endless days" of backbreaking work. To this end, the "young women-laborers counted every kopeck and worked until their strength gave out," Zhak explained. But their meager wages—enough to buy "water for kasha but not the kasha itself"—had to stretch a long way. In order to attract "good men," women needed to be "appropriately dressed," explained one of the women interviewed. Beyond this, "we also need to save something for the future of our fiancés," she continued, for a "good man" could not be secured without a good dowry.

Zhak's interviews suggest that the search for a "good man" was an arduous, highly problematic, rarely rewarding task for a lower-class working woman. According to one laborer, men were more interested in "flibbertigibbets" *(fintifliushki)* who could afford to "go to dance classes" than in working women who "are fading and losing [their] bloom without caresses" thanks to endless hours on the shop floor. Other men, meanwhile, were looking for "profitable wives," milliners or seamstresses who would continue to work after marriage in order to supplement the family income. A seamstress who had in fact married this "type" of husband wrote to the columnist Faust to complain bitterly about her fate. It was thanks to her hard work that the couple was able to pay the rent and buy enough food, the woman declared. Her unemployed husband, meanwhile, "slept until noon" and "never thought about what we were going to eat tomorrow." Her humiliation was complete when, after her husband did find work, he began "betraying" her, "kissing other women [while] his young wife languished behind a machine."[33] This was precisely the situation that the women Zhak interviewed were trying to avoid. "Stupid men! It is not in order to continue to toil that we get married," one woman complained. "If only it was difficult for a good man to find a poor, honest girl. . . . Akh, if only we could find good men!"[34]

Gentlemen-Vampires

Even as they dreamed of their saviors, some of Zhak's subjects displayed a high degree of cynicism about the marriage game. In language reminiscent of that deployed by Flit in "The Little Family," one working woman told Zhak: "You men are all the same. You chatter all kinds of nonsense: 'I love you.' 'I adore you.' And as soon as things get serious, you say: 'Please put the money on the table.'" Unfortunately, Zhak told his readers, such cynicism was justified. It was a "sad fate" that awaited inexperienced gullible women, destined by their naiveté to "fall into the hands of 'professional fiancés'":

I put before you a well-dressed young man, with stiletto heels, snow-white collars, lovely ties, a watch, gloves, etc.

A matchmaker appears to a working girl. "Akh, my dear, do I have a fiancé for you. Oy, oy, what a fiancé! He is a picture! . . . He makes more than 100 rubles a month. You will go to gold with him. Punish me, God, if I lie . . ."

The young woman is electrified. She says she cannot wait. Name a date for the meeting so they can lay eyes on each other face to face.

"Be at the train station today, my dear, in the evening, in the first-class hall," says the matchmaker.

The fiancé appears. He charms the young woman. They start up an acquaintanceship.

Soon it turns out that the fiancé needs 100 or 200 rubles "for business." The young woman draws out from the bank the last of her money and gives it to the fiancé. How can you not trust your future husband? Needing nothing more, the man immediately disappears, probably to woo another.

The crime of the "professional" or "contemporary fiancé" was enabled in part by lower-class women who fervently wanted to believe that these "well-dressed" cavaliers were in fact good men. The women's "light-mindedness in allowing the earnings that they slaved and bled for to be given to a swindling fiancé" was a direct result of their desire to rise, to be lifted out of lives of unrelenting toil, to enter the world of the middle class with its promise of ease and material security.[35] But the danger posed by the "contemporary fiancé" was not limited to young working-class women. Some of the imposter husbands set their caps on the bigger prizes that accompanied middle-class brides, as a certain "B. Ts.," a "marriageable young woman" found out the hard way, when she was wooed, won, robbed, and betrayed by the "assistant pharmacist" Naum Rekhler.[36]

In a scathing attack, the columnist Faust decried the actions of "contemporary fiancés" even as he warned that society itself was to blame for their crimes. "They say that once upon a time there were especially repulsive creatures called vampires who would sneak up to a person and suck out his blood, his strength. . . . Today's vampires are those gentlemen who play the role of 'fiancé.'" These "bloodsuckers . . . operate among all classes of the population," Faust warned, exploiting a set of social conventions that forced women to jump headlong into marriage. "Girls of a certain age have a strong desire to marry," Faust declared. "Countless grandmothers and aunties" badger them relentlessly "almost from the moment of a girl's birth": "Tell me, are you already engaged? Not yet? It's a great pity. Why, aren't you looking for a fiancé? Why are you so discriminating (razborchivaia)?" Such "foolish, useless questions . . . grate upon a girl," bemoaned the columnist. It was "just as if she was on trial and owed every idiot an explanation, as if she had to justify herself to everyone she meets on the street." "Rarely does a girl have the strength to tell these 'dear' acquaintances to go to the devil!" Faust fumed. Instead, the "unlucky girls" try to "save themselves" from the "hell" created by their oppressors; "They run to the kind services of matchmakers and . . . often fall into the hands of professional fiancé-extortionists."[37]

While "contemporary fiancés" victimized people of both middle- and lower-class status, the crimes themselves had to be interpreted differently. The "blood" that was "sucked" from the working woman was not only the blood of her bank account (her hard-earned money). It was the blood of her already anemic body (overtaxed and exhausted by the rigors of blue-collar employment) and the vital fluid of her soul (her dreams of salvation, of rising into the ranks of the middle class). The vampire's bite was thus portrayed as a paralyzing, even mortal wound. In the middle-class context, two victims were bitten, a father and daughter. The blood that was money was sucked from the father, its loss stinging him less than his wounded dignity and imperiled self-esteem. For not only had he been unable to protect his own resources against pillage, he had failed in his role as family defender. By allowing the evil impostor to infiltrate into his home—by not seeing through the villain's mask—the father had acted as an unwitting accomplice, bringing shame to his daughter and revealing his inadequacies not only as a father but as a man. The deserted fiancée had also lost blood. Her pride was tarnished, her reputation perhaps sullied, her fears of spinsterhood resurfacing to taunt her. Yet both father and daughter, if shaken, still stood, the wounds of the vampire serious but not fatal.

At the end of his column on the crimes of the vampire, Faust warned his readers to be on their guard. "We should and must fight against these bloodsuckers. The most important thing is to be careful." Every word that they say should be verified, the writer admonished. And, most important of all: "No money before the wedding. If he insistently demands money before the wedding, be suspicious. . . . If he *haggles* about the dowry, be suspicious." "An honest and decent man will never haggle," Faust told his readers. "He won't degrade himself by trying to get money out of you before the wedding." "Do not confuse the sweet smell of love with the stench of the flea market," the columnist concluded.

The "*Kursistka*" and her "Sexual Mystic"

Returning to the fictional Perel'muters, the family patriarch Jacob was not about to allow such a stench to permeate his good house. And as a man of commerce, he was also not about to let an arrogant *intelligentnyi* "wannabe" and his harridan of a mother get the best of him in a business deal. In the matter of the dowry, Flit gave Jacob the last laugh:

Perel'muter: Well, do you want 15,000?
Elijah: Papa!
Mrs. Perel'muter: Jacob, have you lost your mind?
Perel'muter (smiling): Do you want 15,000?

Mother: That would be another matter. I'd have to think about that . . .

Berman: I do like the girl. I very much sympathize with you. But . . .

Mother: In essence, we are in agreement. Is there really so little in your family? I always respected you, madame.

Perel'muter (laughing): Ha-ha-ha . . . They thought that I would give them
15,000. And you don't want a duel? 15,000, ha-ha-ha! Who am I, Marazli
or Khari?[38] I have two daughters, so one gets everything and the other
nothing? . . . (shouts and hysterics)

Berman: This is a mockery. The impudence. The insult!

Mrs. Perel'muter: Gene, show them to the door. Charlatans!

(Berman and his mother leave. The Perel'muter family stands by the window
showering them with curses.)

Throughout the dowry negotiation process, Flit relentlessly lampooned
his *meshchanskii* characters for their hallmark vulgarities. The play functioned as a biting *intelligentnyi* critique first of Odessa's Jewish
meshchanstvo, and then of western bourgeois pretensions. But it also
touched on issues of Jewish secular identity, on generational differences
between parents and children, and on broader tensions rising as entrenched forms of modernity ran up against changing expectations and
sensibilities, especially in the realms of gender and sexuality. Flit addressed
these themes especially in a subplot that focused on the relationship between the Perel'muter's younger daughter Esther (a *kursistka*) and her "cavalier," a university student and self-proclaimed "sexual mystic."

In Flit's hands, Esther Perel'muter was the farcical embodiment of the Russian "new woman." Like all the other characters in "The Little Family," Esther
was an object of ridicule, an overly serious young woman whose radical ideas
and intellectual pretensions were openly mocked by her parents and siblings
(not to mention, the author). In her turn, Esther sneered at other family
members' opinions and aspirations, which she declared represented the "posi-
tivism" and "repulsive concreteness of the bourgeois order." The character's
pedantic arrogance was on view from the moment Esther first entered the
play in scene 4 and began lecturing her family about political economy, quoting Kant and Hegel. Rachel interjected: "Such good children I have. One
[Mathilda] is an artiste, excuse the expression, and the other is insane." "I'd
rather be crazy than live in such an atmosphere," Esther replied. "My soul is
thirsting for air. I'm suffocating here." Then Mathilda tossed out, "You're suffocating. And only yesterday you stood by the gate for two hours talking to
that student!" "We were talking about immanency and inductive meta-
physics!" Esther replied defensively. Later, when Esther discoursed at length
about the institution of marriage, calling it a "relic of bourgeois love" and a
"synthesis of vulgarity and hypocrisy," her brother Elijah inquired: "And why
do you go out strolling with that student if you think marriage isn't right?"
"You are incapable of understanding," the sister replied haughtily, resisting
her brother's attempts to expose her as a hypocrite.

Esther's self-presentation and the reactions it provoked among her family members were comical in part because the *kursistka* took herself so seriously. But the humor sprang, too, from the fact that Russian society as a whole was still trying to figure out whether women of the type that Esther represented actually had to be taken seriously. As Susan Morrissey points out, societal attitudes toward the *kursistka*, and her possible role in modern Russian society, were profoundly ambivalent. Some perceived her as "an immoral creature, lacking in basic feminine values and manners, [possessing] the sexual desire of a prostitute." Others saw her as a bluestocking, "a stereotype of a sterile old maid." Still others considered her to be an "icon of moral purity . . . the prototype of a progressive new educated mother." These contradictory images exemplified the depth of societal confusion about what to make of the "new woman."[39]

Flit played on the opposition between the avant-garde *kursistka* and the conventional bourgeois lady to humorous effect by contrasting the "qualities" of the two Perel'muter sisters. As is already apparent from her opening scene, Esther considered herself something of a radical, scoffing at anything that in her eyes smacked of bourgeois convention, especially as embodied in Mathilda. But it was the *kursistka*'s unorthodox beliefs, as well as the sincerity of her commitment to them, that came under sharp attack as "The Little Family" progressed, especially in scenes involving Esther's courtship with the self-described "modernist" and "sexual mystic." The "long-haired" student himself made his entrance in scene 8, when the four Perel'muter children were sitting in the living room:

> Student (calling in through the window): Esther, are you home?
> Esther: Ah, is that you? Come in, come in. I'm here. (Fusses excitedly at the mirror, then runs out of the room)
> Gene: She's a philosopher and nonetheless looks in the mirror.
> Student (entering): Hello Mathilda, how are you?
> Mathilda: I want to go to theater school.
> (Student adopts a disappointed pose; he "knows" all about the state of the contemporary dramatic arts)
> Mathilda: I like it. The plays are very funny and there are four schools.
> Student: Yes, there are schools, but lately not as many schools as trends.
> Mathilda: Yes, of course they have different directions. One is on Deribasovskaia Street, another is on Preobrazhenskaia.

From this exchange and subsequent dialog involving the two characters, it was obvious that the majority of the time Mathilda had no idea what the student was talking about and cared even less since she thought him an arrogant know-it-all. Meanwhile, the student condemned Mathilda for her *meshchanskii* lack of culture, although as a good *intelligent*, he did condescend to an effort to civilize her. His attempts to raise Mathilda's level of consciousness about the modern theater led him first to disparage Chekov as "talentless," then to discourse on Oscar Wilde:

> Mathilda: What are you talking about? There are some funny vaudevillians. We saw one at the club. Very funny.
>
> Student: Yes, of course, but Oscar Wilde is a bacchanalia of horrors. You know his *Lady Windermere's Fan*.
>
> Mathilda: No, I didn't see it. It was an operetta, wasn't it?

The lecture then took an unexpected turn when the student disclosed that he himself was a "sexual mystic, like Oscar Wilde." Now it was Mathilda's turn to be horrified: "You should be ashamed to talk like that!" the affronted lady scolded. Gene, the younger Perel'muter son, also could not let such a declaration pass without comment: "You are a sexual mystic, so you pay court to housemaids," implying that sexual mysticism (especially when paired with Oscar Wilde) was synonymous with decadence and promiscuity.[40] In scene 9, it became clear that Mrs. Perel'muter shared her son's view:

> Esther (entering as she dolls herself up): Well, here I am. So, are we going to the meeting of the individualists of sexual neuropathology?
>
> Student: I thought we'd go to the circle for the cultivation of mystical sexual attraction.
>
> Mrs. Perel'muter (flying into the room, infuriated and shouting): What is this you're saying? How can you corrupt my daughter like this? . . .
>
> Student: Madame, don't shout.
>
> Mrs. Perel'muter: What do you mean, don't shout. You are corrupting my children in front of me, and I shouldn't say a word? What are you thinking? You come over here, drink tea, eat jam, smoke cigarettes. Yesterday we even gave you three rubles. But you don't want to marry!
>
> Esther: Mama, for God's sake!
>
> Student: I don't understand . . . I . . .
>
> Mrs. Perel'muter: You don't understand. What you don't understand is that boys like you can't come visiting houses where there are unmarried girls (*devitsy*).
>
> Student: I'm going. This is disgraceful.
>
> Esther: And I am leaving, leaving this house. I'll take care of myself.
>
> [Esther and the student storm out of the room]
>
> Mother: Get out of my house! Out, you scoundrel . . . Get out this minute . . . Get out, you nasty girl (*parshivka*)!

Even if such exchanges were exaggerated to the point that they became ludicrous, Flit used them to poke fun at societal fears of moral degeneracy, especially among youth. The male university student was a special target of those who held that sexual promiscuity and libidinous disorder ran rampant within the *studenchestvo*.[41] "The Stranger" milked those fears for laughs, taking special delight in using them to make Rachel squirm. Rachel treated the young man as an enemy capable of exerting a corrupting force over her daughter. That Esther could have come to hold radical ideas of her own volition seemed impossible for Rachel to contemplate, especially since some of those ideas were explicitly concerned with sex, a topic that to the mother was anathema.

In both idealized western bourgeois and traditional Jewish cultures, sex was reserved exclusively for procreation, coitus was endured by women, the urge for it repressed in men. And yet in Russia's fin-de-siècle era, the general public was treated to generous portions of eroticism served up in popular fiction and film as well as in the venues of Russia's booming urban nightlife scene.[42] As chapter 5 demonstrated, such middle-brow fare was precisely to the taste of Odessa's *meshchanskii* public (much to the chagrin of *intelligentnyi* commentators). But sex was also the topic du jour in the salons of educated society, some of Russia's top thinkers forming circles to discuss sexual pleasures and disorders, all in the name of science.[43] Flit obviously found this highly amusing, since he wanted to send Esther and her suitor off on a date to a "meeting of the individualists of sexual neuropathology." The *kursistka* and her sexual mystic thus provided Flit with a few more arrows to sling at arrogant *intelligents* who claimed to "know."

A Jury of One's Peers

As part of its mission to civilize Russian society, the *intelligentsia* itself undertook to judge for others the kinds of activities that would and would not lead to "spiritual" betterment. Concerned primarily with inner quality rather than external appearance, in practice the *intelligent* nonetheless cultivated a distinct "look" along with a superior attitude. Flit thus gave Esther's "cavalier" long hair and a supercilious posture. Meanwhile, the *kursistka* herself, when she first appeared on the scene, entered the Perel'muter living room with a book in her hands, "walking while reading and making notations with a pencil." The long hair, the posing, the book, and in Elijah's case the briefcase, were indispensable props for Flit's aspiring *intelligents*.

In the world of bourgeois propriety, where outward qualities of dress and manner were thought to mirror inner morality, one's social peers had the power to judge if one was or was not a "cultured" person of quality. In scene 10 of "The Little Family," Flit focused explicitly on the anxieties inherent in a milieu that gave others the power to verify or disown one's own personal identity. The main protagonist in the scene was a certain Mrs. Slavenzon—a "lively lady" *(dama boikaia)* dressed "loudly and pretentiously"—who arrived chez Perel'muter just moments after the screaming fight between Rachel, Esther, and the student:

Slavenzon (entering): Hello dear Madame Perel'muter. Always with the children, always working . . .

Mrs. Perel'muter: Ah, hello Madame Slavenzon. Dunia [the maid] didn't say that you were here. Please sit down. Dunia! Dunia! Oh, that little idiot . . . Please take off your hat.

Slavenzon: No, I can't. I can only stay a minute. How are the children? Your husband?

Mrs. Perel'muter: Fine, thank you. The children are fine. And that acquaintance of ours, the student, he is a nice young man. Mathilda, come here please. Dun'ka, how do you like that nasty good-for-nothing [maid]. I'll be right back. (She leaves.)

Slavenzon: Your mother is always working. What a wonderful housekeeper.

Mathilda: Yes, she . . . Why don't you take off your hat?

The conversation between Mathilda and the guest was then abruptly disturbed as the irate student stormed through the room on his way to the front door: "This is a house of vulgarity. Esther, you are perishing in slime." Esther herself followed in his wake, Flit using the occasion of her exit to gleefully fling out another venomous line: "Look at the situation of the modern family. It is poisonous. It has disordered my central nervous system." "Your sister is so educated," Mrs. Slavenzon commented to Mathilda. "Simply darling! I have a daughter in the music school. And do you play?" "A little," Mathilda demurred. "Please play. I so love music. I always go to the operetta. And the symphony when my husband can get tickets from his musician friend. It is a little boring, but not bad. I so love music. Please play."

The exchanges between the "friends" were filled with social one-upmanship and insults thinly veiled as compliments. For instance, when Slavenzon first entered, she commented that "dear Madame Perelmuter" was always so busy working on the house or dealing with the children. The guest thus implied that both the household and the children were problematic, impugning Rachel's abilities as homemaker and mother. Following the noisy departure of Esther and the student, a flustered Rachel returned to offer refreshment. The tray of appetizers inexpertly delivered by the "good-for-nothing" maid, included some oranges that Rachel made no secret of saying cost eighty kopecks a dozen. Slavenzon refused the delicacies, later pointing out that she normally served her guests not just oranges but candy. Rachel, again chagrined, complained that her household upset was the fault of her "little idiot" of a maid. "You know these servants," she said to her friend. "They will drive you out of your mind." "Fiancés, thieves and drunks," Slavenzon replied in commiseration, sighing about the troubles the privileged had to endure when it came to "the help." "Who is blaming you that you live so sparingly?" Rachel's "friend" consoled.

Slavenzon's last remark insulted not just Rachel, but Jacob who in the guest's opinion, was obviously failing in his duty to provide adequately for his family. Slavenson's husband, on the other hand, was a marvelous provider whose successes enabled her own family to maintain a high-profile social presence. As she had mentioned to Mathilda, she and her husband "always" went to the opera, to the cabaret, to the symphony. In fact, she bragged that her husband could often get free tickets. "You should go to the theater every now and then," Mrs. Slevenzon advised Rachel. "Go out and have fun." The insult was deepened still further when Slavenzon suggested that Jacob's "stinginess" was ruining his own daughters' chances for social advancement: "Why don't you ever take your daughters to the theater or to balls?" she asked. "Do they appear so little?" replied Rachel, desperate to recover some of the family's lost dignity. "It seems that we spend so much time at the theater."

In the scene with Mrs. Slavenzon, Flit put an ironic spin on the bourgeois maxim, "Tell me with whom you are acquainted and I will tell you who you are." Even though Mrs. Slavenzon was vulgarity incarnate, freely violating good form with her insincere compliments and transparent insults (not to mention her appalling costume), Rachel nonetheless coveted her "friend's" approval. "The Stranger" thus mocked Rachel not just for attempting to cover up her own and her family's various inadequacies, but for actually believing that Slavenzon was a social better whose opinion should be valued. While the author ridiculed the idea that individual worth could and should be judged by the exacting yet morally vacant criteria of bourgeois "correctness," he nonetheless acknowledged that adherence to such standards could make or break a reputation.

Conclusion

Oscar Wilde once said that "caricature is the tribute which mediocrity pays to genius."[44] When the student in scene 8 invoked Wilde's specter, Flit tipped his hat to the savage wit and piercing eye of a true master of the comedy of manners genre. If Flit's own efforts fell short of Wilde's brilliance, they nonetheless succeeded in conveying the essence of a sociocultural milieu that enslaved itself to social standards that were brutally exacting yet morally vacant. Precisely because "The Little Family" was a caricature, its plot motifs stood out in especially sharp prominence: status consciousness and anxiety, generational tensions between parents and children, and the crucial importance of marriage and career choices to conceptions of self.

Authors who penned comedies of manners wrote primarily for audiences of their own social peers, satirizing the foibles and follies of the coterie they inhabited. In the case of "The Little Family," the author chose deliberately to obscure his identity. Although he called himself "the Stranger," Flit's comic send-up of the Jewish *meshchanskii* family betrayed an intimate knowledge of the world occupied by his fictional subjects. Notably free of sentiment, Flit's treatment was light hearted, betraying neither anger nor malice. Instead, Flit preferred to laugh at the Perel'-muters' foibles, encouraging his readers to join in the fun. And yet the types he drew on to tell his tale each contained within themselves elements of tragedy.

Mark Steinberg has analyzed the writings of lower-class workers who thought of themselves as strangers in their own world: "In memoirs these writers often recalled feeling alienated from the crass everyday world around them, looking for truth and meaning in isolated reading, wandering, and thinking." In their own writings, such authors described the anguish of "the awakened and sensitive individual" who had nothing in common with the "ordinary people all around them." This profound isolation developed into a "sense of alienation that bordered on a sort of cultural and moral nausea."[45] In the context of "The Little Family," Esther best personified this kind of stranger, "suffocating" in the oppressive environment of her "poisonous" home life. Ridiculed by her mother and mocked by her siblings, Esther sought comfort in the realm of books and ideas. She attempted to flee, too, into the arms of the student. But by declaring himself a "sexual mystic like Oscar Wilde," the long-haired young man opened to speculation the question of whether his carnal desires would incline him toward Esther. Although Flit did not spare the *kursistka* from satire, he did feed her character some of the most scathing lines. At one point, for instance, Esther called bourgeois marriage "a synthesis of vulgarity and hypocrisy," a phrase that aptly summed up the author's overall assessment of the milieu of the Odessa *meshchanstvo.*

There was more than a hint of self-deprecating humor and self-criticism as Flit told the tale of "The Little Family." Despite his sharp wit, it is notable that the author was not wholly unsympathetic to at least some of his characters. He portrayed Jacob, for instance, as browbeaten and harassed but also as honest and essentially kind. While Jacob criticized his children and disparaged their dreams, he at least paid attention to them. Not only that but he sent them to school, ensuring that each had some kind of skill that might help ensure their security. Beyond this, although Jacob's failure as a provider was a theme in the play, he had obviously done well enough to spare his wife and children the indignity of working outside the home and had put enough aside to provide both his daughters with dowries of considerable size. Tellingly, however, in the matter of Mathilda's marriage, Jacob the businessman could not close the deal, unwilling to give in to adversaries he despised. If this, perhaps, made him a momentary hero in his family's eyes, when all was said and done, Mathilda was still twenty-three, still had no husband, and still had only one viable career path, that of being a bourgeois wife. The fear that Mathilda's shelf life might expire before her parents could marry her off, leaving her at sea in a world she was ill-prepared to navigate, might explain why Jacob did not stop Esther from becoming a *kursistka*. Interestingly, Jacob was almost entirely absent from scenes involving his younger daughter. Even though he was in the room when Esther condemned the bourgeois order as "repulsively concrete," he never condemned her radical beliefs. Unlike the other members of the Perel'muter clan, Jacob also refrained from mocking Esther for alliance with the "sexual mystic."

If Flit tempered his representation of Jacob by showing him as a *meshchanin* who was a little bit of a *mentsch*, the author was most ungenerous in his portrayal of Rachel. The socially grasping *meshchanka* was completely self-absorbed, nagging her husband incessantly and shrieking at her children. She was often overwrought to the point of absurdity, had vulgar sensibilities, and poor taste in friends. While she did try to promote her children's security, she did so to enhance her own social prestige. Highly critical of others, she betrayed no capacity for meaningful self-reflection, no visible desire for her own moral improvement. Much like her mother, Mathilda could not see past the material, happy to conform to the "rules" of a society that she never questioned. Similarly, Elijah aspired to rise above his milieu, but only to enhance his status, not to escape a crushing sense of alienation or because he possessed an all-encompassing need to "know."

And where, one may ask, does love fit in to all this? There were very few signs of sincere affection in the Perel'muter home, especially between Jacob and his wife. Yet the family appeared bound by affective ties. In terms of romantic love, Esther clearly had a crush on the "sexual mystic," but he only revealed an intellectual interest in the subject. In Flit's view, the issue of money seemed to make the point moot. What did come across in "The Little Family" was that for both men and women, the process of finding a "proper" spouse was one fraught with possibilities as well as anxieties. While material considerations were often in the spotlight, they seemed to function as proxies for deeper concerns about self-identity. After marriage, too, changes in a couple's material circumstances (whether for better or worse) had the power to impact self-definition, inviting reassessment of one's own as well as a partner's moral character and emotional commitment. Likewise, fluctuations or threats to a family's stability, social status or respectability had the potential to deeply affect all members of that family, adults and children alike. Even if the situations and certainly the dialog of "The Little Family" were purposefully overblown, the trials and tribulations of the fictional characters mirrored real-life anxieties common in middle-class homes. Parents were highly concerned with the security of their own and their children's futures, the struggle for social status and recognition becoming for some an obsession. The safeguarding of family honor was a crucial one here, the disclosure of a scandal powerfully impacting all members of a household. The following chapter examines the extremes some went to in order protect their honor, taking the reader out of the world of crime as metaphor and back to cases involving bloodier forms of villainy.

7

Revenge of the
Queen of Stylish Hairdos

Oil of Vitriol—Concentrated sulfuric acid added to rose liqueur
and American raspberry jam, in both instances to intensify the
red color.

—Entry from a Russian cookbook[1]

• "Here they are together, a comedy of marriage, a staggering drama, and the
revenge of a betrayed woman. Sadness and sorrow, tears and ruined lives, all
are pouring forth. But this is not a movie or far-fetched fantasy. This is life itself. Our main heroes are a husband, a wife, a lodger/lover, and three young
children. The setting is Moldavanka." So opens *Odesskaia pochta's* histrionic
treatment of the trial of El'ka Zaz, the "queen of stylish hairdos," an adulterous
wife arrested for throwing acid in the face of her duplicitous lover, the
"demon-tempter" Belotserkovskii.[2] Like other newspaper accounts in the
"family drama" genre, Zaz's story involved sex, scandal, and bloody violence.
But her tale and its like were also about domesticity, gender roles, and above all,
honor—a woman's honor, the family honor, the honor of a wife and mother.

This chapter examines stories of women at the edge of endurance, journalistic interpretations of their violent acts exposing competing notions
about the nature of femininity and deep ambivalence about women's
changing roles in modern urban society. As will be seen, journalistic tales
of heroines whose conduct was so unexpected or outrageous that it passed
into the realm of spectacle were frequently interpreted in terms of performance. Some of these "dramas" were comparatively benign, focusing on
women who with poise and composure pushed the envelope of polite behavior. For instance, popular excitement at the starting line of the longest-
ever road race in South Russia was heightened dramatically by the arrival
of three "audacious" women—Mesdames Faats, Suruchan, and Alinikova—
all wives of prominent businessmen, who appeared dressed in driving gear,
confidently mounted their vehicles, and actually participated in the race.[3]
But other stories, particularly those carrying headlines such as "Revenge"
and "Scandal," were the stuff of high melodrama, the "stars" of each
episode women such as Zaz, who in contrast to societal expectations, employed "male" techniques of confrontation and violence to save or protect
the honor and reputation of themselves or their families.

The narratives included in this chapter are particularly important because they shed light on how at least some Odessan women rebelled against the limits society imposed on their lives and activities. Despite more than half a century of debate on "the woman question," despite increased opportunities for women to become educated and enter business and professional careers, despite the growing visibility of women in public life, despite the appearance of "new women" bent on leading independent lives, despite the crusades of social critics (including some journalists), mainstream women in Odessa remained triply trapped. First, because the western model of "true womanhood"—idealized in terms of piety, purity, passivity, and domesticity—had the greatest hold on the Odessan popular mind, a woman's behavior and actions were measured against unrealizable expectations. This was as true for middle-class women, whose social peers were highly sensitive to deviations in good form, as it was for lower-class females, trapped by unflattering stereotypes that described them as untrustworthy, immoral, and sexually disorderly.[4] In general, mainstream society held that ladies of the middle class could not exist without male protectors, that women of the lower orders would surely "fall" unless "saved" by their moral and social betters.

A second belief that trapped women was that their respectability, indeed, their very identity, could not be separated from marriage and family life, because their "natural" environment was the home. Certainly a woman might take advantage of the expanding opportunities available to her in the modern city. An educated single woman might begin a ladylike career, perhaps as a teacher or nurse. When the time came, however, she was expected to marry, give up her career, and devote herself to her husband and children. To do otherwise was to reject her femininity and, with it, her respectable status. A widow, too, might venture back into the public world, especially in order to carry on her deceased husband's business. But she, too, was expected to retire in the event of remarriage or with the coming of age of a son who might "unburden" her.[5]

Finally, women in Odessa, as elsewhere, were trapped by the law, legally subjugated first to their father, then to their husband, with few rights and less means upon which to build an independent life for themselves outside of the patriarchal home. Under imperial law, a woman needed a husband's consent to get a job, to enter an institution of higher education, to execute a bill of exchange, or even to receive a separate passport, which itself was often a prerequisite for independent residency and employment.[6] Further, she was legally obliged not only to live with her husband, but to obey and submit to him completely. As William G. Wagner points out, marital strife was "considered a personal affair . . . outside the purview of the law" with husbands having the right to "discipline" their wives in any way they saw fit, including coercion and physical force.[7] A woman's position was made even worse by the fact that, no matter how oppressive her personal situation, marital separations were not legally sanctioned and divorces difficult to obtain.[8]

The following sections examine stories that describe women who not only felt the strain of their entrapment but took active measures to resist it. While their specific grievances and modes of action differed considerably, all of these women shared two things in common: a sense that they had suffered unwarranted shame and dishonor at the hands of an enemy; and the desire to avenge themselves by any means necessary. In spirit, then, the actions of these women mirrored those of gentlemen who—in Russia as in the rest of Europe—had until quite recently routinely answered private insults with public challenges that resulted in duels. But there was a crucial difference. While male dueling was deemed arcane and uncivilized, "heroines" of "family dramas" exercised their prerogatives as modern women with the support and even encouragement of the wider public. Women such as El'ka Zaz successfully protected or saved themselves, while simultaneously airing private grievances and taking vengeance on hated enemies. And thanks largely to the force of popular opinion, they frequently got away with it, even if that meant spilling their own blood in the name of honor.

"Tandochka's Secret"

In July 1914, seventeen-year-old Tat'iana Serdiagina killed herself by self-immolation. The young woman's death was not an average suicide of the kind "noted not less than daily" in newspaper chronicles and generally disregarded by the Odessa public, proclaimed the *Odesskaia pochta* columnist, "M. F." The young woman had not taken her own life for any of the usual reasons—failed romance, a guilty conscience, financial need, or marital strife. The circumstances of this case were "wild, cruel, and incomprehensible," explained M. F. The young Serdiagina had set herself on fire because of the unrelenting "moral and physical torment" she suffered at the hands of her own mother.[9]

As Susan Morrissey notes, "suicide was first and foremost an intimate drama, an exposé of private life."[10] The "drama" in this case was set in the Moldavanka home of Petr and Matrena Serdiagin, a working-class couple with two children, Fedor, nineteen, and the unhappy Tania. With her death, Tania ensured that her family's "abnormal" relations would become the object of intense public scrutiny. M. F.'s initial report of the suicide described a family in which "normal" gender roles were inverted. Petr was a devoted father, "kind and loving." His wife Matrena, on the other hand, was an "evil" woman who beat her children mercilessly, starved them, called them names "from the dictionary of curses," and even threatened to kill them. While both children were victims of her abuse, she especially picked on Tania, who was her father's favorite.

As M. F. explained to his readers, Matrena's wrath was focused on Tania because Petr wanted to help his daughter move up in the world. At one point, for instance, he had gotten a job as a porter at a girls' high school, arranging for Tania to be enrolled there. The girl was thrilled, studied hard, and during her first year, did very well. At that point, however, her mother "categorically refused" to allow Tania to continue her studies. "She is getting educated for nothing," Matrena was quoted as saying. "Let her work with us [at the factory]!" Although Petr acquiesced, he did not want Tania doing manual labor. Instead, he got her into a bookkeeping course. This plan, too, was foiled by Matrena, who "refused to pay for it." After that, things only got worse for Tania, M. F. declared. Her mother continued to abuse her while the father remained a silent witness. On one occasion, when Petr tried to come to his daughter's defense, the wicked Matrena accused him of having an incestuous affair with Tania: "Why do you stand up for her? Do you think I don't know that you are your daughter's lover!" When Tania heard this, she ran out of the house, Matrena yelling after her: "What? Are you waiting for your lover?" The evil rumor started to spread throughout Moldavanka, M. F. explained. Tania was so humiliated that she never left the house. Then, a couple of neighbors who knew the "real" Tania tried to "rehabilitate" her, taking her to a midwife who certified that she was "completely pure." But then Tania's life took another turn for the worse. Her father lost three fingers in an accident at work, forcing him to quit his factory job. Realizing that now she would be completely at her mother's mercy, Tania went to a nearby shop, bought a bottle of alcohol, returned home, burned her letters, photographs, and other personal papers, stood by the window, "let down her hair, doused herself with alcohol, and set herself on fire."

The final scene as described by M. F. is drawn in the colors of high Christian martyrdom:

> Three minutes later the residents of the building were startled by the horrifying picture of the burning girl walking down the corridor. Her hair and clothing were ablaze, glowing in the dark night like some kind of fantastic pageant (*fantasticheskoe zrelishche*).
>
> The burning "Tandochka" walked slowly, holding both of her hands high up to heaven. She did not groan, did not make any sound, did not cry out from her breast.
>
> Everyone was petrified, so lost in the spectacle that no one even ran up to help her, to tear off her burning clothing. Only when the girl solemnly, peacefully moved down the stairwell into the yard did someone pour water on her and extinguish the flames. Then "Tandochka" fell to the ground, those gathered around her hearing only the words: "So hard . . . mother . . ."

Tania was taken to the Jewish Hospital, where she lingered for four days before finally dying, M. F. continued. During that time, several of her girl-friends came to visit, encountering when they did so the cold, heartless Matrena, who reproached them bitterly for their tears. "This is not a mother, this is a wild beast," the friends were quoted as saying. "She doesn't have a heart in her chest, she has a toad." Even at the moment of Tandochka's death, the cruel mother was portrayed as showing no remorse: "Poor Tandochka . . . Go to the devil!"

M. F. followed up his initial report of Serdiagina's death with a second long column titled "Tandochka's Secret," evidently written solely to complete Matrena's vilification.[11] Some people in Moldavanka still did not believe that the mother's cruelty drove Tania to suicide, M. F. claimed. "It can't be that a birth mother could torture her own child," he reported one Moldavankan as saying. "It can't be but it happened," the writer assured his audience. To prove his point, M. F. quoted in full a letter he said Tania herself had written to a friend the day before her death. Whether it was truly written by Tania or was M. F.'s creation, the "letter" remains a fascinating, highly revealing document. First of all, it is a complete condemnation of the mother, whose unspeakable cruelty so tormented Tania. Interestingly, though, it was not Matrena's physical abuse that most affected the young woman. Instead, what Tandochka could not endure were her mother's insinuations regarding the alleged incestuous affair. In the letter, Tania wrote that she was so grievously insulted by this "scandal" that she was prepared for anything, "even for crime."

Tania wanted revenge. "I swear on my honor that I do not intend to put up with such scandal." "I will be patient for a little while longer and then we will see," she wrote. "Later they can pass judgment on me. And I don't care if it is prison or the grave. I agree to anything." The letter's last speech is especially explicit. "Revenge is boiling inside of me," Tania confessed. "I want to take vengeance on my enemy for all the slander, for the lies. This enemy, she is my mother. She is perfidious and predatory like a wild beast. I hate and despise her." "My parents' home has become repulsive to me now," Tania concluded. "The end will come soon. I do not have the strength to endure any longer." In the end, M. F. explains to his readers, Tania was "too tender-hearted to raise her hand against another, even one she considered to be an evil enemy." Though Tania was the one who ended up in the grave, M. F. did his part to ensure that Matrena would also be buried, not in a blaze of martyred glory like Tania but deep in the shame of public condemnation.

Tania's death was not portrayed as suicide but as honorable self-sacrifice, indeed as salvation.[12] In M. F.'s hands, Serdiagina's death became a moral victory for true, "natural" womanly quality over unnatural evil. Even though Tania had contemplated murder, the fact that she was "too tender-hearted" to go through with it was testament to her essential goodness. Tania never realized the dream of living a fully respectable life, a middle-class life of moral as well as material security, a life that her father tried to help her attain. But she died a respectable dignified death, her honor avenged, her reputation cleansed, her enemy vanquished.

"Scandals"

By definition, "scandal" refers to a disgraceful or discreditable action caused by fault or misdeed that damages a person's reputation. It is thus inseparable from notions of "public." As a noted Victorianist points out, "as long as deviant behavior (in the broadest sense) remains private and a superficial moral and social order is preserved, scandal does not exist."[13] It is only when such behavior becomes public that it becomes scandalous. In most cases, this publicity occurred through the mechanisms of confrontation and accusation. In Tandochka's case, her mother spread false accusations that were consumed and reproduced (probably in exaggerated form) by others in the neighborhood. Even though Tandochka herself was portrayed as innocent of the behavior of which she was accused, she nonetheless felt the weight of public shame and disapproval so heavily that she would not leave the house until her friends used public means (expert testimony) to try to restore her reputation.

The neighborhood was a powerful forum for scandal. A larger and even more powerful forum, however, was the newspaper. The popular press was a public arena that thrived on sensationalism; it was in the business of shocking its readers.[14] Thus, the press played a "crucial role . . . in the creation, judgment, and perpetuation of scandal." But it was not just to sell papers that journalists themselves were among the worst scandalmongers. Indeed, as already noted, more than a few columnists used scandal as a way to convey lessons to their readers, "judging, promulgating, or amending standards of acceptable conduct."[15] Tandochka's mother's reputation was mightily impugned by M. F., who reviled Matrena's scandalous behavior and publicly disgraced her for her "unnatural" cruelty. M. F. restored Tandochka's honor even as he stripped away Matrena's.

Press reports suggest that Odessa's women had a highly developed sense of honor and that wounded honor was a powerful force catalyzing women to action. The desire for "public satisfaction" was what motivated one upper-middle-class woman (identified only as the wife of "a well-known property owner and store proprietor") to confront the "well-known broker L." as he sat in the *café-chantant* Alkazar one night in December 1912. The incident took place when the "fashionably dressed woman" entered the crowded café, approached L.'s table, and slapped him. L. responded in turn by picking up a beer bottle and smashing it across her face. According to the report, the assembled public, horrified by L.'s violence, jumped him and held him down until the arrival of the police. When asked later why she had confronted L., the woman said that she wanted "satisfaction," because he had cheated her out of five hundred rubles and, in general, had "acted dishonorably" toward her. The report of L.'s behavior when confronted at the Alkazar lent support to her claim.[16]

The incident at the Alkazar strongly suggests that women themselves were not only keenly aware of the power of scandal but also of how to use it for their own ends. The press was full of stories about "scandals" involving ladies who in the heat of the moment lost their tempers or composure in public.[17] An example of one such woman was a certain "Mrs. G.," who ripped the hat from the head of Tsila Barash as the latter sat in the stands at the hippodrome watching the horse races. According to *Odesskii listok*'s report of the incident, Barash's "desperate scream" caused quite a commotion in the stands, as did the sight of the "struggling" Mrs. G. being "hurriedly taken from the hippodrome and invited to the police station." As it turned out, *Odesskii listok* explained, Barash had lately "been seen everywhere" in seemingly intimate company with Mrs. G.'s husband. When the offended wife found out about this, she "appeared at the hippodrome and here forced Barash to deal with her."[18]

Several interesting points emerge from this report. First, by physically and very publicly attacking Barash, Mrs. G. violated the code of good manners and therein suffered a loss of dignity. It was bad enough for a lady to let her face show signs of annoyance, irritation, or anger. For her to resort to physical violence was unthinkable. Moreover, because she had to be forcibly removed from the scene of the crime and taken to the police station, Mrs. G.'s femininity, too, was to some extent a casualty of the incident. Having said this, it is crucial to note that the newspaper protected the identities of both Mrs. G. and her allegedly philandering husband while at the same time publicly exposing Barash. This highly typical technique provided readers with added information essential to understanding the "real" meaning of the story: Mr. and Mrs. G. were respectable, Barash was not. Mrs. G. employed scandalous behavior in order to make public the larger scandal of her husband's affair. By taking aim at the mistress instead of the husband, however, Mrs. G. attacked her rival's reputation and social legitimacy, suggesting that the mistress was primarily responsible for the husband's "fall," that she was a known "corrupter of family life." Thus, Mrs. G. used "unwomanly" conduct to defend the family honor, her cause aided by the journalist covering the story, who used the scandal to expose and punish Barash's masquerade.

Journalists were not always sympathetic to the causes of female accusers. Take for example an incident, billed as "the usual scandal," that took place one September evening shortly before midnight at the fashionable Severnaia restaurant, where the *chinovnik* "S. D." sat "in the company of two ladies."

> All of sudden, quite unexpectedly, as if from underground, a third lady appeared before them in a highly agitated state. "So then, with whom are you betraying me? With *café-chantant* singers?" the woman cried sharply, appending a string of unflattering Peresyp-like epithets. "I will flood you with sulfuric acid! I will burn your eyes out!" the agitated lady threatened.

Then the scandal became more heated and D. decided "to act." Per his explanation, he only wanted to "push away" from the woman. Instead, he pushed the table so solidly that the woman fell to the floor and lost consciousness.

A doctor and the police were quickly called to the scene. When the woman had recovered from her "strong nervous attack," she explained to police that she was the "artiste" Aleksandra G. and that the *chinovnik* D. was her "lover" *(sozhitel')*.

The *Odesskaia pochta* reporter who wrote the story chalked up the incident to a less than honorable motive—jealousy—which, he claimed, was not an uncommon reason for a lady to publicly confront a gentleman. In this case, however, the journalist did not hide his suspicions about the accuser's respectability. Aleksandra's "unwomanly" conduct was underscored by her use of "Peresyp-like epithets," her morality brought into question further by the fact that she herself was an "artiste" and that the man she accused was not her husband but her lover. In this case, the accuser's behavior was represented as hysterical. Even if both she and the *chinovnik* D. were portrayed as scandalous figures, it was the accuser not the accused who was considered most dangerous. This conclusion was made especially intense not only by Aleksandra's demonstration of "irrational" behavior, but by her bitter threat to "flood" her lover with sulfuric acid.

"Revenge of the 'Queen' of Stylish Hairdos"

The specter of the acid-throwing woman haunted the pages of Odessa's popular press. Represented as an almost exclusively female crime, the incidents, while relatively few in number, were widely and energetically reported.[19] Having said this, it is important to note that there was no such thing as a "typical" *vitrioleuse*. She might appear in any neighborhood, from Bul'varnyi to the outskirts, and could be of any social class or ethnic origin. Some women used acid as a way to take revenge on violent men—husbands or lovers—who had consistently beaten them.[20] Others turned to vitriol to punish men for betrayal or abandonment.[21] Still others found acid to be an effective weapon against female rivals: a jealous wife might fling acid at her husband's mistress, or a mistress at her lover's wife.[22] In yet another case, a mother threw vitriol into the face of her son's fiancée, a woman the mother did not deem worthy of her son's affections.[23] Another mother used acid to punish a brutal son-in-law, who refused to consent to her daughter's repeated requests for a divorce.[24]

Regardless of the specific details of the particular crimes, women who threw acid had several things in common. First, they used vitriol as a means to punish the people they felt responsible for bringing about their unhappiness. Second, in doing so, they displayed a well-developed sense of honor, acid becoming a way for women to answer perceived insults against self-esteem or threats to (real or potential) social position. Third, by choosing acid as a weapon, women sought not to kill their "enemies" but to publicly mark them. In the words of Ruth Harris, who studied the phenomenon in fin-de siècle Paris, "[v]itriol-throwing was the annihilation of individuality, robbing the victim of his distinctive human traits through burning and obliteration. Perhaps even more significantly, it condemned the victim to a life in which his appearance could only evoke repulsion or pity, with the intent to deprive him or her of the possibility of further amorous or sexual activity." Thus, says Harris, the vitrioleuse confers upon her victim "a state of sexual and social impotence, an almost literal 'loss of face,' which was considered to be an appropriate vengeance for the wrongs they had caused."[25]

The act of acid throwing was a guaranteed way to make private grievances publicly visible. Indeed, the crime itself often took place in public. One woman flung vitriol at a man promenading on Nikolaevskii Boulevard because she discovered that, even though he had promised to marry her, he was in fact engaged to someone else.[26] Another woman took revenge on a "contemporary fiancé" outside of the justice of the peace court in Moldavanka. In this case, the assailant was seeking to punish the man who had taken two hundred rubles and other valuables from her on the promise of marriage but then turned out to be already married.[27]

In both of these cases, the woman's public loss of self-esteem when "left at the altar" was avenged when she attacked her betrayer in a very public way. The assailants made no effort to conceal their crimes. On the contrary, they wanted to be seen, were, in fact, seeking publicity. Part of the explanation for this comes from the fact that in addition to the trio of results a woman might accomplish by throwing acid—the punishment, the vengeance, and the marking—one more must be added: the strong possibility of public vindication and acquittal.

Women who attacked their enemies in public did not commit their crimes spontaneously, in the heat of the moment, as it were. Instead, they needed to plan, needed even to stalk their intended victim or at least find a good place to lie in ambush.[28] There is little likelihood that a woman would just happen to have with her a container of sulfuric acid at the precise moment that she ran into her rival on the street. When a vitrioleuse attacked her enemy in private, especially at home, it might be easier to categorize her act as a "crime of passion." One night in June 1912, for instance, Elena Berdyshevskaia was in her kitchen preparing to commit suicide because of her husband's repeated infidelity. According to *Odesskii listok*, the betrayed wife had no sooner succeeded in pouring a bowl of sulfuric acid when in through the door walked Mariia Balasheva, her husband's latest mistress. "When [Berdyshevskaia] unexpectedly saw before her the young woman who had broken up her family life, she decided to take vengeance on her," the report concluded.[29] Such a scenario, however, is not representative of the majority of occurrences.

Evidence suggests that, whether she committed her crime in public or private, the acid-throwing woman took time to plan her attack. Take, for example, the case of Elena Fiialkovskaia, who by 1912 had already endured eleven years of marriage to her husband Mikhail, ten of which she described as "a living hell." The woman reached the breaking point when Mikhail came home one summer evening and took Elena's last good skirt. The suspicious wife followed her errant husband, shadowing him as he sold the skirt to a second-hand clothes dealer, met some of his buddies, picked up a prostitute, and went into a restaurant. Unobserved, she followed him inside the eatery, only to be confronted with the sight of Mikhail, already drunk, with the prostitute in his arms. The betrayed wife returned home, prepared a bowl of sulfuric acid and, several hours later when Mikhail returned, tossed it into her husband's face.[30]

Newspaper representations relied heavily on the potent combination of rejection and jealousy to explain the crimes of the vitrioleuse. A good example of this is the report of a "family drama" revolving around Filipp Galakhov, a man who arrived in Odessa from the countryside in 1910. Unlike many newcomers, Galakhov was lucky, finding a job in the Bul'-varnyi office of a food brokerage firm. Shortly thereafter, Galakhov met and fell in love with Nina Ul'ianskaia and the two set up housekeeping together. Two years later, however, Galakhov's wife came to Odessa with the couple's three small children. When she discovered that Filipp was living with Nina, she left the children with him and decided to try to make it on her own. According to the report, however, the estranged wife was "jealous of her husband's success" and wanted him back. Then one evening, under the pretext of visiting the children, she approached Ul'ianskaia and threw sulfuric acid into her face with the words: "This is for you. Now you'll know!"[31]

"Now you'll know." In the hands of popular press journalists, the statement conveys the pain of rejection, the frustration of jealousy, and a woman's fear of living unprotected in the harsh urban world. Thus the phrase might serve as a vitrioleuse's motto, neatly summing up a trio of motivations, any one of which would be understood in her day as sufficient cause and even justification for her crime. So it was that a jury saw fit to acquit Klavdiia Bashidzhagova, the wife of a customs-artel worker, who was on trial for throwing acid in the face of her husband's mistress, twenty-two-year-old A. Stepel. According to Odesskaia pochta, Bashidzhagova's defense attorneys convinced jurors that the victim herself had sealed her own fate. Stepel's past was "less than irreproachable," said the lawyers Fainshtein and Fridman. In fact, they claimed, Stepel had deliberately broken up a "peaceful" family, causing Bashidzhagova to be "consumed by jealousy" and to fall into a "fit of hysteria," during which time she "ambushed" her rival. Once again, then, the victim became the villain, the newspaper noting that Stepel could never escape the marks of her "crime" now forever inscribed in her once beautiful face.[32]

One of the most revealing examples of the "revenge story" genre starred El'ka Zaz, "the 'queen' of stylish hairdos" introduced at the beginning of this chapter. As in any good melodrama, the author "A. Sh."—the *Odesskaia pochta* reporter who covered Zaz's trial—had to establish a clear opposition between the heroine and her corrupter.[33] In this case, the protagonist's role was filled by the queen: "Everyone in Moldavanka knows her," the journalist explained. "No celebration can take place without her. Be it a wedding, ball, or other special occasion, women hurry to El'ka Zaz." It is crucial to note that from the beginning A. Sh. set out to present El'ka Zaz as someone other than—and distinctly above—the "typical" Moldavankan. Zaz was not a simple hairdresser, a lower-class servant of proficient capabilities. Instead, she was an upwardly mobile entrepreneur, an "experienced hairstylist with a devoted following," who was successful, artistically talented, hard working, and "well mannered." Even though she was definitely a working woman, she was nonetheless portrayed as having a respectable career in service of her family rather than a de-feminizing job that stripped her of her ability to function as a proper wife and mother.

A. Sh. described Zaz as a "womanly" woman, whose personal industriousness promoted appropriately domestic goals. She was "possessed of a good-looking exterior," was married to a hard-working man with whom she lived "quietly . . . peacefully [and] with love," and was the mother of three young children. The greatest ambition of the Zaz couple was "to help the children on in life," to ensure for them a place in respectable society. This "dream" was difficult to realize, however, especially given that Zaz's husband was a beer delivery man with little hope of moving up in the world. Thus, El'ka rather than her husband was portrayed as the family's agent of upward mobility. According to A. Sh., it was in service of the children's future that the Zaz couple decided to bring in a little extra money by taking a lodger. At this point, however, they unwittingly opened the door to a "demon-tempter" destined to "smash" their happy family life and bring down on them "rack and ruin."

Just as it was crucial for A. Sh. to portray El'ka as a good and essentially virtuous heroine, so did he have to present the lodger—Belotserkovskii—as an unambiguous villain. Belotserkovskii was a "young dandy," who "having been abroad, was a master of foreign languages and an artist." Playing El'ka's social aspirations to his advantage, Belotserkovskii "zealously flirted" with her, using his charms, his "passionate sweet talk," his "vows of love," and, above all, his pretentious claims to *intelligentnyi* cultural status to seduce the impressionable Zaz. The "demon-tempter took possession" of his victim. Under Belotserkovskii's evil influence, Zaz completely forgot her husband and children, the narrator continued. She allowed her "beloved" to caress and kiss her, even "in the presence of the children," whom she bribed with candy so that they would not tell all to their daddy. She was, wrote the author, "intoxicated" by a "crazy passion" that completely "overpowered common sense," an "ardent passion" so strong that it drove her into an adulterous affair that was obvious to everyone except, of course, her faithful husband.

The heroine's fall successfully accomplished, all that remained was her final ruin. "The beginning of the end" came, the narrator continued, when Zaz's husband of ten years discovered that "the woman in whom his soul rested" had "set herself up with a lover." At that point, the husband confronted his "wife-betrayer" and ordered her out of his house. "In despair, Zaz rushed to her lover, but he did not know her," A. Sh. explained. "Belotserkovskii had already cooled to her and gone on to another woman, whom he intended to marry."

The "stormy encounter" when the "wife-betrayer" was herself betrayed by the "demon-tempter" forms the "stupendous finale" of A. Sh.'s melodrama of "real life." For it was at that moment, the author revealed, that Zaz showered her lover with sulfuric acid and Belotserkovskii was severely disfigured. "The upper half of his once handsome face had turned into an unbroken blue bubble," wrote the journalist. "He lost all sight in his right eye and his left one was injured." In the aftermath of the attack, Zaz was arrested and held in custody pending trial. The period of her incarceration was one of utter despair for all of the family, the narrator explained. The "queen" herself became ill "from all of this," said A. Sh. Meanwhile, "the children became orphans and the husband a 'widower' of a living wife and mother."

The melodramatic tone of A. Sh.'s representation of the case was even more pronounced in his narration of Zaz's trial. The image presented to readers was that of a good-hearted husband, a penitent wife, and three suffering children, all of whom wanted nothing more than a chance to rebuild their shattered family life. El'ka took the stand, "crying and sobbing" as she told the jury "about her love for Belotserkovskii, who boorishly betrayed her, and about the anguish of the children, left at the mercy of fate." Even as she spoke, A. Sh. told readers, these selfsame children also cried, "trembling from worry" as they sat in the lobby, waiting for the court to deliver the decision that would "cut them off from their mother" forever. The husband, too, was described as "unable to hold back his tears," when his turn came to testify. Rather than speaking against his wife, however, he explained to the jury that he had forgiven her for "everything" and, in fact, "tried his hardest to shield her."

Then it was Belotserkovskii's turn to tell his side of the matter. "Brought into court on the arm of his legal wife," the partially blind, badly disfigured man "poured out on the accused a sea of dirt. He denied the liaison with the accused and called her a debauched and depraved woman." He even went so far as to tell jurors that El'ka had confessed to him "that she had already been cheating on her husband for seven years." According to the narrator, Belotserkovskii's testimony so effected Zaz that she succumbed to a faint. "A recess in the proceedings ensued and a physician was called to tend to the accused." When Zaz had revived, her attorney took the floor to sum up the case, stressing to the jury the "moral suffering" already endured by the defendant. With these words, Zaz again lost her composure: she "fell into hysterics and started loudly sobbing." And so ended the trial.

The jury did not have to deliberate for long before they returned a verdict of "not guilty," the journalist reported. The final scene was one of a "joyous" family reunion as the happy cries of El'ka's children "filled the hall," and the loving husband "gave heartfelt thanks to the defense attorney." The "victim," meanwhile, the "half blind" Belotserkovskii— "deprived" by the vitrioleuse of both his handsome face and "his ability to work"—"sighed heavily as he left the courtroom on the arm of his wife and dragged himself home."

Throughout his narration of the case of El'ka Zaz, A. Sh. presented a story of unambiguous opposition. The heroine was a good and essentially virtuous woman driven to commit horrible deeds by a deceitful, villainous man, who ruined, shamed, and dishonored her. In the end, Zaz was the clear victor. Her honor was avenged, her actions vindicated, her enemy marked, his punishment assured. Belotserkovskii, on the other hand, was completely vanquished. He was exposed as dishonorable, mendacious, and cruel, his immorality forever etched in the living flesh of his distorted face. By playing up Zaz's role as forgiven wife and much-loved mother, *Odesskaia pochta* elicited the sympathies of readers toward a woman who, while clearly guilty of both adultery and mayhem, was represented as having already suffered enough. The way the paper told it, the real villain of the story was not the perpetrator of the horrible crime but the evil lover who seduced then abandoned her. The reader was left with the impression that since her husband had forgiven her moral indiscretions, how could the jury do otherwise than acquit her? Zaz's actions were deemed irrational rather than premeditated, rash but not criminal. A victim of feminine hysteria, she was temporarily out of control, overwrought by the deception and betrayal of her lover and her own guilty conscience.

Unflattering representations of a *vitrioleuse's* motives and character only appeared in the paper on the rare occasions when a woman was actually found guilty. Such was the case in the summer of 1914, when Agafiia Guseva was convicted for the crime of pouring sulfuric acid on her sleeping lover, the port worker P. Khlypov.[34] The reporter covering the story for *Odesskaia pochta* described Guseva in highly critical terms. She was "not a pretty woman," the author told readers, using the familiar tactic of equating physical appearance with moral quality in order to instantly cast doubt upon the woman's character. Further, Guseva was described not as hysterical (an ambiguous classification that implied some claim to femininity) but as "insanely jealous." Guseva testified that Khlypov was "a drunk, living on my money and setting himself up with lovers." However, she did not provide evidence that might have persuaded the jury that her "unwomanly" actions were in fact motivated by "feminine" fears. She had not caught her lover *in flagrante delicto*. Neither did she claim to have suffered gross mistreatment at his hands. Instead, she was portrayed as angry because she *thought* he was betraying her, because she *thought* that he did not love her any more. Tellingly, press reports represented Gusaeva as a "fallen" woman (the port worker's lover, not his wife), whose immorality was perceived as empowering her criminality. The jury in the case did not believe that Guseva was creditably feminine. Her actions, therefore, were deemed unjustifiable. Hence the victim remained the victim. Guseva was deprived of her rights and sentenced to four years' hard labor.

As this example suggests, society's responses to acid-throwing women were determined as much by the character of the victim as by that of the villain. Unsympathetic portrayals of violent women only seemed to appear if the villainess was deemed to be of dubious moral character. For the most part, however, even when plenty of evidence existed to implicate a woman in a violent crime, reporters and perhaps society as a whole had a hard time envisioning robust female villainy. Mitigating circumstances were frequently presented to readers to soften or even erase the villainess' criminality in the public mind. More times than not, the villainess herself was brought forward as the true victim of the "drama" while the men who were attacked were judged as deserving of their fate. While rarely actually condoned, the actions of violent women were nevertheless presented in such a way as to make them less abhorrent than they might actually have been.

It is crucial to emphasize again at this juncture that social-class status was absolutely key when it came to interpreting women's actions. This becomes eminently clear in discussions of a case that juxtaposed a cast of well-established gender types: a financially successful but morally weak-willed bourgeois husband, a virtuous but passive wife, an evilly seductive lower-class mistress, and a good son driven to murder to protect the family honor. Unlike the other stories in this chapter, here a male is cast in the starring role. And yet it was the women in the tale whose interests were most at stake, their story offering strong testimony that reporters and jurors alike considered violations of the sanctity of marriage and family life to be nothing short of an assault on civilization itself.

"For the Family Honor"

In April 1914, the *Odesskaia pochta* columnist Faust printed a letter from a female reader under the title "Types of Odessa Husbands." The "desperate" wife confided to the columnist that when she and her children were away on vacation, her husband had "taken up with a 'dirty woman' *(griaznaia zhenshchina)*" who "by artful practices completely took possession of his will." The evil mistress was "bringing horrors" to the family, inciting the husband against his loyal wife and children. When her husband did come home, he "barely recognizes me or the children," the wife reported.

Further, he withdrew his support from the family, who subsequently fell into need: "He does not give me and the children anything to live on," the exhausted wife proclaimed. "I cannot stand anymore. I am sick, the little children are tormented. But I am afraid that if I undertake anything against this woman or open a scandal, things will get even worse," she continued. "Your feuilleton is my last hope."[35]

Faust's anonymous writer did not want to damage her own or her family's reputation by openly accusing either her husband or his mistress. At the same time, however, she understood that Faust's column provided her with a powerful means to condemn "Delilahs" who used their femininity to corrupt "good" men and destroy respectable families. The columnist himself was highly sympathetic to the woman's plight, judging her to be a respectable wife whose interests and honor needed to be protected. By exercising a relatively mild form of public confrontation, the letter writer was able to air her personal grievance in a public forum while still protecting her own femininity.

A story that so closely mirrored the one told to Faust by the distraught wife that it may, in fact, have been the same one, involved in the "Delilah" role an eighteen-year-old Moldavankan named Raia Plotitsa, whose "attack" on the respectable middle-class Grinshtein family was forcefully and fatally rebuffed. The basics of the story are these. Fifty-year-old Lev Grinshtein was a well-known businessman in Odessa's central city, where he lived with his wife and five children. At some point in 1911, Grinshtein met and fell in love with Plotitsa, who became his mistress. Grinshtein's oldest son, Froim, who strongly disapproved of his father's behavior, defended his mother strenuously against her new rival and demanded that his father give up the affair. When the elder Grinshtein refused to do so, the son petitioned the mistress to break off the relationship. Plotitsa also refused. Finally, in November 1914, Froim took matters into his own hands, murdering Plotitsa as she sat in the kitchen of her mother's Moldavanka home.

The details of the events leading up to Plotitsa's murder were first conveyed to *Odesskaia pochta*'s reading public in a sweeping melodramatic article, titled "For the Family Honor: A Drama in Moldavanka," written by the columnist "M. K." Far from being hidden in the fine print, the initial report of the murder filled more than half a tabloid page, including a series of allegedly verbatim accounts of conversations and confrontations that had taken place between key participants in the drama during the preceding three years.[36]

"How many terrifying dramas take place every day inside the gloomy walls of the big city," M. K. began. And how many people "carefully protect their secrets" from outsiders' eyes, "afraid of malicious rumors" and the possibility of disgrace. "Who wants to bring their unhappiness and suffering out onto the street?" "But there comes a time when such feelings are crowded out by more serious ordeals," the writer continued, ordeals "no one has the strength to endure in silence. "That is when the secrets come out," M. K. declared. M. K.'s narration of the "drama in Molda-vanka" was stunningly unambiguous. Froim was represented as an "inno-cent" murderer, who heroically defended his tragic but saintly mother. Lev, meanwhile, was portrayed as a prurient adulterer, blind to the cruelty and selfishness of his manipulative mistress.

When M. K. introduced the elder Grinshtein's name into the story, his words were laudatory: "Who in the world of Odessa commerce does not know Lev Grinshtein . . . one of the elders of the Odessa fruit trade." This initial praise soon turned to scorn, however, as M. K. revealed that the out-wardly respectable man was in fact an adulterer. For many long years, Grinshtein had been an "exemplary husband and father" whose "family life was the envy of everyone," M. K. told his readers. But then, for some inexplicable reason, "the head of the family grew cold to his wife and chil-dren," renouncing "his attachment for them." The "sudden change in his character naturally worried his wife and children," the writer continued. Then, after "a year of excruciating suffering," Lev's secret finally came out.

From this point on in the story, M. K. represented Lev as a social coun-terfeit, as a "fallen" man with no legitimate claims to respectability. "They had already been saying for a long time . . . in the city that Grinshtein was going around everywhere with a good-looking young woman who was practically a teenager," M. K. told his readers. "He began to absent himself from the store, went out in the evenings, and spent significantly more money than usual." The virtuous Froim "started to investigate," the writer explained, discovering that his father had "taken a lover whom he had set up in a private apartment" in a secluded corner of the Aleksandrovskii dis-trict. "Waiting for the right moment, the son confronted his father." "Papa! You should be ashamed of yourself. Aren't you the father of a fam-ily? Why are you destroying us? Why are you tormenting our poor mama? She's already sick with grief. Have mercy on us and throw away your pas-sion." "It's none of your business! I can't allow you to interfere in my pri-vate affairs," the irate father declared in a tone that did not allow for reply.

Grinshtein's crimes were compounded still further when he was por-trayed lying blatantly to his kindly wife, who was devastated by rumors of her husband's infidelity. "I am simply helping out a poor but very nice girl," the adulterer claimed. It is true that the young woman had "fallen," Lev admitted. "But I raised her up from the depths. I only want to save her, put her on the right path." "That's the truth?" his wife inquired. "I swear," exclaimed the mendacious husband. As M. K. noted, however, "later on it became obvious that there was far more going on than 'philanthropy.'"

If Lev was portrayed as straying from the bourgeois straight and nar-row, his wife was represented as the pinnacle of respectability and a model of morality. Not only did she believe Lev when he said that he was trying to help the "poor girl," she graciously and "affectionately" wel-comed the stranger into the household. From the outset, then, the wife was represented as a "suffering innocent," a defenseless victim bereft of the means to protect herself or otherwise influence the unfortunate course her life was taking. Plotitsa, meanwhile, was represented from the start as the complete antithesis of the good and kindly wife. After a brief nod to Raia's sad home life—her father died when she was only three, she was raised by her mother who barely made enough to keep the family going—M. K. proceeded to vilify the young woman, portraying her as a selfish, money-grubbing whore who would stop at nothing to destroy the Grinshteins' happy home life.

M. K.'s characterization of Froim himself was from the start highly sympathetic. The writer began his tale by transporting the reader to a Moldavanka street corner at the very moment when a pale young man, with a "terrible fire" burning in his eyes, ran up to a policeman and shouted, "Arrest me! I killed her!" The as-yet-unnamed murderer then surrendered his revolver and "surprisingly" started crying like a baby, his tears and obvious remorse immediately setting the man apart from the "typical" Moldavanka murderer. Once at the police station, the tearful young man reiterated his confession: "I killed my father's lover, killed her because she destroyed my mother's life, our family life."

M. K.'s sympathy for Froim deepened still further as the writer sketched a series of confrontations between the heroic son and his nemesis, Plotitsa. During their initial encounter, Froim reproached the woman for encouraging the affair. "You know he is an old man and you are a young woman. You should be ashamed to tear someone else's family apart." But the young man's moral appeal fell lifeless on the field of hard-edged materialism. "But what about me? It's profitable for me and I'm content. I don't give a damn about his children. I have to take care of myself."

The tension between the good, loyal bourgeois son and the manipulative, acquisitive lower-class mistress formed the core of M. K.'s drama. At several points in his narrative, the cultural struggle between these two protagonists centered on Plotitsa's material aspirations as symbolized in her lust for a piano, a classic mark of respectability. The first time the issue came up was during an early conversation between Froim and Raia in which the young woman explained that she had no intention of supporting herself by working in a factory. Instead, she planned to remain in Lev's care, regardless of the ramifications for her lover's legitimate family. "If your papa doesn't have money enough to support two families, then he can stop feeding you," Plotitsa said bitingly. "In general, he is very sparing in his relations with me," she complained. "I dare say you have a piano at home, but I don't have one. Ah, but I will. You might not eat for a whole year but I will get a piano!"

The piano reappeared again in a part of M. K.'s story subtitled, "A Nightmarish Life," a section devoted to Plotitsa's vilification. "Life for the Grinshtein family was like a bad dream," M. K. declared. "In the end, the head of the family cut his family off and lived openly with his mistress," taking her along even when the family retired as usual to their summer-time dacha. It was then that things went from bad to worse, explained M. K. The brazen mistress asserted her power, "conducting herself as if she were the lady of the house!" When it became clear to everyone that things would only get worse, the family offered Plotitsa money, promising to support her if she would relinquish her immoral claim. But in answer to their proposition, she laughed in their faces. After that, "Grinshtein bought her a piano and quickly satisfied her every whim," M. K. claimed.

The last straw fell when the wayward husband, who "was not in the least embarrassed by his gray hairs," decided to forget his duty and file for divorce. This was the beginning of the end for young Froim, said M. K. "What am I going to do? What will become of me? I cannot go on like this any longer!" the humiliated son repeated to himself over and over again. He could not stand by and watch the family ripped asunder, the reporter emphasized. He could not continue to watch his innocent mother suffering. Worst of all, M. K. continued, he could no longer endure the endless taunts of people on the streets, all of whom seemed to know about his father's indiscretions:

> "So, how is Mama No. 2? Does your father's mistress rule it over you, too? Tell your papa he's got good taste!" These snide remarks worked on the youth like poison. They unnerved him, influenced his psyche, his mind. "Don't cry, mama," he said comforting her. "Trust in God. Maybe He will help." But deliverance did not come.

It was one of those comments that finally drove Froim to confront Raia as she visited her mother's Moldavanka apartment: "Why have you come?" Plotitsa demanded. "I came to ask you when all this will end," Froim retorted. "It's never going to end," sneered Raia. "Get out of here, you fool!" Froim slapped her face. Raia burst out with a stream of insults and cursed Froim's mother. Then Froim reached into his pocket, pulled out a small revolver, and shot Plotitsa twice at point-blank range. Subtly linking the twin passions of father and son toward the young woman, on the one hand erotic, on the other deadly, the reporter pointed out to his readers that one of the bullets entered Raia's body "a little above her left nipple."

M. K. ended his treatise by quoting the testimony given by father and son to the police:

> "She was not my mistress," Grinshtein declared. "I simply helped her out as if she were a good daughter. I cannot help what people thought. And I cannot understand why my son killed her."
>
> "I shot her in a fit of rage," the son explained. "She ruined our lives. She ruined the peace in our family. She was leading us all to destruction. How many tears she caused my mother! How much pain and suffering came down on us because of her!"

Even though Raia Plotitsa was the victim of murder, she was nonetheless a villain in the eyes of M. K., who represented her mercilessly as a self-centered woman without morals or conscience. At one point or another, Plotitsa was portrayed as blatantly mocking all of the ideals held most dear by respectable society. Yet her aspirations were in many ways similar to those of other lower-class women. What Plotitsa wanted was material security and social recognition. She wanted a man to take care of her, to provide for her, to raise her status. To M. K., however, such desires were misplaced. Even if Plotitsa got her piano, she was still nothing but a lower-class whore. No amount of material possessions or pretensions to status would change the fact that morally the woman from Moldavanka had no claim to respectability.

Beyond this, Plotitsa was depicted as devious and cunning, a "typical" Moldavankan who made a business of misrepresentation. When she first met the Grinshteins, she tried to pass herself off as an orphan in order to gain sympathy. When Froim investigated and discovered her family, Plotitsa came up with a new story, claiming that her mother tried to force her into prostitution. Lev, meanwhile, was completely taken in by her masquerade, so much so that he committed the ultimate sin, deserting his family in order to make his mistress into a lady, trying to reinvent in the prostitute a good bourgeois wife. "I will never leave him," Raia said at one point. "Isn't he solicitous? Isn't he attentive? And furthermore, I love him, all the more since he bought me this beautiful little silver bag! Is this really a crime?" To M. K. the answer was obviously yes. Plotitsa was guilty of the crime of cultural transgression, guilty of insolently pretending to be a lady (something the reporter firmly believed she was not and could never be). Moreover, she was guilty of maliciously and systematically attempting to destroy the heart of the middle-class world: the family.

In the eyes of M. K., Lev, too, was guilty. If at first Lev was simply a dupe, falling for his mistress's manipulations, in the end he was fully criminalized. He turned his back on the world of the respectable when he turned his back on his virtuous, morally upright wife. As far as the reporter was concerned, the cultural criminal deserved neither respect nor sympathy. Froim, meanwhile, was portrayed as morality's champion, defending not only his mother, a "suffering innocent," but all of respectable society. The Froim preserved by M. K.'s pen was an accomplished social detective, uncovering the ugly immorality hidden behind a young woman's beautiful face. But by unmasking the mistress, he denuded his father and thus destroyed himself. In a world where reputation was social currency, the disgrace of the father spelled the ruin of the family. When Froim, in agony, asked himself the question, "What will become of me?" his fears were for himself, not for his mother. At the same time, however, his anxiety was greater than himself, his anguish giving voice to the fears of respectable people battling for control of a hostile environment. What will become of us if we cannot defend ourselves (and our mothers, wives, and children) against the evil intrigues of immorality? What are we going to do if we cannot find a way to keep control of our turf? "I killed her. People saw it. But the suffering, the suffering, how we all suffered. Who can tell you about that!" said the young Grinshtein as he was led away by police. "He has a kind, gentle, expressive face," said M. K. "He doesn't look at all like a murderer." "Evidently he suffered more than a little to be driven to crime."

For two weeks following the initial report of Plotitsa's death, *Odesskaia pochta*'s feuilletonist Faust turned his column into a forum for public discussion of the issues raised by the "Drama in Moldavanka."[37] The flurry of public responses to the story provides a wealth of evidence concerning popular perceptions of proper gender and family roles as well as a window onto contemporary notions of respectability, morality, and cultural identity. While there was some variation in the tone of the letters selected by Faust for inclusion in his column, the dominant themes first expressed by M. K. generally seemed to prevail. Especially clear was the notion that Odessans were, in Faust's words, clearly conscious "of the holy duty and inviolability of the family hearth."

Several letters focused on the proper role of the father, expressing views very much in keeping with the culture of respectability embraced by the middle class. Lev had "no moral right to get mixed up with a girl when he knows that his pernicious passion will offend and disgrace himself and his family," one writer pronounced. "He should be led by a strong sense of duty. A man's spirit should be stronger than his sensual instincts. He should be able to keep himself from *wanting*" [original emphasis]. An entirely different opinion was expressed by a man who defended the father's traditional role as undisputed head of the household: "Does the son have the right to get involved in his father's intimate life, even if that life threatens the unity of the family? For me, at least, the answer is clearly no!" Plotitsa's mother came under attack from a male writer who claimed that the daughter's wayward actions were the product of a bad upbringing. This writer's voice was joined by that of a female respondent who claimed that Raia's mother should never have allowed the girl "to accept presents from old men who have families."

The figure of Plotitsa herself drew the bulk of the letter writers' attentions. A number of primarily female respondents had harsh criticism for young women who pretended to be in love with older married men in order to gain personal wealth. One writer claimed that Raia could not have possibly loved "such an old man. . . . It is clear that this was simply a material calculation on her part." A female respondent added, "Hasn't life shown us that many women's love ends when the money ends? I know of many such cases." Another author judged men like Lev to be "ridiculous" for "trying to save girls who are just using them for mercenary ends." Another woman respondent said Raia was motivated not by love, but by pure "personal interest," adding that the young woman's sad end should serve "as an example to other girls and women in general," and that it is always best "to live honestly and not build happiness upon someone else's misery."

A number of readers echoed the view that at the heart of the story was a message to women. In the words of one author, Froim Grinshtein should be freed from prison while Raia Plotitsa's death should "be an example for other such women whose 'love' breaks up families." A women writer concurred: "Let this drama serve as an example to all girls who get involved in matters of family love." In another letter, though, the audience for the message was not women like Plotitsa, but men like Lev. In this case, the story should serve as an example "to all men who leave home for an hour and forget what they have got."

Through the lens of Faust's editorial eye, public opinion overwhelmingly supported Froim for doing his best to protect the family honor. Readers also seemed to sympathize heartily with the highly moral middle-class mother, whose purity and defenselessness stood in marked contrast to her husband's betrayal and her rival's evil aggression. The public apparently loathed the adulterous father, who could not control his sexual urges and thus abdicated moral leadership of the family. Finally, they condemned the manipulative lower-class mistress for insinuating herself into a place where she did not belong and for cold-heartedly plotting to bring about the ruin of a respectable family. Although a few readers thought it was unfortunate that the young woman was killed, most seemed to think that she deserved her fate. This view was confirmed in no uncertain terms when, in mid-April 1915, the jury in the Grinstein case acquitted Froim of all charges, the crowd in the courtroom greeting the verdict with hearty cheers of "bravo!"[38]

While there is no denying that Froim was the protagonist in the Grinshtein's family drama, the central opposition in the story was actually between the villainous Raia Plotitsa and Froim's mother, whose name was never mentioned, even in passing. The fact that the virtuous "true" woman was mute as well as nameless is suggestive on several levels. First, her anonymity can be read as a form of protection, M.K.'s reluctance to "know" her name providing the mother with yet another shield behind which to hide her shame from public view. A second reading of this absence might be that the mother had no need of her own name because her individual identity had long since ceased to exist. Indeed, her "self" had faded to such an extent that it was only the ideal she represented that raised Froim from the role of murderer to avenger. In a sense, then, Froim *became* his mother recast as a modern woman taking extreme measures to protect herself and her family. In M.K.'s representation, it was Froim who suffered most from Lev's adulterous relationship, Froim who shed tears over his shame and lost honor, Froim who escaped the entrapments of social convention, bourgeois propriety, and even the law so that justice could be done, and Froim who was ultimately exonerated and valorized. Thus M.K. feminized the good son. Importantly, however, at the end of the story the hero's masculinity was confirmed in no uncertain terms. After the trial ended, Froim did not return to the domestic hearth. Instead, he was delivered directly from the investigative police into the hands of the army, having three months previously received his draft notice. After successfully defending his family's honor, Froim Grinstein thus transformed again, from son to mother to warrior.

Conclusion

Newspaper contributors were fascinated by stories of women who bent or broke the rules of polite society while still maintaining their femininity and respectability. Such figures were rarely represented as "new women," who encroached dangerously on male turf in the public political sense (as radicals, community organizers, or suffragettes), or even economically (as professionals or entrepreneurs). What made heroines like El'ka Zaz compelling was that they were by all accounts properly "domestic" women. In reporting such incidents, journalists faced the problem of having to explain women's apparently aberrant, even abhorrent actions. In order to do so, writers focused especially on the problems women faced and the solutions they employed to solve them. The narratives these commentators constructed, while no doubt highly embellished to heighten their sensationalistic qualities, were nonetheless highly revealing of social expectations for female behavior. Stories about women who took (or attempted to take) control of their own lives through independent action turned on journalists' judgments of women's moral character, motives, claims to respectability, and femininity. If a woman was unrespectable, the treatment of her case by journalists was decidedly negative. But when journalists deemed their female subjects to be worthy, they attempted to understand and excuse "unwomanly" behavior by explaining mitigating circumstances that revealed the women were either of high moral character or the "true" victims in dramas that threatened feminine respectability.

A key ingredient was acceptance of the idea that women had the right to defend their own honor and could use almost any means at their disposal to do so. While ideally it was a man's job to protect women both physically and morally, if a woman had no male champion or if the man who should play that role (a father or husband) was the source of her problem or was disloyal, weak, or otherwise incompetent, society empowered her to take matters into her own hands. This said, it is crucial to note that journalists stressed the exceptional nature of such cases, seldom calling into question the core belief that women and men were "naturally" different. Social commentators were extremely reluctant to acknowledge that the lines separating masculinity and femininity were in any way blurred, even if the stories they were discussing strongly indicated that they were. Interestingly, this attitude, along with the apparent inability of social observers to imagine that "respectable" women were in fact capable of truly criminal actions, combined to create an atmosphere in which women could stretch the limits of acceptable female behavior, could behave in "male" ways and get away with it. Indeed, evidence suggests that some women actively subverted dominant stereotypes, safe in the knowledge that their actions were likely to be excused.

Stories about women's behavior both in public and private were a central feature of Odessa's popular press, revealing competing notions about what women were supposed to be like, how they were supposed to behave, what kinds of things they were supposed to do and say. On one level, the discourse on the nature of femininity exposed profound anxieties about women's changing roles in society. On another level, it revealed deep concerns about the changing relationship of bodies, power, and identity in the modern urban world. As the next chapter shows, these themes reappeared again in an epic drama that played out in 1914, one starring an unlikely hero, the elephant Iambo.

8 | Iambo's Fate

The population of Odessa is increasing . . . not by the day but literally by the hour. . . . Soon the really full-blooded Odessan will
become a rarity here, like a bison or elephant. The old poetic
Odessa is disappearing, the pure-blooded Odessan is denigrated,
and coming to take its place is—Modern, crowded, smoke-
stacked Odessa, stinking of automobiles with their bothersome
droning, the rumble of the *electrichka* and the blinding but cold
brightness of electricity. Now the "Odessan" is an imitation.
—"Faust"[1]

• "Elephant Sentenced to Death" screamed a two-inch-high banner headline in an April 1914 edition of *Odesskaia pochta.*[2] The condemned was
Iambo, a high-strung pachyderm charged with the crime of attempted
murder. Iambo's fate was Odessa's biggest cause célèbre in that tense prewar spring, the elephant's infamy rivaling that of Barnum's famous
Jumbo.[3] In his few months of limelight, Iambo was more than just an object of curiosity. As journalists picked up on his story, he became a powerful symbol, a metaphorical incarnation of the multifaceted anxieties of
Odessa society, a nine-thousand-pound vessel filled with conjured "others." The columns that appeared during the Iambo days were sometimes
direct, sometimes ironic, sometimes satirical. Regardless of the style of narration, however, commentary about Iambo served to reflect public preoccupation with questions of respectability and morality, modernity and urbanity, freedom and oppression.

The common denominator in all of these stories was the crucial question: Who was Iambo? What kind of a "person" was he? Was he victim,
villain, or avenger? Criminal or madman? What were his goals, aspirations, anxieties, and fears? In what did he believe and in whom did he
trust? For Odessa's journalists, Iambo was more than just an elephant; he
was an instrument for the expression of identity, a means through which
writers confronted the complex and troubling question of man's role in
the modern city. In allegories woven by popular press columnists, Iambo
played varying parts, represented by turns as righteous, persecuted, altruis-
tic, and cynical. A mute martyr, Iambo was on the one hand a projection

of "everyman," a malleable surrogate for social critics of every stripe. On the other hand, though, he was an analog, especially for the middle-class man whose struggle for control of himself and the city so preoccupied contributors to Odessa's popular press.

Both in the real world and in the realm of journalistic imagination, Iambo's "identity" was highly scrutinized, with reporters and politicians, military officers and medical experts all seeking to uncover Iambo's true character. The elephant was the object of public dissection, his fate the focus of intense speculation. The troubled animal's story in all of its manifestations is thus highly revealing of the tensions and anxieties riddling Odessan society at a moment of growing economic uncertainty and heightened political and social unrest.

Iambo's Crime

Iambo was introduced to the Odessa public as a "peaceful," "intelligent," "wonderfully trained" animal, the "talented" star attraction of Monsieur Lorberbaum's menagerie, which was appearing on Kulikovo Field[4] as part of the city's annual spring festival. By early April, however, the elephant's image underwent a dramatic transformation. Now newspapers reported that Iambo was a menace, a dangerous criminal who might at any moment break out of his cell and "take a stroll down Deribasovskaia"[5] leaving havoc in his wake.[6]

The trouble began when the animal became unusually agitated, announced one of his trainers. For some unknown reason, "a change took place in Iambo's character." He began trumpeting in a "sinister" manner, flapping his ears, and bending back the bars of his cage. The trainer responded to the elephant's "misbehavior" with a few heavy blows of an iron rod. Iambo in turn retaliated, repeatedly striking the trainer in the head with his trunk, the blows severe enough to render the man unconscious and send him to the hospital for over a week.[7]

Iambo's violent outburst "raised great alarm among circus administrators, who started to monitor the elephant's behavior especially attentively." When several nights later an "enraged" Iambo was again ferociously ripping at his chains, the elephant's worried owner, Monsieur Lorberbaum, determined that the animal was out of control. Like the parent of a delinquent child, Lorberbaum then decided to seek the help of local authorities. Odessa's chief of police, Baron S. V. fon-der-Khoven, soon arrived on Kulikovo Field to assess the situation, bringing with him a coterie of assistants, "a collection of supervisors, and a mass of constables and mounted officers" with pistols at the ready.[8]

After taking the testimony of eyewitnesses and fully reviewing the evidence, fon-der-Khoven declared that the "brutal" felon should be put to death. Once the sentence was pronounced, however, the impromptu execution committee[9] was faced with a practical problem: How does one go about killing an elephant? Various methods were debated. "A knife would not hurt him and his skin was so thick that a bullet would feel like a pin-prick to him." The problem was further complicated by the belief that Iambo was "an intelligent animal [who] knew by instinct that something [was] being planned against him." In the end, the authorities opted for poison, agreeing that a dose of twenty-five grams of potassium cyanide would be sufficient to do in the beast.[10]

The means being agreed upon, the executioners next had to figure out a way to administer the lethal dose. They introduced poison into an orange that they lobbed to the elephant. Iambo picked up the fruit, lifted it to his mouth, then promptly tossed it back. A second orange, injected with a lesser dose, was inspected by the elephant and immediately crushed. The committee then offered an unpoisoned fruit that Iambo consumed with-out hesitation. Similar attempts using Iambo's favorite cakes were likewise unsuccessful. Changing its tactics, the committee next tried vodka, a drink for which Iambo reportedly had a weakness. While it was somewhat diffi-cult to find that commodity at 6:00 a.m., the police apparently knew where to look. Shortly after sunrise, Iambo was presented with a barrel of cyanide-spiked spirits. He stuck his trunk in the barrel, then kicked it over with all his might. Exasperated, the committee abandoned its original plan, deciding instead to try shooting the animal. The big guns were called in: Odessa's resident military commander appeared on the scene only to put the kibosh on the plan. Iambo's skin was too tough, the official de-clared. There was no guarantee that the bullets would penetrate the ani-mal's durable hide. Indeed, the shots might bounce off or go awry, endan-gering the lives of other animals, not to mention people who might be in the vicinity.[11]

Things were at an impasse. It looked as though Iambo, foreshadowing Rasputin, was one of those distinctly Russian creatures whose mystical powers made him immune to assassination. In consternation, the parties on the scene decided to pass the buck. The city prefect, I. V. Sosnovskii, was called to the field to take charge of the situation. Sosnovskii's first ac-tion was to post a couple of armed guards around the prisoner's enclosure. Then, in a move that will surprise no one familiar with the state of Russian bureaucracy at the time, Sosnovskii announced his intention to call a spe-cial commission to investigate the Iambo problem.[12]

As these events transpired, the news rapidly spread that Iambo was in a state of high agitation and might at any moment break out of his cage and go on a rampage. "To many, of course, such news was frightening," *Iuzh-naia mysl'* reported. "Others, on the contrary, were not averse to seeing so rare a spectacle." Thousands of curious onlookers of every social class turned up on the scene, some coming on foot, others arriving in a never-ending line of droshkies, carriages, and automobiles. "And with the speed of lightening, various rumors, one more fantastic than the next, spread among the crowd."[13] Naturally, the sensational coverage only heightened public interest, drawing thousands more Odessans to Kulikovo Field. Sosnovskii, meanwhile, continued to view the elephant with suspicion, ordering that a moat be dug around the cage to create an additional obstacle for Iambo to overcome, just in case the animal did manage to escape.[14]

A "Slave of the City and Culture"

Odesskie novosti's "L. Dumskii" was one of the first columnists to use the elephant as a vehicle for the expression of social criticism. The tale he related was an impassioned, highly metaphorical one, centering on the question of "why elephants sometimes go mad." Iambo himself was incarnated by the narrator as "an *intelligentnyi* elephant," who while still an "untrained" youth, decided to leave behind "the warm rays of the African sun" and seek his fortune in the cold, modern metropolis. Obviously equating Iambo's life story with those of human "bipeds," Dumskii's column resonates with concerns about the evils of city life, the corrupting influence of materialism, the emasculating effects of complacency, and the oppressive nature of autocracy. When "the free son of the wilderness" first arrived in Odessa, his "way of life sharply changed," Dumskii explained. Iambo became a "slave to the City and Culture;" he was "settled into a cage and chained to his place."[15]

The animal's "cage" was a multilayered construction. On one level, it was an enclosure formed by unrelenting autocracy, the "bars" of which were state controls on individual freedom. "Gentlemen, here in the twentieth century, it is foolish to deprive a blameless elephant of the right of movement," Iambo said, trying to reason with his "captors." "In Africa we have nothing like this!" In answer, the "foolish bipeds" explained that without a proper residency permit, Iambo had no rights. The elephant "waved his trunk contemptuously and remained in chains." Thus Iambo became acquainted with "the charms of the Pale of Settlement," Dumskii wrote.

If the "cage" was the state, it was also the city, the modern commercial metropolis, a place both empowered and corrupted by money. Like so many others, Iambo quickly adapted to the venal environment. He "fell under the power of bipeds," learning to imitate "the most human of traits: parasitism." Soon Iambo realized that "only fools procure their bread by the sweat of their brows. The intelligent ones skim off other people's milk."

The third layer of the "cage" was "Culture," in this case meaning the highly idealized behavioral and "spiritual" expectations so thoroughly and unforgivingly articulated by the mavens of polite society. Iambo's keepers assigned him a "tutor" who instructed the elephant on the rules of good form. He became a highly refined elephant, well bred and polite, a master of the art of "correctness." Thus Iambo matured "from a foolish young little elephant, full of joie de vivre" into a full-blown "biped." Once Iambo had completed his education, he was ready to begin his career. The elephant became an entertainer, astounding the public with elegant displays of manners and grace. Even though he himself considered his "numbers" to be "foolish," it was not long before the act made Iambo a star, his performances attended by "all Odessa."

With the coming of "success," Iambo became content in his confinement. "What is so bad about my life now?" the elephant reasoned. "I am satisfied. I do not have to be afraid of bad weather. My hide is safe from the shot of English rifles. The authorities love me and, yes, I have popularity." "Is it true that in the wilderness I would be more valued?" Iambo continued. "Here I am not simply an elephant. No, I am Mr. Iambo!" But every now and then, "on hot summer nights," the captive elephant was tormented by "bright visions of the free wilderness" of his youth, Dumskii confided. "Maybe the young Iambo even reminisced about some young, happy, grand she-elephant," the columnist mused. "But he stubbornly drove these uncomfortable thoughts from his mind." "I must forget these nostalgic dreams once and for all," said Iambo. "Freedom—that is a fairy tale for children."

Then, one "drunken, voluptuous spring night," Iambo had an epiphany. "Suddenly, unexpectedly, clearly, distinctly, and mercilessly," Iambo came to understand "that a horrible crime had been committed against him." He could not at first formulate his feelings exactly. ("Elephants do not read Chekhov, you know.") After much consideration, he realized that "his material security was a crime." With "burning hot shame," he understood that he had come to care more for the safety of his own hide than for his freedom. Suddenly everything was clear: "Freedom cannot be confined by iron chains. Freedom is life, fear for what tomorrow's day will bring." With these thoughts, Iambo realized that he needed to act now or risk being a slave forever. "And with all the strength of awakening instincts of freedom, he started to tear spitefully at his chains. He summoned up all of his forgotten and unneeded strength to help. Was he sick? Sick of remaining in slavery!"

His keepers were "alarmed" by the elephant's unaccustomed behavior. "Armed bipeds arrived and started threatening Iambo," but the animal's cunning instincts saved his life. "And what now?" Dumskii concluded with a declaration poignant of hopelessness. "Now in the country of the bipeds, there are those who aspire to freedom. But poor Iambo is already condemned! And if he remains alive, then he will be a slave forever and ever. Even in his dreams he will not see freedom. That is why elephants sometimes go mad."

Dumskii used Iambo's troubles to present to the reader a sharp discussion of some of the more burning themes of his day. The column is full of tension between traditional romantic populism and oppressive urban modernity. The elephant began life in the countryside, where he could be "wild," "free," and "joyful." Once he was "trapped" in the city, however, he became a "slave" and a "parasite."

Dumskii's narrative touches on crucial issues of the expression of middle-class identity within an environment—the city—which was at once a site of transformation and a venue for performance. When Iambo first came to the city, he was *intelligentnyi* but untrained. With the help of the tutor, he rose in society, becoming an expert in the art of "correctness." Once he acquired this new talent, Iambo was hailed as a celebrity, his heightened status and respectability acknowledged by an appreciative public, who conferred on him respect and dignity. But, Dumskii continued, Iambo paid a high price for his "success." Indeed, the columnist portrayed the elephant as exchanging moral integrity for material security. Instead of risking all to fight for freedom, Iambo acquiesced to his captors, thus sacrificing not only his personal liberty but also his manhood. It is not until after his epiphany that the elephant reclaimed his "forgotten and unneeded strength," throwing off the kid gloves of refinement to take on his oppressors.

"The Most Topical Theme in Odessa"

The day after Dumskii's column appeared in *Odesskie novosti,* similar tensions were revealed in a satirical feuilleton penned by the *Iuzhnaia mysl'* contributor, "S. Krainii," who took up "the most topical theme in Odessa." "The whole city is talking about the elephant who understands poison better than your average pharmacist," the column began. "Yesterday there was good weather and everywhere, at the dachas . . . in private homes and on the streets, everyone was asking the same question: 'Why is the elephant enraged?'" Krainii set out to uncover the "true cause" of Iambo's distress, conducting "interviews" with those "in a position to know."[16]

In the "answers" supplied by Krainii's various "respondents," Iambo appeared in many different guises. Interestingly, though, the columnist's various characterizations of the elephant himself are not what is most revealing. Instead, it was Krainii's acerbic commentary on the viability of the liberal social project that dominated the narrative. The columnist caricatured his subjects, ridiculing them through sarcasm and cynicism. The interviewees' "answers" thus became condemnations, not of those they blamed for Iambo's condition, but of themselves.

The first to be "questioned" was Monsieur Lorberbaum, "the owner of the establishment in which such colossally important events are taking place," Krainii announced, establishing early the facetious tone that was to permeate the column. The writer represented the businessman as "evasive" and defensive, emphatic in his desire to clear his own reputation (thus blackening it) and to assert his civic-mindedness (exposing his self interest). "Affairs in my menagerie are in wonderful shape. I do not in the least need the advertising," Lorberbaum declared. He did not put together the menagerie in order to make a profit, Lorberbaum continued. Instead, he was motivated by a "love of science" and "national pride."[17]

In Lorberbaum's opinion, Iambo was upset because of the rude behavior of the Odessa public. "You know that Odessans are genteel [*svetskii*] people," he said sarcastically. "They come to the menagerie and conduct themselves as if they were in their own homes. They pinch and torment the animals as if they were their own children," as if the living animals were stuffed exhibits in a museum. "My animals are obedient and dutiful," Lorberbaum declared. "They endure any unpleasantness that befalls them." But, he continued, the unrelenting abuse was taking its toll. "Yesterday one tiger even started crying." Iambo was especially sensitive. "He is a real elephant, not a stuffed one made of wood with a rubber trunk."

Krainii thus invoked a much-visited motif in which a haughty *intelligent* (Lorberbaum) accuses the *(meshchanstvo)* public of philistinism. The public was "tiresome," Lorberbaum complained. "They are constantly trying to chew without teeth" (aspiring to a social position they were not adequately prepared to assume). While Krainii may well have intended to satirize the public's rough edges, so too did he aim to deflate the pretensions of the educated elite. Further, the writer lampooned Lorberbaum for hypocritical paternalism, thus criticizing all such employers, who in the interests of profit, exposed their "obedient and dutiful" children (workers) to mistreatment.

Through Lorberbaum's "answer," Krainii raised concerns about civic-mindedness, business ethics, and commitment to the improvement of self and society. In his interview with a "Bureaucrat," the columnist turned his attention to criticism of the state. "There are no such things as wild elephants," said the Bureaucrat, equating the elephant with a minority nationalist. "All the wild animals are now peaceful." As for elephants demanding freedom, he continued, "this is absurd. There can be no freedom whatsoever for elephants. And there can be no demonstrations of any kind, or else we will act sternly." "All elephants must sit in their cages and calmly chew their food," said the representative of the state. If they do otherwise, they will "get acquainted with the Iakut [Siberian] frosts. That will keep them from going mad."

Another "respondent," a "Pedagogue," was used by Krainii to expose ambivalent attitudes about the "civilizing" potential of education and the appropriation of western values. In this context, Iambo was a "wild animal"–cum-peasant who had not yet been "tamed" by education. The "upset and disobedient" elephant was among the last of his kind, the Pedagogue declared. In his opinion, all such "animals" should be required to go to a special school where "conduct-books, marks, and exams" would bring them under control. But too much knowledge acquired too quickly could be dangerous and destabilizing, he warned. "Cramming" caused "elephant disease" ("swelling of the brain"), a condition that was running rampant among people in Russia, knowledge thus "spreading among us in a manner opposite to the natural and practical way it spreads in the West."

In his interview with a "Municipal Official," Krainii revealed scorn for reactionary censorship policies while simultaneously satirizing himself and his journalistic colleagues. Iambo's ire had been stirred up by the revolutionary press, claimed the official. "In my opinion it should be forbidden for elephants to read the left newspapers. Let them read *Znamia* and *Russkaia Rech'*," he suggested, citing a pair of reactionary right-wing publications. "Better literature for elephants cannot be found." Moreover, given the current state of affairs, "the entrance to the menagerie should be locked against journalists," advised the official. "The elephant is not a business manager. He does not appear on the streets in a tail coat." If Iambo's name could be kept out of the papers, he would certainly calm down. The better solution yet would be to make an artificial copy of Iambo using synthetic rubber, which "looks natural and will not shine." "A rubber elephant is the ideal, truly Odessan wild animal," the official concluded.

Yet another of Krainii's "respondents" was a "Broker from Fankoni"[18] who saw in Iambo the famous independent spirit of the Odessa entrepreneur. The Broker himself, however, was disdained for his self-aggrandizement. "When I had a trading house on Deribasovskaia and 200,000 on my personal account, I often went to Berlin," the Broker explained. "There at the Tiergarten was an elephant who let everyone lead him around by the nose." Iambo would not accept that kind of treatment, the Broker continued, for "in Odessa it is impossible to lead anyone by the nose."

The last to be "interviewed" by Krainii was Iambo himself, the only character in the columnist's gallery who was represented as sincere. Iambo was a "peaceful" animal who "respected openness," quoted the works of the great poets (including, of course, Pushkin), and was in all respects thoroughly civilized. In other words, he was genuinely *intelligentnyi*. "I am . . . not a troublemaker," the elephant declared. "My trainer Pastushka insulted my elephant dignity so I protested. Freedom for elephants is as necessary as it is for people," said Iambo. "Give me freedom and give me cakes, but without cyanide."

Both Dumskii and Krainii used Iambo to touch on matters of concern to a public struggling to make sense of a rapidly changing world. *Odesskii listok* followed up on some of those issues in an overtly political, if allegorical, feuilleton titled "Memoirs of a Black Panther," in which the elephant appeared as the leader of a working-class rebellion. Thus, Iambo provided an opportunity for the liberal paper to express its sympathies with the plight of the oppressed and to demand political action.

The tale began with Iambo overseeing a secret gathering held one night in Lorberbaum's menagerie. As the meeting got under way, "the quiet, methodical Iambo was in a strangely excited state," the "black panther" began. "Knowing that he needed to speak his mind, we elected him chairman." "The nerves of the noble beasts were strained to maximum," the panther continued. Then Iambo himself took the floor, "call[ing] for the overthrow of the existing system," rallying his "comrades" around issues of insulted dignity, poor living and working conditions, and the intolerable repression of authoritarianism.

> Comrades, everyone without exception, from the great lion to the guinea pigs, unite! We no longer have the strength to endure the human yoke. They beat us for the slightest misunderstanding and they torture us for disobedience. . . . They hold us in cramped cages, with nowhere to stretch out our limbs. We have an endless working day. . . . The human's iron rod rules everywhere and if it would not be for the stunning pain of its touch, we would have breakfasted on our keepers long ago. Comrades, enough of this yoke. Overthrow it. Remember there is strength in unity. . . . "Down with humans!"[19]

A Troubled Body

The same day that *Odesskii listok* ran "Memoirs of a Black Panther," they printed a second column focusing not on questions of the body of the state but rather on the state of the body of the elephant. Iambo's behavior was erratic because he feared for his hide, said Leri, the column's author. "They want to kill me! For what? For nothing. They are afraid that I will get my freedom," "Iambo" wrote in his diary. But freedom was not really the issue. "Practical considerations" also came into play. Iambo's body was a valuable commodity, his skin and tusks coveted by "greedy" Odessans. "Elephant skin goes at a high price now," Iambo declared, adding that he had heard two elegantly dressed young men saying that an elephant-skin purse at Vagner's store cost close to twenty rubles. "Since I possess such a treasure, it is dangerous to live among people, especially among such practical people as Odessans." They are clever, these Odessans. "They will not skin a living elephant." Their goal was to convince everyone that Iambo was crazy so that they would have an excuse for assassinating him.[20]

Leri thus cast Iambo not so much as a person but as a product, using the elephant to voice anxieties about the growing commodification of identity. Not only did "clever Odessans" want to deprive Iambo of his material possessions, they also tried to strip him of his moral worth, especially his dignity, Iambo complained. "They thought an elephant would be stupid enough to swallow cyanide. What a comedy. . . . Thirty years in the society of bipeds taught me something." They were the ones who lost face, the elephant declared. "They gave me poisoned oranges and cakes, then left in disgrace." "What bothers me most is the story with the vodka," he continued. "What vandalism! They spoiled a whole barrel with their idiotic poison! I am not an alcoholic and cannot drink more than an ordinary person, but I was truly sorry when I had to spill out all that vodka. Imagine, a whole barrel!"

But it was neither fear for the safety of his hide nor indignation in the face of insult that was the root of Iambo's distress. His was the springtime madness of erotic dreams, Leri asserted. Iambo was desirous of female companionship. Yet he was a respectable elephant, not an extremist: "I heard something about Professor Merezhkovskii," Iambo said. "This professor is a sixty-year-old man, and what things he has done! I raised my trunk in horror when I read in detail about the Kazan professor's erotic madness. And did they kill him? Was he executed? Tried? Nothing of the kind." So why should he, Iambo, strong and vital, be cut down in the flower of youth? Unlike some of his contemporaries, who delighted in the currently chic fad of self-destruction, Iambo was "not a person that in childhood dreamed about death. I never looked at a vial of poison with secret excitement. And do not worry, I am not part of the suicide club." Instead of killing him, Iambo concluded, the humans should help find him a good wife, a "sweet" she-elephant who might "calm [his] agitated nerves" and "heal [his] tortured heart" with her caresses. The best thing to do would be to run an advertisement in *Novoe vremia*, Iambo reasoned. "Young, strong elephant seeks reciprocity in ardent love from a beautiful she-elephant. Odessa, Kulikovo Field, the menagerie. Come!"[21]

Leri's assertion that Iambo's madness had an erotic basis foreshadowed the real-world opinion voiced by some of the myriad of experts consulted by the city prefect's special commission. The views put forward by the specialists to explain the elephant's condition drew heavily on various medical and psychological theories in vogue at the time. Fritz Shpifman, a top animal trainer from the famous Hagenbeck Zoo in Hamburg, concluded that the elephant's "insubordination" was the result of "sexual excitement," a condition that might only be "cured" by execution. Another expert diagnosed the problem as "neurasthenia," prescribing solid doses of morphine and opium.[22] Yet another specialist, seemingly a follower of Cesare Lombroso,[23] determined that Iambo had "dangerous eyes," adding that anyone going near the elephant's enclosure was gravely threatened.[24]

"Is it Possible to Save Iambo?"

According to *Odesskaia pochta*, within a week of the initial report of the elephant's troubles, Iambo's story had been picked up by newspapers throughout Russia, with public opinion firmly on the side of the besieged pachyderm.[25] Even Sosnovskii's special commission sympathized with the elephant, reporting to the city prefect that Iambo "acts like a person, thinks like a person, knows what people are trying to do to him, and knows his fate is in the balance."[26]

Iambo supporters put forward various plans to try to save him, most of which involved moving the elephant to the Moscow Zoo. Such hopes were fueled when A. A. Tobolkin, the zoo's chief veterinarian, judged Iambo to be "completely normal." Citing a view sure to be popular with reform-minded members of educated society, Tobolkin claimed that the elephant's misconduct was the direct result of the highly unsanitary conditions in which he was forced to live. If Iambo could be moved to more hospitable quarters in Moscow, he would surely recover completely. Tobolkin met with Sosnovskii and V. F. Dzhunkovskii, an assistant minister of internal affairs, to discuss the possibility of transferring the elephant to Moscow. In the end, however, the logistical problems involved in moving the massive animal proved insurmountable. Moscow reluctantly declined to rescue Iambo, and the newspapers again spoke of the elephant's imminent demise.[27]

So it was that the debate returned to the relative merits of various methods of extermination. Some advocated electrocution as efficient and humane.[28] Others thought a dose of fifteen hundred sleeping pills would do the trick.[29] Shpifman, the expert from the Hamburg Zoo, advocated hanging.[30] The hunting society suggested exploding bullets.[31] Still others remained loyal supporters of potassium cyanide.[32]

Odesskaia pochta's Faust, who was far more concerned with human than animal psychology, pointed a horrified finger at those individuals who were so gleefully contemplating Iambo's demise. "Hunters have come forward ready to kill the elephant. I myself overheard this conversation near the elephant's enclosure: 'He would be kaput if we shot him in the eye!' 'No, better to poison him with curare. It will work magnificently.'" As it turned out, the immorality of Iambo's captors and would-be executioners was to be a theme revisited by other commentators during the Iambo days.[33]

"What If . . ."

The passion and absurdity of the "elephant question" was not lost on local comedians.[34] Neither was Faust immune to the episode's ironic humor. "Last week was elephant week," when all anyone could talk about was Iambo, Faust said in the introduction to a whimsical column, complete with illustrations, titled "What If . . ." So what would happen if the elephant did escape, the columnist mused? He let his imagination wander through commentary that, while light, was nonetheless infused with serious reflections about the complexities and anxieties of modern urban life.[35]

Faust began the story of Iambo's day out with the elephant's triumphant escape from Kulikovo Field. Once clear of the menagerie grounds, Iambo headed for a nearby tram stop, his appearance meeting with a typically gruff response from the conductor: "All full! Don't detain the tram!" Unlike the average Odessan, however, Iambo's great strength provided him with a means to exact revenge from the rude conductor. He pushed over a telegraph pole, climbed onto the roof of the tram car, and swiftly crushed it. "This would be a first in Odessa," Faust declared. "Not someone being crushed by the *'elektrichka'* but someone crushing it."

Iambo's next stop was a fashionable central café, where he decided to stop for a cup of hot chocolate and some pastries. But once again the elephant's plans were foiled, this time by a snooty waiter who refused to serve him because he was improperly dressed, daring to appear in public without a white collar. Iambo answered the pretension with a fit of laughter that sent tables flying "as if blown by a hurricane." The adventurous pachyderm wreaked similar havoc on meetings of the duma, the rabbinate, and the association of Jewish salesclerks.

As evening fell, Iambo was ready for entertainment so he headed to a local estrada theater. Much to his surprise, he himself wound up as the star attraction, asked by an impresario to perform in a special "number" with one of Odessa's most famous "artistes." "Today! Ladies, free of charge!!! Only here! The inimitable Khenkin celebrating his 34,876th farewell benefit. The elephant 'Iambo' and Khenkin will perform the tango."

Iambo's debut attracted the attention of a beautiful *café-chantant* singer, with whom the elephant became instantly enamored. He made a date to escort her to a fine restaurant. In order to afford such an extravagance, however, Iambo was forced to pawn his tusks. Then, knowing that in a private dining room his money would buy "smells but no food," the elephant decided that he had best eat his fill at a cheap buffet. Unfortunately, the comestibles he ingested had been sitting too long; the poisonous provisions worked better than potassium cyanide. Iambo soon became violently ill and, in the end, "turned up his toes." As the final illustration showed, Iambo's day ended when the poor elephant died alone in the gutter without a kopeck to his name.

Faust's fantasy showed Iambo tilting at the windmills of modern urban life, at first finding success and then losing it. He started the day as everyman's avenging hero, crushing the tram, laughing at snobbery, and mocking those in positions of authority. At his height, it seemed that Iambo had conquered Odessa, glorying in the sensational spotlight, dancing the tango with Khenkin. But as the "poor elephant" discovered, Odessa herself could be a femme fatale; she set him up and did him in. He was seduced by the city's entertainments, indulging in the sexual license of the urban milieu. He sought to live above his proper station in life, asserting an identity to which he was not entitled. Like so many others who tried but failed to conquer the city, he was destined to die on the street, another victim of a city that made promises to many but only delivered to a few.

Iambo's Fate

Back in the real world, the public continued to wait anxiously for some resolution of the Iambo problem. "It is Iambo's fate to become an epic," *Odesskaia pochta* claimed. "It seems that no other public event in recent times has attracted as much attention." Everyone in Russia knew about the "ordinary elephant from Lorberbaum's menagerie." Iambo's popularity was "greater than that of many celebrities," the article continued. Every newspaper in the country had "dedicated several articles and feuilletons to Iambo," the elephant's portrait gracing the pages of "dozens of publications." A local cinematography firm had even made a movie about the elephant to be shown in local cinemas.[36]

"There is fervent opposition to Iambo's death sentence among the public," *Odesskaia pochta* reiterated.[37] Indeed, the elephant had a mass of sympathizers and even a few avengers, as Iambo's owner Lorberbaum discovered when he received a death threat claiming that the day Iambo died would be the menagerie owner's last.[38] Other menagerie employees, too, received threatening letters, including several reportedly written by *intelligentnyi* people.[39] A particularly loyal fan went so far as to attack one of Lorberbaum's animal handlers. "Ah I've got you at last!" the assailant cried. "You'll die before Iambo. I'll finish you off myself!"[40]

Lorberbaum himself became an object of increased suspicion, with many observers ascribing sinister motives to the menagerie owner. Some believed that Lorberbaum wanted to have the elephant killed in order to collect on a large insurance policy. Others claimed Lorberbaum was torturing Iambo by night and not feeding the animal properly. Lorberbaum vehemently denied all such accusations. Nonetheless, probably on Sosnovskii's orders, police conducted a thorough investigation of the menagerie owner's "reliability."[41]

In a final effort to steady the nerves of the agitated pachyderm (not to mention the public), Lorberbaum bought a pair of female elephants who arrived by train in early June. The transfer of the "she-elephants" to their new home did not go without a hitch, however. As they were disembarking from the train, one of the pair escaped from her handlers and bolted toward Pushkinskaia Street. As one might imagine, the sight of the stampeding elephant in the crowded square outside the station created a panic. It took quite some time for the public to realize that Iambo himself was not on the loose. Iambo's "girlfriend" was soon recaptured and placed in an enclosure close to her intended beau.[42]

Contrary to hopes, the womanly influence of the "she-elephant" was not powerful enough to soothe the troubled Iambo. On Monday, June 9th, three days after the arrival of his would-be mate, Iambo again "started raging with unbelievable strength." He attacked his new trainer, broke off an iron bar from the side of his cage, and thrashed at the enclosure's ceiling with his trunk, reducing it to rubble. A senior veterinary inspector examined Iambo, "conferred by telephone with higher authorities," then announced that the time had come to put the elephant to death. A firing squad was quickly assembled and a variety of "precautionary measures" taken.[43]

The shooting began at 3:00 p.m. According to initial reports, 261 bullets were pumped into the unfortunate elephant during a barrage that lasted between fifteen and thirty minutes. Thus Iambo met his seemingly inevitable fate.[44]

The word hit the streets almost instantly—"They are shooting Iambo!" The public raced to the grounds to find out what was happening. Many of those who came were Iambo supporters, moaning, crying, and full of regret for the embattled elephant. The shooting went on for so long as to be "excruciating." "When will it end?" someone shouted from the crowd. "Poor Iambo!" The relentless gunfire agitated the other animals in the menagerie, one reporter observed. Members of the firing squad were also reportedly appalled by the scene: "What a horrible picture! It is staggering!" Lorberbaum himself did not have "sufficient strength" to watch the proceedings. Instead, Iambo's master sat in the foyer of the menagerie, his face "distorted and pale." "It is a calamity," Lorberbaum moaned. Meanwhile, at the gates, thousands of locked-out "mourners" clamored for entry.[45]

"Iambo's Funeral"

Odesskaia pochta provided readers with full coverage of "Iambo's funeral," beginning with a detailed description of the difficulties encountered by the team of artel workers brought in by Lorberbaum to remove the elephant's body. The men labored all night to free Iambo from his chains, lift him onto a cart, and manhandle the load through a sticky field of mud to at last reach the paved street.

Lorberbaum and city authorities wanted to transport the "hero" with little fanfare. This proved to be impossible, however. By 6:00 a.m., thousands of Odessans crowded around the dead elephant, accompanying the "hearse" as it processed down the main streets of central Odessa from Kulikovo Field to Iambo's "final resting place" outside the university's anatomical institute building. Once there, police again tried to control the crowd, severely restricting entrance into the yard. The "public tried in vain to see at least from afar" the hideously disfigured, blood-covered corpse. Meanwhile, other members of the public poured into the menagerie to view the site of the execution. But there on the spot where Iambo had so recently stood, the mourners saw only the newly arrived female elephants, who were described much as Iambo himself had been only two months before: "completely tame" and "freely eating from the hands of the public."[46]

The results of the "postmortem" were reported in the newspaper in gruesome detail, including a reference to the "positively unbearable" stench surrounding the rotting corpse. During the course of the autopsy, over a hundred bullets were removed from the body, most of which failed to penetrate the elephant's tough skin. The fatal missiles were those that had entered through his eyes and ears. The final assemblage of experts to evaluate the elephant determined that there was no medical evidence to support the view that Iambo's violent behavior had been caused by disease. The elephant had been in good health at the time of his death. He "had a strong heart," the official report proclaimed.[47] Once the autopsy was complete, the remains of Iambo were duly disposed of. The "meat" was taken to the city salvage factory. Iambo's hide and skin were taken to a local taxidermist who was charged with the task of turning the "hero of the day" into a stuffed trophy.[48]

"People Like You and Me"

"Even as Iambo's corpse begins to decompose, his name will not soon cease to provoke endless conversations, rumors, and arguments," proclaimed *Odesskaia pochta,* a paper that devoted half a page to a poignant obituary full of Iambo's thoughts and feelings. The death itself, so long expected, seemed to take the public by surprise. In its aftermath, everyone seemed to be contemplating the same questions: "Was it impossible to save Iambo? Was it really necessary to do him in? Why was there such a big hurry to shoot him?"[49]

One story introduced the possibility of foul play. It turned out that Iambo's new handler, Charlie Ileneb, was a longtime employee of Lorberbaum's and had, in fact, up until two years before been the elephant's primary attendant. At that point, however, Iambo had broken Ileneb's wife's rib. "She has been sick ever since," Ileneb claimed. Given that Iambo's final rage was directed against Ileneb, the allegation hanging in the air was that the trainer might have provoked the incident in order to exact his revenge.[50]

A rare report that represented Iambo as deserving of his fate saw the execution as just punishment for the elephant's various crimes. Iambo had a "dark past," the author of the piece noted. He was a savage beast, who in his time had "broken more than a few human ribs and killed one person outright." Then there was the incident with Iambo's "girlfriend," the reporter continued, the one whom the pachyderm had met eleven years earlier while still in Kharkov. "Iambo took an instant dislike to her," the journalist claimed. "If menagerie workers left her alone with him even for a few minutes, Iambo would strike her zealously with his tusks." He continued to "torment" the female for three months until, in the end, he finally succeeded in murdering her. "After that, Iambo became cheerful and lively," the author concluded.[51]

Such negative portrayals of Iambo's character were uncommon in the press. Instead of vilifying the dead elephant, most journalists extolled his virtues, representing him as decidedly more humane than the "savage beasts" who senselessly and brutally annihilated him. "The public was deeply agitated by the behavior of the gun-lovers who with sensual pleasure prepared for the murder of the unlucky animal," a *Iuzhnaia mysl'* columnist wrote. During the execution itself, the shooters reached a state of madness, wailing like wild beasts and "losing any likeness to human beings." Horror was also expressed by a local hunter who wrote to *Odesskie novosti* to lodge a "deeply felt protest against the profanity and abuse of the word 'sportsman'" to refer to the hunters who had participated in the shooting squad. "These were not sportsmen but butchers from some third-rate slaughterhouse," the impassioned writer fumed.[52] A similar reaction was voiced by the columnist Leri. "I shuddered with horror when I read the description of the execution of the unlucky Iambo," Leri began. "One question came to mind: Who are they, these inhuman shooters? . . . Hottentots? Comanches?" Leri's invocation of language normally reserved by journalists to describe the worst kinds of urban "barbarians" is testament to the outrage engendered among the public by the elephant's execution. But Iambo's "murderers" were not hardened criminals or "insolent" hooligans, Leri emphasized. They had not surfaced from the urban depths. Instead, they were "people of culture, conscious and reasonable beings of the twentieth century . . . members of our society, people like you and me."[53]

Conclusion

Iambo's image and the facts of his story were pressed into service for a variety of causes, many of which exposed Odessans' anxieties about living in the modern urban world. A martyr of the middle-class self, Iambo was a sacrifice on the altar of the City and Culture, his death symbolizing the distance between the ideals and the reality of the world of the middle class in Odessa. In his drive for respectability, the middle-class man struggled to conquer his environment, control his body, and develop his soul. Yet, like Iambo, he might at any moment succumb, driven to madness or even crime by the strict expectations of society, by the corrupt influence of his urban surroundings, or, more terrifying still, by the savage within. "The wild animal in man is far from dead and will not soon die," one columnist wrote. "All of the instincts of wild beasts, right up to the thirst for blood and the insatiable desire for murder" remain alive in us." "Who is worse off," he continued. "The elephant, who even after thirty years, remained unadapted to life in a cage . . . or us, tightly laced in the stone corset of the city."[54]

In death as in life, Iambo was frequently portrayed as a respectable, *intelligentnyi*, profoundly moral yet constantly besieged figure, the epitome of the modern middle-class man. "Poor Iambo! Just day before yesterday I feasted my eyes upon the sight of his gentle, well-behaved conduct as he decorously and politely ate from the hand of his new trainer," one columnist wrote. "But today . . . today he lies a lifeless corpse."[55] "He has gone to that world where there is neither sorrow nor lament," another commentator noted. "And when he died, when his clear, intelligent eyes were covered with the haze of approaching death, one could read in them a mute, bewildered question: For what? Poor, poor Iambo!"[56] Many a writer represented the elephant as a model citizen, contrasting Iambo's sterling character traits against those of the excessively acquisitive and status-obsessed *meshchanin*, whose lack of personal integrity compromised the public good. The columnist Satana made this point well in a piece aimed at publicly chastising a local merchant, a certain Lazarev, who refused to allow a poor street vendor to set up a stand on the pavement outside his store. "No words will move him to tears, for his thick-skinned heart is armored against any 'tenderness,'" Satana wrote. "That skin is a blessed memory of Iambo. But under poor Iambo's thick elephant skin beat a sensitive, magnanimous heart, while in the place where Lazarev's heart should be, there is nothing but a sign reading: 'Here is a heart.'" Lazarev "only understands one language," Satana concluded, "the language of money."[57]

Some writers resisted such eulogizing, seeing the Iambo phenomenon in more ambiguous terms as a manifestation of the uncertainties and doubts of an aggressive but still insecure middle class. For instance, *Odesskaia pochta*'s editor-publisher A. Finkel' invoked Iambo in a stinging column meant to reprove the Odessa public for its vulgar tastes, specifically condemning an audience at the posh City Theater for its undisciplined behavior during a performance of a touring drama company. The fact that the troupe itself, which had been extensively hyped in advance, was only "mediocre" did not excuse theatergoers for visibly displaying their discontent, said Finkel. The crux of the problem was that the public expected too much, it "wants something bigger, more grandiose; it wants Iambo."[58] Further proof to the point was offered within a month of Finkel's column when the Malevich circus advertised the appearance of the famous wrestler Foss, billing him as "Iambo II." Perhaps even more telling (and condemning) was the description of a local prostitute, whose colossal figure was described as "Iamboesque" [*iamboobraznaia*].[59]

In July 1914, with spring turned to summer, *Odesskaia pochta* published one last story to end the Iambo days. It seems that during the annual sea festival at the Arkadia beach resort, a kite bearing the elephant's name and likeness burst into flames in midair, dropped from the sky, and subsequently sank. "Iambo is unlucky," someone in the crowd was overheard saying.[60]

Epilogue

A Moment in the Sun

> Odessa had its moment in the sun, but now it is fading—a
> poetic, slow, lighthearted, helpless fading.
> —Isaak Babel (1916)[1]

• For better or worse, Odessa was a modern city, savvy and irresistible, dangerous in its pleasures, comfortable in its conceits, concerted in its efforts to remain a place unto itself. Odessa's "light and easy atmosphere [made] the typical Odessan . . . the exact opposite of the typical Petrogradian," Isaak Babel wrote.[2] Indeed, well into the twentieth century, contemporary accounts upheld the view that Odessans preferred the sunny secular side of modernity to the "joyful horror" and spiritual decadence that marked St. Petersburg's dark fin-de-siècle mood.[3] Yet it cannot be denied that by the 1910s, some Odessans were having their doubts.

On the pages of the popular press, the *electrichka* in many ways symbolized ambiguous attitudes about modernity. Government officials and business leaders had lobbied hard for the building of the modern urban transportation system, citing the many advantages that streetcars would provide for individuals and businesses alike. Once the system was in place, however, complaints about it were legion. People complained that the *electrichka* was noisy, that tram stops were in the wrong places, that service was too slow, that hours of operation were too short, that conductors were rude or dishonest, that tram cars were overcrowded, that transfers were impossible to make.[4] The biggest complaint, however, was that the trams were dangerous. Pickpockets and "children of the street" exploited crowded conditions to steal the purses and wallets of the unwary.[5] Plus the tram itself could be deadly, the so-called Belgian guillotine spooking horses, running over pedestrians, dragging slow-moving oldsters and children along its rails.[6] Indeed, more than four hundred people were injured by the *electrichka* in 1912 alone, a statistic that prompted one journalist to dub the streetcar "a tool for the modern death penalty."[7]

Automobiles were another sign of the times. On the one hand, the car was the ultimate status symbol, imparting to its owner instant recognition of his or her high position in society, with the streets of the center especially functioning as a showcase for the ostentatious display of wealth.[8] Indeed, the entire city was a "center of automobilism," a testament to Odessa's reputation as a mecca of modernity.[9] To some observers, however, automobiles were menacing threats. Newspaper reports condemned drivers who operated their vehicles unsafely, motored too quickly, or ran horse-drawn conveyances off the road.[10] Plus automobiles were shockingly loud and unsanitary, contaminating the environment. One reporter decried the presence of the machines in Aleksandrovskii Park, complaining that "cars roll nonstop along the park's main alleys filling the air with the asphyxiating stench of gasoline [which] detracts from a nice stroll in the park. Now the public goes out of its way to avoid what used to be the best spot in town for a walk. It is deplorable."[11]

If the technologies of modernity gave some Odessans pause, the apocalyptic horrors of the Great War did much to dampen the collective spirit. As elsewhere in Russia, the public greeted initial calls for mobilization with breathless elation. An impromptu prowar demonstration broke out on Cathedral Square, complete with political and patriotic speeches. The gathering crowd then marched down Deribasovskaia, proudly displaying a portrait of Nicholas II, singing patriotic songs, and chanting "Down with Germans!" and "God Save the Tsar!" "Life has never been so red-hot, boiling, seething," one newspaper commentator wrote a week after the call to arms. Thousands of people, soldiers and civilians alike, gathered near public monuments and government buildings in the central city to discuss the latest news, every telegram issuing forth more rumors than facts. Even Odessa's notoriously brazen thieves were caught up in the patriotic fervor, one columnist noted. Despite the presence of large crowds everywhere on the streets, even highly accomplished pickpockets seemed reluctant to ply their trades. "There is an explanation," the writer suggested. First, "there is earnest surveillance on the part of police." Second, "the thieves themselves fear reprisals from the side of the public."[12]

The euphoria of late summer 1914 quickly devolved into something decidedly darker as Odessans tried to contend with wild fluctuations in the stock market, skyrocketing prices, rampant speculation in fuel and foodstuffs, mounting defeats at the front, and massive unemployment on the docks thanks to the final closing of the Black Sea straits with Ottoman entry into the war. By January 1915, conditions in Odessa were so desperate that close to three thousand soldiers' wives assembled outside the city duma building to demand that local government officials provide them with grants. In a move illustrative of increasing tensions in Odessa, city prefect Sosnovskii ordered that mounted police be called in to break up the demonstration.[13] But at this stage in its history, Odessa was spared one torment. With the exception of a short bombardment of the port on the night of September 17, 1914, executed by Ottoman gunboats under German command, the city remained out of the line of fire. This is not to say that city life was unaffected by the war effort. On the contrary, Odessa was a major staging ground for the military, a key supply collection point, and an important site for civilian volunteer efforts. Moreover, the city was an asylum for tens of thousands of war refugees, who poured into Odessa from Poland, Lithuania, Belorussia, and Rumania, putting additional stress on the city's already overtaxed infrastructure.[14]

Tellingly, even in these grim times, the Odessan propensity for fun was not easily extinguished. For instance, in mid-March 1915, when word came through the wires that Russian forces had beaten back the Austrians at the Peremyshlia fortress, Odessa erupted in unrestrained celebration. "Joy shone on everyone's face. Strangers kissed and congratulated each other on the victory. Old borders that separated people of different classes and social conditions were worn down."[15] Hoping to capitalize on momentarily high spirits, Odessa's lively theatrical and entertainment community quickly organized a large-scale street carnival as a fundraiser for the families of poor soldiers. Deribasovskaia and other central streets were bedecked with flags, portraits of the tsar, and banners bearing patriotic slogans. The main hall of the city duma building was likewise decorated, becoming (not unironically) the main headquarters of the carnival. On the day of the great event, people flocked to the scene to watch famous wrestlers from the Malevich circus take each other on in bouts staged on the street. Musicians roamed through the crowds collecting donations as they went. Masked entertainers were also at work, favoring the assembled with spicy anecdotes and playing practical jokes on those who did not give or donated less than their appearance suggested they should.[16]

Such festivities were especially welcome, since in general, the war had so diminished Odessa's normally vibrant nightlife scene. Businesses were shutting down throughout the city, one columnist lamented, and thanks to wartime prohibition of the sale of hard liquor "slowly, before our eyes, the Odessa tavern is becoming extinct. The huge halls have become deserted. The machines that throw out the sounds of polkas and waltzes rarely cry out, and in the evenings . . . the tavern is half sunk in darkness, without the usual noise and animation." Anyone can drink tea at home, the journalist sighed, but where can one go to drink vodka in the company of friends, away from disapproving wives. But even without strong drink, men continued to gather in taverns to talk about the war, read the papers, dissect rumors, and listen to veterans tell their tales.[17]

Unsurprisingly, restrictions on the manufacture and sale of hard liquor led to an upsurge in the production and distribution of "moonshine."[18] But this was only part of the story of civic disorder during the war years.[19] Massive unemployment drove many to petty theft. Business in false passports picked up considerably, as did counterfeiting and forgery of all kinds, from coins and stamps to labels and military orders.[20] Meanwhile, papers reported hysterically that hooligans ruled the streets and that groups of runaway soldiers became gangs of armed bandits.[21] Moreover, labor militancy in the city was reaching new heights. Under the auspices of Odessa's hastily formed War Industries Committee, more than fifty new industrial enterprises had been established since the outbreak of war, most of them metal processing plants named for their products: "Grenade," "Shrapnel," "Shell." While on the one hand the new factories served to buttress a critically flagging economy, they also proved to be fertile soil for the spread of revolution.[22]

By 1916, Odessa was a city out of balance, its identity challenged by pressures beyond its control. A sign of rising anxiety among the Odessan population was distrust of foreigners and other strangers, something that in former times would have been utterly antithetical to the whole idea of being Odessan. The erosion of tolerance began early in the war when local patriots—many of them businessmen, many of them Jewish—began to co-operate with the police to identify and detain Austrians, Germans, and Ottomans working in Odessa.[23] Some newspapers tried to cast these new attitudes into a humorous light. For instance, a March 1915 report told of a popular animal act that, until the outbreak of the war, had been playing at Lorberbaum's menagerie. As it transpired, the stars of the show, six lions and four tigers, had been working with a German trainer, who fled Odessa with the declaration of war. Because they only understood the language of the enemy, the "German-national wild animals" had to be "Russified" by a new trainer before they could again perform in public.[24]

Symptomatic of the larger problem were the changing sensibilities of journalists, including Jews, who conceived of themselves as "real" Odessans even as they riled up hatred against foreigners, refugees, and any newcomers who arrived in the city without visible means of support. Reporters turned suspicious eyes on female refugees who hoped to enter domestic service, dubbing them as runaways "not from enemy-occupied territory . . . but from penal battalions." Likewise, papers reported that male refugees (many of whom were older and thus not subject to the draft) were turned down for positions as porters, *dvorniki*, and guards based solely on the fact that they were thought likely to be "fugitives from hard labor."[25] Even if some newspaper columnists reminded readers that more than a few "real refugees [were] honest people" deserving of aid and sympathy, fear ruled the day. Even in *Odesskaia pochta*, the organ of Odessa's Jewish "every-man," press reports screamed about the criminal activities of the "Polish and Lithuanian rats" who were "infesting" Odessan shores.[26] "The war has changed everything," one columnist bemoaned in 1915. "It touches even the most remote corners of our lives and habits."[27]

A short three years later—in the aftermath of the Great October Revolution, and within days of the Ukrainian Rada's declaration of independence, the creation of the Red Army, and the signing of the Treaty of Brest-Litovsk, which put Odessa inside the Austrian sphere of occupation—Isaak Babel published a short essay declaring that "Odessa stands strong, she hasn't lost her astonishing knack for assimilating people." After all the newcomers retreated to their former domains, Babel wrote, "the horns of ocean liners will once more blare in our harbor, and in our taverns old gramophones will once more croak words about Britannia ruling the waves. Our storehouses will be filled with oranges, coconuts, pepper, and

Málaga wine, and in our granaries the greenish dust of pouring grain will rise."[28] By 1921, when a severely battered Odessa emerged from the trauma of revolution and civil war, its once-vibrant middle class lay in ruins. But just as Babel predicted, old Odessa lived on, not only in the sensibilities of the southwestern school of writers but also in the ethos of *meshchanstvo* that, in reinvented form, came to dominate Soviet society in the era of "developed socialism."[29]

Now in post-Soviet times, Odessans draw on popular images of their city's storied past to rekindle the mood of "old" Odessa and assert a powerful local identity. New versions of the "Gambrinus" and the "Café Frankoni" have risen in the environs of Deribasovskaia, which is once again a boulevard of high fashion and conspicuous consumption.[30] Local museums display artifacts from Odessa's heyday, popular histories of the city tell of its moment in the sun, and the mayor's office distributes a slick CD-rom featuring images of Odessa then and now (focusing on the years 1869, 1912, and 2002).[31] Two of the monuments erected in the city since the fall of communism celebrate the Odessan spirit of playful irreverence: Il'f and Petrov's "Twelfth Chair" has a place of honor in the city garden; while nearby a life-sized statue of the entertainer Leonid Utesov sits smiling warmly on a park bench as if inviting passersby to sit down and listen to a story. And every year around April 1, Odessa hosts an annual festival of humor, featuring comic performances on the Potemkin steps, a carnival on Deribasovskaia, and other "lively" entertainments. Finally, and perhaps most tellingly, Odessans near and far gather in a virtual city on the Web, with pages devoted to compilations of Odessa anecdotes, dictionaries of the Odessan language, "who's who" listings of famous Odessans, and chronicles of local news items, including the latest stories about crime.[32] Sites such as these facilitate communication between diaspora Odessans and those who remain on the shores of the Black Sea. But most of all they celebrate a shared identity rooted in a past most Odessans never knew: the world brought to life so vividly by journalists—Faust, Satana, Flit, and the rest—in their newspaper tales of "old Odessa."

Notes

Introduction—The Modern Odessan

1. "The *Nakaz*, or Instruction, of Catherine II to the Legislative Commission of 1767–1968," in *Imperial Russia: A Source Book, 1700–1917*, ed. Basil Dmytryshyn (Hinsdale, IL, 1974), 83.

2. Vladimir Jabotinsky, "Memoirs by My Typewriter," in *The Golden Tradition: Jewish Life and Thought in Eastern Europe*, ed. Lucy S. Dawidowicz (New York, 1967), 397–98.

3. For a recent bibliography of works on Odessa, compiled by Patricia Herlihy, see Nicolas V. Iljine, ed., *Odessa Memories* (Seattle, WA, 2003), 129–33.

4. Vlas Doroshevich, *Odessa, odessity: odessitki-Ocherki, nabbroski, eskizy*, quoted in Robert A. Rothstein, "How It Was Sung in Odessa: At the Intersection of Russian and Yiddish Folk Culture," *Slavic Review* 60, no. 1 (2001): 783.

5. Richard Stites, *Russian Popular Culture: Entertainment and Society since 1900* (Cambridge, 1992), 4, 19, and 21.

6. While scholars continue to debate the definitions of "modern" and "modernity," I find Marshall Berman's conceptualization to be most compelling. See Marshall Berman, *All that Is Solid Melts into Air: The Experience of Modernity* (New York, 1982).

7. The seminal work of Judith Walkowitz, *City of Dreadful Delight: Narratives of Sexual Danger in Late-Victorian London* (Chicago, IL, 1992), powerfully demonstrates the revelatory possibilities of close analysis of stories in the mass press for historians of the modern European city. Joan Neuberger, *Hooliganism: Crime, Culture, and Power in St. Petersburg, 1900–1914* (Berkeley, CA, 1993), is an early and influential example within the historiography of late-imperial Russia.

8. Inspired especially by the work of Michel Foucault, scholars in a variety of fields have begun to study crime and criminality as cultural constructs. For an overview of recent work, see the introduction to Margaret L. Arnot and Cornelie Usborne, eds., *Gender and Crime in Modern Europe* (London, 1999). The most thorough treatment of the subject for late-imperial Russia is Stephen P. Frank, *Crime, Cultural Conflict, and Justice in Rural Russia, 1856–1914* (Berkeley, CA, 1999).

9. On Chicago, see David E. Ruth, *Inventing the Public Enemy: The Gangster in American Culture, 1918–1934* (Chicago, IL, 1996), 120–22.

10. For other discussions of crime in late-imperial Russian cities, see Neuberger, *Hooliganism;* Hubertus Jahn, "Der St. Petersburger Heumarkt im 19. Jahrhundert. Metamorphosen eines Stadtviertels," *Jahrbücher für Geschichte Osteuropas* 44 (1996): 162–77; Henri Troyat, *Daily Life in Russia under the Last Tsar* (Stanford, CA, 1961), 56–62; Daniel R. Brower, *The Russian City between Tradition and Modernity, 1850–1900* (Berkeley, CA, 1990), 178 and 197; Joseph Bradley, "Once You've Eaten Khitrov Soup,

You'll Never Leave," *Russian History* 11, no. 1 (1984): 1-28; Michael Hamm, *Kiev: A Portrait, 1800–1917* (Princeton, NJ, 1993), 156–59; and Stephen D. Corrsin, "Warsaw: Poles and Jews in a Conquered City," in *The City in Late Imperial Russia*, ed. Michael F. Hamm (Bloomington, IN, 1986), 139.

11. Recent work by geographers points out the need to investigate the "differential historical geographies of modernity" especially beyond well-studied metropolitan areas such as London, Paris, and New York. See Brian Graham and Catherine Nash, eds., *Modern Historical Geographies* (New York, 2000), 2.

12. The notion that identity is culturally constructed is now so widely accepted in academic circles that it no longer needs supporting citation. Students and others unfamiliar with the standard canon of critical cultural theory and its impact on the field of history might begin with two excellent review articles, both somewhat out of date but still quite useful: Sarah Maza, "Stories in History: Cultural Narratives in Recent Works in European History," *American Historical Review* 101, no. 5 (1996): 1493–1515; and Mark D. Steinberg, "Stories and Voices: History and Theory," *Russian Review* 55, no. 3 (1996): 347–54.

13. Louise McReynolds has been the most vocal advocate of this position, most recently in her book *Russia at Play: Leisure Activities at the End of the Tsarist Era* (Ithaca, NY, 2003).

14. *Vsia Odessa. Adresnaia i spravochnaia kniga vsei Odessy* (Odessa, 1914), 139–41. While the vast majority of those listed were in the Russian language, there were categories also for publications in Yiddish, German, and Polish.

15. Sales figures are from L. N. Beliaeva et al., eds., *Bibliografiia periodicheskikh iz-danii Rossii, 1901–1916* (Leningrad, 1959); S. M. Kovbasiuk et al., eds., *Odessa. Ocherk istorii goroda-geroia* (Odessa, 1957), 113; and *Obzor odesskogo gradonachalstva za 1912* (hereafter cited as *OOG za 1912*) (Odessa, 1913), 35. *Odesskaia pochta* (hereafter cited as *OP*), 6 July 1914, claims that the newspaper's average daily sales increased from 61,000 in 1912 to 68,000 in 1913 to 79,000 in 1914, making for annual sales of well over 20 million copies. This would put it on a par with the best-selling newspapers in St. Petersburg in the same year. See Louise McReynolds, *The News Under Russia's Old Regime: The Development of a Mass-Circulation Press* (Princeton, NJ, 1991), 296.

16. Aggregate statistics included in the annual reports of the city prefect (*OOG za 1912*, and for 1913 and 1914) confirm that young males of lower-class background were the most likely to be convicted of crime. However, as Stephen Frank reminds us, conviction statistics especially tend to obscure the participation in crime of women and those of the higher social classes. See Frank, *Crime, Cultural Conflict, and Justice in Rural Russia*.

17. We owe our knowledge of *Krokodil* to the singular efforts of Sergei Lushchik, who has published several essays on the history of the journal and its contributors based on archival materials as well as interviews with participants. Lushchik, "Odesskii 'Krokodil,'" *Al'manakh bibliofila* 10 (1981): 254–64, and especially "Odesskii zhurnal 'Krokodil' i ego avtory," in *Odesskii zhurnal 'Krokodil' i ego avtory. Izbrannye stranitsy (1911–1912)*, ed. O. F. Botushanskaia (Odessa, 1998): 231–310.

18. Elias's ideas, which first appeared in print in Germany in the mid-1930s, did not find an audience among American scholars until translated into English in the late 1970s. These days, he is au courant, especially in Russian history circles. The definitive English-language version is Norbert Elias, *The Civilizing Process: Sociogenetic and Psychogenetic Investigations*, rev. ed. (Malden, MA, 2000). Erving Goffman was among the first to argue that modern identity is at root a performance. His seminal work, *The Presentation of Self in Everyday Life*, has come out in many editions since it was originally published in 1956 as a monograph by the University of Edinburgh's Social Sciences Research Centre.

19. On the traditional disdain of the intelligentsia for the bourgeoisie, see Catriona Kelly and David Shepherd, eds., *Constructing Russian Culture in the Age of Revolution, 1881–1940* (New York, 1998), 134 passim.

20. Neuberger, *Hooliganism,* 18 passim.

21. Wayne Morrison, *Theoretical Criminology* (London, 1995), 3–4.

22. Mark Steinberg, "'Black Masks': Performance, Image, and Identity on the Streets of the City." Conference paper delivered at the Spring 2004 meeting of the Midwest Russian History Workshop. A published version is forthcoming as part of the proceedings of the June 2004 St. Petersburg conference on the culture of fin-de-siècle Russian cities. See also Efrat Tseëlon, ed., *Masquerade and Identities: Essays on Gender, Sexuality, and Marginality* (London, 2001), 3.

23. Sheila Fitzpatrick's work demonstrates that the concept is also quite fruitful when discussing the early Soviet period. A collection of her essays on this theme is published under the title *Tear Off the Masks! Identity and Imposture in Twentieth-Century Russia* (Princeton, NJ, 2005).

24. John F. Kasson, *Rudeness and Civility: Manners in Nineteenth-Century Urban America* (New York, 1990), 99–111.

25. "Passing" has been most heavily theorized in relation to race, ethnicity, and gender rather than class. For a recent discussion see the introduction to Elaine K. Ginsberg, ed., *Passing and the Fictions of Identity* (Durham, NC, 1996).

26. The city directory *Vsia Odessa,* section 1, p. 182, provides a list of executive-board members in 1914. Occupations of individual members, as shown in the directory's alphabetical listing of city residents, were as follows: four *Odesskie novosti* journalists (including both that paper's managing editor and its publisher, also a lawyer), three contributors to *Odesskii listok* (one of them a lawyer), three more lawyers, two merchants (one of the first guild, one of the second), one physician, one *chinovnik* working in the customs department, and one member whose occupation was not listed.

27. "Gde intelligentsiia (Iz pis'ma v redaktsiiu)," *Odesskii listok* (hereafter *OL*), 6 March 1912.

28. Grigorii Moskvich, *Putevoditel' po Odesse* (Odessa: 1913), 30.

29. Moskvich, *Putevoditel'.* A brief version of the club's charter is included in the listing for "Literaturno-artisticheckii klub" under the heading "Kluby i Sobraniia" in *Vsia Odessa,* section 1, p. 182.

30. "Gde intelligentsia."

31. "Vecher Iumora," *OL,* 19 February 1912.

32. "Gde intelligentsia."

33. The club's annual report for 1917 shows that regular members were primarily *intelligentnyi,* its guest members almost all "middle *meshchanstvo.*" See *Otchet pravleniia Odesskago literaturno-artisticheskago obshchestva za 1917 god* (Odessa, 1918), 16 and 30–39.

34. Richard Holt, "Social History and Bourgeois Culture in Nineteenth-Century France," *Comparative Study of Society and History* 27, no. 4 (October 1985), 717, talks about the association of particular titles with social class in nineteenth-century France.

35. Benjamin Nathans, *Beyond the Pale: The Jewish Encounter with Late Imperial Russia* (Berkeley, CA, 2002), 5.

36. John D. Klier, "A Port, Not a Shtetl: Reflections on the Distinctiveness of Odessa," *Jewish Culture and History* 4, no. 2 (2001): 175.

37. Nathans, *Beyond the Pale,* 126.

38. Ilya Gerasimov, "'My ubivaem tol'ko svoikh': Prestupnost' kak marker mezhetnicheskikh granits v Odesse nachala XX veka (1907–1917 gg.)," *Ab Imperio* 1 (2003): 260.

39. Nathans, *Beyond the Pale,* 11.

40. A notable exception is Yuri Slezkine's recent declaration that "moderniza-tion . . . is about everyone becoming Jewish." Yuri Slezkine, *The Jewish Century* (Princeton, NJ, 2004), 1.

41. My calculations show that Russians and Jews split the middle class roughly in half, with the probable edge going to Jews. For a detailed discussion of Odessa's

202 | NOTES TO PAGES 14–20

class composition, including an explanation of how these figures were arrived at, see my Ph.D. dissertation. Roshanna P. Sylvester, "Crime, Masquerade, and Anxiety: The Public Creation of Middle-Class Identity in Pre-Revolutionary Odessa, 1912–1916" (Yale University, 1998), 48–55.

42. David Cesarani, "Port Jews: Concepts, Cases, and Questions," *Jewish Culture and History* 4, no. 2 (2001): 2.

43. David Sorkin, "The Port Jew: Notes Toward a Social Type" *Journal of Jewish Studies* 50, no. 1 (Spring 1999): 87–97; Lois Dubin, *The Port Jews of Habsburg Trieste* (Stanford, 1999); Patricia Herlihy, "Port Jews of Odessa and Trieste—A Tale of Two Cities," *Jahrbuch des Simon-Dubnow-Instituts* 2 (2003): 183–98; Klier, "A Port, Not a Shtetl"; Maria Vassilikou, "Greeks and Jews in Salonika and Odessa: Inter-Ethnic Relations in Cosmopolitan Port Cities," *Jewish Culture and History* 4, no. 2 (2001): 155–72.

44. Cesarani, "Port Jews," 2–3.

1—Dangertown

1. Jabotinsky, "Memoirs by My Typewriter," 399.

2. On Odessa as El Dorado, see Robert Weinberg, *The Revolution of 1905 in Odessa: Blood on the Steps* (Bloomington, IN, 1993), 1–12.

3. *Pervaia vseobshchaia perepis' naseleniia Rossiiskoi Imperii, 1897 g.*, vol. 47, *Gorod Odessa* (St. Petersburg, 1904), 2–3 (hereafter *Census of 1897*), recorded a population of 403,815 for city and suburbs, 380,541 for the city alone. See also Patricia Herlihy, "The Ethnic Composition of the City of Odessa in the Nineteenth Century," *Harvard Ukrainian Studies* 1 (1977): 53–78.

4. Moskvich, *Putevoditel'*, 1, cited "little Paris" as one of Odessa's many monikers. The city was also known as the "pearl on the Black Sea," the "southern beauty," the "Palmyra of the south," the "capital of the south," and "Little Vienna."

5. Patricia Herlihy, *Odessa: A History, 1794–1914* (Cambridge, MA, 1986), 7.

6. On these visions of Moscow and St. Petersburg, see Joseph Bradley, *Muzhik and Muscovite: Urbanization in Late Imperial Russia* (Berkeley, CA, 1985), 59–69; Yuri M. Lotman, *Universe of the Mind: A Semiotic Theory of Culture* (Bloomington, IN, 1990), 191–203; and Katerina Clark, *Petersburg, Crucible of Cultural Revolution* (Cambridge, MA, 1995), 3–16.

7. Quote from Frederick W. Skinner, "City Planning in Russia: The Development of Odessa, 1789–1892" (Ph.D. diss., Princeton University, 1973), 174.

8. M. L. Harvey, "The Development of Russian Commerce on the Black Sea and Its Significance" (Ph.D. diss., University of California, 1938), 159.

9. Frederick W. Skinner, "Odessa and the Problem of Urban Modernization," in *The City in Late Imperial Russia*, ed. Michael F. Hamm (Bloomington, IN, 1986), 213.

10. Weinberg, *Revolution of 1905*, 13.

11. Patricia Herlihy, "Commerce and Architecture in Odessa in Late Imperial Russia," in *Commerce in Russian Urban Culture, 1861–1914*, ed. William Craft Brumfield et al. (Washington, DC, 2001), 180–83.

12. Herlihy, *Odessa*, 125–27 and 258–62.

13. *Census of 1897*, 152–53. For comparative figures, see A. G. Rashin, *Naselenie Rossii za 100 let (1811–1913 g.g.). Statisticheskie ocherki* (Moscow, 1956).

14. Zvi Gitelman, *A Century of Ambivalence: The Jews of Russia and the Soviet Union, 1881 to the Present* (New York, 1988), 59.

15. Steven J. Zipperstein, *The Jews of Odessa: A Cultural History, 1794–1881* (Stanford, CA, 1985), especially 70–113.

16. Lucy S. Dawidowicz, "Introduction: The World of East European Jewry," in *The Golden Tradition: Jewish Life and Thought in Eastern Europe*, ed. Lucy S. Dawidowicz (New York, 1967), 26.

17. Skinner, "Odessa and the Problem of Urban Modernization," 214 and 229.

See also Weinberg, *Revolution of 1905*, 16–18. The *Census of 1897*, 137, also shows that Jews were firmly in control of some of the leading sectors of the city's economy.

18. Skinner, "City Planning," 281–95, describes the construction boom of the 1870s, 1880s, and 1890s.

19. Weinberg, *Revolution of 1905*, 13.

20. N. Vasilevskii, *Ocherk sanitarnogo polozheniia g. Odessy* (Odessa, 1901).

21. Patricia Herlihy, "Odessa Memories," in *Odessa Memories*, ed. Nicolas V. Iljine, 8–9.

22. Skinner, "Odessa and the Problem of Urban Modernization," 216; Weinberg, *Revolution of 1905*, 20–21.

23. For a detailed description of economic development during the second half of the nineteenth century, see S. Ia. Borovoi, "Polozhenie rabochego klassa Odessi v XIX i nachale XX v. Istochnikovedcheskie zametki," in *Iz istorii rabochego klassa revoliutsionnogo dvizheniia* (Moscow, 1958), 308–18. See also Skinner, "City Planning," 295–307 and 325-26. On foreign investment, see Herlihy, *Odessa*, 190–93; and Skinner, "Odessa and the Problem of Urban Modernization," 216. Health spas and treatments offered are listed in *Vsia Odessa*, 81–101. On the development of Odessa's tourist industry, see McReynolds, *Russia at Play*, 165, 174, and 190–92.

24. Quoted in Skinner, "Odessa and the Problem of Urban Modernization," 231.

25. Herlihy, *Odessa*, 283–94.

26. The events of the 1905–1907 period are well-covered in the literature, especially in Weinberg, *Revolution of 1905*. See also Skinner, "Odessa and the Problem of Urban Modernization," 230–33; Jeremiah Schneiderman, *Sergei Zubatov and Revolutionary Marxism: The Struggle for the Working Class in Tsarist Russia* (Ithaca, NY, 1976), 286–332; and Kovbasiuk, *Odessa*, 79–87.

27. Anti-Jewish pogroms occurred in Odessa in 1821, 1849, 1859, 1871, 1881, and 1905. On nineteenth-century pogroms, see Zipperstein, *Jews of Odessa*, 20, 112, and 114–128; Herlihy, *Odessa*, 258, 281, 293, 295, 297, 299–308, 311, 335, 351, 353, and 354; and Jonathan Frankel, *Prophecy and Politics: Socialism, Nationalism, and the Russian Jews, 1862–1917* (Cambridge, 1981), 51, 54, and 135. On the 1905 pogrom, see especially Weinberg, *Revolution of 1905*, 164–87. See also John Klier and Shlomo Lambroza, eds., *Pogroms: Anti-Jewish Violence in Modern Russian History* (Cambridge, 1992).

28. Skinner, in "Odessa and the Problem of Urban Modernization," 216, reports that grain exports fell from 147 million pood in 1903 to 45.5 million in 1908. Meanwhile, membership in the first two merchants' guilds declined from 956 in 1906 to 639 in 1909.

29. Quoted in Kovbasiuk, *Odessa*, 106.

30. Herlihy, *Odessa*, 309–10.

31. Guido Hausmann, "Der Numerus clausus für jüdische Studenten im Zarenreich," *Jahrbücher für Geschichte Osteuropas* 41, no. 4 (1993): 509–31.

32. Christoph Gassenschmidt, *Jewish Liberal Politics in Tsarist Russia, 1900–1914: The Modernization of Russian Jewry* (New York, 1995), 115.

33. Herlihy, *Odessa*, 273.

34. Skinner, "Odessa and the Problem of Urban Modernization," p. 218.

35. For some of the many complaints lodged by foreign sea captains regarding large-scale theft and corruption in Odessa's port, see Great Britain, Foreign Office, F. O. 371, *General Correspondence, Political: Russia*, especially 1907, vol. 322, 311–27, 330–36, and 337–40; and 1911, vol. 1218, 62–63.

36. For evidence of police corruption, see Gosudarstvennyi arkhiv Rossiiskoi federatsii (hereafter GARF), *f.* 102, *op.* 215, *d.* 43, "O zloupotrebleniiakh chinov Odesskoi politsii po vydachy zagranichnykh pasportov nachal 24 marta 1909." For an example of official discussion of the activities of Odessan thieves outside Odessa, see GARF, *f.* 102, *op.* 215, *d.* 50, *ch.* 2, "O grabezhykh i razboiakh sovershennykh shaiki Saitskago." For one of many reports of thieves impersonating investigative police

agents in Odessa, see Gosudarstvennyi arkhiv Odesskoi oblasti (hereafter GAOO), f. 314, op. 2, d. 9, ll. 246–47.

37. See, for example, S. P. Beletskii, *Rozysknoi al'bom*, vyp. 1, *Vory-Karmanniki (Marvikhery)* (St. Petersburg, 1913). See also GARF, f. 1742, "Kollektsiia fotoportretov i fotografii lits, prokhodivshikh po delam politseiskikh uchrezhdenii."

38. See, for example, an article detailing the capture in Moldavanka of a gang of eleven thieves implicated in the murder of an Odessa merchant. *Vestnik politsii*, 20 January 1908, 22.

39. "Vstrecha Novago goda," *OL*, 1 January 1912; "Mimokhodom," *OL*, 3 January 1912; and "Novogodnyi pozhar," *OL*, 1 January 1912.

40. Sosnovskii's personal listing in the 1914 city directory shows that he was a member of more than a dozen charitable associations. *Vsia Odessa*, 383.

41. "Mimokhodom," *OL*, 3 January 1912.

42. On *obshchestvennost'* as "educated society," see Edith W. Clowes, Samuel D. Kassow, and James L. West, eds., *Between Tsar and People: Educated Society and the Quest for Public Identity in Late Imperial Russia* (Princeton, NJ, 1991), 3–6.

43. "Obshchestvennost' v Odesse," *OL*, 1 January 1912.

44. "Slukhi i fakti," *OL*, 8 January 1912.

45. "Odessa pod vodoi," *OL*, 29 May 1912.

46. Skinner, "Odessa and the Problem of Urban Modernization," 216.

47. "Nashi besedy. O krazhakh" *OL*, 16 December 1912.

48. For coverage of election-day happenings including reported disturbances, see *OP*, 25 and 26 October 1912, and "Zhaloby izbiratelei," 31 October 1912.

49. Gassenschmidt, *Jewish Liberal Politics in Tsarist Russia*, 115 and 205. See also Kovbasiuk, *Odessa*, 107–8.

50. "Novaia Duma" and "Vybory glasnykh dumy. Rezul'taty," *OL*, 5 May 1913, 4. See also GAOO, f. 2, op. 11, d. 58, "Spiski kuptsev i vladeltsev torgovykh zavedenii. Raporty i perepiska vyborakh glasnykh Odesskoi Gor. Dumy".

51. For participation of ROPiT and other port workers in the uprisings of 1905, see Weinberg, *Revolution of 1905*, 64–65, 110–11, 120, 129, 171, and 214–15. On reports of strikes and worker demands in the 1912–1914 period, see the following articles entitled "Zabastovki" in *OL*: 14 April and 5 and 12 June 1912; and *OP*, 11 July 1914. See also Kovbasiuk, *Odessa*, 112 and 118.

52. For strikes in Slobodka-Romanovka, see articles entitled "Zabastovka v probochnom zavode," *OL*, 9 June 1912; and *OP*, 29 March 1914; and "Zabastovki i aresty," *OP*, 27 April 1914, 4; and others.

53. Of the many reports of strikes in Peresyp, see "Zabastovka," *OL*, 14 and 17 April 1912; "Na fabrikakh, na zavodakh, i v masterskikh," *OL*, 2 May 1912; "Zabastovki," *OL*, 12 June 1912; and "Den' 1 maia v Odesse," *OP*, 2 May 1914.

2—Horrors of Life

1. Leonid Utesov, "Moia Odessa," *Moskva* 9 (1964): 134.

2. Moskvich, *Putevoditel'*, 1, 47, and 57. Moskvich was a prolific writer, author of a series of travelogues covering major tourist sites in imperial Russia including Moscow, St. Petersburg, Warsaw, the Crimea, the Caucasus, the Volga, and Finland. For general discussion of his work in Odessa, see G. Zlenko, "Moskvich iz Odessy," *Vecherniaia Odessa*, 2 October 1982; M. Bel'skii, "Putevoditeli Grigoriia Moskvicha," *Vecherniaia Odessa*, 14 July 1990; and S. Muranov and A. Popov, "S Moskvichom po Odesse," *Vecherniaia Odessa*, 17–20 September 1994.

3. Moskvich, *Putevoditel'*, 1–10, 53–56.

4. Moskvich, *Putevoditel'*, 82–83 and 119.

5. Jacob A. Riis, *How the Other Half Lives* (New York, 1997). On Sims and other crusading London writers who joined the rhetoric of colonialism with calls for urban reform, see Walkowitz, *City of Dreadful Delight*, 15–39. On the political implications of

"legibility" and "illegibility" in the urban environment, see James C. Scott, *Seeing Like a State: How Certain Schemes to Improve the Human Condition Have Failed* (New Haven, CT, 1998), 54.

6. *OOG za 1912*, 11, includes a full accounting of ship traffic into Odessa in 1912. Moskvich, *Putevoditel'*, 3–4, includes information on passenger service.

7. Skinner, "City Planning," 303–4. For more on Boffo, see Herlihy, "Commerce and Architecture in Odessa in Late Imperial Russia," 184–85.

8. For demographic information on port residents, see the *Census of 1897*, iv, 2–3, and 160–61.

9. Schneiderman, *Sergei Zubatov and Revolutionary Marxism*, 287.

10. V. K. Vasil'evskii, "Polozhenie portovykh rabochikh v Odesse," *Trudy Odesskogo otdela Russkogo obshchestva okhraneniia narodnogo zdraviia* 4 (1904).

11. Weinberg, *Revolution of 1905*, 46.

12. "Portovye rabochie," *OL*, 1 May 1912.

13. On severe competition for work forcing down wages, see articles entitled "Portovye rabochie," in *OL*, 19 and 25 January, and 5 February 1912. Many of the five million Jews living in the Pale of Settlement—a group of provinces in western Russia acquired in the partitions of Poland—resided in small market towns called *shtetls*.

14. Weinberg, *Revolution of 1905*, 45.

15. Vasil'evskii, "Polozhenie portovykh rabochikh v Odesse," 36–49, states that the majority of day laborers on the docks made less than 10 rubles a month, with average expenses for food and lodging running at between 5 and 6 rubles, not including vodka. "Portovye rabochie," *OL*, 25 January 1912, says that during times of high unemployment, the average pay for an hour of unloading would fall from 30–35k (kopecks) to around 25k. When work was in short supply, many workers earned less than 75k per day. In good times, however, a port worker might earn as much as 3–4 rubles per day. See "Portovye rabochie," *OL*, 19 September 1912. GAOO, *f.* 314, *op.* 2, *d.* 11, *l.* 67, lists 14 cafeterias, 9 restaurants, 10 taverns licensed to sell only tea and soft drinks, 2 taverns selling hard liquor, and 4 food stalls. In terms of short-term housing, there was 1 hotel, 3 boarding houses, and 8 flophouses in the district.

16. For some of the many examples of *OL* stories that invoked such images, see "Dnevnik proisshestvii" (hereafter "DP"), 2 March 1912; "DP," 19 January 1912; "Napadeniia," 6 November 1912; "Grabezhi," 5 September 1912; "DP," 5 September 1912; "Ubiitsa-simuliant," 22 March 1912; and "Ubiistvo," 13 January 1912.

17. "Nochlezhki v portu," *OL*, 15 February 1912.

18. "Osmotr nochlezhnykh priiutov," *OL*, 21 March 1912.

19. "Nochlezhnye doma," *OL*, 4 February 1912.

20. These raids were particularly common in the summertime. See, for example, *OL*, "Oblava," 5 July 1912; "Eksploatator," 17 July 1912; and "Oblava," 2 August 1912.

21. "'Merzavchik' i polushki," *OL*, 4 February 1912. Annual revenue from such sales was estimated at more than 7,500 rubles, "enough to feed lunch to 1,260 people every day for a year (at an average cost of 6k a day for lunch)."

22. "Tainye prodavtsy vodki," *OL*, 1 June 1912.

23. The quotations included in the following discussion are drawn from *OL* articles by Isaev: "V nochnom traktire," 14 February 1912; "Nochlevzhki v portu," 15 February 1912; "V portovoi nochlezhke," 14 March 1912; "Portovaia obzhorka," 29 March 1912; "Sredi portovykh rabochikh," 2 May 1912; "Sredi portovykh rabochikh," 5 August 1912; and "V nochnom traktire," 18 August 1912.

24. "V portovoi chitalne," *OL*, 16 March 1912.

25. "Sredi portovykh rabochikh," *OL*, 2 May and 5 August 1912.

26. "Traktir i portovyi rabochii (Iz pis'ma v redaktsiiu)," *OL*, 23 March 1912; and "Portovyia nochlezhni," *OL*, 12 April 1912.

27. For expression of these views in *OL*, see the columns by Isaev and Degterev cited above. The paper campaigned quite vigorously for the institution of insurance

for port workers. See, "Strakhovanie portovykh rabochikh," *OL*, 8, 10, and 14 February 1912; and "Nashi besedy. Strakhovanie portovykh rabochikh," *OL*, 16 February 1912. For a story regarding the failure of private charities to provide necessary services to port district residents, see "Slukhi i fakty," *OL*, 25 January 1912.

28. "Osmotr nochlezhnykh priiutov," *OL*, 21 March 1912.

29. "Slukhi i fakty," *OL*, 24 and 25 January 1912.

30. "Portovyia nochlezhni," *OL*, 4 April 1912.

31. See in *OL:* "Portovye rabochie," 19 January and 5 February 1912; "Sredi portovykh rabochikh," 4 March and 7 April 1912; "V Odesskom portu," 8 April 1912; "Naplyv rabochikh," 4 July 1912; and "Portovye rabochie," 19 September 1912.

32. "K ustroistvu khlebnoi gavani," *OL*, 3 January 1912; and "Portovye rabochie," *OL*, 1 May 1912.

33. "Sredi portovykh rabochikh," *OL*, 4 March 1912.

34. "Pomoshch portovym rabochim," *OL*, 12 May 1912.

35. "Sredi portovykh rabochikh," *OL*, 12 April 1912; "Bezplatnye obedy dlia portovykh rabochikh," *OL*, 12 May 1912.

36. "Sredi portovykh rabochikh," *OL*, 12 April 1912.

37. "Nashi besedy. O krazhakh" *OL*, 16 December 1912.

38. See note 35, chapter 1, above.

39. Weinberg, *Revolution of 1905*, 5–6. For demographic information on Slobodka-Romanovka residents, see the *Census of 1897*, iv and 12–13; and "Sud i Slobodka," *OL*, 19 February 1912.

40. Utesov, "Moia Odessa," 135. While no statistical evidence exists to support this, the raw census data from 1919 show that 75 per cent of district residents were Ukrainian, with Russian comprising another 15 per cent. Jews and Poles were the next most populous groups in Peresyp, each making up about 3 per cent of the total. See GAOO, *f.* 16, *op.* 124, *d.* 8997, "Uchet naseleniia 1919 g. po Peresypskom uchastku".

41. "Dni nashei zhizni. Iarmarka," *OP*, 15 September 1915, reported that "all the city" came to Peresyp's annual autumn fair but that, with the outbreak of the war, the fair lost much of its former luster.

42. GAOO, *f.* 314, *op.* 2, *d.* 11, *l.* 64–65.

43. GAOO, *f.* 316, *op.* 2, *d.* 11, *l.* 50–54.

44. Moskvich, *Putevoditel'*, 83.

45. "Deputatsiia u g. Odesskago gradonachalnika," *OL*, 7 February 1912.

46. Weinberg, *Revolution of 1905*, 39.

47. "Dni nashei zhizni," *OP*, 23 January 1914.

48. Weinberg, *Revolution of 1905*, 5–6, 8, 36–37, 40, and 49.

49. "Torzhestvo na Peresypi," *OL*, 7 October 1912.

50. Vasil'evskii, N. *Ocherk sanitarnogo polozheniia g. Odessy* (Odessa, 1901), 17.

51. "O postroike zdaniia deshevykh kvartir," *OL*, 10 January 1912.

52. "Pavlovskiia zdaniia deshevykh kvartir," *OL*, 23 February 1912.

53. Weinberg, *Revolution of 1905*, 35–36.

54. Skinner, "Odessa and the Problem of Urban Modernization," 222–23.

55. Skinner, "City Planning," 318–21.

56. On bathing in polluted waters, see "Slukhi i fakty," *OL*, 1 June 1912. For reports of epidemics, see especially *Epidemiia chumy i kholery 1910 goda v Odesse* (Odessa, 1911). On industrial accidents, see "Slukhi i fakty," *OL*, 6 October 1912.

57. "Dni nashei zhizni. V lodke-po Slobodke!" *OP*, 9 July 1914. *Odesskaia pochta* made the point graphically in a 1912 editorial cartoon captioned "Public Improvements in the Odessa Outskirts." In the first cell, under the phrase "A funeral procession in the city," a group of well-dressed people are shown walking on a paved road. The second cell, titled "A funeral procession in the outskirts," depicts a couple slogging through thigh-high mud. See [editorial cartoon], *OP*, 25 December 1912. For discussion of the political ramifications during the 1905 revolution of official neglect of

the outskirts, see Weinberg, *Revolution of 1905*, 87, 90–91, 125, and 229.

58. Skinner, "City Planning," 322.

59. "Dni nashei zhizni. V lodke-po Slobodke!" Sirkis, who also wrote for the Odessa satirical journal, *Krokodil*, was the father of Osip Kolychev, a Soviet poet popular in the 1930s, especially for the hit song, "Young Guard." Many thanks to Elena Karakina of the Odessa Literary Museum and especially to Sergei Lushchik for providing this information.

60. "Dni nashei zhizni. Golos," *OP*, 10 April 1915.

61. Of the many reports of violent incidents on Peresyp's Moskovskaia Street in 1912, see "DP" articles in *OL* on 26 January, 1 February, 7 February, 1 August, 2 November, and 6 November. For an example of an incident on Gorodskaia Street in Slobodka-Romanovka, see "Napadeniia i grabezhi," *OL*, 2 October 1912. For sample reports of muggings on other Slobodka streets in 1912, see "DP" articles in *OL* on 2 October and 7 November.

62. See, for example, "Na pochve revnosti," *OL*, 1 May 1912; and "Otnusil nos," *OL*, 21 February 1912.

63. "DP," *OL*, 4 November 1912.

64. "DP," *OL*, 4 September 1912.

65. "Ubiistvo na Peresypi," *OL*, 31 October 1912.

66. "Draka," *OL*, 3 May 1912.

67. "Raskrytie zverskago ubiistva," *OL*, 9 August 1912, 3.

68. "Perestrelka na Peresypi," *OP*, 2 January 1916.

69. All quotations in my discussion of the Stefanovskii case here and below are from: "Brat na brata (krovavaia drama)," *OP*, 17 May 1915; and "Za oskorblenie materi (Drama na Slobodke-Romanovke)," *OP*, 14 November 1915.

70. "Uzhasy zhizni (Iz zaly okruzhnago suda)," *OP*, 1 March 1914.

71. Laura Engelstein, *The Keys to Happiness: Sex and the Search for Modernity in Fin-de-Siècle Russia* (Ithaca, NY, 1992), 360 passim, discusses the public's fascination with sex, pointing specifically to the popular press as a location for the exploration of sexual practices "unrelated to family life and free from community control."

72. See Neuberger, *Hooliganism*, 60–63 and 264–72 passim.

73. *OOG* figures show a significant jump in convictions for disorderly conduct, from 55 in 1911 and 65 in 1912 to 589 in 1913 and 470 in 1914, a difference directly attributable to arrests associated with increasing labor unrest.

74. For examples of other cases of rape in Peresyp and Slobodka-Romanovka, see "Uzhasy zhizni," *OP*, 12 June 1914; "Nasiliia," *OL*, 4 April 1912; "Dikari," *OL*, 12 September 1912; "DP," *OL*, 1 September 1912; and "DP," *OL*, 5 May 1912. For an example of coverage of fights over women, see "Otnosil nos," *OL*, 21 February 1912; and "Na pochve revnosti," *OL*, 1 May 1912.

75. For sample stories regarding domestic violence against women, see "Semeinaia drama," *OL*, 28 April 1912; "Zverskoe ubiistvo," *OL*, 10 June 1912; and "Ubiistvo i samoubiistvo," *OL*, 20 July 1912. For an extreme case of child abuse, see "Istiazanie," *OL*, 22 April 1912. On fistfights, see Schneiderman, *Sergei Zubatov*, 292.

76. "Uzhasy zhizni," *OP*, 12 June 1914.

3—City of Thieves

1. Quotation from Isaak Babel's story, "The King," in *The Collected Stories of Isaac Babel*, trans. Walter Morrison (New York, 1955), 205.

2. "Dni nashei zhizni. V mire prestupnikov," *OP*, 7 September 1912.

3. The character of the gangster "king" Benya [Benia] Krik appears in a number of Babel's stories: "The King," "How It Was Done in Odessa," "The Father," "Lyubka [Liubka] the Cossack," "Odessa," "Sunset," "Froim Grach," and "Justice in Brackets."

4. Herlihy, *Odessa*, 273. See also Tat'iana Dontsova, *Moldavanka: Zapiski Kraeveda* (Odessa, 2001).

5. On industrial development in the 1880s and 1890s, see Weinberg, *Revolution of 1905*, 5.

6. See Moskvich, *Putevoditel'*, 80, and Herlihy, *Odessa*, 273.

7. Moskvich, *Putevoditel'*, 81.

8. GAOO, *f.* 316, *op.* 2, *d.* 11, *ll.* 56–61.

9. For examples of stories focusing on the lack of adequate public services in Moldavanka, see "Slukhi i fakty," *OL*, 1 June 1912; "Interesy Moldavanki," *OL*, 28 April 1912; and "Slukhi i fakty," *OL*, 2 February 1912.

10. "Dni nashei zhizni. Moldavanka noch'iu," *OP*, 6 April 1912.

11. For a sampling of *OL* reports from early 1912 that relate to deaths or injuries resulting from poor housing conditions, see "DP" on 5, 11, and 29 January, and 10 March.

12. Quotations in this section are from the following Isaev pieces appearing in *OL*: "Na tolkuchem rynke," 20 April 1912; "Nosilshchiki tolkuchago rynka," 18 May 1912; and "'Tolkuchii,'" 9 September 1912.

13. "Na tolkuchem rynke," *OL*, 24 June 1912.

14. "Slukhi i fakty," *OL*, 22 January 1912.

15. For a smattering of the many possible examples reported in 1912 of the presence of thieves, prostitutes, and fencers of stolen goods at the flea market, see "DP" articles in *OL* on 11, 29, and 31 January, 9 February, 9 March, 5 July, and 2 December. For reports of rapes in the flea market, see "DP," *OL*, 2 December 1912; and "Gnusnoe nasilie," *OL*, 17 July 1912.

16. "Nosilshchiki tolkuchago rynka," *OL*, 18 May 1912.

17. See "Khodataistvo torgovtsev tolkuchago rynka," *OL*, 23 February 1912; "'Tolchok' i Moldavanka," *OL*, 18 February 1912; and "Ekran zhizni," *OP*, 7 May 1914.

18. Gerasimov, "'My ubivaem tol'ko svoikh'," 212–14, shows that while in terms of statistics Jews in Odessa were actually less likely than Russians to commit crime, investigative police records nonetheless demonstrate preoccupation with Jewish criminality.

19. "Dni nashei zhizni. V mire prestupnikov," *OP*, 7 September 1912.

20. "Slukhy i fakty," *OL*, 5 January 1912. "Belyi raby," *OP*, 7 September 1912, estimated that there were around 8,000 dvorniki working in Odessa, including some building owners in Moldavanka and Slobodka-Romanovka who personally acted in that capacity.

21. Of the many raids conducted in Moldavanka in 1912, see the articles in *OL*: "Arest vorov," 8 March; "'Skhodka' vorov," 22 June; and "Vorovskaia 'khovira'," 1 July.

22. See, for example, "Oblava," *OL*, 5 July 1912; "Eksploatator," *OL*, 17 July 1912; "Oblava," *OL*, 2 August 1912; and "Oblava," *OL*, 16 December 1912.

23. "Grandioznaia "oblava," *OL*, 4 December 1912.

24. The names of various "specialists" are drawn from several installments of a multipart series, "Dni nashei zhizni. V mire pristupnikov," that appeared in *OP* on 11 and 28 September 1912.

25. According to Beletskii, *Rozysknoi al'bom*, 9, this category of thieves (whom he refers to by a slighly different name, *marvikhery*) was made up primarily of non-Russians (Jews, Poles, and Greeks), who were especially prevalent "in the southern and western regions of Russia."

26. Per Beletskii, *Rozysknoi al'bom*, 11, the female equivalent "would offer to help a lady with her garment, which had gone asunder, and while doing so pick her pocket."

27. The term *kliukvenniki* may be derived from the slang phrase *razvesistaia kliukva* (often shortened simply to *kliukva*), which in translation means a spreading cranberry tree. In its common usage, the term is a farcical oxymoron referring to things that are not what they seem. My thanks to Mark Steinberg for making this connection.

28. For discussion of female shoplifting in New York, see Elaine Abelson, *When Ladies Go A-Thieving: Middle Class Shoplifters in the Victorian Department Store* (New York, 1989).

29. Counterfeiting was another crime closely associated with Moldavanka. See, for example, GAOO, *f.* 314, *op.* 2, *d.* 9, *ll.* 12–13 and 291–95

30. See, for example, "Gastroli," *OL,* 11 March 1912.

31. "Slukhi i fakty," *OL,* 26 January 1912.

32. "Pereodetyi v shansonetku vor," *OP,* 8 April 1914.

33. See "Arest 'korolevy' vorov," *OL,* 7 November 1912; and "Pokhopedenia 'korolevy vorovok,'" *OL,* 13 July 1912.

34. "Priezd 'korolia' vorov," *OL,* 8 March 1912.

35. "DP," *OL,* 5 January 1912.

36. "Kartinki Moldavanki," *OP,* 4 June 1915.

37. "Kartinki Moldavanki," *OP,* 4 June 1915.

38. "Odesskie vory i Borodinskiia torzhestva," *OP,* 27 August 1912. The thief known as "Morozhenshchik," whom Faust mentioned above, was also arrested at this occasion as were his two nephews.

39. "'Blagorodnyi' otprysk," *OL,* 19 August 1912.

40. "Dni nashei zhizni. V mire prestipnikov," *OP,* 18 September 1912.

41. Boris Briker, "The Underworld of Benia Krik and I. Babel's *Odessa Stories,*" *Canadian Slavonic Papers* 36, nos. 1–2 (1994): 119–22.

42. "Dni nashei zhizni. V mire prestipnikov," *OP,* 21 September 1912.

43. Among the many reports of muggings in Moldavanka in early 1912, see "DP" articles in *OL* for 3, 17, and 24 January, 1 and 21 February, and 10 March. For examples of violent street fights and assaults in 1912, see "DP" articles in *OL* for 10 and 24 January, 9 February, 5 June, and 6 November. See also "Izbieniia," *OL,* 22 May 1912; and "Ulichnaia rasprava," *OL,* 24 February 1912. For examples of murders and attempted murders on the street, see "Ubiistvo," *OL,* 11 September and 20 June 1912; "Pokushenie na ubiistvo," *OL,* 11 April 1912; and below.

44. "Dikie nravy," *OL,* 4 September 1912.

45. Many of the rapes reported in Moldavanka involved the attack by two or more males on young women or girls. The flea market was an especially common venue for such rapes. See, for example, "DP," *OL,* 2 December 1912; and "Gnusnoe nasilie," *OL,* 17 July 1912. For other instances of gang rape in Moldavanka see "DP," *OL,* 6 May 1912; "Nasilie," *OL,* 16 May 1912; and "Gnusnoe nasilie," *OP,* 8 May 1914. For instances of child molestation, see "Nasilie," *OL,* 16 May 1912; and "DP," *OL,* 2 August 1912. For cases of domestic violence, see "Ottseubiistvo," *OL,* 8 January 1912; "Koshmarnaia drama," *OL,* 13 June 1912; "DP," *OL,* 10 March 1912; "Mat' i doch' (Krovovaia drama)," *OP,* 25 May 1915; and "DP," *OL,* 6 December 1912.

46. "Zverskoe ubiistvo vorami nevinnago cheloveka," *OP,* 2 March 1914.

47. "Kalendar Odesskoi kopeiki. Dokole?" *Odesskaia kopeika,* 8 March 1914.

48. See, for example, "DP," *OL,* 14 January 1912; "DP," *OL,* 24 January 1912; and "Deti ulitsy," *OL,* 22 March 1912.

49. See "Uzhasy zhizni," *OL,* 23 May 1912; and "Nashi deti," *OL,* 21 June 1912.

50. "Dni nashei zhizni," *OP,* 11 April 1914.

51. "Kartinki Moldavanki," *OP,* 4 June 1915.

52. "Neschastnyia deti," *OL,* 22 March 1912,. For another example, see "Arest shaiki maloletnykh prestupnikov," *OP,* 23 January 1914.

53. Engelstein, *Keys to Happiness,* 274–98, analyzes the powerful symbolism of the juvenile prostitute who personified contemporary concerns about "the urban sexual threat" as well as the disintegration of morality associated with the "chaotic state" of urban lower-class family life.

54. "Na dne Odessy (Detskaia prostitutsiia)," *OP,* 4 June 1912, p. 4. Laurie Bernstein, *Sonia's Daughters: Prostitutes and Their Regulation in Imperial Russia* (Berkeley, CA,

1995), 43, notes that "[o]n the one hand, observers were outraged and disgusted by the idea of young girls catering to the sexual fancies of adult men. At the same time though, privileged society found something exciting and prurient about child prostitution."

55. "Kartinki Moldavanki," *OP,* 4 June 1915. Faust quotes some words of the little song: "Oy, mama I want to get married. Oy, mama, arrange me a marriage. I can't wait anymore, I need a young fiance!"

56. For more on such stereotypes, see Bernstein, *Sonia's Daughters,* 161–66 and below.

57. "Na dne Odessy (Detskaia prostitutsiia)," *OP,* 4 June 1912.

58. For more on concern about children of the street in St. Petersburg, see Neuberger, *Hooliganism,* 158–215. On the phenomenon in New York, see Christine Stansell, *City of Women: Sex and Class in New York, 1789–1860* (Urbana, IL, 1987), 193–216.

59. "'Moldavanka,' eia vragi i druz'ia," *OP,* 12 October 1915.

60. "Deti ulitsy," *OL,* 23 February 1912.

61. "Dni nashei zhizni. V mire prestipnikov," *OP,* 11 September 1912.

62. "Kartinki Moldavanki," *OP,* 4 June 1915.

63. "Dni nashei zhizni. V mire prestipnikov," *OP,* 11 September 1912.

64. "K borbe s nishchenstvom," *OL,* 1 March 1912.

65. See, for instance, "Iniia vorovki," *OL,* 11 February 1912; "Sovershennye krazhi," *OL,* 31 January 1912; "Krazha i zaderzheniia," *OL,* 11 January 1912; "Arest shaiki maloletnykh prestupnikov," *OP,* 23 January 1914; and "Devochka-vorovka," *OL,* 28 July 1912.

66. "Byket (Vorovki—'znamenitosti')," *OP,* 8 January 1915.

67. "Dni nashei zhizni. V mire prestipnikov," *OP,* 11 September 1912.

68. "Deti ulitsakh," *OL,* 1 May 1912.

69. "Deti ulitsakh," *OL,* 1 May 1912.

70. The various competing, contradictory and overlapping explanations of juvenile crime offered by Russian journalists, jurists, criminologists, social reformers, and other contemporary observers stressed biological and moral as well as social factors. For more on this, see especially Neuberger, *Hooliganism,* and Engelstein, *Keys to Happiness.*

71. "Kartinki Moldavanki," *OP,* 4 June 1915.

72. "Kartinki Moldavanki," *OP,* 4 June 1915.

73. "'Moldavanka,' eia vragi i druz'ia," *OP,* 14 October 1915.

74. Sam Bass Warner, Jr., "Slums and Skyscrapers: Urban Images, Symbols, and Ideology," in *Cities of the Mind: Images and Themes of the City in the Social Sciences,* ed. Lloyd Rodwin and Robert M. Hollister (New York, 1984), 186.

75. "Kartinki Moldavanki," *OP,* 4 June 1915.

76. "'Moldavanka,' eia vragi i druz'ia," *OP,* 14 October 1915.

77. "'Moldavanka,' eia vragi i druz'ia," *OP,* 15 October 1915.

78. "'Moldavanka,' eia vragi i druz'ia," *OP,* 16 October 1915.

79. "Dom No. 28," *OP,* 13 August 1915.

80. "Dom No. 28" *OP,* 13 August 1915.

81. "Obratite vnimanie!" *OP,* 7 March 1914.

82. "Kartinki Moldavanki," *OP,* 4 June 1915.

83. "Kartinki Moldavanki," *OP,* 4 June 1915.

84. "Dni nashei zhizni. Otkliki," *OP,* 6 September 1912.

85. "Dni nashei zhizni. Popularnye," *OP,* 9 January 1915.

86. "Dni nashei zhizni," *OP,* 1 February 1912.

87. "Rodnaia kartinka," *OP,* 1 June 1913.

88. See, among others, "Dni nashei zhizni," *OP,* on 1 February and 1 June 1912; and "Alekseevskii bazar," *OL,* 16 June 1912.

89. "K delam moldavanskago ssudo-sberegatelnago tovairshchestva," *OL*, 1 March 1912. For a listing of officially chartered organizations and associations, see "Mestnyia uchrezhdeniia," *Vsia Odessa*, 142–77. For a discussion of labor organizations before and during 1905, see Weinberg, *Revolution of 1905*, 54–82 passim.

90. Weinberg, *Revolution of 1905*, 205.

91. For more on Jewish criminality as a means to construct a modern identity distinct to Odessa, see Gerasimov, "'My ubivaem tol'ko svoikh.'"

92. For a comparative example, see Danil Buyarin, "*Goyim Naches*, or Modernity and the Manliness of the Mentsh," in *Modernity, Culture, and "the Jew,"'* ed. Bryan Cheyette and Laura Marcus (Stanford, CA, 1998), 63–87.

93. Babel, *Collected Stories*, 212.

4—Under the Cover of Night

1. Valentin Kataev, *A White Sail Gleams* (Moscow, 1954), 64.

2. Quotations in this and the following paragraph are drawn from: "Dni nashei zhizni. Iz nabliudenii," *OP*, 10 November 1914; "Ulitsa," *OP*, 18 June 1915; and "Khodataistvo o vyselenii 'meblirashek,'" *OP*, 26 August 1915.

3. "Pornografiia," *OL*, 7 March 1912; and "Slukhi i fakty," *OL*, 27 January 1912.

4. "Ulitsa," *OP*, 18 June 1915.

5. Kasson, *Rudeness and Civility*, 100.

6. Ruth Harris, *Murders and Madness: Medicine, Law, and Society in the Fin de Siècle* (Oxford, 1989), 328. See also Walkowitz, *City of Dreadful Delight*, 20. For similar views in St. Petersburg, see Neuberger, *Hooliganism*. On Paris, see the pioneering study by Louis Chevalier, *Laboring Classes and Dangerous Classes in Paris during the First Half of the Nineteenth Century*, (New York, 1973).

7. T. J. Clark, *The Painting of Modern Life: Paris in the Art of Manet and His Followers* (Princeton, NJ, 1984), 79.

8. Clark, *Painting of Modern Life*. See also Walkowitz, *City of Dreadful Delight*.

9. See Moskvich, *Putevoditel'*, 11–15; Skinner, "City Planning," 281–95; GAOO, *f. 2, op.* 11, *d.* 58, "Spiski kuptsev i vladeltsev torgovykh zavedenii," 59–108; and *Spravochnaia kniga ob Odesskikh soslovnykh kuptsakh i voobshche o litsakh i uchrezhdeniiakh torgovo-promyshlennago klassa po g. Odessa na 1916 god* (Odessa, 1916).

10. Moskvich, *Putevoditel'*, 11–12, 19–21. The rate for one night at a suite at the Londonskaia was approximately the same as a month's rent, with maid service and tea, at a boarding house.

11. Moskvich, *Putevotidel'*, 21–22 and 25.

12. On living conditions, see Vasil'evskii, *Ocherk*, 17. Conclusions about participation of central city residents in government and voluntary associations derived from analysis of *Vsia Odessa*.

13. *Census of 1897*, 2–3.

14. On living conditions of university students, see "V studencheskoi 'stolovke,'" *OL*, 21 January 1912; "Studencheskoe zhit'e-byte," *OL*, 5 February 1912; and "Zhizn' studenta," *OP*, 2 June 1916.

15. *Census of 1897*, 2–3; and Vasil'evskii, *Ocherk*, 6–7 and 17.

16. Moskvich, *Putevoditel'*, 80.

17. See, for example, "Na Privoze," *OL*, 20 December 1912; and "Predprazdnichnyi bazar," *OL*, 23 March 1912.

18. GAOO, *f.* 314, *op.* 2, *d.* 11, ll. 41–48.

19. For a sampling of reports of theft at Old Bazaar, see "DP" articles in *OL* for 3 and 4 October and 3 November 1912. For thefts at Privoz, see "DP" articles for 5 September and 6 December 1912; and others.

20. See, for example, "DP," *OL*, 26 February 1912; "Kreditor i dolzhnik," *OL*, 4 January 1912; "DP," *OL*, 19 February 1912 and 2 December 1912; "Ubiistvo," *OL*, 6 January 1912; "Pokushenie na ubiistvo," *OL*, 24 July 1912; and "DP," *OL*, 7 September 1912.

21. "Slukhi i fakty," *OL*, 22 August 1912.

22. The tavern was described in vivid detail by Kuprin in his short story, "Sasha" (originally titled in Russian as "Gambrinus.") See A. Kuprin, *Sasha*, trans. Douglas Ashby (London, 1920), 9–38.

23. Herlihy, *Odessa*, 264–65.

24. This description of the clientele of various drinking establishments draws heavily on Skinner, "Odessa and the Problem of Urban Modernization," 227.

25. See, for example, "DP," *OL* for 16 March 1912, 4 July 1912, 2 November 1912, and 24 February 1913. See also "Iz-za kopeiki," *OL*, 3 October 1912.

26. For the theft report, see "DP," *OL*, 20 January 1912. For an example of robbery, see "Napadeniia i grabezhi," *OL*, 2 October 1912. On the exploits of Krasnoglav, see "DP," *OL*, 3 October 1912. Krasnoglav's victim died a short time later. See "Nozhevyia raspravy," *OL*, 6 October 1912.

27. "Debosh v 'Iubilei,'" *OP*, 30 April 1914.

28. "Zhenshchina," *OP*, 10 June 1914.

29. For contemporary views on a woman's "natural" morality, see Stephen P. Frank, "Narratives within Numbers: Women, Crime, and Judicial Statistics in Imperial Russia, 1834–1913," *Russian Review* 55, no. 4 (1996): 544.

30. "Pod pokrovnom nochi," *OP*, 5 April 1915.

31. "Dni nashei zhizni. Traktirnoe zlo," *OP*, 6 April 1915.

32. From the mid-nineteenth century onward, the tsarist government regulated commercial sex through a system that licensed brothels and individual prostitutes. Clandestine prostitutes were those who worked without a "yellow ticket," as the licenses were known. For a thorough analysis of this practice, see Bernstein, *Sonia's Daughters*.

33. See especially "Kulisy Odessy," *OP*, 22 May 1912.

34. "Nochnoi osmotr," *OP*, 5 January 1913.

35. "Bor'ba s prostitutsiei, sutenerami i nochym razvratom. (Iz prikaza odessck. politsiimeistera)," *OP*, 25 June 1914.

36. Bernstein, *Sonia's Daughters*, 50–51.

37. See "Kak-zhe byt'?" *OP*, 27 June 1914; "Ulitsa," *OP*, 18 June 1915; and "Dni nashei zhizni. V mire prestipnikov," *OP*, 11 September 1912.

38. "Kulisy Odessy," *OP*, 22 May 1912.

39. "Na dne Odessy (Oblava na prostitutok)," *OP*, 26 June 1914.

40. "O tom, o sem," *OP*, 26 June 1914.

41. "Bystrotechnost'," *Krokodil*, no. 15, March 1912.

42. "Kulisy Odessy," *OP*, 22 May 1912.

43. Engelstein, *Keys to Happiness*, 186.

44. For the use of these terms, see "O tom, o sem," *OP*, 26 June 1914; and "Dni nashei zhizni," *OP*, 18 December 1914. Bernstein, *Sonia's Daughters*, 146, finds that such attitudes were common throughout Russia.

45. "Kulisy Odessy," *OP*, 22 May 1912; "Na dne Odessy (Detskaia prostitutsiia)," *OP*, 4 June 1912; "Dni nashei zhizni," *OP*, 18 December 1914.

46. "Lektsiia o prostitutsii," *OL*, 15, 26, and 28 February 1912. On the association of domestic servants with prostitution, see also Bernstein, *Sonia's Daughters*, 107–8; and Barbara Alpern Engel, *Between the Fields and the City: Women, Work, and Family in Russia, 1861–1914* (Cambridge, 1994), 177.

47. "Kulisy Odessy," *OP*, 22 May 1912.

48. "Mat' i syn," *OP*, 5 November 1914.

49. "Na dne Odessy (Oblava na prostitutok)," *OP*, 26 June 1914.

50. "Drama zhizni," *OL*, 15 February 1912.

51. See, for example, "Uzhasy nashikh dnei," *OP*, 15 January 1914; and "Prodavtsy zhivogo tovara," *OL*, 25 May 1912. For discussions of "white slavery" in Russia, see Bernstein, *Sonia's Daughters*, 147–49; and Engelstein, *Keys to Happiness*, 279–80, 304, and 308.

52. For stories about young women from Odessa ending up in Constantinople, Calcutta, and Buenos Aires as well as for analysis of the "white slave" trade in general, see Edward J. Bristow, *Prostitution and Prejudice: The Jewish Fight against White Slavery, 1870–1939* (New York, 1983), 99, 107, 120, 124, 133, 190, 192, and 202.

53. "Belaia rabynia, "*OP,* 2 February 1915.

54. "Arest prodavtsa zhivogo tovara," *OL,* 9 October 1912.

55. See Bernstein, *Sonia's Daughters,* 161–66.

56. See Bristow, *Prostitution and Prejudice.*

57. See Bristow, *Prostitution and Prejudice.*

58. All quotations included in this section are from the following articles: "'Muzh vernulsia!'" *OP,* 20 March 1914; "Arest 'Khipesnits,'" *OL,* 16 February 1912; "Khipesnitsy," *OL,* 17 July and 14 October 1912; and "DP," *OL,* 11 March 1912.

59. "Zhiteiskaia drama," *OL,* 30 September 1912.

60. Moskvich, *Putevoditel',* 78–79.

61. "Kulisy Odessy," *OP,* 22 May 1912; and "O tom, o sem," *OP,* 26 June 1914.

62. "Nasilie," *OL,* 6 July 1912.

63. "Skromnyia rechi. Gluboe nasilie," *OL,* 7 July 1912.

64. GAOO, *f.* 314, *op.* 2, *d.* 11, *ll.* 22–25, lists the addresses of dozens of licensed brothels and boarding houses operating in the neighborhood, as well as a wide variety of known criminal "haunts."

65. See, for example, Odesskaia gorodskaia duma, *Izvestiia Odesskoi gorodskoi dumy,* September 1911, 2009–2014.

66. See, for example, "DP," *OL,* 4 September 1912.

67. See, for example, "Ubiistvo prostitutki," *OP,* 12 April 1913. The details of a full-scale investigation leading to the arrest of a former lover for the murder of another prostitute in the area appear in GAOO, *f.* 314, *op.* 2, *d.* 9, 124–35. Even if prostitutes sometimes suffered at the hands of their lovers, Laurie Bernstein found that they were much more likely to be brutalized by their madams and pimps. See Bernstein, *Sonia's Daughters,* 146–61. For an example of this in Odessa, see "Rasprava," *OL,* 8 April 1912.

68. "V krovavom koshmare," *OP,* 24 April 1915. See also the extensive follow-up pieces that appeared in subsequent issues.

69. "V krovavom koshmare," *OP,* 24 April 1915.

70. The trial of Mendel Beilis, a Jew falsely accused of the ritual murder of a Christian boy in Kiev, was one of the most highly visible national crime stories of the decade. For a discussion of how various newspapers represented the case, see McReynolds, *The News,* 226–27 and 249–50.

71. "Sud. Delo Maiorki Strokera," *OP,* 26 July 1915.

72. "Sud idet," *OP,* 18 September 1915.

73. "Bezumets ili prestupnik?" *OP,* 19 September 1915.

74. I was not able to discover the eventual outcome of the case.

75. Joan Neuberger, "Culture Besieged: Hooliganism and Futurism," in *Cultures in Flux: Lower-Class Values, Practices, and Resistance in Late Imperial Russia,* ed. Stephen P. Frank and Mark D. Steinberg (Princeton, NJ, 1994), 188–90.

76. "Khuliganskoe napadenie na nachal'nika sysknoi politsii I. P. fon-Kliugel'-gen i ego suprugu," *OP,* 18 September 1913. For examples of reports of armed attacks by "hooligans" on lone women, see "Nozhevyia raspravy," *OL,* 9 October 1912; "DP," *OL,* 6 December 1912; and "Pokushenie na ubiistve," *OL,* 5 April 1912.

77. "Ulichnoe khuliganstvo," *OL,* 27 May 1912.

78. For examples of reports in Alexandrovskii Park, see "Napadeniia i grabezhi," *OL,* 2 October 1912; "Grabezhi v Aleksandrovskom parke," *OL,* 22 June 1912; "Grabezh," *OL,* 12 June 1912; and "Khuliganstvo v Aleksandrovskom parke," *OP,* 4 April 1914. For incidents at the central city garden, see "DP," *OL,* 1 and 3 August 1912. The garden's reputation as a safe haven for children was further impugned by a

report that perverts were lurking inside the public lavatories there. See "DP," *OL* , 2 October 1912.

79. The incident was initially reported in "Debosh khuliganov," *OP,* 22 April 1914. The columnist's response appeared in "Ekran zhizni," *OP,* 2 May 1914.

80. "Khuliganskoe napadenie na nachal'nika sysknoi politsii I. P. fon-Kliugel'-gen i ego suprugu," *OP,* 18 September 1913.

81. "Buistvo," *OL,* 11 May 1912. See also "V p'ianom vide," *OL,* 2 March 1912.

82. The incident was described in a letter to the city prefect from the head of the Odessa Education District. See GAOO, *f.* 2, *op.* 4, *ch.* 2, *v.* 973, *d.* 9251, 70–74.

83. "Deboshiry," *OP,* 14 September 1914; and "Skandal u Robina," *OP,* 30 September 1914.

84. "K skandalu u Robina," *OP,* 1 October 1914.

85. Official surveillance of Odessa students suspected of radical tendencies was on the rise during this period. See, for example, GARF, *f.* 102, *op.* 244, 1914 g., *d,* 3, 4, 5, 6, 9, 12, 14, 17, 20, 24, 25, 44, 59, 65, 74, 98, 149, 163, 289, and 345. Non-Russian students (Jews, Georgians, foreigners) were especially suspect. See also Susan K. Morrissey, "More 'Stories About the New People': Student Radicalism, Higher Education, and Social Identity in Russia, 1899–1921" (Ph.D. diss., University of California, 1993).

86. Samuel D. Kassow, *Students, Professors, and the State in Tsarist Russia* (Berkeley, CA, 1989), 410. On attitudes toward the rising number of Jewish students, see Hausmann, "Der Numerus clausus für jüdische Studenten im Zarenreich," 509–31.

87. For broader analysis of changing images of students and student radicalism in late imperial society, see Susan Morrissey, *Heralds of Revolution: Russian Students and the Mythologies of Radicalism* (New York, 1998).

88. This idea was certainly not unique to Odessa. See A. Izgoev, "Ob intelligent-noi molodezhi," in *Vekhi,* ed. Nikolai Berdiaev et al. (Armonk, NY, 1994), 97–124. See also Morrissey, "More 'Stories About the New People,'" 248–49.

89. "Dni nashei zhizni. Gorkiia istiny," *OP,* 4 October 1912.

90. See Walkowitz, *City of Dreadful Delight,* 15–19, for a discussion of the seductive powers of dangerous urban spaces for the bourgeois male "explorer."

91. "O tom, o sem," *OP,* 26 June 1914.

92. For a theoretical discussion of spectacle, see Guy Debord, *Society of the Spectacle* (Detroit, 1983). For an approach inspired by Debord that has comparative relevance, see Vanessa R. Schwartz, *Spectacular Realities: Early Mass Culture in Fin-de-Siècle Paris* (Berkeley, CA, 1998).

5—Making an Appearance

1. "Slukhi i fakty," *OL,* 23 March 1912.

2. Moskvich, *Putevoditel',* 47–49.

3. Moskvich, *Putevoditel',* 47–49.

4. Moskvich, *Putevoditel',* 49.

5. "Gde intelligentsiia (Iz pis'ma v redaktsiuu)," *OL,* 6 March 1912.

6. On the figure of the Russian middle-class woman becoming in various senses more publicly visible, see Adele Lindenmeyr, *Poverty Is Not a Vice: Charity, Society, and the State in Imperial Russia* (Princeton, 1996); Louise McReynolds, "'The Incomparable' Anastasiia Vial'tseva and the Culture of Personality," in *Russia—Women—Culture,* ed. Helena Goscilo and Beth Holmgren (Bloomington, IN, 1996), 273–94; Christine Ruane, "Clothes Shopping in Imperial Russia: The Development of a Consumer Culture," *Journal of Social History* 28, no. 4 (1995): 765–82; and Sally West, "Constructing Consumer Culture: Advertising in Imperial Russia to 1914" (Ph.D. diss., University of Illinois, 1995).

7. Quotations are from the reprint of the 1889 edition of a popular etiquette guide: Iur'ev and Vladimirskii, *Khoroshii ton. Pravila svetskoi zhizni i etika. Sbornik sove-*

tov i nastavlenii. (Moscow, 1991). See also Catriona Kelly, *Refining Russia: Advice Literature, Polite Culture, and Gender from Catherine to Yeltsin* (New York, 2001).

8. Valentin Katayev [Kataev], *A Mosaic of Life, or The Magic Horn of Oberon: Memoirs of a Russian Childhood,* trans. Moira Budberg and Gordon Latta (Chicago, IL, 1976), 388–89.

9. A mythological three-headed dog who guarded the entrance to the infernal regions.

10. "O tom, o sem. Dvornik d. No. 51," *OP,* 17 October 1914.

11. "Itogi dnia 'belago tsvetka,'" *OL,* 29 April 1912. Odessa was not the only city to host "Flower Days." Around the same time as Odessa's White Flower Day in 1912, a St. Petersburg children's charity held a similar and equally successful event, "Blue Flower Day." See Lindenmeyr, *Poverty Is Not a Vice,* 215.

12. "Nashi besedy. Rol zhenshchiny v dele protivotuberkuleznoi bor'by," *OL,* 21 April 1912; "Den 'belago tsvetka,'" *OL,* 21 April 1912; "'Belyi tsvetok' v Odesse," *OL,* 24 April 1912; "Slukhi i fakty," *OL,* 25 April 1912; "Itogi dnia 'belago tsvetka,'" *OL,* 29 April 1912.

13. "'Belyi tsvetok' v Odesse," *OL,* 24 April 1912.

14. "O tom, o cem," *OP,* 26 June 1914.

15. On women, especially lower-class women, being mistaken for prostitutes, see Bernstein, *Sonia's Daughters,* 51, 116, and 304. See also Walkowitz, *City of Dreadful Delight,* 50–52.

16. Iur'ev and Vladimirskii, *Khoroshii ton,* 69–75.

17. "Zvuki dnia. Damskaia boltovnia," *OL,* 7 April 1912.

18. Unless otherwise specified, all quotations included in this section are drawn from the following articles: "Den odessita," *OP,* 4 March 1912; "Dni nashei zhizni," *OP,* 6 August 1912; "U 'Robina,'" *OP,* 2 August 1915; and "Robina, Fankoni, ofitsianty i . . . publika," *OP,* 26 August 1915.

19. Olga Vainshtein, "Russian Dandyism: Constructing a Man of Fashion," in *Russian Masculinities in History and Culture,* ed. Barbara Evans Clements, Rebecca Friedman, and Dan Healey (London, 2002), 69–70. My reading stands in contrast to Vainshtein's argument that dandies employed "the semantics of bourgeois masculinity" in order to create a positive impression, accentuating their "propriety, responsibility, reliability, and respectability".

20. "O tom, o sem: Robinisti," *OP,* 17 October 1915.

21. Iur'ev and Vladimirskii, *Khoroshii ton,* 40 and 71.

22. "Monolog 'robinista,'" *Odesskaia kopeika,* 7 January 1914.

23. *Odesskoe obozrenie teatrov,* no. 99, 5 September 1912.

24. "Gore odesskoi materi," *OP,* 13 September 1914.

25. "Zvuki dnia," *OL,* 1 August 1912.

26. "Dni nashei zhizni," *OP,* 6 August 1912.

27. Iur'ev and Vladimirskii, *Khoroshii ton,* 261–63.

28. Iur'ev and Vladimirskii, *Khoroshii ton,* 262–63. David Blackbourn, "The Discreet Charm of the Bourgeoisie: Reappraising German History in the Nineteenth Century," in *The Peculiarities of German History: Bourgeois Society and Politics in Nineteenth-Century Germany,* by David Blackbourn and Geoff Eley (Oxford, 1992), 201, finds that similar audience etiquette was practiced in Germany from the mid-nineteenth century onward.

29. "Pechal'nyi intsident," *OP,* 17 February 1914.

30. "Gospodin Khenkin ne razschitel," *OP,* Sunday, 6 July 1914. See also "Skandal v teatre Bolgarovoi," *OL,* 19 March 1912.

31. For the most complete treatment of Russian nightlife, see McReynolds, *Russia at Play.*

32. Moskvich, *Putevoditel',* 19.

33. "Gospodin Khenkin ne razschital," *OP,* 6 July 1914. Quote is from Stites, *Russian Popular Culture,* 21.

34. "Nikolai Panin," *OP*, 6 February 1915. The article goes on to explain that Panin's career came to an abrupt halt when the local investigative police discovered that the performer had avoided military service by using a false passport. After an unsuccessful suicide attempt, Panin was arrested, sentenced to a month in jail, then inducted into the army. Vial'tseva herself, the woman Panin so successfully impersonated, was a huge favorite with middle-class audiences across Russia. On the implications of her fame for the development of middle-class culture in Russia, see McReynolds, "'The Incomparable' Anastasiia Vial'tseva," and *Russia at Play*.

35. Stites, *Russian Popular Culture*, 13. See also I. V. Nest'ev, "A Bit of History," in Louise McReynolds, ed., "Russian Nightlife, Fin-de-Siècle," *Russian Studies in History* 31, no. 3 (1992–1993): 25–49.

36. "Var'ete," *Antrakt*, no. 1 (1913–1914).

37. Catriona Kelly, "'Better Halves': Representations of Women in Russian Urban Popular Entertainments, 1870–1910," in *Women and Society in Russia and the Soviet Union*, ed. Linda Edmondson (Cambridge, 1992), 12, describes *café-chantants* as venues where "the slur of prostitution hung over not only performers, but audience."

38. For a scandal featuring the antics of a drunken police officer, see "Skandal v 'Severnoi,'" *OL*, 1 May 1912. For a story concerning the jealous rage of a "betrayed" woman against her lover, see "Skandal v 'Severnoi,'" *OP*, 5 September 1915. For a tongue-in-cheek story about a "typical" Severnaia patron, see "Posle Severnoi," *Iumoristicheskii pulemet*, no. 3, May 1915.

39. "Skandal v 'Severnoi,'" *OL*, 17 June 1912.

40. "Zvuki dnia," *OL*, 1 June 1913.

41. "Tsirk," *OL*, 7 October 1912.

42. Katayev, *Mosaic of Life*, 19.

43. Stites, *Russian Popular Culture*, 19.

44. "Sport," *OL*, 14 February 1912. The writer Valentin Kataev recalled how the announcer of a wrestling match he attended at the circus introduced Zaikin: "World Champion Ivan Zaikin, hero of the Volga, who threw the unbeatable champion of the Polish tsardom, Pitliasinsky, who then, shattered by his defeat, gave up wrestling and opened a private gymnasium in Odessa for the benefit of under-developed youth." See Katayev, *Mosaic of Life*, 21.

45. Kataev says in *Mosaic of Life*, 26, that his father, a schoolteacher, was one of the local *intelligents* who believed wrestling to be an insult to any "intelligent human being." For analysis of similar reactions in the West, see Allen Guttman, *The Erotic in Sports* (New York, 1996).

46. On the appeal of wrestling to middle-class society, see, McReynolds, *Russia at Play*, chapter 4.

47. Katayev, *Mosaic of Life*, 20–21 and 26.

48. Unless otherwise noted, all quotations included in this section are drawn from the following articles: "Foss v Odesse," *OP*, 28 June 1914; "Foss v Odesse," *OP*, 29 June 1914; "O Fosse," *OP*, 30 June 1914; "Eshche o Fosse," *OP*, 1 July 1914; "'Gastroli' Fossa," *OP*, 2 July 1914; and "Gastroli Fossa," *OP*, 6 July 1914.

49. On Sandow, see John F. Kasson, *Houdini, Tarzan, and the Perfect Man: The White Male Body and the Challenge of Modernity in America* (New York, 2001), 21–76. See also David L. Chapman, *Sandow the Magnificent: Eugen Sandow and the Beginnings of Bodybuilding* (Urbana, IL, 1994). On Poddubnyi, see McReynolds, *Russia at Play*, especially 131–43. On Breitbart, see Sharon Gillerman, "Samson in Vienna: The Theatrics of Jewish Masculinity," *Jewish Social Studies* 9, no. 2 (2003): 65–98.

50. "Dni nashei zhizni. Okolo 'geroi' (Razgovory)," *OP*, 8 July 1914. For similar imagery associated with excessive appetite, see Kasson, *Rudeness and Civility*, 195–201.

51. Patrick J. Rollins, "Imperial Russia's African Colony," *Russian Review* 27, no. 4 (October 1968): 432–51.

52. The performers were referred to as both "Somalians" and "Ethiopians." All

quotations included in this section are drawn from the following articles: "Efiopy v Odessa," *OL*, 4 September 1912; "Dni nashei zhizni," *OP*, 5 September 1912; "Zvuki dnia: Efiopy," *OL*, 7 September 1912; and a series of articles and advertisements running in *Odesskoe obozrenie teatrov* (hereafter *OOT*) on 4, 6, 9/10, 16/17, and 26 September 1912.

6—The Little Family

1. "Samoubiistvo," *Krokodil*, no. 19, April 1912.

2. "Zvuki dnia. Letniaia entsiklopediia (Neobkhodimoe rukovodstvo dlia priezzhikh)," *OL*, 1 June 1912.

3. "'Semeika' ili 'Gospoda Odessity,'" *Krokodil*, April 1912, nos. 18, 19, and 20.

4. For the convenience of the reader, I have anglicized these names. In the original, the characters are: Iakov L'vovich Perel'muter, Rakhil' Markovna, Iliusha, Zhenia, Esfir', and Matil'da.

5. Richard J. Evans, "Family and Class in the Hamburg Grand Bourgeoisie, 1815–1914," in *The German Bourgeoisie: Essays on the Social History of the German Middle Class from the Late Eighteenth to the Early Twentieth Century*, ed. David Blackbourn and Richard J. Evans (London: 1991), 115.

6. For a concise summary of proper bourgeois family roles as defined in the western context, see Alan Trachtenberg's introduction to the section titled, "Home as Place and Center for Private and Family Life," in *Home: A Place in the World*, ed. Arien Mack (New York, 1993).

7. Lushchik, "Odesskii zhurnal 'Krokodil,'" 242–57. Lushchik quotes circulation figures from archival records of the Provisional Committee for Printing Affairs *(Vremennyi komitet po delam pechati)*, GAOO, f. 10, op. 1, ed. khr. 60, l. 20ob.; ed. khr. 106, l. 25ob.

8. A dowry of 10,000 rubles was comparatively large given that, according to ChaeRan Freeze, *Jewish Marriage and Divorce in Imperial Russia* (Boston, 2002), 30, "in late-nineteenth-century Russia a typical dowry ranged between one hundred and several thousand rubles."

9. See for instance, "Zvuki dnia. Letniaia entsiklopediia (Neobkhodimoe rukovodstvo dlia priezzhikh)," *OL*, 1 June 1912. A prospective bride's age did in fact make a difference to would-be suitors and their families, but age was on the rise in the early twentieth century. See Marion A. Kaplan, *Making of the Jewish Middle Class: Women, Family, and Identity in Imperial Germany* (Oxford, 1991), 96; and Freeze, *Jewish Marriage*, 55–58 and 60.

10. On the appeal of actresses as role models for "modern" young women, see McReynolds, *Russia at Play*, chapter 4.

11. Morrissey, *Heralds of Revolution*, 163, shows that the single largest group of women enrolled as auditors at St. Petersburg University in 1906–1907 were daughters of the *meshchanstvo*. While Morrissey finds that some female students did in fact marry while at the university, contemporary surveys concluded that women chose to become students because they "sought knowledge primarily for its own sake," not because they were looking for husbands. See Morrissey, 171–72.

12. Freeze, *Jewish Marriage*, 71.

13. Freeze, *Jewish Marriage*, 20–21, points out that distrust of matchmakers was common among enlightened Jews. On family lineage and wealth as traditional criteria for spousal selection in Jewish society, see 25–33.

14. Guido Hausmann, *Universität und städtische Gesellschaft in Odessa, 1865–1917: Soziale und nationale Selbstorganisation and der Peripherie des Zarenreiches* (Stuttgart: Franz Steiner Verlag, 1998), 184, shows that in 1912, the year "The Little Family" was published, admissions quotas capped the size of the Jewish student body at Novorossiiskii University at 15 percent. On the status afforded to Jewish lawyers in Russia, see Nathans, *Beyond the Pale*, chapters 6 and 7; and Gassenschmidt, *Jewish Liberal Politics*.

15. Bolshaia-Arnautskaia was arguably the most *meshchanskii* street in all Odessa, certainly not an address that a refined person would brag about.

16. Kaplan, *Making of the Jewish Middle Class*, 97.

17. Iur'ev and Vladimirskii, *Khoroshii ton*, 52–54.

18. On the persistence of negative stereotypes associated with Jewish women's commercial activities, see Freeze, *Jewish Marriage*, 68.

19. Iur'ev and Vladimirskii, *Khoroshii ton*, 99–101.

20. There were actually several such publications in Odessa: *Odesskii brachnyi listok* (hereafter *OBL*) and *Odesskaia i iuga Rossii brachnaia gazeta* (hereafter *OIRBG*). As Freeze, *Jewish Marriage*, 24, points out, such publications also existed in other parts of the empire, personal ads in the secular press having "a major impact on matchmaking."

21. A survey of eighteen issues of *OBL* in the 1912–1914 period (nos. 40–41, 43–44, 46–50, 55–57, 60, 62–66) contained 263 ads in which the author spoke about his or her financial status and/or the material circumstances required of a potential spouse.

22. "Slukhi i fakty," *OL*, 7 April 1912.

23. My survey of *OBL* found 182 ads in which the author specified "intelligent-nyi" as a quality of self or one sought after in a prospective spouse. Both male and female authors invoked the term in roughly equal numbers suggesting the degree to which "intelligentnyi" was employed as a synonym for respectable.

24. Freeze, *Jewish Marriage*, 24.

25. *OBL*. Gerasimov, "'My ubivaem tol'ko svoikh,'" 248, quoted ads from two 1910 issues (no. 10 and no. 12) of *OIRBG* that likewise emphasized a man's material prospects.

26. Freeze, *Jewish Marriage*, 24.

27. *OIRBG*, no. 6, 7 February 1910, quoted in Gerasimov, "'My ubivaem tol'ko svoikh,'" 248 (my translation).

28. *OIRBG*, no. 10, 7 March 1910, quoted in Gerasimov, "'My ubivaem tol'ko svoikh,'" 248 (my translation).

29. My *OBL* survey found 103 ads referred explicitly to religion. Of these, only 13 said that religious persuasion did not matter.

30. Gerasimov, "'My ubivaem tol'ko svoikh,'" 248.

31. "V ob-ve 'Pridanoe,'" *OP*, 21 April 1914. On similar organizations in Germany, see Kaplan, *Making of the Jewish Middle Class*, 98.

32. "Zhenikhi i nevesty (Odesskiia nabliudeniia)," *OP*, 21 April 1914.

33. "Tipy odesskikh muzhei," *OP*, 17 April 1914.

34. "Zhenikhi i nevesty."

35. "Zhenikhi i nevesty." See also "Sovremennyi zhenikh," *OL*, 20 March 1912.

36. "Sovremennyi zhenikh," *OP*, 18 May 1915.

37. "Krovopiitsvy," *OP*, 19 May 1915.

38. The Marazli family, originally headed by a Greek entrepreneur who came to Odessa and made a fortune, was among the richest and most successful in the city. A. R. Khari was the director of a local bank, a wealthy, high-powered financeer and philanthropist.

39. Morrissey, "More 'Stories about the New People,'" 328–29. See also Morrissey, *Heralds of Revolution*, chapter 6.

40. As Evgenii Bershtein points out in "The Russian Myth of Oscar Wilde," in *Self and Story in Russian History*, ed. Laura Engelstein and Stephanie Sandler (Ithaca, NY, 2000), 175, in the aftermath of Wilde's trial, Wilde's name became "the standard euphemism for modern homosexuality" in the Russian press.

41. Morrissey, *Heralds of Revolution*, 173. For evidence of these views in Odessa, see chapter 3 above.

42. McReynolds, *Russia at Play*.

43. Engelstein, *Keys to Happiness*, discusses the Foucauldian implications of the discourse of sexuality in late imperial Russia.

44. Quoted in Mark Nicholls, *The Importance of Being Oscar* (New York, 1980), 10.

45. Mark D. Steinberg, *Proletarian Imagination: Self, Modernity, and the Sacred in Russia, 1910–1925* (Ithaca, NY, 2002), 89–90.

7—Revenge of the Queen of Stylish Hairdos

1. Adapted from Joyce Toomre, trans., *Classic Russian Cooking: Elena Molokhovets' A Gift to Young Housewives* (Bloomington, IN, 1992), 107.

2. "Mest 'korolevy' modnykh prichesok," *OP*, 11 February 1916.

3. *OOT*, 6 September 1912. A group photo of club members (including the women) was published in *OL*'s illustrated supplement on 8 September 1912.

4. For a discussion of literary representations of gentry and bourgeois women trapped in this way, see Barbara Heldt, *Terrible Perfection: Women in Russian Literature* (Bloomington, IN, 1987).

5. On the expectation that professional women would give up their careers after marriage, see Christine Ruane, *Gender, Class, and the Professionalization of Russian City Teachers, 1860–1914* (Pittsburgh, PA, 1994), 81–82 and 115–20.

6. William G. Wagner, "The Trojan Mare: Women's Rights and Civil Rights in Late Imperial Russia," in *Civil Rights in Imperial Russia,* ed. Olga Crisp and Linda Edmondson (Oxford, 1989), 66.

7. Wagner, "Trojan Mare," 67.

8. William G. Wagner, *Marriage, Property, and Law in Late Imperial Russia* (Oxford: Clarendon Press, 1994), 67.

9. "Taina odnoi molodoi zhizni," *OP*, 16 July 1914.

10. Morrissey, "More 'Stories about the New People,'" 293.

11. "Taina Tandochki," *OP*, 17 July 1914.

12. Barbara T. Gates, *Victorian Suicide: Mad Crimes and Sad Histories* (Princeton, NJ, 1988), 70, discusses the distinction made in various Victorian literary texts between "ignoble and noble suicide."

13. Kristine Ottesen Garrigan, *Victorian Scandals: Representations of Gender and Class* (Athens, OH, 1992), 5.

14. McReynolds, *The News.*

15. Garrigan, *Victorian Scandals,* 5.

16. "Skandal v 'Alkazar,'" *OL*, 6 December 1912.

17. In addition to those described here and below, see "Dni nashei zhizni," *OP*, 6 June 1912; "DP," *OL*, 11 September 1912; and "Zvuki dnia," *OL*, 1 June 1913.

18. "Dva skandala na begakh," *OL*, 24 April 1912.

19. Of the eighteen cases I examined, all but one were perpetrated by women. For the exception, see "Neudavshaiasia mest'," *OL*, 1 February 1912.

20. "DP," *OL*, 10 March 1912; "Mest' zheny," *OL*, 10 June 1912; "Predupredila," *OL*, 18 July 1912.

21. "Mest'," *OL*, 29 April 1912; and "Mest'," *OL*, 11 May 1912.

22. "Semeinaia drama," *OL*, 2 June 1912; and "Mest'," *OL*, 14 June 1912.

23. "Dikaia mest'," *OL*, 4 November 1912.

24. "Zhiteiskaia drama," *OL*, 18 July 1912. Three years before the acid-throwing incident, the victim in this "drama," the salesclerk Dmitrii Makeev, had stabbed his own young wife twelve times near the gate of the Evropeiskaia Hotel on Pushkinskaia Street in Bul'varnyi. Regardless of this, the reporter claimed that Makeev still hoped to reconcile with his estranged wife.

25. Harris, *Murders and Madness,* 238–39.

26. "Mest'," *OL*, 10 April 1912.

27. "Mest'," *OL*, 16 May 1912.

28. For other examples of public attacks of this kind, see "Mest'," *OL*, 11 May 1912; "Dikaia mest'," *OL*, 4 November 1912; and "Zhiteiskaia drama," *OP*, 26 April 1914.

29. "Mest'," *OL*, 14 June 1912.
30. "Semeinaia drama," *OL*, 20 June 1912.
31. "Semeinaia drama," *OL*, 2 June 1912.
32. "Zhiteiskaia drama," *OP*, 26 April 1914.
33. "Mest' 'korolevy' modnykh prichesok," *OP*, 11 February 1916.
34. "Sud. Revnost'," *OP*, 12 June 1914.
35. "Tipy odesskikh muzhei," *OP*, 7 April 1914.
36. "Za chest' sem'i. Drama na Moldavanke," *OP*, 25 November 1914.
37. The following discussion draws on letters excerpted by Faust in "Dni nashei zhizni. Ubiistvo na Moldavanke," *OP*, 27 November 1914, and "Dni nashei zhizni. V chadu strasti," *OP*, 28 November 1914. Other letters were excerpted in Faust's columns on 1 and 8 December 1914.
38. See various reports in *Odesskie novosti*, 17–19 April 1915.

8—Iambo's Fate

1. "Dni nashei zhizni," *OP*, 26 April 1914.
2. "Slon, prigovorennyi k smerti," *OP*, 14 April 1914.
3. "Jumbo" was one of Barnum's star attractions in the 1870s. Jumbo's popularity was so great that, after the elephant was accidently killed by a train, Barnum decided to turn the elephant's skeleton, hide, and tusks into a permanent display to travel with the circus. See Harvey Rachlin, *Jumbo's Hide, Elvis's Ride, and the Tooth of Buddha: More Marvelous Tales of Historical Artifacts* (New York, 2000).
4. Kulikovo Field was located on the edge of Odessa's central city, immediately adjacent to the main passenger railway station.
5. Deribasovskaia Street was the main street of the city, Odessa's Nevskii Prospekt.
6. "Slon, prigovorennyi k smerti," *OP*, 14 April 1914; "Vzbesivshiisia slon," *Iuzhnaia mysl'*, 14 April 1914.
7. *OP* reported that the trainer beat the elephant with an iron rod. See "Slon, prigovorennyi k smerti." The *Iuzhnaia mysl'* report said that the man whipped Iambo. See "Vzbesivshiisia slon." For other early reports of the incident see "Tragediia slona Iambo," *Odesskie novosti*, 14 April 1914; and "Tragediia slona," *OL*, 14 April 1914. Valentin Kataev's memoirs offer an impressionistic but not wholly accurate recollection of these events. See Katayev, "The Elephant Jumbo," in *Mosaic of Life*, 164–70.
8. "Vzbesivshiisia slon"; "Slon prigovorennyi k smerti."
9. The committee was made up of fon-der-Khoven, Lorberbaum, the menagerie veterinarian, and a few animal handlers.
10. "Slon, prigovorennyi k smerti." There seems to have been some confusion on what dosage was necessary to kill a person. *OP* reported that 25 grams was enough to kill "tens of thousands of people." *Iuzhnaia mysl'* reported that the cyanide, purchased at Gaevskii's pharmacy, was capable of poisoning more than a hundred people, not tens of thousands. See "Vzbesivshiisia slon."
11. "Slon prigovorennyi k smerti."
12. The special commission was comprised of two architects, the city's medical inspector, military and civic doctors, and a veterinarian.
13. "Vzbesivshiisia slon."
14. "Iambo," *OP*, 17 April 1914.
15. "Krugi na vode. Otchego inogda besiatsia slony," *Odesskaia novosti*, 14 April 1914.
16. "Otchego vzbesilsia slon?" *Iuzhnaia mysl'*, 15 April 1914.
17. Such were the motivations actually articulated by another menagerie owner, the famous Carl Hagenbeck, a pioneer in the development of modern, open zoological gardens. See Blackbourn, "Discreet Charm of the Bourgeoisie," 200–201.
18. The Café Fankoni, located in the heart of the central city, was popular with members of Odessa's financial circles.

19. "Memuary chernoi pantery," *OL*, 15 April 1914.

20. "Zvuki dnia. Zapiski slona," *OL*, 15 April 1914.

21. A harsh reply to Leri's column appeared the following day in the ultra-right, blatantly anti-Semitic daily *Rossiianin*. The vitriolic feuilletonist "Svoi" concurred that Iambo had succumbed to the influence of the spring air, falling in love with "some disgracefully fat Jewess *(zhidka)* whose external appearance so reminded him of a she-elephant that he got excited." This was not the first time the elephant had been involved with such a woman, the acid-tongued Svoi asserted. "The noble elephant got his higher education in Hamburg in the Hagenbeck Zoo, where he soiled himself with some mangy, stinking Jewess, who in the end, even lost her human shape." Now that Iambo was facing execution, the columnist went on, the "Yid" Lorberbaum would no longer "permit the public to be entertained by the wild animals for fear that one after the other all the better and most expensive examples might perish" thanks to similar corrupting influences. See "'Beshennyi' slon," *Rossiianin*, 16 April 1914.

22. "Neurasthenia" was a popular diagnosis at the time for any patients (especially women) with "nervous complaints."

23. Cesare Lombroso was an Italian forensic psychiatrist, who in the 1880s and 1890s devised a system to identify deviant types by physical features.

24. "Vokrug 'Iambo,'" *OP*, 15 May 1914; "'Iambo' nelzia spasti!" *OP*, 25 April 1914.

25. "Dni 'Iambo' sochteny," *OP*, 19 April 1914.

26. "Slon 'Iambo,'" *OP*, 15 April 1914.

27. "Iambo," *OP*, 20 April 1914; "'Iambo' mozhno spasti," *OP*, 14 May 1914; "Vokrug slona 'Iambo,'" *OP*, 2 May 1914.

28. Electrocution was the means of execution employed in 1903 by the owners of "Topsy," a bad-tempered elephant who had killed three men in three years during her tenure at Coney Island's Luna Park.

29. "Dni 'Iambo' sochteny," *OP*, 19 April 1914.

30. "'Iambo' nakanune gibeli," *OP*, 21 April 1914.

31. "'Iambo' nelzia spasti!"

32. "Iambo," *OP*, 4 May 1914.

33. "Dni nashei zhizni," *OP*, 16 April 1914.

34. "Dni 'Iambo' sochteny."

35. "Esli-by," *OP*, 20 April 1914.

36. "Poslednaia popytki spasti 'Iambo,'" *OP*, 27 April 1914; "Iambo nakaune gibeli."

37. "Sud'ba 'Iambo,'" *OP*, 23 April 1914.

38. "Sud'ba 'Iambo.'"

39. "Napadenie na uktrotitelia zverintsa," *OP*, 15 May 1914.

40. "Napadenie na uktrotitelia zverintsa."

41. The first report concerning an alleged insurance policy on Iambo appeared in "Iambo nakaune gibeli," *OP*, 21 April 1914. Iambo's value was estimated at 20,000 rubles. See "Iambo," *OP*, 17 April 1914.

42. "Podrugi 'Iambo,'" *OP*, 6 June 1914. See also "'Iambo' i 'Gibzi,'" *OP*, 7 June 1914.

43. "Razstrel slona," *Russkaia rech'*, 10 June 1914.

44. "Razstrel slona 'Iambo,'" *OP*, 9 June 1914.

45. "Razstrel slona 'Iambo.'" For another description of Iambo's execution and subsequent removal to the university, see "Rastrel slona," *Russkaia rech'*, 10 June 1914. *Odesskie novosti* ran three separate stories on Iambo's death in their Tuesday, 10 June issue. See "Lebedinaia pesn' Iambo," "Eshche o razstrele Iambo," and "Pogibshii Iambo," *Odesskie novosti*, 10 June 1914.

46. "Pokhorony 'Iambo,'" *OP*, 11 June 1914.

47. "Vskrytie 'Iambo,'" *OP*, 12 June 1914.

48. "Preparirovanie 'Iambo,'" *OP,* 18 June 1914.
49. "K razstrelu 'Iambo,'" *OP,* 10 June 1914.
50. "K razstrelu 'Iambo.'"
51. "Iz proshlago 'Iambo,'" *OP,* 13 June 1914.
52. "Sport ili zhestokost'?" *Odesskie novosti,* 11 June 1914. For more on this theme, see "Okhotniki" and "Protestu okhotnikov," *Odesskie novosti,* 12 June 1914.
53. "Zvuki dnia," *OL,* 10 June 1914.
54. "Moi kino," *Iuzhnaia mysl',* 11 June 1914.
55. "Razstrel slona 'Iambo,'" *OP,* 9 June 1914; "Pamiati Iambo," *OP,* 9 June 1914; "Pokhorony 'Iambo,'" *OP,* 11 June 1914.
56. "Pamiati Iambo."
57. "O tom, o sem," *OP,* 13 June 1914.
58. "Karnaval zhizni," *OP,* 12 June 1914.
59. For the reference to the prostitute, see "Na dne Odessy (Oblava na prostitutok)," *OP,* 26 June 1914. For the reference to the wrestler, see "Gastroli Fossa," *OP,* 6 July 1914.
60. "Sluchai s Iambo," *OP,* 1 July 1914.

Epilogue—A Moment in the Sun

1. *The Complete Works of Isaac Babel,* ed. Nathalie Babel, trans. Peter Constantine (New York, 2002), 77.
2. Babel, *Complete Works,* 75.
3. The phrase is Aleksandr Blok's. For more on St. Petersburg, see Clark, *Petersburg, Crucible of Revolution;* and Mark D. Steinberg's forthcoming book, *St. Petersburg Fin de Siecle.*
4. "Slukhi i fakty," *OL,* 6 and 24 January and 5 February 1912.
5. For detailed discussion of this problem, see chapter 4.
6. The nickname "Belgian guillotine" came from the fact that a Belgian company built, owned, and operated the tram system. See "Slukhi i fakty," *OL,* 17 January 1912. On the many reports of accidents involving the tram, see "Stolknovenie vagonov tramvaia," *OL,* 7 February 1912; "Pod vagonom tramvaia," *OL,* 24 February 1912; "Tragicheskaia smert' starika," *OL,* 2 September 1912; "Khronika tramvaia," *OL,* 3 November 1912; "Neschastnyi sluchai na rel'sakh," *OL,* 8 January 1912; "Uzhasnaia smert' pod tramvaem," *OL,* 15 January 1912; and "Zhertva tramvaia," *OL,* 31 January 1912.
7. "Itogi odesskoi 'elektrichki' za 1912 god," *OP,* 1 January 1913, reported that 422 people had been injured by the *electrichka* in 1912, 20 of them fatally. Quoted from "Dni nashei zhizni. Moi slovar'," *OP,* 12 July 1912.
8. The vast majority of automobiles in Odessa were registered to private individuals and businesses in the central districts, especially in Bul'varnyi. Automobile registration records are included in GAOO, *f.* 314, *op.* 2, *d.* 10.
9. *Iuzhnyi avtomobilist,* no. 1, January 1914, p. 11.
10. See especially "Ezda na avtomobiliakh," *OL,* 31 March 1912; and "Bor'ba s bystroi ezdoi na avtomobiliakh," *OL,* 1 April 1912. For reports of accidents, see "Sluchai s semei g. odess. gradonachalnika kamergera I. V. Sosnovskago," *OL,* 30 March 1912; "Pod avtomobilem," *OL,* 1 May 1912; "Ne vezet," *OL,* 5 May 1912; "Pod avtomobilem," *OL,* 6 September 1912; "Avtomobil'naia katastrofa," *OP,* 4 June 1913.
11. "Slukhi i fakty," *OL,* 25 May 1912.
12. Odessa's daily newspapers were filled with stories about such activities. For a sampling of *OP's* coverage, see "Po gorodu (Nabroski)," *OP,* 24 July 1914; "Vysochaishchaia blagodarnost' zhiteliam goroda Odessy," *OP,* 25 July 1914; "Molebstvie v sinagoge," *OP,* 27 July 1914; and "Detskaia manufestatsiia," *OP,* 5 August 1914. For the report about thieves' response to the war, see "Odesskii prestupnoi mir i voina," *OP,* 29 July 1914. On students, see "Manifestatsiia studentov," *OP,* 10 October 1914, 4.

13. Kovbasiuk, *Odessa*, 116–17.

14. "O tom, o sem. 'Nochlezhki' dlia bezhentsev," *OP*, 30 June 1915.

15. "Orazdnik pobedy," *OP*, 10 March 1915.

16. "Artisty-voinam," *OP*, 13 March 1915; "Artisty-voinam: Vpechatleniia," *OP*, 14 March 1915; "Karnaval," *OP*, 14 March 1915; "Vchera na ulitsakh Odessy," *OP*, 14 March 1915. For discussion of the various kinds of patriotism demonstrated by performing artists during the war years, see Hubertus F. Jahn, *Patriotic Culture in Russia during World War One* (Ithaca, NY, 1995), 85–149.

17. "Odesskie traktiry," *OP*, 20 February 1915, 3–4.

18. "Tainy vodochnyi zavod," *OP*, 16 September 1915; "'Alkogol'naia' panama v Odesse," *OP*, 26 February 1915; "Tainy kabaki na Moldavanke," *OP*, 2 September 1915, 3.

19. "Bezumnyi pryzhok," *OP*, 13 January 1915.

20. See, for example, GAOO, *f.* 314, *op.* 2, *d.* 9, *l.* 73, 78, 82, 85, 94, and 97. See also "Fabrikatsiia podlozhnykh pasportov," *OP*, 20 June 1916.

21. GAOO, *f.* 314, *op.* 2, *d.* 9, *ll.* 83, 98, and 239–42. See also "Vorovskoi 'miting,'" *OP*, 12 September 1915.

22. Kovbasiuk, *Odessa*, 117–18, shows that, as a proportion of total industrial output, metal processing grew from 12 percent in 1914 to over 33 percent in 1915 to 44 percent by 1917.

23. On the roundup of enemy nationals, see GAOO, *f.* 16, *op.* 124, *d.* 17332, "Svedeniia o nedvizhimykh imushchestbakh prinadlezhashchikh turetsko-paddannym, avstrovengerskim i germansko-poddannym."

24. "Vo vlasti khishchnikov," *OP*, 5 March 1915.

25. "Registratsiia prislugi v Odesse," *OP*, 30 September 1915.

26. "Tipy bezhentsev," *OP*, 29 January 1916.

27. "Odesskie traktiry."

28. Babel, *Complete Works*, 82.

29. For more on Soviet notions of *meshchanstvo*, see Vera S. Dunham, *In Stalin's Time: Middleclass Values in Soviet Fiction* (Durham, NC, 1990), and Svetlana Boym, *Common Places: Mythologies of Everyday Life in Russia* (Cambridge, MA, 1994).

30. In an irony worthy of Babel, the rebuilding of the central city since 1991 has been made possible in part thanks to the largesse of successful Odessan gangsters in emigration, some of whom made their fortunes in the "Little Odessa" of Brighton Beach.

31. "Odessa: Puteshestvie vo vremeni," CD-ROM (Odessa, 2002).

32. See for example, the Odessa Globe Web site [www.odessaglobe.com] and the official Web site of the Worldwide Club of Odessans [*Vsemirnyi klub Odessitov:* www.woc.tora.ru]. The latter offers extensive news about city life, publicizes publications about the city and its history, and provides listings of local events and club activities.

Bibliography

Archival Sources

Gosudarstvennyi arkhiv Odesskoi oblasti (GAOO)
    fond 2, Kantseliariia odesskogo gradonachalnika
    fond 16, Odesskaia gorodskaia uprava
    fond 314, Kantseliariia odesskogo politsmeistera
Gosudarstvennyi arkhiv Rossiiskoi Federatsii (GARF)
    fond 102, Departament politsii Ministerstva vnutrennikh del
    fond 1742, Kollektsiia fotoportretov i fotografiia lits, prokhodivshikh po delam
        politseiskikh uchrezhdenii

Newspapers, Journals, and Other Periodicals

Antrakt
Gudok
Iuzhnaia mysl
Iuzhnyi avtomobilist
Izvestiia odesskoi gorodskoi dumy
Krokodil
Odesskaia kopeika
Odesskaia pochta
Odesskie novosti
Odesskii brachnyi listok
Odesskii listok
Odesskoe obozrenie teatrov
Rossiianin
Russkaia rech'
Vestnik politsii (St. Petersburg)
Zaria aviatsii
Zhenskaia gazeta

Selected Books and Articles

Abelson, Elaine S. *When Ladies Go A-Thieving: Middle-Class Shoplifters in the Victorian Department Store.* New York, 1989.
Arnot, Margaret L., and Cornelie Usborne, eds. *Gender and Crime in Modern Europe.* London, 1999.
Atlas, D. *Staraia Odessa. Ee druz'ia i nedrugi.* Odessa, 1911.
Babel, Isaac. *The Collected Stories of Isaac Babel.* Translated by Walter Morrison. New York, 1955.

———. *The Complete Works of Isaac Babel.* Edited by Nathalie Babel. Translated by Peter Constantine. New York, 2002.

Bakhtin, Mikhail. *Rabelais and His World.* Translated by Helene Iswolsky. Bloomington, IN, 1984.

Barbakaru, Anatolii. *Gop-Stop: Odessa Banditskaia.* Moscow, 2000.

———. *Odessa-mama: Kataly, kidaly, shulera.* Moscow, 1999.

Bater, James. *St. Petersburg: Industrialization and Change.* London, 1976.

Beletskii, S. P. *Rozysknoi al'bom.* Vypusk 1, *Vory-karmanniki (Marvikhery).* St. Petersburg, 1913.

Beliaeva, L. N., et al., eds. *Bibliografiia periodicheskikh izdanii Rossii, 1901–1916.* Leningrad, 1959.

Berdiaev, Nikolai, et al., eds. *Vekhi: Landmarks.* Armonk, NY, 1994.

Berman, Marshall. *All that Is Solid Melts Into Air: The Experience of Modernity.* New York, 1982.

Bernstein, Laurie. *Sonia's Daughters: Prostitutes and Their Regulation in Imperial Russia.* Berkeley, CA, 1995.

Bershtein, Evgenii. "The Russian Myth of Oscar Wilde." In *Self and Story in Russian History,* edited by Laura Engelstein and Stephanie Sandler, 168–88. Ithaca, NY, 2000.

Blackbourn, David, and Geoff Eley. *The Peculiarities of German History: Bourgeois Society and Politics in Nineteenth-Century Germany.* Oxford, 1984.

Blackbourn, David, and Richard J. Evans, eds. *The German Bourgeoisie: Essays on the Social History of the German Middle Class from the Late Eighteenth to the Early Twentieth Century.* London, 1991.

Blumin, Stuart M. *The Emergence of the Middle Class: Social Experience in the American City, 1760–1900.* Cambridge, 1989.

———. "The Hypothesis of Middle-Class Formation in Nineteenth-Century America: A Critique and Some Proposals." *American Historical Review* 90, no. 2 (April 1985): 299–338.

Borovoi, S. IA. "Polozhenie rabochego klassa Odessy v XIX i nachale XX v.: Istochnikovedcheskie zametki." In *Iz istorii rabochego klassa revoliutsionnogo dvizheniia,* edited by V. V. Altman, 308–18. Moscow, 1958.

Boym, Svetlana. *Common Places: Mythologies of Everyday Life in Russia.* Cambridge, MA, 1994.

Bradley, Joseph. *Muzhik and Muscovite: Urbanization in Late Imperial Russia.* Berkeley, CA, 1985.

———. "Once You've Eaten Khitrov Soup, You'll Never Leave." *Russian History* 11, no. 1 (1984): 1–28.

Brenner, David A. *Marketing Identities: The Invention of Jewish Ethnicity in Ost und West.* Detroit, MI, 1998

Briker, Boris. "The Underworld of Benia Krik and I. Babel's *Odessa Stories.*" *Canadian Slavonic Papers* 36, nos. 1–2 (1994): 115–34.

Bristow, Edward J. *Prostitution and Prejudice: The Jewish Fight against White Slavery, 1870–1939.* New York, 1983.

Brooks, Jeffrey. "Popular Philistinism and the Course of Russian Modernism." In *Literature and History: Theoretical Problems and Russian Case Studies,* edited by Gary Saul Morson, 90–110. Stanford, CA, 1986.

———. *When Russia Learned to Read: Literacy and Popular Literature, 1861–1917.* Princeton, NJ, 1985.

Brower, Daniel R. *The Russian City between Tradition and Modernity, 1850–1900.* Berkeley, CA, 1990.

Certeau, Michel de. *The Practice of Everyday Life.* Translated by Steven F. Rendall, Steven. Berkeley, CA, 1984.

Cesarani, David. "Port Jews: Concepts, Cases, and Questions." *Jewish Culture and History* 4, no. 2 (2001): 1–11.

Chapman, David L. *Sandow the Magnificent: Eugen Sandow and the Beginnings of Body-building.* Urbana, IL, 1994.

Chartier, Roger. *Cultural History: Between Practices and Representations.* Translated by Lydia G. Cochrane. Cambridge, 1988.

———. "Culture as Appropriation: Popular Culture Uses in Early Modern France." In *Understanding Popular Culture: Europe from the Middle Ages to the Nineteenth Century,* edited by Steven L. Kaplan, 230–53. Berlin, 1984.

Chevalier, Louis. *Laboring Classes and Dangerous Classes in Paris during the First Half of the Nineteenth Century.* New York, 1973.

Cheyette, Bryan, and Laura Marcus, eds. *Modernity, Culture, and 'the Jew.'* Stanford, CA, 1998.

Clark, Katerina. *Petersburg, Crucible of Cultural Revolution.* Cambridge, MA, 1995.

Clark, T. J. *The Painting of Modern Life: Paris in the Art of Manet and His Followers.* New York, 1985.

Clements, Barbara Evans, Barbara Alpern Engel, and Christine D. Worobec, eds. *Russia's Women: Accommodation, Resistance, Transformation.* Berkeley, CA, 1991.

Clements, Barbara Evans, Rebecca Friedman, and Dan Healey, eds. *Russian Masculinities in History and Culture.* London, 2002.

Clowes, Edith W., Samuel D. Kassow, and James L. West, eds. *Between Tsar and People: Educated Society and the Quest for Public Identity in Late Imperial Russia.* Princeton, NJ, 1991.

Costlow, Jane T., Stephanie Sandler, and Judith Vowles, eds. *Sexuality and the Body in Russian Culture.* Stanford, CA, 1993.

Crisp, Olga, and Linda Edmondson, eds. *Civil Rights in Imperial Russia.* Oxford, 1989.

Dawidowicz, Lucy S. "Introduction: The World of East European Jewry." In *The Golden Tradition: Jewish Life and Thought in Eastern Europe,* edited by Lucy S. Dawidowicz, 5–92. New York, 1967.

Debord, Guy. *Society of the Spectacle.* Detroit, MI, 1983.

Dontsova, Tat'iana. *Moldavanka: Zapiski kraeveda.* Odessa, 2001.

Dubin, Lois. *The Port Jews of Habsburg Trieste.* Stanford, CA, 1999.

Dunham, Vera S. *In Stalin's Time: Middleclass Values in Soviet Fiction.* Durham, NC, 1990.

Elias, Norbert. *The Civilizing Process: Sociogenetic and Psychogenetic Investigations.* Rev. ed. Malden, MA, 2000.

Engel, Barbara Alpern. *Between the Fields and the City: Women, Work, and the Family in Russia, 1861–1914.* Cambridge, 1994.

Engelstein, Laura. *The Keys to Happiness: Sex and the Search for Modernity in Fin-de-Siècle Russia.* Ithaca, NY, 1992.

Epidemiia chumy i kholery 1910 goda v Odesse. Odessa, 1911.

Evans, Richard. *Tales from the German Underworld: Crime and Punishment in the Nineteenth Century.* New Haven, CT, 1998.

Faitel'berg-Blank, Viktor. *Banditskaia Odessa-2: Nochnye naletchiki.* Moscow, 2002.

Faitel'berg-Blank, Viktor, and Valerii Shestachenko. *Banditskaia Odessa: "Dvoinoe dno" Iuzhnoi Pal'miry".* Odessa, 1999.

Filippov, Boris. *Actors without Make-Up.* Moscow, 1977.

Fitzpatrick, Sheila. *Tear Off the Masks! Identity and Imposture in Twentieth-Century Russia.* Princeton, NJ, 2005.

Foucault, Michel. *Discipline and Punish: The Birth of the Prison.* Translated by Alan Sheridan. New York, 1977.

Frank, Stephen P. *Crime, Cultural Conflict, and Justice in Rural Russia, 1856–1914.* Berkeley, CA, 1999.

———. "Narratives within Numbers: Women, Crime, and Judicial Statistics in Imperial Russia, 1834–1913." *Russian Review* 55, no. 4 (1996): 541–66.

Frank, Stephen P., and Mark D. Steinberg, eds. *Cultures in Flux: Lower-Class Values,*

Practices, and Resistance in Late Imperial Russia. Princeton, NJ, 1994.

Frankel, Jonathan. *Prophecy and Politics: Socialism, Nationalism, and the Russian Jews, 1862–1917.* Cambridge, 1981.

Freeze, ChaeRan. *Jewish Marriage and Divorce in Imperial Russia.* Boston, 2002.

Fried, Albert. *The Rise and Fall of the Jewish Gangster in America.* New York, 1980.

Garrigan, Kristine Ottesen, ed. *Victorian Scandals: Representations of Gender and Class.* Athens, OH, 1992.

Gassenschmidt, Christoph. *Jewish Liberal Politics in Tsarist Russia, 1900–1914: The Modernization of Russian Jewry.* New York, 1995.

Gates, Barbara T. *Victorian Suicide: Mad Crimes and Sad Histories.* Princeton, NJ, 1988.

Gay, Peter. *The Bourgeois Experience: Victoria to Freud.* 5 Vols. New York, 1984–1998.

Geertz, Clifford. *The Interpretation of Cultures.* New York, 1973.

Gerasimov, Ilya. "'My ubivaem tol'ko svoikh': prestupnost' kak marker mezhetnicheckikh granits v Odesse nachala XX veka (1907–1917 gg.)." *Ab Imperio* 1 (2003): 209–60.

Gillerman, Sharon. "Samson in Vienna: The Theatrics of Jewish Masculinity." *Jewish Social Studies* 9, no. 2 (2003): 65–98.

Ginsberg, Elaine K., ed. *Passing and the Fictions of Identity.* Durham, NC, 1996.

Gitelman, Zvi. *A Century of Ambivalence: The Jews of Russia and the Soviet Union, 1881 to the Present.* New York, 1988.

Glickman, Rose. *Russian Factory Women: Workplace and Society, 1880–1914.* Berkeley, CA, 1984.

Goffman, Erving. *The Presentation of Self in Everyday Life.* New York, 1959.

Graham, Brian, and Catherine Nash, eds. *Modern Historical Geographies.* New York, 2000.

Great Britain. Foreign Office. *General Correspondence: Russia.*

Guttmann, Allen. *The Erotic in Sports.* New York, 1996.

Habermas, Jürgen. *The Structural Transformation of the Public Sphere: An Inquiry into a Category of Bourgeois Society.* Translated by Thomas Burger. Cambridge, MA, 1992.

Haimson, Leopold H. "The Problem of Social Identities in Early-Twentieth-Century Russia." *Slavic Review* 47, no. 1 (1988): 1–20.

Haine, W. Scott. *The World of the Paris Café: Sociability among the French Working Class, 1789–1914.* Baltimore, MD, 1996.

Hamm, Michael F. *Kiev: A Portrait, 1800–1917.* Princeton, NJ, 1993.

———, ed. *The City in Late Imperial Russia.* Bloomington, IN, 1986.

———, ed. *The City in Russian History.* Lexington, KY, 1976.

Harris, Ruth. *Murders and Madness: Medicine, Law, and Society in the Fin-de-Siècle.* Oxford, 1989.

Harvey, David. *Paris, Capital of Modernity.* New York, 2003.

———. *The Urban Experience.* Baltimore, MD, 1989.

Harvey, M. L. "The Development of Russian Commerce on the Black Sea and Its Significance." Ph.D. diss., University of California, 1938.

Hausmann, Guido. "Der Numerus clausus für jüdische Studenten im Zarenreich." *Jahrbücher für Geschichte Osteuropas* 41, no.4 (1993): 509–31.

———. *Universität und städtische Gesellschaft in Odessa, 1865–1917. Soziale und nationale Selbstorganisation an der Peripherie des Zarenreiches.* Stuttgart, 1999.

Healy, Dan. *Homosexual Desire in Revolutionary Russia: The Regulation of Sexual and Gender Dissent.* Chicago, IL, 2001.

Heldt, Barbara. *Terrible Perfection: Women in Russian Literature.* Bloomington, IN, 1987.

Hendershot, Cynthia. *The Animal Within: Masculinity and the Gothic.* Ann Arbor, MI, 1998.

Herlihy, Patricia. "Commerce and Architecture in Odessa during the Late Imperial Period." In *Commerce in Russian Urban Culture, 1861–1914,* edited by William

Craft Brumfield et al., 180–94. Washington, DC, 2001.
———. "The Ethnic Composition of the City of Odessa in the Nineteenth Century." *Harvard Ukrainian Studies* 1 (1977): 53–78.
———. *Odessa: A History, 1794–1914*. Cambridge, MA, 1986.
———. "Port Jews of Odessa and Trieste: A Tale of Two Cities." *Jahrbuch des Simon-Dubnow-Instituts* 2 (2003): 183–98.
Hildermeier, Manfred. *Bürgertum und Stadt in Russland, 1760–1870. Rechtliche Lage und soziale Struktur*. Köln, 1986.
Holt, Richard. "Social History and Bourgeois Culture in Nineteenth-Century France: A Review Article." *Comparative Studies in Society and History* 27, no. 4 (October 1985): 713–26.
Holt, Richard, J. A. Mangan, and Pierre Lanfranchi, eds. *European Heroes: Myth, Identity, Sport*. London, 1996.
Hyman, Paula, and Deborah Dash Moore, eds. *The Modern Jewish Experience*. Bloomington, IN, 1983.
Iljine, Nicolas V., ed. *Odessa Memories*. Seattle, WA, 2003.
Iur'ev and Vladimirskii. *Khoroshii ton. Pravila svetskoi zhizni i etiketa*. St. Petersburg, 1889. Reprint, Moscow, 1991.
Jabotinsky, Vladimir. "Memoirs by My Typewriter." In *The Golden Tradition: Jewish Life and Thought in Eastern Europe*, edited by Lucy S. Dawidowicz, 394–401. New York, 1967.
Jahn, Hubertus. *Patriotic Culture in Russia during World War I*. Ithaca, NY, 1995.
———. "Der St. Petersburger Heumarkt im 19. Jahrhundert. Metarmophosen eines Stadtviertels." *Jahrbücher für Geschichte Osteuropas* 44, no. 2 (1996): 162–77.
Johnson, Eric A. *Urbanization and Crime: Germany, 1871–1914*. Cambridge, 1995.
———. "Women as Victims and Criminals: Female Homicide and Criminality in Imperial Germany, 1873–1914." *Criminal Justice History* 6 (1985): 151–75.
Joselit, Jenna Weissman. *Our Gang: Jewish Crime and the New York Jewish Community, 1900–1940*. Bloomington, IN, 1983.
Kaplan, Marion A. *The Making of the Jewish Middle Class: Women, Family, and Identity in Imperial Germany*. Oxford, 1991.
Karpovich, Michael. "Two Types of Russian Liberalism: Maklakov and Miliukov." In *Continuity and Change in Russian and Soviet Thought*, edited by Ernest J. Simmons, 129–43. Cambridge, MA, 1955.
Kasson, John F. *Amusing the Million: Coney Island at the Turn of the Century*. New York, 1978.
———. *Houdini, Tarzan, and the Perfect Man: The White Male Body and the Challenge of Modernity in America*. New York, 2001.
———. *Rudeness and Civility: Manners in Nineteenth-Century Urban America*. New York, 1990.
Kassow, Samuel D. *Students, Professors, and the State in Tsarist Russia*. Berkeley, CA, 1989.
Katayev [Kataev], Valentin. *A Mosaic of Life, or The Magic Horn of Oberon: Memoirs of a Russian Childhood*. Translated by Moira Budberg and Gordon Latta. Chicago, IL, 1976.
———. *A White Sail Gleams*. Moscow, 1954.
Kelly, Catriona. "'Better Halves'? Representations of Women in Russian Urban Popular Entertainments, 1870–1910." In *Women and Society in Russia and the Soviet Union*, edited by Linda Edmondson, 5–13. Cambridge, 1992.
———. *Refining Russia: Advice Literature, Polite Culture, and Gender from Catherine to Yeltsin*. New York, 2001.
———. "Teacups and Coffins: The Culture of Russian Merchant Women, 1850–1917." In *Women in Russia and Ukraine*, edited by Rosalind Marsh, 55–77. Cambridge, 1996.

Kelly, Catriona, and David Shepherd, eds. *Constructing Russian Culture in the Age of Revolution, 1881–1940*. New York, 1998.

Klier, John D. "A Port, Not a Shtetl: Reflections on the Distinctiveness of Odessa." *Jewish Culture and History* 4, no. 2 (2001): 173–78.

Klier, John D., and Shlomo Lambroza, eds. *Pogroms: Anti-Jewish Violence in Modern Russian History*. Cambridge, 1992.

Kocka, Jürgen. "The Middle Classes in Europe." *Journal of Modern History* 67, no. 4 (1995): 783–806.

Kocka, Jürgen, and Allen Mitchell, eds. *Bourgeois Society in Nineteenth-Century Europe*. Oxford, 1988.

Kovalenko, Konstantin Stepanovich, ed. *Iz istorii Odesskoi partiinoi organizatsii. Ocherki*. Odessa, 1964.

Kovbasiuk, S. M., ed. *Odessa. Ocherk istorii goroda-geroia*. Odessa: 1957.

Kuprin, A. *Sasha*. Translated by Douglas Ashby. London, 1920.

Kuznetsov, Evgenii. *Iz proshlogo russkoi estrady. Istoricheskie ocherki*. Moscow, 1958.

Langland, Elizabeth. *Nobody's Angels: Middle-Class Women and Domestic Ideology in Victorian Culture*. Ithaca, NY, 1995.

Leikina-Svirskaia, V. R. *Russkaia intelligentsiia v 1900–1917 godakh*. Moscow, 1981.

Levenstein, Harvey. *Paradox of Plenty: A Social History of Eating in Modern America*. Oxford, 1993.

Levine, Lawrence W. *Highbrow/Lowbrow: The Emergence of Cultural Hierarchy in America*. Cambridge, MA, 1988.

Lindenmeyr, Adele. *Poverty Is Not a Vice: Charity, Society, and the State in Imperial Russia*. Princeton, NJ, 1996.

Lombroso, Caesar, and William Ferrero. *The Female Offender*. New York, 1897.

Lotman, Yuri M. *Universe of the Mind: A Semiotic Theory of Culture*. Bloomington, IN, 1990.

Löwe, Heinz-Dietrich. *The Tsars and the Jews: Reform, Reaction, and Anti-Semitism in Imperial Russia, 1772–1917*. Chur, Switzerland, 1993.

Lushchik, Sergei Z. "Odesskii 'Krokodil'." *Al'manakh bibliofila* 10 (1981): 254–64.

———. "Odesskii zhurnal 'Krokodil' i ego avtory." In *Odesskii zhurnal 'Krokodil" i ego avtory. Izbrannye stranitsy (1911–1912)*, edited by O. F. Botushanskaia, 231–310. Odessa, 1998.

Mack, Arien, ed. *Home: A Place in the World*. New York, 1993.

Mancoff, Debra N., and D. J. Trela, eds. *Victorian Urban Settings: Essays on the Nineteenth-Century City and Its Contexts*. New York, 1996.

Mangan, J. A., ed. *Making European Masculinities: Sport, Europe, Gender*. London, 2000.

Maza, Sarah. "Stories in History: Cultural Narratives in Recent Works in European History." *American Historical Review* 101, no. 5 (1996): 1493–1515.

McReynolds, Louise. "'The Incomparable' Anastasiia Vial'tseva and the Culture of Personality." In *Russia—Women—Power*, edited by Helena Goscilo and Beth Holmgren, 273–94. Bloomington, IN, 1996.

———. *The News under Russia's Old Regime: The Development of a Mass-Circulation Press*. Princeton, NJ, 1991.

———. *Russia at Play: Leisure Activities at the End of the Tsarist Era*. Ithaca, NY, 2003.

———. "Russian Nightlife, Fin-de-Siècle." *Russian Studies in History* 31, no. 3 (1992–1993).

Messerschmidt, James W. *Masculinities and Crime: Critique and Reconceptualization of Theory*. Lanham, MD: 1993.

Mironov, B. N. "Prestupnost' v Rossii v XIX—nachale XX veka." *Otechestvennaia istoriia* 1 (1998): 24–42.

Morrison, Wayne. *Theoretical Criminology*. London, 1995.

Morrissey, Susan K. *Heralds of Revolution: Russian Students and the Mythologies of Radicalism*. New York, 1998.

Morson, Gary Saul, ed. *Literature and History: Theoretical Problems and Russian Case Studies*. Stanford, CA, 1986.

Moskvich, Grigorii. *Putevoditel' po Odesse*. Odessa, 1913.

Muir, Edward, and Guido Ruggiero, eds. *History from Crime*. Selections from Quaderni Storici. Baltimore, MD, 1994.

Nathans, Benjamin. *Beyond the Pale: The Jewish Encounter with Late Imperial Russia*. Berkeley, CA, 2002.

Neuberger, Joan. "Culture Besieged: Hooliganism and Futurism." In *Cultures in Flux: Lower-Class Values, Practices, and Resistance in Late Imperial Russia*, edited by Stephen P. Frank and Mark D. Steinberg, 185–204. Princeton, NJ, 1994.

———. *Hooliganism: Crime, Culture, and Power in St. Petersburg, 1900–1914*. Berkeley, CA, 1993.

Nord, Deborah Epstein. "The City as Theater: From Georgian to Early Victorian London." *Victorian Studies* 31, no. 2 (1988): 159–88.

Novikov, A. I. *Meshchanstvo i meshchane*. Leningrad, 1983.

Obzor odesskogo gradonachalstva (za 1912–1914). Odessa, 1913–1916.

Ostroumov, S. S. *Prestupnost' i ee prichiny v dorevoliutsionnoi Rossii*. Moscow, 1980.

Otchet odesskogo aero-kluba (za 1912). Odessa, 1912.

Otchet pravleniia odesskago literaturno-artisticheskago obshchestva za 1917 g. Odessa, 1918.

Pendergast, Tom. *Creating the Modern Man: American Magazines and Consumer Culture, 1900–1950*. Columbia, MO, 2000.

Penter, Tanja. *Odessa 1917: Revolution an der Peripherie*. Köln, 2000.

Perrot, Philippe. *Fashioning the Bourgeoisie: A History of Clothing in the Nineteenth Century*. Princeton, NJ, 1994.

Pervaia vseobshchaia perepis' naseleniia Rossiiskoi Imperii 1897 g., vol. 47, *Gorod Odessa* (St. Petersburg, 1904).

Prestupnik i prestupnost'. Sbornik 2. Moscow, 1927.

Rachlin, Harvey. *Jumbo's Hide, Elvis's Ride, and the Tooth of Buddha: More Marvelous Tales of Historical Artifacts*. New York, 2000.

Rashin, A. G. *Naselenie Rossii za 100 let (1811–1913 g.g.). Statisticheskie ocherki*. Moscow, 1956.

Ribeiro, Aileen. *Dress and Morality*. New York, 1986.

Riis, Jacob A. *How the Other Half Lives*. New York, 1997.

Rivosh, Ia. N. *Vremia i veshchi. Ocherki po istorii material'noi kul'tury v Rossii nachala XX veka*. Moscow: 1990.

Rodwin, Lloyd, and Robert M. Hollister, eds. *Cities of the Mind: Images and Themes of the City in the Social Sciences*. New York, 1984.

Rollins, Patrick J. "Imperial Russia's African Colony." *Russian Review* 27, no. 4 (October 1968): 432–51.

Rosenberg, William G. "Identities, Power, and Social Interactions in Revolutionary Russia." *Slavic Review* 47, no. 1 (Spring 1988): 21–28.

———. *The Liberals in the Russian Revolution*. Princeton, NJ, 1974.

Rothstein, Robert A. "How It Was Sung in Odessa: At the Intersection of Russian and Yiddish Folk Culture." *Slavic Review* 60, no. 4 (Winter 2001): 781–801.

Ruane, Christine. "Clothes Shopping in Imperial Russia: The Development of a Consumer Culture." *Journal of Social History* 28, no. 4 (Summer 1995): 765–82.

———. *Gender, Class, and the Professionalization of Russian City Teachers, 1860–1914*. Pittsburgh, PA, 1994.

Rubin, Joan Shelley. *The Making of Middlebrow Culture*. Chapel Hill, NC, 1992.

Rubin, Rachel. *Jewish Gangsters of Modern Literature*. Urbana, IL, 2000.

Rubinstein, Ruth P. *Dress Codes: Meanings and Messages in American Culture*. Boulder, CO, 1995.

Ruth, David E. *Inventing the Public Enemy: The Gangster in American Culture, 1918–1934*. Chicago, IL, 1996.

Sabatos, Charles. "Crossing the 'Exaggerated Boundaries' of Black Sea Culture: Turkish Themes in the Work of Odessa Natives Ilf and Petrov." *New Perspectives on Turkey* 24 (2001): 83–104.

Sargeant, Lynn Mary. "Middle-Class Culture: Music and Identity in Late Imperial Russia." Ph.D. diss., Indiana University, 2001.

Scanlon, Jennifer. *Inarticulate Longings: The Ladies' Home Journal, Gender, and the Promises of Consumer Culture*. New York, 1995.

Schneiderman, Jeremiah. *Sergei Zubatov and Revolutionary Marxism: The Struggle for the Working Class in Tsarist Russia*. Ithaca, NY, 1976.

Schwartz, Vanessa R. *Spectacular Realities: Early Mass Culture in Fin-de-Siècle Paris*. Berkeley, CA, 1998.

Scott, James C. *Seeing Like a State: How Certain Schemes to Improve the Human Condition Have Failed*. New Haven, CT, 1998.

Scott, Joan Wallach. *Gender and the Politics of History*. New York, 1988.

Sennett, Richard. *The Fall of Public Man*. New York, 1977.

———. *Flesh and Stone: The Body and the City in Western Civilization*. New York, 1994.

Sharpe, William, and Leonard Wallock, eds. *Visions of the Modern City: Essays in History, Art, and Literature*. Baltimore, MD, 1987.

Sindall, Rob. "Middle-Class Crime in Nineteenth-Century England." *Criminal Justice History* 4 (1983): 23–40.

Skinner, Frederick W. "City Planning in Russia: The Development of Odessa, 1789–1892." Ph.D. diss., Princeton University, 1973.

———. "Odessa and the Problem of Urban Modernization." In *The City in Late Imperial Russia*, edited by Michael F. Hamm, 209–48. Bloomington, IN, 1986.

———. "Trends in Planning Practices: The Building of Odessa, 1794–1917." In *The City in Russian History*, edited by Michael F. Hamm, 139–59. Lexington, KY, 1976.

Slezkine, Yuri. *The Jewish Century*. Princeton, NJ, 2004.

Smith-Rosenberg, Carroll. *Disorderly Conduct: Visions of Gender in Victorian America*. New York, 1985.

Snow, George E. "Perceptions of the Link between Alcoholism and Crime in Pre-Revolutionary Russia." *Criminal Justice History* 8 (1987): 37–51.

Sorkin, David. "The Port Jew: Notes Toward a Social Type." *Journal of Jewish Studies* 50, no. 1 (Spring 1999): 87–97.

Spierenburg, Pieter, ed. *Men and Violence: Gender, Honor, and Rituals in Modern Europe and America*. Columbus, OH, 1998.

Spravochnaia kniga ob Odesskikh soslovnykh kuptsakh i voobshche o litsakh i uchrezhdeniiakh torgovo-promyshlennago klassa po g. Odessa na 1916 god. Odessa, 1916.

Stansell, Christine. *City of Women: Sex and Class in New York, 1789–1860*. Urbana, IL, 1987.

Steinberg, Mark D. *Moral Communities: The Culture of Class Relations in the Russian Printing Industry, 1867–1907*. Berkeley, CA, 1992.

———. *Proletarian Imagination: Self, Modernity, and the Sacred in Russia, 1910–1925*. Ithaca, NY, 2002.

———. "Stories and Voices: History and Theory." *Russian Review* 55, no. 3 (1996): 347–54.

———. "Workers on the Cross: Religious Imagination in the Writings of Russian Workers, 1910–1924." *Russian Review* 53, no. 2 (1994): 213–39.

Stites, Richard. *Russian Popular Culture: Entertainment and Society since 1900*. Cambridge, 1992.

———. *The Women's Liberation Movement in Russia: Feminism, Nihilism, and Bolshevism, 1860–1930*. Princeton, NJ, 1978.

Sussman, Herbert L. *Victorian Masculinities: Manhood and Masculine Poetics in Early Victorian Literature and Art*. Cambridge, 1995.

Sylvester, Roshanna P. "City of Thieves: Moldavanka, Criminality, and Respectability in Prerevolutionary Odessa." *Journal of Urban History* 27, no. 2 (January 2001): 131–57.

———. "Crime, Masquerade, and Anxiety: The Public Creation of Middle-Class Identity in Pre-Revolutionary Odessa, 1912–1916." Ph.D. diss., Yale University, 1998.

———. "Cultural Transgressions, Bourgeois Fears: Violent Crime in Odessa's Central

Entertainment District." *Jahrbücher für Geschichte Osteuropas* 44 (1996): 503–22.
———. "Making an Appearance: Urban 'Types' and the Creation of Respectability in Odessa's Popular Press, 1912–1914." *Slavic Review* 59, no. 4 (Winter 2000): 802–24.
Thompson, F. M. L. *The Rise of Respectable Society: A Social History of Victorian Britain, 1830–1900*. Cambridge, MA, 1988.
Thurston, Robert W. *Liberal City, Conservative State: Moscow and Russia's Urban Crisis, 1906–1914*. Oxford, 1987.
———. "Police and People in Moscow, 1906–1914." *Russian Review* 39, no. 3 (1980): 320–38.
Timberlake, Charles E. "The Middle Classes in Late Tsarist Russia." In *Social Orders and Social Classes in Europe since 1500: Studies in Social Stratification,* edited by M. L. Bush, 86–113. London, 1992.
Tobias, J. J. *Urban Crime in Victorian England.* New York, NY 1972.
Toomre, Joyce. *Classic Russian Cooking: Elena Molokhovets' A Gift to Young Housewives.* Bloomington, IN, 1992.
Tosh, John. *A Man's Place: Masculinity and the Middle-Class Home in Victorian England.* New Haven, CT, 1999.
Trice, Thomas Reed. "The 'Body Politic': Russian Funerals and the Politics of Representation, 1841–1921." Ph.D. diss., University of Illinois, 1998.
Troyat, Henri. *Daily Life in Russia under the Last Tsar.* Stanford, CA, 1959.
Tseëlon, Efrat, ed. *Masquerade and Identities: Essays on Gender, Sexuality, and Marginality.* London, 2001.
Ustav obshchestva odesskii soiuz russkikh liudei. Odessa, 1913.
Utesov, Leonid. "Moia Odessa." *Moskva* 9 (1964): 121–42.
Vasil'evskii, N. *Ocherk sanitarnogo polozheniia g. Odessy.* Odessa, 1901.
Vasil'evskii, V. K. "Polozhenie portovykh rabochikh v Odesse." *Trudy Odesskogo otdela Russkogo ovshchestva okhraneniia narodnogo zdraviia.* No. 4 (1904): 36–49.
Vassilikou, Maria. "Greeks and Jews in Salonika and Odessa: Inter-Ethnic Relations in Cosmopolitan Port Cities." *Jewish Culture and History* 4, no. 2 (2001): 155–72.
von Geldern, James. "Life In-Between: Migration and Popular Culture in Late Imperial Russia." *Russian Review* 55, no. 3 (July 1996): 365–83.
Vsia Odessa. Adresnaia i spravochnaia kniga vsei Odessy, s otdelom Odesskii uezd na 1914 g. Odessa, 1914.
Wagner, William G. *Marriage, Property, and Law in Late Imperial Russia.* Oxford, 1994.
———. "The Trojan Mare: Women's Rights and Civil Rights in Late Imperial Russia." In *Civil Rights in Imperial Russia,* edited by Olga Crisp and Linda Edmondson, 65–84. Oxford, 1989.
Walkowitz, Judith R. *City of Dreadful Delight: Narratives of Sexual Danger in Late-Victorian London.* Chicago, IL, 1992.
Weinberg, Robert. *The Revolution of 1905 in Odessa: Blood on the Steps.* Bloomington, IN, 1993.
Werheimer, Jack, ed. *The Modern Jewish Experience.* New York, 1993.
West, Sally. "Constructing Consumer Culture: Advertising in Imperial Russia to 1914." Ph.D. diss., University of Illinois, 1995.
Wilson, Elizabeth. *Adorned in Dreams: Fashion and Modernity.* Berkeley, CA, 1985.
Wirtschafter, Elise Kimerling. *Structures of Society: Imperial Russia's "People of Various Ranks."* DeKalb, IL, 1994.
Worobec, Christine D. *Peasant Russia: Family and Community in the Post-Emancipation Period.* Princeton, NJ, 1991.
Zedner, Lucia. *Women, Crime, and Custody in Victorian England.* Oxford, 1991.
Zeleva, T. V., ed. *Iz istorii burzhuazii v Rossii.* Tomsk, 1982.
Zipperstein, Steven J. *The Jews of Odessa: A Cultural History, 1794–1881.* Stanford, CA, 1985.
Zorkaia, N. M. *Na rubezhe stoletii. U istokov massovogo iskusstva v Rossii, 1900–1910 godov.* Moscow, 1976.

Index

DATE DUE